Palgrave Studies in Sport and Politics

Series Editor
Martin Polley, International Centre for Sports History and Culture
De Montfort University, Leicester, Leicestershire, UK

Palgrave Studies in Sport and Politics aims to nurture new research, both historical and contemporary, to the complex inter-relationships between sport and politics. The books in this series will range in their focus from the local to the global, and will embody a broad approach to politics, encompassing the ways in which sport has interacted with the state, dissidence, ideology, war, human rights, diplomacy, security, policy, identities, the law, and many other forms of politics. It includes approaches from a range of disciplines, and promotes work by new and established scholars from around the world.

Mark Orton

Football and National Identity in Twentieth-Century Argentina

La Nuestra

Mark Orton
Newport, UK

ISSN 2365-998X ISSN 2365-9998 (electronic)
Palgrave Studies in Sport and Politics
ISBN 978-3-031-20588-0 ISBN 978-3-031-20589-7 (eBook)
https://doi.org/10.1007/978-3-031-20589-7

© The Editor(s) (if applicable) and The Author(s), under exclusive license to Springer Nature Switzerland AG 2023

This work is subject to copyright. All rights are solely and exclusively licensed by the Publisher, whether the whole or part of the material is concerned, specifically the rights of translation, reprinting, reuse of illustrations, recitation, broadcasting, reproduction on microfilms or in any other physical way, and transmission or information storage and retrieval, electronic adaptation, computer software, or by similar or dissimilar methodology now known or hereafter developed.

The use of general descriptive names, registered names, trademarks, service marks, etc. in this publication does not imply, even in the absence of a specific statement, that such names are exempt from the relevant protective laws and regulations and therefore free for general use.

The publisher, the authors, and the editors are safe to assume that the advice and information in this book are believed to be true and accurate at the date of publication. Neither the publisher nor the authors or the editors give a warranty, expressed or implied, with respect to the material contained herein or for any errors or omissions that may have been made. The publisher remains neutral with regard to jurisdictional claims in published maps and institutional affiliations.

Cover illustration: @Hans Neleman/Getty Images

This Palgrave Macmillan imprint is published by the registered company Springer Nature Switzerland AG
The registered company address is: Gewerbestrasse 11, 6330 Cham, Switzerland

Acknowledgements

There are numerous people who I would like to thank for bringing this project to a successful conclusion. Primarily, I would like to thank my Ph.D. supervisors at De Montfort University, Matt Taylor and Martin Polley for their guidance in bringing the thesis on which this book builds, to fruition. Grateful thanks are also due to Liz Crolley for her comments as examiner on where to build on the findings of the thesis. I would also like to thank scholars, in both the UK and Argentina such as Pierre Lanfranchi, Julio Frydenberg, Rodrigo Bunster and Rodrigo Daskal for giving me the benefit of their thoughts on the direction my research was taking and for making suggestions about areas to investigate.

I am also indebted to those who have helped grow my academic interest in Latin America over the years, notably Ann Matear and Andy Thorpe at the University of Portsmouth and to Kristie Robinson and Lucy Cousins who gave me the opportunity to spend a year in Argentina working on the sadly missed Argentina Independent newspaper.

I am thankful to all the staff who have assisted me at libraries and archives on both sides of the Atlantic. I am particularly grateful too for the hours of assistance and interest in the project on the part of Rodrigo Spiess at the TEA archive in Buenos Aires and to Carolina Rossi Romero at Museo River Plate and Bernardo Bertelloni at Vélez Sarsfield for enabling me to access their respective club archives.

I would like to thank De Montfort University for their financial assistance in granting me a fees bursary to undertake Ph.D. research as well as funding for field work in Argentina and Uruguay. I am also grateful to work colleagues, past and present, over the past eight years who have enabled me to attend conferences and tutorials and undertake fieldwork.

I would like to thank my father for his continued support throughout this project, giving encouragement and financial support towards field visits to Argentina as well as proof-reading numerous drafts. I also dedicate this work to the memory of my mother, who passed away at the outset of this project. I am also grateful to my brother Neil and friends, Terry Sullivan, Erin McNamara, María Agustina Izurieta, Livvy Davies, Lee Treagus, Sharon Dahn and Sue Norman who have provided enormous emotional support and belief in this project when I most doubted myself. Finally, I am indebted to Dave Branfield for his technical support and proof reading, and to Lynnie Sharon at Springer Publishing Company for her tireless support in promptly responding to all my queries during the publishing process.

Contents

1 Introduction — 1
2 'The Virile English Game': The Origins of Argentine Football 1867–1912 — 17
3 Creating Argentinidad Through Football 1913–1930 — 55
4 Flying the Flag: Football and the International Projection of Argentinidad 1913–1930 — 97
5 Political Football: The Age of Decline? 1931–1958 — 123
6 The Age of Social and Footballing Revolution 1959–1976 — 169
7 In the Shadow of the Proceso 1976–1983 — 209
8 False Dawn: From Democratic Restoration to Economic Armageddon 1983–2002 — 247
9 Conclusion — 287

Index — 301

Abbreviations

AAA	Alianza Anticomunista Argentina
AAAF	Asociación Amateur Argentina de Football
AAF	Asociación Argentina de Football
AAFAP	Asociación Argentina de Football (Amateur y Profesionales)
AAFL	Argentine Association Football League
AAmF	Asociación Amateurs de Football
AFA	Asociación del Fútbol Argentino
BAEHS	Buenos Aires English High School
CBD	Confederação Brasileira de Desportos
EAM	Ente Autárquico Mundial '78
ERP	Ejercito Revolucionario del Pueblo
FAA	Futbolistas Argentinos Agremiados
FIFA	Fédération Internationale de Football Association
FMLN	Farabundo Martí National Liberation Front
GAA	Gaelic Athletic Association
GOU	Grupo de Oficiales Unidos
IMF	International Monetary Fund
IOC	International Olympic Committee
PFA	Professional Footballers' Association
TyC	Torneos y Competencias
UCR	Unión Cívica Radical
UTA	Unión Tranviarios Automotor

List of Figures

Fig. 5.1 Number of players earning the maximum wage in Argentina in 1948 by Club — 151

Fig. 6.1 National Team Debutants 1959–1978 by Province of Club as percentage — 203

List of Tables

Table 2.1   Net immigration to Argentina 1857–1914 by nationality   39
Table 4.1   Italo-Argentines in the Italian National Team 1914–1935   114

CHAPTER 1

Introduction

The outpouring of grief following Diego Maradona's death in November 2020 confirmed the symbiosis between football and Argentine society. As journalist Marcela Mora y Araujo highlighted at the time, 'Maradona became an emblem of *Argentinianess*, more so than other sports stars or celebrities.'[1] With the passage of time, a myth has emerged conflating Argentina's destiny as a nation with the performance of its men's national football team, with victories confirming Argentina as 'first among equals,' whilst losses become a collective tragedy.[2] Taking Argentina as its case study, this book focuses on the long twentieth century, from the establishment of British economic hegemony during the late nineteenth century to the catastrophic 2001–2002 financial crisis that so affected Argentine society and led to a reappraisal of the country's identity as the hegemonic neo-liberal economic model of the previous quarter century became decisively discredited. It analyses how football became so entrenched within society that alongside the tango, it became an important cultural signifier of that Argentine identity. It demonstrates how football functioned as an agent for assimilation in a nation transformed by massive European migration at the turn of the twentieth century, as well as echoing

[1] *The Guardian*, 26 November 2020, 45.
[2] *Vein ti tres*, 30 June 2016, 3.

© The Author(s), under exclusive license to Springer Nature Switzerland AG 2023
M. Orton, *Football and National Identity in Twentieth-Century Argentina*, Palgrave Studies in Sport and Politics,
https://doi.org/10.1007/978-3-031-20589-7_1

Argentina's economic, political and social development throughout the remainder of the twentieth century as competing discourses surrounding national identity vied for supremacy.

Whilst this phenomenon is not new or exclusive to Argentina, using sport as a lens for viewing society has fascinated scholars since the mid-1970s, demonstrated by works such as Robert Malcolmson's *Popular Recreations in English Society 1700–1850* and James Walvin's *The People Game*.[3] More recently, academics have broadened their range, utilising sport to analyse immigration, politics, socio-economic organisation and other issues relating to national identity construction. These are most evidently linked to global sporting events such as the Olympic Games, where national teams characterise what Benedict Anderson describes as an 'imagined political community' representing tenuous notions of shared values.[4]

Whilst scholars such as Michael Goebel, María Sáenz Quesada, Luis Alberto Romero and Colin MacLachlan have offered a wider understanding of identity creation in Argentina, Goebel acknowledged in 2011 that there was a need for academic attention to the role of football in this process given, 'the weight attached to footballers and their style of play as the embodiment of Argentiness.'[5] Though Goebel chose not to follow this up himself, others have done so with mixed success. In his popular history of Argentine football, *Angels with Dirty Faces*, Jonathan Wilson provides a synthesis of the existing historiography without adding much new analysis in the first half of the book, although this is partially remedied through his first-person interviews with actors from later in the twentieth century.[6] Sociologist Pablo Alabarces contends that narratives of national identity around football in Argentina complement official narratives, rejecting any role for British pioneers of the game in 'contributing to that identity.'[7] Alejandro Molinari and Roberto Martínez have made the case that historians should take into account all the cultural universe of a people when analysing the concept of identity, whilst

---

[3] Malcolmson (1973) and Walvin (1975).

[4] Anderson (1983, 6).

[5] Goebel (2011, 198), Sáenz Quesada (2012), Romero (2004), and MacLachlan (2006).

[6] Wilson (2016).

[7] Alabarces (2006, 3).

absenting women, indigenous and *mestizo* people, and Afro-Argentines—the 'voiceless others'—from their investigation of how football became *the* national passion in Argentina.[8]

Taking an explicitly historical approach, drawing upon primary newspaper and magazine sources as well as archival material from football clubs, governing bodies and governmental records, *La Nuestra* looks at the evolution of football's relationship with Argentine society and how it helped a diverse population think about concepts of the national without losing sight of their ethnic origins. It also examines the role of these 'voiceless others' in using football as a way of imposing themselves on the national consciousness, as well as highlighting the complexities of dual identity in the opening decades of the twentieth century as football was becoming a symbol of hybrid *argentinidad* or Argentineness.

As well as assessing Argentine identity through football in a domestic setting, this book examines how the game provided a way for Argentina to be perceived abroad, especially in Europe, through the mythology of an idiosyncratic style of play known as *la nuestra* 'our way' and how deviations from this in the 1960s and late 1980s changed opinions abroad of Argentina more widely. It illustrates how despite being able to produce some of the best footballers the world has ever seen such as Alfredo Di Stéfano and Diego Maradona, football also reflected Argentina's economic weakness in the wider global economy at key points in the twentieth century such as the 1930s and in the final quarter of the twentieth century.

Representations of the role of football in constructions of Argentine identity have hitherto inclined towards a nationalist, revisionist interpretation of the country's history in which immigrants were assimilated into a unified Argentine 'race' that was European and white in contrast to neighbouring Brazil in which as Roger Kittleson describes, 'Conceptions of *brasildade* in soccer depended on theories that Brazil had a mixed-race culture.'[9] This assimilationist approach has led to the acceptance amongst historians of Argentine football of what Eric Hobsbawm identified as 'invented tradition.'[10] By creating and venerating symbols

---

[8] Molinari and Martínez (2013, 11–14).
[9] Kittleson (2014, 6–8).
[10] Hobsbawm (2014, 1–2).

such as the *pibe* and the *potrero* and in creating an idiosyncratic Argentine playing style known as *la nuestra* ('our way'), during the 1920s, writers such as Borocotó fulfilled what Hobsbawm described as 'continuity with a suitable historic past' in which such symbols 'reflect the entire background, thought and culture of a nation,' something that has influenced the subsequent historiography.[11] Developing his synthesisation of the construction of an Argentine playing style during the 1920s with its accompanying lexicon of *criollo* footballing terms from a survey of contemporary articles in *El Gráfico*, the anthropologist Eduardo Archetti posited in *Masculinities*, 'football is a powerful expression of national capabilities and potentialities,' without fully challenging their underlying precepts.[12]

This nationalist viewpoint makes no consideration of the positive contribution to this process by the British footballing pioneers of football or their Argentine-born descendants, nor the possibility of dual identity amongst other immigrant communities. Alabarces suggests in *Fútbol y patria* that Argentine identity is based upon plurality and the coexistence of varied stories that allow for multiple constructions, without clarifying what they are, especially in the case of dual identities.[13] Whilst Ranaan Rein has contributed to filling this historiographical gap in *Fútbol, Jews and the Making of Argentina*, by focusing solely on the Jewish community he gives no sense of the contribution of larger and more influential immigratory communities.[14]

The symbiotic relationship between football, civic identity and Argentine politics has also been a fertile area for scholarship. For example, Julio Frydenberg has identified that this relationship began as 'team-clubs' morphed into more complex 'member-clubs' that became embedded in the local community.[15] Meanwhile, Vic Duke and Liz Crolley have noted that democratic participation within football clubs predated that of Argentina more widely by several years.[16] In his exploration of Argentine football's governing body, *AFA*, Sergio Levinsky highlights the centrality

[11] Ibid., 11.
[12] Archetti (1999, 15).
[13] Alabarces (2007, 28).
[14] Rein (2015, 15).
[15] Frydenberg (2011, 45–70).
[16] Duke and Crolley (2014, 100).

of this relationship. Quoting the boast of 1960's Asociación del Fútbol Argentino (AFA) leader, Valentín Suárez that 'the state will never lower the curtain on football,' he argues that this meant that no matter what financial problems Argentine football got into, the government would always rescue it due to its importance to Argentine society.[17]

Areas remain in need of greater interpretation. The conjunction of football's professionalisation with a period of democratic deficit in Argentina's political landscape at the start of the 1930s has been unsatisfactorily dealt with by scholars. Levinsky makes a loose connection between the arrival in football club boardrooms of erstwhile elected politicians following the 1930 military coup that ejected President Hipólito Yrigoyen, but does so without further elaboration.[18] Meanwhile, Alabarces claims that the inauguration of professional football in Argentina in 1931 was an important political act in that, 'it functioned as the only way of democratising sporting practice.'[19] By placing professionalism and the subsequent commodification of the game in Argentina in its wider political context, *La Nuestra* argues that in the case of Argentine football, the classic interpretation that professionalism was the origin of all ills, as the start of corruption and mercantilism in the game still has merit, despite Alabarces' rejection of it.[20]

Much of the existing scholarship concerning the link between football and politics rightly focuses on the transformational 1946–1955 presidency of Juan Domingo Perón. With the assimilation of immigrants accomplished by the 1940s, the way was open for Perón to develop new concepts of national identity, free of ethnic differences after his 1946 election. For almost a decade, Peronism, based on a nebulous ideal of social justice, revolutionised Argentine society, bringing previously marginalised sectors such as the working class firmly into the political process. Rein sustains that, 'Peronism used sports for the dual purpose of reshaping Argentine national consciousness … and mobilizing support for and loyalty to the regime.'[21] For his part, Alabarces highlights the role of cinema in supporting Peronist narratives of social mobility through the

---

[17] Levinsky (2016, 20).
[18] Ibid., 45.
[19] Alabarces (2007, 55–57).
[20] Ibid., 55.
[21] Rein (2015, 95).

release of films like *Pelota de Trapo* (1948) and *Escuela de Campeones* (1950).[22] This book complements this research by investigating the overlooked pedagogical role played by the Peronist press in support of these political goals, particularly the incorporation of working-class internal migrants into the political process, who had hitherto been dismissed by *porteño* elites as *cabecitas negras* or 'little blackheads.'

Another area of the relationship between Peronism and football where there is room for further analysis surrounds the 1948–1949 players' strike which had long-term consequences for Argentine game. Investigations by Julio Frydenberg and Daniel Sazbon have focused on the political aspects of the dispute, whilst Enrico Montenari has concentrated on the strike's effect on football fans.[23] *La Nuestra* adds to these findings by focusing on the role of footballers as members of the labour movement and how the dispute contributed to shifting ideas of national identity through resulting migrations.

A further contentious theme from the Peronist era was the absence of Argentine participation in international competition between 1947 and 1955. Levinsky attributes this policy—especially withdrawal from the 1950 World Cup in Brazil—to footballing diplomatic disagreements between the two nations, highlighted by Argentina's attempt to usurp Brazil's hosting of the tournament.[24] Building on this interpretation, this book places these decisions in the context of wider Peronist foreign policy and linking the period to previous examples of diplomatic failure on the part of Argentina's footballing authorities in explaining a pattern of dysfunction.

Following Perón's overthrow in 1955, the 1960s and 1970s were a turbulent period in Argentina as repressive military regimes sought to suppress alleged subversion. In his exploration of Estudiantes de la Plata as the archetype of *antifútbol* and the modernisation of Argentine football, Alabarces has conflated the violence committed by the team with that of the regime of General Juan Carlos Onganía. *La Nuestra*

---

[22] Alabarces (2007, 65–80).
[23] Frydenberg and Sazbon (2015, 65–80) and Montenari (2018, 191–204).
[24] Levinsky (2016, 84).

alternatively views the rise of Estudiantes as a case study for better understanding generational change in Argentina that functioned as a metaphor for youthful resistance to hegemonic forces.[25]

Scholars have long explored the use of major sporting events by national leaders for political ends, with Matthew Brown noting of the Tlatelolco massacre of unarmed students by Mexican security forces days before the opening ceremony of the 1968 Olympics in Mexico City, 'The government's subsequent cover-up of the extent to which its agents had caused the violence themselves served to show how important international opinion, and the role of sporting events in directing that attention, had become.'[26] Argentina's hosting of the 1978 World Cup was just such a seminal moment, both in a sporting sense and in a societal one, with the country in the grip of a military dictatorship at war with a significant proportion of its own population considered 'subversives.' Existing interpretations have failed to fully evaluate the moral ambiguity of the period. Levinsky suggests that a unified identity emerged during the tournament driven by a pliant press in support of the regime that negated any criticism of the government by human rights groups as being 'anti-Argentine.'[27]

By contrast, the analysis of Alabarces is rooted instead in revisionist post-democratic norms of morality. He argues that during the competition the conflation of football success and patriotic representation reached hyperbolic levels due to the association with the 'aggressive and fascistic' nationalism of the dictatorship, although accepting that later interpretations following the 1983 restoration of democracy in Argentina have changed the way scholars now view the tournament.[28] By contrast, viewing the 1978 World Cup through a purely contemporary historical context rather than the approaches employed by other scholars, this book arrives at new interpretations based on the actions of participants at the time, adding to the body of knowledge relating to this important juncture in Argentine history.

La Nuestra also amplifies the voices of previously under-represented sectors of society—women, Black people, *mestizos*, the interior and the young, showing how football provided a route to being heard in the

---

[25] Alabarces (2007, 95–104).
[26] Brown (2014, 145–146).
[27] Levinsky (2016, 186–187).
[28] Alabarces (2007, 111–126).

national discourse that was not available through other ways. Indeed, their stories are weaved through the chronology of the twentieth century, reaching public consciousness at various points as they intersect with wider processes of Argentine political, cultural and socio-economic transformation.

The role of women in Argentine football, especially as players, is a facet of the game that has grown in academic attention in recent years, especially Brenda Elsey and Joshua Nadel's 2019 collaboration, *Futbolera* and Ayelén Puyol's book *Que jugadora*, although David Wood's investigation of literary representations of female football in South America highlights how little has been written in contrast to that of the development of the women's game in Argentina compared with neighbouring Brazil.[29] Much of this research focuses on Argentina's participation in the 1971 Women's World Cup in Mexico, and this book adds to a better understanding of the thread running through the history of women in Argentine football.

Attempts to examine themes of race and provincial identity through football have been less convincing. In the existing literature, these themes barely get a passing mention. Jeffrey Richey's doctoral study of press coverage of race, ethnicity and provincial identity in Argentine football between 1912 and 1931 identifies a pejorative discourse amongst populist sectors of the Buenos Aires press, true of *Crítica*, a newspaper which applied stereotypes of backwardness to those of Indigenous and *mestizo* background from the northern provinces of Argentina. Other findings regarding the 'benevolent' role played by central authorities are contestable though.[30]

In terms of race, the sociologist Grant Farred argues that much of what has passed for racial discourse in relation to football in Argentina has come in counterpoint with neighbouring nations, describing the depiction of Brazilian players as *macacos* or 'monkeys' in the Argentine press during the 1920s as being a 'Darwinian trope that signifies Brazilian racial inferiority.'[31]

---

[29] Elsey and Nadel (2019), Pujol (2019), and Wood (2018, 569).
[30] Richey (2013, 117–119).
[31] Farred (2005, 104–105).

STRUCTURE

The thematic chapters are structured chronologically reflecting on different elements of national identity construction with supporting case studies as the century progressed, with some themes such as the role of women, race and the interior interweaving through the whole book.

Chapter 2 investigates football's arrival and diffusion in Argentina, arguing that a supportive environment on the part of Argentine elites and nation builders encouraged the arrival of British investment, which combined with a rapidly growing working class proved fertile ground for the spread of football in Argentine. It argues that there were three key disseminators of the game in Argentina in which British immigrants were at the forefront, or at least heavily involved: the private school system, the railway industry and neighbourhood clubs.

Chapter 3 examines how football contributed to constructions of *Argentinidad* within Argentina from the First World War until 1930. It deconstructs some of the myths surrounding the creation of *la nuestra* as a metaphor for an assimilated Argentine society arguing that Anglo-Criollos played a significant role that has hitherto been rejected. It also makes the case that following the decline in influence of the British community in Argentine football, the baton was picked up by the Italo-Argentine collective on the pitch, in the boardroom and on the terraces in a way that did not entirely forego expressions of Italian identity. Case studies of the Santiago del Estero provincial team in the Campeonato Argentino, the Afro-Argentine footballer Alejandro de los Santos and the first women's game in 1923 reflect on the difficulties encountered by 'voiceless others' in forcing themselves into the national discourse.

By contrast, whilst covering the same timeframe as the previous chapter, Chapter 4 focuses on how displays by Argentine teams on the international stage informed opinions of how the country was perceived abroad. Additionally, it shows how transnational relationships developed with Danubian football during the 1920s that helped shape Argentine football over the following two decades. As *rioplatense* football came to dominate international football in the 1920s and early 1930s, *La Nuestra* demonstrates how perceived footballing styles and national characteristics expressed through football were used as a means of separating Argentine and Uruguayan identity which had hitherto been viewed as a united entity.

Central to Chapter 5 is the relationship between politics and football in Argentina. Beginning with the introduction of professionalism in 1931, it shows how an oligopoly of economically powerful clubs, the so-called *cinco grandes*: Boca Juniors, Independiente, Racing Club de Avellaneda, River Plate and San Lorenzo, came to dominate Argentine football in a manner that reflected the wider democratic deficit in the country at the time. Whilst the link between Peronism and sport has been well documented, this chapter re-evaluates some of the lesser covered aspects of this relationship, firstly the promotion of the working class with the changing demography and demonisation of internal migrants as *cabecitas negras*, the role of footballers as workers highlighted by the 1948–49 Players' Strike, the weakness and inconsistencies in foreign policy that saw the national team withdrawn from international competition. Arguing that rather than being the 'Golden Age' of Argentine football as most writers contend, this chapter suggests the 1940s presaged the 'Age of Decline' that reached its nadir with humiliating World Cup defeat at the 1958 World Cup that became known as the 'Disaster of Sweden.'

Chapter 6, 'The Age of Revolution,' analyses the turbulent period between Juan Peron's overthrow in 1955 and his return to power in 1973. Beginning with the response to the 'Disaster of Sweden,' it investigates how Argentine football, like the wider nation struggled with processes of modernisation, raising with it existential questions about national identity. The chapter shows how this tempestuous period was reflected by changes in playing style as football became an arena for the political struggles and violence of the late 1960s and early 1970s. It also examines how societal changes in terms of the radicalisation of youth and increasing rights for women were illuminated through football through case studies of Estudiantes de La Plata's rise to prominence and Argentine involvement at the second Women's World Cup in 1971.

Chapter 7 explores Argentina under the *Proceso* and how the country lived through the paradox of its most important footballing moment, hosting the 1978 World Cup, coinciding with the government being in a state of war against sections of its own people, and how the tournament provided an arena for different concepts of national identity to be competed for. It also examines the role of football in maintaining the morale (or not) of the Argentine people during the *junta*'s doomed 1982 military adventure in the Falklands/Malvinas.

The final thematic chapter concludes by looking at the final two decades of the twentieth century in Argentina, highlighting how the international performances of the country's leading clubs, as well as the national team's 1986 World Cup victory, helped re-assert the nation's reintegration into the global community following the restoration of democracy in 1983. It assesses the transformation of Argentina under President Carlos Menem's neo-liberal economic policies, in which economic autonomy was surrendered to foreign capital for the sake of short-term riches, but which ended in *el crisis* of 2001–2002 which plunged huge swathes of the Argentine population into poverty. As such, it highlights how Argentine football faithfully reflected this process of globalisation, as the export of footballers and uniquely Argentine methods of player commodification reflected a neo-liberal economy based on 'competitive advantage' in what could be termed the 'Argentine Football Factory.'

Methodology and Sources

As an historical investigation that gets to the heart of understanding national identity construction over long twentieth century, *La Nuestra* has relied upon a range of primary written sources to better understand and interpret this phenomenon. The primary sources used have been contemporary newspapers, magazines, government publications, football clubs' and governing bodies' annual reports as well as personal papers. Given the century-long scope of this project, these sources best support the arguments presented by this book in displaying first-hand the opinions and actions of actors involved in the themes under investigation.

Archival research at the Biblioteca Nacional de Argentina and Tea y Deportea journalism school in Buenos Aires helped narrow down the choice of two key titles: *El Gráfico* and *La Nación* as the main underpinning of the research for *La Nuestra*. The main reason for their suitability is that both publications cover the entire chronological span of this book, something that cannot be said for other titles such as *Crítica*, *La Cancha* and *Goles*, allowing for a greater consistency of analysis. The editorial reputations of these titles mean they are both renowned for the depth and journalistic quality of their reporting, with *La Nación* being similar in editorial style to *The Times* in Britain and achieving what Daniel Lewis describes as 'international attention and prestige.'[32] Whilst it is true that

---

[32] Lewis (2001, 70).

other scholars, most notably Archetti and Alabarces, have heavily utilised *El Gráfico* in the course of their own research, the magazine's use in this book remains valid since it reinterprets material from the magazine used by other scholars, especially in the case study of Estudiantes in Chapter 5, as well as utilising previously unused articles.

Supplementing these key sources, other titles have supported individual case studies according to chronological relevance. For example, *Crítica* under the editorship of Natalio Botana during the 1920s had highly opinionated journalists pontificating on a range of footballing issues as he challenged for office in the footballing corridors of power. Argentine regional newspapers have also been referenced when examining the relationship between the capital and the interior. Titles such as *El Litoral* in Rosario and *El Liberal* in Santiago del Estero present a provincial perspective alongside those originating from Buenos Aires, especially in terms of agitating for greater provincial involvement in the national governance of Argentine football. More populist magazines such as *La Cancha* and *Goles* and the sports newspaper, *Olé*, are used given their self-appointed roles as the 'voice of the terraces,' enabling the consideration of opinions not always apparent in the two main sources. In a similar vein, as the sporting mouthpiece of the Peronist regime, *El Mundo Deportivo* is also referenced to better understand the link between Peronism and football. Uruguayan dailies such as *Mundo Uruguayo* and *El País* are used in the case study contrasting footballing identities between Argentina and its *rioplatense* neighbour. *La Nuestra* also analyses British and European national and local newspapers in examining footballing interactions between Argentine and European sides, to gain an outsider's perspective on constructions of Argentine identity through football and also to interpret the 1978 World Cup when the Argentine press was heavily censored by the prevailing military dictatorship.

To better understand the strategies of key institutions in Argentine football, the archives of the AFA, the game's governing body, available online in digitised format, as well as those of club sides River Plate and Vélez Sarsfield were accessed. Most documents accessed from these archives were *memorias y balances*, a combination of correspondence, annual accounts and reports in a single volume which facilitate the analysis of trends from year to year and changes and continuities in policy, as well as being a way of examining how these institutions have been affected by economic and political factors impacting Argentine society more widely.

The choice of River Plate and Vélez Sarsfield was predicated on the issue of availability, given that few clubs have written records available from the early decades of the twentieth century. These records illuminate the organisational identity of the respective bodies in terms of their corporate values, as well as mediating their opinions on issues of the day such as the introduction of professionalism. By analysing the commercial contracts entered for things such as land purchase and rental from railway companies, these sources highlight the role played by these companies in the development of Argentine football. Similarly, by recording who competed for office, they provide a point of departure for investigating wider political links between the governing body, clubs and political parties and state institutions. From the data contained in annual reports, such as membership lists, it has been possible to extrapolate further information related to the ethnic make-up of support bases. This proved extremely helpful when for example gauging the magnitude of the Italo-Argentine community in Argentine football. Furthermore, government records such as census data have been particularly useful for understanding immigratory patterns and government policies on issues such as naturalisation of foreigners.

In terms of personal sources, the diary of William Heald who participated in the first game played in Argentina, and player autobiographies such as those by Alfredo Di Stéfano and Osvaldo Ardiles give an insight into key periods such as the 1948–1949 players' strike and the 1976–1983 dictatorship through the thoughts and feelings of actors who participated during these events.[33]

References

Alabarces, Pablo. 2006. Boundaries and Stereotypes (or What Is the Use of Football, if Any Indeed?). Sociedad (Buenos Aires), January: 112.

Alabarces, Pablo. 2007. *Fútbol y patria. El fútbol y las narrativas de la Nación en la Argentina*, 4th ed. Buenos Aires: Prometeo Libros.

Anderson, Benjamin. 1983. *Imagined Communities: Reflections on the Origin and Spread of Nationalism*. New York: Verso.

Archetti, Eduardo. 1999. *Masculinities: Football, Polo and the Tango in Argentina*. Oxford: Berg.

Ardiles, Ossie. 2010. *Ossie's Dream*. London: Corgi Books.

---

[33] Heald (1867), Di Stéfano (2000), and Ardiles (2010).

Brown, Matthew. 2014. *From Frontiers to Football: An Alternative History of Latin America Since 1800*. London: Reaktion Books.
Di Stéfano, Alfredo. 2000. *Gracias, Vieja*. Madrid: Aguilar.
Duke, Vic, and Liz Crolley. 2014. *Football, Nationality and the State*. Abingdon: Routledge.
Elsey, Brenda, and Joshua Nadel. 2019. *Futbolera*. Austin: University of Texas Press.
Farred, Grant. 2005. Race and Silence in Argentine Football. In *In the Game*, ed. Amy Bass, 95–115. New York: AIAA.
Frydenberg, Julio. 2011. *Historia Social del Fútbol: Del amateurismo a la profesionalización*. Buenos Aires: Siglo Veintiuno Editores.
Frydenberg, Julio, and Daniel Sazbon. 2015. La huelga de jugadores de 1948. In *La cancha peronista: Fútbol y política (1946–1955)*, ed. Ranaan Rein, 65–80. San Martín: UNSAM Edita.
Goebel, Michael. 2011. *Argentina's Partisan Past*. Liverpool: Liverpool University Press.
Heald, Walter. 1867. *Diary of Walter Heald, Volume 1, 7 March 1866–13 September 1867*. John Rylands Library, University of Manchester.
Hobsbawm, Eric. 2014. Introduction: Inventing Traditions. In *The Invention of Tradition*, ed. Eric Hobsbawm and Terence Ranger, 1–14. Cambridge: Cambridge University Press.
Kittleson, Roger. 2014. *The Country of Football: Soccer and the Making of Modern Brazil*. Berkeley: University of California Press.
Levinsky, Sergio. 2016. *AFA. El fútbol pasa, los negocios quedan: Una historia política y deportiva*. Buenos Aires: Autoria Editorial.
Lewis, Daniel K. 2001. *The History of Argentina*. New York: Greenwood Press.
MacLachlan, Colin M. 2006. *Argentina: What Went Wrong*. Westport: Praeger.
Malcolmson, Robert. 1973. *Popular Recreations in English Society, 1700–1850*. Cambridge: Cambridge University Press.
Molinari, Alejandro, and Roberto L. Martínez. 2013. *El Fútbol. La conquista popular de una pasión argentina*. Avellaneda: Editorial de la Cultura Urbana.
Montenari, Enrico. 2018. '¡Hoy no hay fútbol!' La huelga de futbolistas de 1948 de la prensa Peronista. *Revista Historia Autónoma* 12: 91–204.
Pujol, Ayelén. 2019. *¡Qué jugadora! Un siglo de fútbol femenino en la Argentina*. Buenos Aires: Ariel.
Rein, Ranaan. 2015. *Fútbol, Jews, and the Making of Argentina*. Stanford: Stanford University Press.
Richey, Jeffrey W. 2013. Playing at Nation: Soccer Institutions, Racial Ideology and National Integration in Argentina 1912–31. Unpublished PhD thesis, University of North Carolina, Chapel Hill.
Romero, Luis Alberto. 2004. *A History of Argentina in the Twentieth Century*. University Park, PA: Penn State University Press.

Sáenz Quesada, María. 2012. *La Argentina. Historia del País y de su Gente*. Buenos Aires: Editorial Sudamericana.
Walvin, James. 1975. *The People's Game*. Bristol: Allen Lane.
Wilson, Jonathan. 2016. *Angels with Dirty Faces: The Footballing History of Argentina*. London: Orion Books.
Wood, David. 2018. The Beautiful Game? Hegemonic Masculinity, Women and Football in Brazil and Argentina. *Bulletin of Latin American Research* 37 (5): 567–581.

CHAPTER 2

'The Virile English Game': The Origins of Argentine Football 1867–1912

Football's arrival in Argentina was heavily shaped by the outcome of the civil wars which bedevilled the country from independence from Spain in 1816 that went the way of liberal national builders, who solicited foreign investment and immigrant labour to modernise the Argentine economy. The British responded with alacrity, and its economic influence was accompanied by the arrival into Argentina of other cultural and sporting practices such as football, disseminated through British community social clubs, schools and industries, especially the railway industry. Historians have considered this to be representative of British 'informal empire,' a term imbued with pejorative connotations, but this chapter argues that of the positive aspects to this relationship, the diffusion of football was one of its most benign and efficacious features.[1]

As with other sporting foundations, such as William Webb Ellis picking up and running with the ball at Rugby School in 1823, football's entrance to Argentina is surrounded by myth. Repeated ad nauseam by writers, especially outside Argentina, Tony Mason's 1995 assertion that football was popularised by the local population watching groups of British sailors kicking a ball about whilst waiting for their ships to be loaded or unloaded

---

[1] Brown (2014, 61), Knight (2008, 30), and Alabarces (2007, 39–46).

© The Author(s), under exclusive license to Springer Nature Switzerland AG 2023
M. Orton, *Football and National Identity in Twentieth-Century Argentina*, Palgrave Studies in Sport and Politics,
https://doi.org/10.1007/978-3-031-20589-7_2

remains remarkably resilient.[2] Despite Argentine-based scholars such as Julio Frydenberg confirming that there is 'no verifiable evidence' of this being the case, the sailor myth has become rooted because it supports later historical outlooks in which the arrival of football was part of a British neo-colonial project to dominate Argentina.[3] This populist revisionism provided for notions of worker to worker transmission of football, but is not rooted in any historical chronology, and has been designed to divert attention from what Alabarces considers to be a top-down diffusion from the dominant to the popular classes.[4]

By contrast, this chapter contends that football was diffused through a combination of both top-down and horizontal transfer at the end of the nineteenth century. These transfers were initially established through British private schools, railway works' teams and *barrio* (neighbourhood) teams in which the British mixed with other nationalities, enabling miscegenation and the production of new shared identities founded on a common cultural practice. Football became therefore such an integrative force once disseminated to the Argentine popular classes that it became a useful conduit for the organic creation of local identities amongst people from diverse backgrounds, independent of state-led attempts at assimilation into Argentine society.

The Third British 'Invasion' of Argentina

In 1806 and 1807, British military commanders, General William Carr Beresford, Commodore Sir Home Popham and Lieutenant-General John Whitelocke, exploited Spanish involvement in the Napoleonic Wars by attempting to usurp Spain's colonial rule in Argentina. Unprotected by Spanish forces, these unlicenced military actions were repelled by the inhabitants of Buenos Aires, in the process developing nascent ideas of Argentine national identity that ultimately achieved independence from Spain in 1816.[5] A succession of civil wars threatened to strangle the embryonic nation almost at birth, but victory by Justo José Urquiza over his erstwhile Federalist ally Juan Manuel de Rosas at the Battle of

---

[2] Mason (1995, 1–7) and Goldblatt (2007, 125–128).

[3] Frydenberg (2011, 25) and Brown (2014, 65–68).

[4] Alabarces (2018, 51–54).

[5] Harvey (2002, 12–13) and Knight (2008, 37).

Caseros in 1852 paved the way for the adoption of a new liberal constitution a year later, providing the basis for Argentina's economic and demographic transformation into a modern, multi-ethnic nation with full political control over its entire territory.

The overthrow of Rosas saw Argentina become more global in outlook as it sought to maximise the economic potential available exporting from its agriculturally rich pampas to markets in Europe. With Argentina's oligarchic land-owning elite loathe to invest the necessary capital expenditure on modernising the country's transport system and other infrastructure, economically liberal Argentine nation builders such as Juan Bautista Alberdi, Domingo Faustino Sarmiento and Bartolomé Mitre instead sought overseas investment. British investors filled the void, using capital accumulation from Britain's own successful industrial revolution to help construct Argentina's nascent infrastructure. British capital was particularly essential to railway construction, which Argentina desperately needed to get its agricultural produce to port and onwards to international markets, given the lack of natural communications like navigable rivers in the vast pampas. Between 1865 and 1913, trade between the UK and Latin America trebled as Argentina became Britain's leading trading partner, accounting for almost half of its overseas investment. This upgrading of Argentina's transport network alongside technological advances in shipping facilitated quicker and cheaper transatlantic trade with key European markets, as Liverpool supplanted Cadiz as the main destination for Argentine goods.[6]

Another reason for constructing the railway system, especially in the late 1880s when the network grew from 5,836 km to 9,432 km, was to assert government authority over all Argentine territory. With speculators reticent to invest in economically unviable routes, Argentine authorities offered concessions to construct lines to remote parts of the country. Under President Juárez Celman, Argentina indebted itself with loans from Barings Bank in London, offering profit guarantees to those foreign capitalists prepared to build them. Unfortunately for the government, the level of agricultural production required to service the loans failed to keep pace with repayments, accelerating the 1890 Barings Crisis in which only the intervention of the Bank of England as 'lender of last resort' saved Barings from bankruptcy.

---

[6] Rock (2019, xi), Sáenz Quesada (2012, 359–360), and Brown (2014, 61).

1890 was a point of inflection for Anglo-Argentine relations, as British banks called in their Argentine loans crippling the local economy, forcing the resignation of Juarez Celman. To re-open now harder to obtain lines of credit, the Argentine state sold its controlling interest in the railways to the British companies running them. Whilst Britain did not exercise formal political power in Argentina, the Barings Crisis demonstrated that through its commercial relationship, Britain could use economic leverage to ensure that its interests were not endangered by political decisions taken by the Argentine government. With the headquarters of the Ferrocarril Oeste and Ferrocarril Sur based at River Plate House, it is easy to see why this centre of British investment invited comparison with other colonial enterprises like East India Company and the Hudson Bay Company.

Despite this hegemony being described by some scholars as 'informal empire' in which Argentina simply exchanged one colonial ruler for another, with Argentina tied to Britain for the purchase of manufactured goods in return for its primary exports, the benefits of the arrangement did not all flow Britain's way. Since Latin American republics possessed neither the economic, technological, nor social capital to achieve the aspired level of modernisation, had the British not filled the void, then other competitors such as the United States, France and Germany would have replaced Britain as the hegemonic power instead.[7] As the nineteenth-century British Liberal politician Richard Cobden claimed, 'our miraculous railroads, that are the talk of all nations, are the advertisements and vouchers for the value of our enlightened institutions.'[8] As Colin Lewis notes, narratives of British economic dominance 'have disguised, diminished and deflected attention from the *anglo-criollo* character of initial funding in these activities.'[9] It was this sense of co-operation between Briton and Argentine that helped in the later popular diffusion of football.

Britain's exertion of soft hegemonic power also expressed itself culturally, accounting for the game's establishment. In 1895, the British community in Argentina stood at 21,788. Barely accounting for 1% of the population, the economic power they exercised meant that key individuals

---

[7] Williamson (1992, 280–285), Bakewell (2004, 441 and 491), Hobsbawm (1994, 39–40), and Lewis (2007, 228–229 and 261).

[8] Cited in Ferguson (2004, xviii–xix).

[9] Lewis (2007, 232).

in Anglo-Argentine commerce, such as George Drabble, president of the London and River Plate Bank and pioneer of corned beef exportation, held considerable influence within local society.[10] María Sáenz Quesada has suggested that the British collectively stood aloof from their host community as a result, maintaining customs such as taking afternoon tea at 5 o'clock sharp, and practising sports like tennis, golf, football, rugby and rowing as they did at home. They did this in newly built British suburbs carrying anglicised names such as Banfield, Hurlingham and Kimberley.[11] Divided by language and the Protestant faith from Argentines and other immigrants alike, the British maintained what Archetti describes as 'segregated cultural boundaries.'[12]

Despite these stereotypical representations, British migrants to Argentina were not a homogenous group. Markers like class and regional origin accounted for the extent to which Britons assimilated into Argentine society. The earliest arrivals tended to be upper- and middle-class English merchants, seizing upon commercial opportunities in the nascent republic's immediate post-independence period, confining themselves largely to Buenos Aires. From the 1850s, their numbers grew significantly as young Englishmen arrived to work on the railways, in banks, and other ancillary service industries that now thrived in support of British capital in Argentina. Often, they were public school or Oxbridge educated, 'Conservative in their political views and imperialist in sentiment' and 'great enthusiasts for sports,' according to David Rock.[13] Later in the century, they also settled in provincial cities like Rosario, Mendoza and Tucumán as these cities became better connected by rail with the capital, and in the pampas as estancia managers as cattle-rearing and wheat cultivation became transformed into modern agrobusinesses.

Soon after they were joined by working-class Britons who came to Argentina from the English midland and southern counties, attracted by the availability of work in the railway industry, a sector in which they were richly experienced.[14] Similarly, significant numbers of immigrants arrived from Scotland, initially working on the *pampas* as small farmers or

---

[10] *The Buenos Aires Herald*, 10 January 1893.
[11] Sáenz Quesada (2012, 232).
[12] Archetti (1999, 2).
[13] Rock (2017, 359).
[14] Rock (2019, 189–198), Buján (2015, 324–339), and Belich (2011, 524–528).

agricultural labourers in the mid-nineteenth century, and later as labourers on infrastructure projects in the capital and as railway workers. Again, the lure of improved economic opportunities not otherwise available in the populous central lowland belt of Scotland was the main driver for migration, whilst adherence to the Presbyterian strand of Protestantism also marked Scots out as different from the English in Argentina.[15]

Up to 30,000 people from Ireland emigrated to Argentina during the nineteenth century as part of a much larger emigration to the New World, triggered by the 1845–49 Potato Famine which decimated the population of the Irish midland and western counties. Largely agrarian in origin, Irish immigrants initially settled in the *pampas* hinterland of Buenos Aires, where they tended sheep and worked the land, effectively replicating their original status in their homeland. Thousands more migrated to Argentina as an alternative to the United States from the 1860s, escaping grinding poverty in Ireland's urban centres such as Dublin and Limerick, enticed by the promise of free passage and the job opportunities. Like other immigrant communities in Argentina such as the Italians and Spanish, the Irish set up their own banking, hospitals, Catholic educational and mutual aid institutions. Furthermore, Hiberno-Argentines took a greater interest in local politics than expatriates from the other side of the Irish Sea, joining the Radical Party (UCR) in significant numbers, pushing for electoral reform that eventually gave political rights to immigrants.[16] Hundreds of Welsh settlers arrived from 1865 to establish an agricultural colony in the barren southern Chubut region of Patagonia, 1000 miles south of Buenos Aires, but their remoteness from the capital meant they had minimal influence on wider Argentine affairs.[17]

Football's Arrival and Early Diffusion in Argentina

Football first arrived in Argentina in 1867, four years after the first rules were codified at a meeting in London's Freemasons' Tavern that founded the Football Association. Edward Mulhall, editor of *The Standard* in

---

[15] Rock (2019, 152–155).

[16] McKenna (1997, 77–81 and 388–390), Sáenz Quesada (2012, 325), Rock (2019, 144–145 and 197–198), and Kelly (2009, 182).

[17] Davies (2015, n.p.).

Buenos Aires, received a copy of these rules from friends in the UK and in turn passed them onto his friend Thomas Hogg, a fervent sportsman and member of Buenos Ayres Cricket Club. In England, cricket clubs had often been the source of football clubs as cricketers sought winter recreation, as the examples of Accrington Stanley, Sheffield United and Preston North End attest.

Keen to try the game, Hogg placed an advert in *The Standard* on 6 May 1867, encouraging potential players to meet three days later to decide on the rules for football matches to be played at the cricket ground. The meeting duly took place, where the rules were settled by those present, who elected Hogg's friend, Walter Heald, as secretary and treasurer of the new football section of the Cricket Club. Heald did much to promote this novel sport: his diary providing a unique insight into sport's importance amongst the British expatriate community. Heald proactively sought out new members and provided copy for *The Standard* which gave the new entity essential publicity. As he recorded gleefully the day after the meeting, 'got nine new ones, most of whom paid up on the spot.'[18]

After an initial attempt to play on the 25 May national holiday was foiled due to a waterlogged pitch, the first match eventually took place on the Corpus Christi holiday of 20 June 1867, on the pitch of the Buenos Ayres Cricket Club in the upmarket neighbourhood of Palermo. After a delay discussing the etiquette of wearing shorts in front of the ladies present, players were eventually split into two teams: the *Blancos* wearing white caps, captained by Hogg, and the *Colorados*, led by Heald sporting red ones. The *Blancos* triumphed 4-0 in a game played in two halves of 50 minutes.

Despite Argentine football's fuse being lit, it took another quarter of a century for it to fully catch light with early enthusiasm waning within a few months. As Heald recorded in his diary entry for 6 September 1867, a meeting of the football club was curtailed by a lack of attendees as club members preferred the alternative attractions of 'cards, boxing and cock-fighting.'[19] Numerous reasons account for this delay, one being confusion over the rules, with the rugby code gaining popularity in some clubs. The Yellow Fever epidemic of the early 1870s also led to the dispersal of the

---

[18] Heald (1867, n.p.).
[19] Ibid., n.p.

British population to the outer extremities of the Buenos Aires conurbation. The Buenos Ayres Cricket Club ultimately opted for the rugby code, but its footballing pioneer Hogg expressed in a letter to Mulhall his opinion that although it would take time for football to catch on, he intended to 'persevere' as it was the 'best pastime.'[20]

Clubs also started to open their doors to members of the Argentine elite, who perceived anything culturally British as the height of modernity, beginning football's gradual diffusion beyond the British community. By inviting privileged Argentines to play their sports, the British not only disseminated football in terms of rules and regulations and the promotion of healthy athletic activity, but also the *way* it was played. Argentine elites later adapted this model of sporting club for their own purposes. Gimnasia y Esgrima de Buenos Aires, initially founded as a gymnastics and fencing club in 1880, was emblematic of this development, with fencing being an elitist sport practised by the officer class of the military. The social element was also important to these elites, with *tertulias* or social gatherings an essential part of club life. Gimnasia acted as a catalyst for other clubs of the same name, the most prominent coming from the recently constructed provincial capital of Buenos Aires, Gimnasia y Esgrima de La Plata, formed on 3 June 1887. Four years after its foundation, it added football to its sporting activities.

Even within the wider British community, there were splits along regional and national lines. The Presbyterian Church was prominent in this respect, catering for the pastoral care of the Scottish contingent as well as organising social activities for its parishioners. One such activity was the 1890 foundation of St. Andrew's Athletic Club by Rev. J. W. Fleming as recreation for the Scottish railway workers amongst his congregation, who a year later became Argentina's first football league champions. St. Andrew's followed the example of churches and chapels in Britain such as the Aston Villa Wesleyan Chapel which gave rise to a football club of the same name in the Lozells district of Birmingham in 1874.

There were also sporting and social clubs that catered to specifically Irish tastes and concerns; indeed two of them: Lobos Athletic, the first football club to be formed in the rural pampas, and Porteño were founder

---

[20] Taylor (1998, 23–25).

members of the Argentine Amateur Football League's second incarnation in 1893. Porteño, formed in July 1895 as Club Atlético Capital, before renaming themselves after a winning bet on a horse named *Porteño* that enabled them to buy their first kit, were particularly emblematic. Porteño's links to the wider Irish community were reflected in 1899, when *The Standard* reported that club were holding a fundraising concert at Buenos Aires' Catholic Club.[21] Despite serving the Hiberno-Argentine community, Porteño were not institutionally strong advocates of Irish nationalism, something that gained currency amongst sections of the Irish diaspora in Argentina. Non-Irish players and members were welcome, as the presence in their ranks of the likes of Juan José Rithner, Juan Presta and Eduardo Uslenghi shows. Instead, those of a Nationalist bent opted for the sport of hurling, linked to the Gaelic Athletic Association (GAA) back in Ireland, which enabled the Irish community to come together without including their Argentine hosts.[22]

Mens sana in corpore sano

The primary agents for the propagation of football beyond the British community in Argentina were the British-run private schools. In contrast to Argentine state schools which focused physical education on individual gymnastics, those operated by the British instead placed great emphasis on the practice of team sports.

The incorporation of team sports such as football and rugby by British-run schools mirrored practices employed by mid-Victorian educational leaders both in the UK and in its colonies. The aim was to prepare the young men of the elites for their adult responsibilities as military officers, industrialists and administrators of the British Empire, or in Argentina's case to run its railways and estancias in what Alabarces considers as another example of football fomenting 'informal empire.'[23]

Ideas of Social Darwinism and 'survival of the fittest' underpinned this philosophy, with Herbert Spencer's 1861 treatise *Education, Intellectual, Moral and Physical* being influential in terms of propounding the improvement of the race, something that found resonance amongst

---

[21] *The Standard*, 28 July 1899 and Raffo (2008, 15).
[22] McKenna (1997, 77–79).
[23] Alabarces (2007, 50–51).

Argentine nation builders like Alberdi.[24] Argentine elites sent their children to be educated at these British schools in the hope that their youngsters would also be inculcated in these values to prepare them for public office and lead Argentine commerce and administration, giving something of a lie to the 'informal empire' rhetoric of Alabarces, since Argentine opinion formers actively emulated the British of their own volition. Some had been educated at British public schools themselves. Carlos Pellegrini, Argentine president in the 1890s, was an Old Harrovian and planned to establish his own version of the British public school in Buenos Aires, so that, 'young men may receive the intellectual and moral education to make them worthy citizens of a liberal cultured democracy.' The idea was eventually thwarted by his death in July 1906.[25]

This movement became known as 'muscular Christianity,' a term used in 1857 by a reviewer of Thomas Hughes' *Tom Brown's School Days*, in which Hughes recounts how young men were shaped by the public school system, and how the pastoral side of education was reinforced by the playing of sports in the pursuit of *mens sana in corpore sano*, 'healthy minds in healthy bodies.' It was a view upheld by an 1864 Royal Commission on public schools which argued that school sports helped form 'some of the most valuable social qualities and manly virtues.'[26]

Church schools were at the vanguard, with St. Andrew's Presbyterian Church, founding the Scotch National School, later St. Andrew's Scotch School in 1838, something that would have long-lasting consequences for Argentine football. Initially, the school only catered for the Scottish expatriate community. According to the school's founder, Rev. William Brown, education was best done within the community because, 'A new generation is springing up [speaking] the language of the natives.' Displaying an attitude of cultural superiority common amongst early British settlers towards their host community, Brown argued that his parishioners would otherwise, 'assimilate … in manners and ideas … Must they, whether old or young, be suffered to fall a prey to this evil?'[27] It was the later arrival to St. Andrew's of Alexander Watson Hutton as a teacher that gave impetus to the routine practice of sports at the school.

---

[24] Cashmore (2000, 299–300).
[25] *The Standard*, 11 September 1906.
[26] Holt (1989, 71–76) and Taylor (2011, 9–10).
[27] Dodds (1897, 25).

Born in the working-class Gorbals district of Glasgow, an area susceptible to emigration, Watson Hutton arrived in Buenos Aires on 25 February 1882 after graduating from Edinburgh University.

In 1884, Watson Hutton set up his own Buenos Aires English High School (BAEHS) in the southern Buenos Aires *barrio* of Barracas, giving fundamental importance to the teaching of physical education. The Scotsman strived to make his BAEHS more secular than St. Andrew's had been, where he had grown frustrated with the strictly sectarian and clerical policies of his Presbyterian superiors, teaching in Spanish alongside English in a bid to also attract Argentine and other immigrant students in what was becoming an increasingly competitive market for private education in Buenos Aires, as attitudes towards the host community became more progressive. In contrast to the narrow ethnicity propagated by St. Andrew's, Watson Hutton aspired to, 'bridge over that chasm which all too often separates persons of different nationality.'[28] As Watson Hutton, by now a naturalised Argentine, argued when retiring from the school in 1910, 'I have done everything in my power to mould [students] both physically and mentally to take their place as leading citizens of this great Republic.'[29]

Watson Hutton brought the first leather footballs to Argentina in 1885. When asked by customs officials what they were amongst his luggage, he replied, 'They are games for the boys of the college,' completely bemusing said officials.[30] A year later, he recruited the son of his former Glasgow landlady, William Waters, as a specialist sports master, the first to be hired in Argentina solely for that purpose. Watson Hutton opted for the association code of football over rugby, considering it less dangerous to his students. The Scotsman's focus was not just on the physical well-being of his male students, with BAEHS providing the first school swimming pool in Argentina, as well as the first girls' tennis courts, ensuring that his female students had sporting provision too. Indeed, these were selling points to the parents of prospective pupils. An advertisement in the *Buenos Aires Herald* in 1893 boasted of BAEHS being the 'Largest Private School in the Country,' highlighting its sporting offering, 'Gardens with Lawn Tennis for girls, Cricket and Football Field

---

[28] *The Standard*, 18 December 1901.
[29] *The Standard*, 21 April 1910.
[30] *El Gráfico*, 3 June 1933, 12–13.

and Gymnasium for Boys.'[31] These facilities led *The Standard* to report in 1902, 'athletics are carefully attended to at Mr Watson Hutton's school. He fully understands the importance of bodily training and gives it place of honour.'[32]

BAEHS were founder members of the second and more enduring version of the Argentine Association Football League (AAFL) established in 1893 by Watson Hutton, prompting contemporary Argentine sportswriter Félix Frascara to describe him as the 'Father of Argentine Football.'[33] After being forced change from name from BAEHS to Alumni because it was considered by the AAFL to be advertising for the school, Watson Hutton's rebranded club became the first great club of Argentine football, dominating the first decade of the twentieth century. Their record of ten league titles has only subsequently been surpassed by the *cinco grandes* ('big five'): Racing Club de Avellaneda, River Plate, Independiente, Boca Juniors and San Lorenzo. Alumni exhibited all the physical rigour and vestiges of fair play expected from students and graduates of a British private school. According to one of Alumni's former players, Carlos Lett, the team was more than the sum of its parts, with the close comradeship amongst the players a key aspect in the club's success.[34]

It was not just in Buenos Aires that British educationalists encouraged football to be played. In Rosario, 400 km north-west of the capital, Isaac Newell was a keen advocate of the game at his Anglo-Argentine Commercial School who catered for both Argentine and Anglo-Argentine in preparation for the world of business. With a similar lower-middle-class background to Watson Hutton, Newell arrived in Argentina from Rochester in Kent to improve his economic prospects, working as a telegraph operator for sixteen years before turning his attentions to teaching. In 1903, some current and former pupils banded together to form a club, which they named, in English, Newell's Old Boys, both as an act of respect for their mentor and in emulation of the old boys' clubs prevalent in English football at the end of the nineteenth century like Old Etonians and Old Carthusians.

---

[31] *The Buenos Aires Herald*, 8 January 1893.
[32] *The Standard*, 20 December 1902.
[33] *El Gráfico*, 3 June 1933, 12–13.
[34] Clarin.com (2003).

Again, Argentine elites emulated the British. Estudiantes de Buenos Aires, formed by students of the Colegio Nacional Central in 1898, were amongst the pioneers of *criollo* clubs. Amid their founders were some of the first *criollos* to represent the Argentine national team: Tristán González, José Buruca Laforia and José Susán. Anglo-Criollos such as Juan FitzSimon (who became the club's first president), Hansen and McHardy also featured amongst the student body, and as founding players for the club, reinforcing the part this group played in the dissemination of football in Argentina.

By 1900, the standard of football played by these schools had reached such a level that the AAFL added a División Escolar to its league competition. Whilst some like King Edward's College, St George's High School and BAEHS were clearly British-run schools, the presence of Instituto Americano and the Escuela Nacional de Comercio confirms that those competing were not exclusively so.[35] Central to the appearance of the Escuela Superior de Comercio was the work of headmaster, Irishman Dr James FitzSimons, a keen sports enthusiast in his own right, who contracted his compatriot, 29-year-old Paddy McCarthy, as a sports and mathematics teacher in 1900. FitzSimons was also instrumental in bringing sports into the Argentine state school system in his role as Inspector-General of Secondary Education.

State schools which were attended by Argentines and the children of immigrants alike become increasingly pervasive in Argentina following the 1884 Law of Public Education. Physical education in these state schools followed European models of individual gymnastics imported from Germany, Sweden and France, rather than British team sports, which according to Diego Armus and Pablo Scharagrodsky were perceived by pedagogues as 'an atrocious and savage physical practice and a vehicle for moral corruption, physical violence and questionable values from the street, not what young children should be learning.'[36]

Another reason individual gymnastic activity was preferred by state schools was that since physical education played such a small part of the curriculum, amounting to just two hours a week at most, the training of teachers in more complex sports was not the most productive use of scarce resources. This was further exacerbated by the fact that 80% of

---

[35] *La Nación*, 4 June 1904, 7.
[36] Armus and Scharagrodsky (2014, 85–86).

those entering the teaching profession in the early decades of the twentieth century were women, who were culturally excluded from football anyway. By way of comparison, Richard Holt has suggested that a similar emphasis on uncomplicated physical training compared with team sports, albeit with a military aspect, was present in British state schools in the second half of the nineteenth century too. The simplicity of military drills and marches was easy to both teach and learn, enabling the provision of physical education to a large number of students simultaneously as well as providing a basic grounding for the discipline that would be expected of them as the foot-soldiers in Britain's numerous colonial wars.[37] The chief ideologue of this gymnastic approach was Enrique Romero Brest, founder of the Instituto Nacional de Educación Física in 1906. Romero Brest argued that 'Sport and physical education are different concepts and, at times antagonistic,' further arguing that football was 'a suffocating exercise.'[38] This emphasis was challenged in Congress by the Radical deputy Le Breton, who argued in 1915 that football helped 'physical and moral development' and should therefore be promoted in the school system.[39] It would not be until the 1920s that football became an integral part of state school physical education in Argentina.

A similar story applied in the armed forces where physical training of conscripts followed the gymnastic theme. By contrast, team sports were thought by the British military to be essential for forming an *esprits de corps* in soldiers.[40] In 1933, Watson Hutton highlighted their success in the physical condition of the boys graduating from his school and the role of exercise in improving the fitness of conscripts over the previous half century.[41]

School football was therefore a method for the successful integration of young men of diverse backgrounds into the army, an important agent of national identity in Argentina at the turn of the twentieth century. Although the state's role in terms of using football for this purpose was non-existent at this juncture, private schools, both British and Argentine,

[37] Holt (1989, 135–142).
[38] Romero Brest (1905, 434).
[39] Congreso de la Nación (1915).
[40] Mason and Riedi (2010, 64).
[41] *El Gráfico*, 3 June 1933, 12–13.

used sport as a way of inculcating young men in the ideals of what national identity should be in Argentina.

Loco for Football

If British-run schools offered a limited space for children from diverse backgrounds to mix, British-run companies, especially in the railway industry—which provided 73% of direct foreign investment in Argentina in 1910—did so for adults on a far larger scale. As a result, the railway industry played a fundamental role in football's diffusion throughout Argentina.[42]

Works' teams were important in the diffusion of football around the world, not least in the game's English birthplace. As Mike Huggins and John Tolson have argued of the British case, the railways were especially important in the rapid diffusion and development of late Victorian sport.[43] This pattern was replicated in Argentina, with most companies engaged in constructing Argentina's infrastructure giving rise to football clubs being British owned. For example, Old Caledonians were formed by Scottish workers at the Bataume, Pearson Bataume sewerage works, whilst Reformer Athletic Club was founded by employees of the Smithfield refrigeration plant in Campana. Managers positively encouraged workers to play sports in their breaks and free time as a means of integrating men from different backgrounds into a common cause, as well as maintaining their physical fitness for employment. These management practices were linked to forms of welfare capitalism commonplace in early twentieth-century Britain, not only aiding staff morale but also acting as an inducement for recruitment. Shift rotation ensured there was a regular pool of players involved in these ad hoc games from which teams could be formed, whilst the integration of the *sábado inglés* or 'English Saturday' into the working week gave workers more time to indulge in their preferred leisure pursuit, enabling games to be played against other clubs on a weekly basis. Whilst this was not formally introduced into Argentine labour law until 1932, British companies started introducing a 1 pm end

---

[42] Lewis (2007, 234).

[43] Huggins and Tolson (2001, 2, 22 and 99).

to the working week on Saturday in the 1900s, replicating changing work practices in Britain formalised in 1911.[44]

Whilst Mason has suggested that there is no clear evidence in the English case about whether any particular industry was prolific in producing football clubs, it is evident that railway companies were certainly prominent, with Newton Heath, the antecedents of Manchester United formed in 1878 by workers of the Lancashire and Yorkshire Railway arguably the most famous example.[45] In Argentina, the railways played an even more central role, not only in terms of club formation but also in facilitating football's geographic spread, as 25,000 km of track linked Buenos Aires to virtually every urbanised area of the country from Salta in the north to Comodoro Rivadavia in the south.[46]

The employment opportunities and those for associated supply chains in Argentina were summarised by the *Railway Times* in 1888, which noted the need for 500 stations to be manned and maintained as well as 2,000 locomotives, alongside the need for rolling stock, drivers, guards and stokers.[47] The resultant arrival of British managers and workers provided another branch-line for football's development, enabling swifter diffusion to the local *criollo* and immigrant populations who worked alongside them. This impetus was largely horizontal, driven by employees themselves in the first instance.

The benefits of football were significant for workers, especially those engaged in the back-breaking toil of physically laying the new tracks, with excavation done by shovel and pickaxe, and removal of earth done by wheelbarrow. Given that these men were paid piecework wages per cubic yard of earth excavated, playing football contributed to good health and fitness, essential to workers in ensuring continuity of a good level of pay. Management looked favourably on football for numerous reasons, offering financial and logistical assistance to the formation of clubs by their employees. A 1927 *Railway Gazette* article acknowledged the benefits of football for railway companies, arguing that football was propitious for employee health and assisted in the integration of staff from differing

---

[44] Rock (2019) and Mason (1980, 28; 1995, 15–19).

[45] Ibid., 30.

[46] Zalduendo (1968, 269) and Rock (2019, 177).

[47] Cited in *South American Journal*, 7 January 1888.

ethnic backgrounds, aiding the creation of an *ésprits de corps* amongst workers.[48]

Arguably, the archetypal railway football club was Ferro Carril Oeste from the Buenos Aires *barrio* of Caballito at the geographic centre of the capital, where the first stretch of railway line in Argentina was constructed in 1857. Ferro were founded on 28 July 1904 by ninety-five workers of the Buenos Aires Western Railway at the encouragement of two of its British managers, David Simson and John Hardy. According to the club's founding statute, it was formed to promote 'physical exercise and football in particular,' amongst employees.[49] Ferro built their stadium on land ceded by the railway company alongside the Cucha Cucha to Avellaneda line, constructing a wooden club house from the packing cases that locomotive parts arrived in. This corporate largesse meant that whilst other clubs were frantically moving from place to place in search of a home, the club has remained at the site until this day.

The growth of commuter settlements, especially to the south of the capital, proved fertile ground for the diffusion of football as railway companies sought to popularise their newly constructed lines. Running south-east from Constitución Station through Avellaneda and out into Greater Buenos Aires, these satellite towns were initially populated by railway workers and their families. Station stops on Ferrocarril del Sud's branch lines gave rise to several clubs whose names remain inextricably linked to the railways, such as Quilmes, Lanús, Talleres de Remedios de Escalada, Banfield and Temperley. This is best exemplified in the case of Banfield. The settlement, named after the Ferrocarril del Sud's manager, was founded in 1873 in the municipality of Lomas de Zamora and populated mainly by workers of the company and their families. On 21 January 1896, local British residents formed a football club of the same name, playing matches on land adjacent to the railway line. This mode of diffusion mirrors the findings of Matthew Brown and Gloria Lenci in their survey of football's sport's dispersal in São Paulo in neighbouring Brazil, in which the development of the tram system between 1899 and 1910 acted as the catalyst for the construction of the city's sporting infrastructure.[50]

---

[48] Scher et al. (2010, 90–92).
[49] Mazzitelli (2011, 63–65).
[50] Brown and Lenci (2016, 175).

The railways were also essential to wider notions of consolidating and integrating the national territory. In addition to being a physical embodiment of Argentina's modernisation, the railways facilitated the expansion of the country's industrial base beyond the capital. The development of Argentina's railway network is a matter of some controversy. Juan Alberdi claimed in 1852, 'the railways will bring about the unity of the Argentine Republic better than all the congresses.'[51] By contrast, Ezequiel Martínez Estrada's 1933 treatise *X-Ray of the Pampa* complained that the railway system in Argentina resembled a spider's web, with Buenos Aires placed firmly at the centre at the expense of linking provincial centres, suggesting that it illustrated Argentina's dependency on foreign [British] investment.[52]

This view takes little account of the reality of railway construction into the interior of Argentina, without which the game could not have spread beyond the capital in the way that it did. Without state intervention in promoting the construction of branch lines connecting provincial towns and cities, given the reticence of British capital to invest in less economically viable routes, it is unlikely that football would have extended to these parts so quickly. It was the profit guarantees for foreign railway companies, combined with artificially reduced ticket prices, which ensured the heavy presence of the industry in the northern and central provinces that enabled the game's wider diffusion.

Progress began in the agriculturally important provinces of Buenos Aires, where no substantive settlement was further than 40 km from a railway line by 1920, and Santa Fe. This enabled Lobos Athletic, 102 km from Buenos Aires, in 1892 to form the first club in the pampas, their pitch being adjacent to the railway station facilitating their ability to compete in the AAFL against teams from the capital. Rosario, 400 km north-west of Buenos Aires, became the second most important footballing centre in Argentina thanks to the railways. All the city's major clubs—Newell's Old Boys, Rosario Central, Rosario Athletic and Central Córdoba—had origins linked to the industry.

Like Buenos Aires, Rosario had its own archetypal railway club, Rosario Central, formed following a meeting called by an English railway worker, Thomas Mutton, and attended by seventy colleagues on Christmas Eve

---

[51] Alberdi (2013, 143).
[52] Martínez Estrada (2002, 259).

1889. The selection of Colin Blain Calder, a manager with the Central Argentine Railway, as Central's first president reflected the tight control that the Railway's British owners exerted over Central and its multinational playing staff. Following the merger of the Central Argentine Railway and the Rosario to Buenos Aires Railway, club membership almost doubled from 70 to 130, but the strictness of Central's membership policy—restricted to just railway employees—hindered the growth of its playing and support base. It was only on the insistence of one of the players and founder members, Miguel Green, at the club's 1903 assembly that this rule was relaxed, and membership broadened to the wider community of their northern Rosario heartland of Arroyito.

Elsewhere in the interior, the heavy influence of the railways was also seen in the football of Argentina's second most populous city, Córdoba, which acted as a major interconnecting hub for the national network. The city's two biggest clubs, Talleres (meaning workshop) and Instituto, both originated from the Ferrocarril Central Córdoba railway company that connected the city with Rosario. This formation of football clubs under the umbrella of railway companies was a pattern replicated right across the north of Argentina. Workers of the Ferrocarril Central Córdoba, assisted by local residents, founded a club in Santiago del Estero in 1919 and were later one of the first provincial clubs to play in the Campeonato Nacional in 1967. In Salta and Tucumán, it was employees of the Central Norte railway company that provided the impulse for clubs of the same name. It was a similar story in Patagonia in the south where workers of the Ferrocarril del Estado established a club in Comodoro Rivadavia and those of Ferrocarril Patagónico did similarly in Puerto Madryn.

By way of gauging the influence of the railways on club formation in Argentina compared to other South American countries, a survey of all the clubs to have played in the continent-wide Copa Libertadores reveals that of the 21 clubs to represent Argentina in the competition, a quarter—Quilmes, Banfield, Ferro Carril Oeste, Rosario Central and Talleres de Córdoba—owe their origins directly to railway workers, with others having more tangential links. By contrast, amongst the other competitors, only Oruro Royal of Bolivia, Brazil's Jundiahy, Junior Barranquilla of Colombia and the Central Uruguay Railway Cricket Club (now Peñarol) can claim a similar direct lineage.[53] This was due to the geographical

[53] Fabbri (2012, 16–339).

advantages Argentina had over its neighbours for railway construction. The lack of mountains, large rivers and other natural impediments in the wide central belt of the *pampas*—the most economically productive area of the country—meant the need for tunnels, bridges and curves was drastically reduced, making railway construction relatively cheap compared with the rest of the continent and Europe. Whilst the work of Diego M. Gutiérrez, Marco Bettine and Borja García suggests that there was a similar pattern of railway diffusion in the Brazilian state of São Paulo, none of the clubs they cite had a similar level of national profile as the clubs identified in Argentina except for Jundiahy.[54]

The role of railway companies in football's diffusion also manifested itself in less obvious ways. By the first decade of the twentieth century, formal and informal football pitches were often located in the vacant lots besides railway lines, particularly adjacent to stations and repair sheds. This source of land became essential as municipal authorities in cities like Buenos Aires and Rosario failed to provide public spaces for recreational team sports, doing everything in their power to prevent the playing of football in public green spaces like parks and plazas to maintain their aesthetic aspect, and prevent groups of sportsmen from disturbing the peace of promenading citizens.[55] This contrasted with other major South American cities such as Montevideo and São Paulo, where the provision of recreational facilities with associated transport links was part of integrated city planning policies by municipal authorities. Developers forced clubs to move their grounds further and further away from the city centre in search of spaces to play, as land was used up for building. In this context of land shortage, accessibility to plots provided by the railways was essential for the continuation of such clubs. As the example of Ferro Carril Oeste shows, the ability to procure land on which to not only construct a football pitch, but also proper changing and clubhouse facilities, was a crucial factor in gaining admission to the league structure, the aim of most clubs in Buenos Aires in this period. For many clubs, the lack of available space on which to construct such facilities led to a peregrination around the city in search of a permanent home. In a city where laissez-faire planning regulations saw the construction of houses and factories grow exponentially at the turn of the twentieth century, the railway companies who

[54] Gutiérrez et al. (2021, 321).
[55] *La Capital*, 24 April 1929, 5.

owned the land adjacent to the increasing mileage of tracks around the Greater Buenos Aires area therefore became an important provider of playing space.

Railway companies drove a hard bargain where non-employee clubs were involved. Attempts by Temperley to rent land from the Southern Railway to build a ground were rebuffed by the railway company until personal financial guarantees were given by the club's president, Alfredo Beranger, in 1917 that it could fulfil its obligations. Others from the capital who rented from the railways included River Plate, who inaugurated their new home in the Recoleta *barrio* of Buenos Aires in 1923, after the club had led a nomadic existence moving from ground to ground in its native La Boca and the southern suburb of Sarandí. Thanks to the contacts of club president, José Bacigaluppi, the club struck a deal with the Ferrocarril Buenos Aires al Pacifico to move to the site on avenida Alvear and calle Tagle. The move brought River much needed stability as its membership grew from 1,080 in 1921 to 3,493 just one year after the move, as it constructed a stadium with room for 58,000 spectators.[56] The potential fragility of the arrangement was reflected in May 1923 when *Crítica* newspaper warned that whilst the club may have constructed a 'magnificent' stadium, their progress may have all been for nothing if the railway company declined to renew the rental agreement.[57]

By the 1930s, railway founded clubs had outgrown their British roots, becoming creolised to reflect the changes in society that saw second generation immigrants accepted as Argentines by *criollos*. The rules that only railway employees could become members of clubs became restrictive to their growth and development, and so they became more secular, broadening their appeal to the wider communities in which they were situated. Ferro Carril Oeste, for example, shortened its name from Club Atlético de los empleados del Ferrocarril Oeste de Buenos Aires to reflect its independence from the railway company. Likewise, by the 1920s as many of the members of Rosario Central had no connection to the railway as employees, the economic support given by the parent company waned. At a special assembly in 1925, the members declared themselves fully independent of the Central Argentine Railway. The response of the

---

[56] *Boletin Oficial de River Plate*, Año 1, No. 3, January 1929, 23.

[57] *Crítica*, 23 May 1923.

company was to evict Central from its land which it had loaned since 1918, obliging it to find an alternative ground.

As a key part of Argentina's infrastructural development, the railway industry was also an important agent in the creation of national identity through football directly by bringing together people from diverse backgrounds and acting as a catalyst for the game's diffusion into the interior. It also did so secondarily through the promotion of suburban lines and provision of playing spaces in substitution for state and municipal bodies.

CRISOL DE RAZAS: FOOTBALL, IMMIGRATION AND NATIONAL IDENTITY CONSTRUCTION

Immigration was a key factor in the social and economic transformation of Argentina in the early twentieth century, with football again acting as an agent in helping to assimilate immigrants into *criollo* society and in the organic creation of a new Argentine identity from these disparate elements.

To exploit the opportunities afforded by the opening of the *pampas* for cattle and sheep ranching, and cereal cultivation for the transatlantic export market, Argentina needed labour and lots of it. Influenced by Social Darwinism and Herbert Spencer's theories of racial determinism, Alberdi argued that the route to Argentine progress lay in 'improving the blood line' of its population, with immigration from Europe perceived as the answer. In 1852, he wrote presciently that from the assimilation of people with different linguistic and cultural backgrounds, a new Argentine nationality would emerge.[58]

State financial assistance was made available for immigrants attracted by Argentina's temperate climate to cross the Atlantic following passage of the 1876 Avellaneda Law. Argentina's 1869 population of 1.8 million more than quadrupled to 7.8 million by 1914, as foreigners accounted for half of the inhabitants of the capital, Buenos Aires, even allowing for the number of Argentine-born offspring born to earlier immigrants.[59] Whilst some immigrants settled in provincial cities such as Rosario, Córdoba and Mendoza, or worked in the countryside, the vast majority remained at their first point of arrival, Buenos Aires, where the greatest demand

[58] Alberdi (2002, 95–101).
[59] República Argentina (1916, 403–417).

Table 2.1 Net immigration to Argentina 1857–1914 by nationality

Italians	2,283,882
Spanish	1,472,579
French	214,198
Russians	160,672
Ottomans	136,079
Austro-Hungarians	87,108
Germans	62,006
British	55,055

Source República Argentina (1916, 201)

for labour existed. Better skilled and endowed with greater literacy than the existing *criollo* inhabitants from the popular classes, these immigrants therefore improved the human capital available in Argentina. Collectively nicknamed *gringos*, European immigrants had myriad reasons for going to Argentina. Some went to escape persecution, to escape poverty and to make a new life for themselves, whilst other *golondrinas* ('swallows') migrated back and forth across the Atlantic back to capitalise on the opportunity to earn money during the harvest seasons of both Argentina and Europe. Crucially, each contributed to new understandings of national identity.

Italian immigration was the most numerous in Argentina, accounting for almost half of all foreigners there by 1914 (see Table 2.1). Early immigrants came from the more prosperous, northern regions of Italy such as Liguria, Sardinia, Piedmont and Tuscany, but later arrivals in the late nineteenth century originated from the poorer southern regions of Apulia, Calabria, Campania and Sicily. Italian entrepreneurs dominated Argentina's incipient industrialisation at the end of the nineteenth century, owning more than half of the country's factories and becoming key players in the Argentine economy. As with other immigrant groups, the Italian community formed their own mutual aid societies, banks and newspapers, the most prominent being *La patria degli Italiani*, published between 1877 and 1930.[60]

The next most influential group were the Spanish community, who migrated primarily from the Atlantic provinces of Galicia (giving rise to all Spanish immigrants to Argentina being called *gallegos*), the Basque Country and the Canary Islands. By virtue of their shared language

[60] Orton (2022).

and Hispanic heritage, in some ways the Spanish had the easiest job of integrating into Argentine society. However, suspicions arising from Argentina's colonial experience, and *criollo* perceptions of them having limited intelligence, meant *gallegos* found themselves at the lower end of the social scale, consigned mainly to menial jobs such as street cleaners or dockworkers, although many achieved a measure of social mobility by progressing into the world of retailing and commerce. With the centenary of self-government in 1910, the standing of the Spanish community in Argentina underwent something of a renaissance as shared notions of Hispanicism became popularised by prominent *criollo* intellectuals such as Manuel Ugarte and Joaquín González, who claimed that *gallegos* were more desirable immigrants than those from other European origins.[61]

Another significant contingent came from France, working the land and investing in wineries, refrigeration plants and ancillary services such as the Banco Francés del Río del Plata. In a comparable way to the British, French influence in Argentina went beyond the economic to include the cultural, as Argentine elites consumed French literature and fashion.

For others, like Jewish immigrants arriving from Russia, and Lebanese and Syrians from the Levant, Argentina was a place of refuge from the pogroms of Tsar Alexander III and persecution by the Ottoman Empire, respectively. Ironically, the perverse descriptions of these communities as *rusos* and *turcos* cast some doubt about the level of sanctuary provided as both were marginalised in Argentine society.

The impact of mass immigration aroused debates about the country's identity within Argentine intelligentsia, as the government wrestled with how best to assimilate these arrivals into a common purpose. Those born on Argentine soil, regardless of parentage, were automatically granted citizenship based on *jus soli*. Therefore, the idea of being *criollo* or a native Argentine was being reinterpreted as the result of mass immigration. The conventional and original understanding of the term *criollo*, 'Creole' related to the white Argentine-born descendants of Spanish colonists, dating back to the sixteenth century. State-led attempts at assimilating these 'new' *criollos* came with the instruments directly under its control, principally education and the military as they sought to incorporate immigrant populations into a 'hyphen-less' Argentine nation.[62]

[61] Solberg (1970, 119–120).
[62] Goebel (2011, 43) and Gabaccia and Ottanelli (2001, 3).

The introduction of free, mandatory and secular state primary schooling in 1884 meant that the children of immigrants, whether they originated from Italy or Spain, were inculcated with Argentine patriotism. This was done through the teaching of *mitrismo*, a historiographical current based on the writings of former President Bartolomé Mitre which created a pantheon of national military and civic leaders in what became known as the 'Official History' of Argentina. Used in schoolbooks, this civic version of national identity was designed to elicit an emotional response in which the newly arrived immigrant and the *criollo* could unite in a sense of *argentinidad*. Argentine-born sons of immigrants became liable for a year's military conscription at the age of twenty, with policy being to mix conscripts from different areas of the nation and socio-economic backgrounds to accelerate assimilation. Nationalist intellectual Manuel Gálvez even suggested that this road to assimilation would be most quickly achieved in military combat, claiming that a war would invoke 'vast patriotic fervour' amongst foreign-born Argentines.[63]

Whilst encouraging the assimilation of youngsters, these policies largely passed by large swathes of the adult immigrant population, who in many cases lacked sufficient knowledge of Spanish to absorb it. Despite many immigrants arriving in Argentina with the intention of making a new life for themselves, only 2.25% of the foreign-born population took Argentine citizenship. Two key reasons account for this: firstly, with citizenship came certain civic responsibilities, including military service; secondly, their status as foreigners meant immigrants retained the legal protection of the diplomatic missions of their original countries whilst simultaneously enjoying the safeguards of the Argentine Civil Code.[64] For many immigrants, this was a price worth paying for not having access to direct political participation. This reticence to become citizens created tensions between *criollos* and immigrants, who in the 1900s and 1910s were held to blame by *criollos* for increasing social conflict within Argentina as the introducers of socialism and anarchism, with workers acting collectively in a meaningful way for the first time. By contrast, industrious *gringos* were equally scornful of what they saw as the idle nature of the *criollos*. In 1909, the Italo-Argentine writer Eduardo Maglione argued that immigrants had improved Argentina culturally and economically, and

---

[63] Gálvez (1910, 78).
[64] Sáenz Quesada (2012, 325).

that attempts to assimilate them to the 'indolent and ignorant creole mentality' would set back this improvement.[65]

In attempting to square the circle of forming a national citizenry out of these distinct social groupings of *criollos*, immigrants and descendants of immigrants, President Roque Sáenz Peña introduced the 1912 electoral reform law bearing his name. In addition to the introduction of secret ballots, the Sáenz Peña Law granted the vote to all men holding Argentine citizenship. As a result, far more immigrants became naturalised, whilst their Argentine-born children felt a greater kinship to the land of their birth than those of their forebears, giving rise to a more civically active and homogenous society.

Despite the concerns of nationalists, a discernible identity emerged from the cosmopolitanism of Buenos Aires at the most basic level. Immigrants from different backgrounds intermixed with working-class and middle-class *criollos* on a neighbourhood basis to create an organic hybrid civic society rather than disperse into ethnic ghettos, as happened in other countries of high immigration such as the United States. The lack of cultural homogeneity enabled the incorporation of immigrant customs and words, principally from Italian, such as *chau* (goodbye) and *pibe* (street kid), contributing to a new vernacular known as *lunfardo* and the emergence of new cultural expressions like the tango (which also incorporated Afro-Argentine influences).[66] The mutation of Spanish into this local slang became the de facto language of the street and was transformed into the written word with its adoption in popular media outlets such as the magazine *Caras y Caretas* as it competed for sales with others in a changed cultural market place.[67] It was within these rapidly urbanised cosmopolitan *barrios* of Buenos Aires and other Argentine cities that football became an agent for the establishment of a shared local identity. Football supplemented and to an extent, supplanted extant national identities, acting as an agent for integration and assimilation as the Genoan, Asturian, *criollo* and Englishman played side by side or stood together on the terraces.

Central to football's broader diffusion across both ethnic and class boundaries was its simplicity. Language was not implicitly a barrier, as

---

[65] Maglione (1909, 320–326).
[66] Scobie (1971, 190–195).
[67] Rogers (2008, 230–232).

this could be overcome with mutually understood gestures and body language, whilst the background noise from the crowd often rendered talking on the pitch redundant. As a new cultural phenomenon (to working-class Argentina), participants had no pre-existing notions of how the game should be played, allowing for home-grown idiosyncrasies to evolve, eventually forming a footballing identity that became apparent when transposed against foreign touring teams. Economically, football was a cheap sport, requiring only a ball, goal posts and space to play, enabling participation by the popular classes who were otherwise excluded from other elitist sports such as golf, tennis and rowing. Neither was it necessary to be a player to feel part of the collective experience. One could also do so as a spectator, expressing partisanship for those wearing the shirt of their local neighbourhood or co-workers.

It was this simplicity that enabled football to take a foothold amongst the popular classes. Whilst Chris Gaffney has suggested that football was able to develop unopposed by other sports, the popularity of pelota—a high-speed racquet game—amongst the Basque community did offer just such a challenge to football at the end of the nineteenth century as matches achieved attendances commensurate with football games.[68] The first pelota court in Argentina was opened in Buenos Aires in 1882 at Plaza Euskara and an 1885 match between two of the era's biggest pelota stars, Pedro Zavaleta and Indalecio Sarasqueta, attracted a crowd of 8,000, much larger than any attending football at this time.[69] Where the two sports diverged was the ability of football to break across ethnic lines, something that pelota was not able to do with such success. The technical nature of pelota, like cricket in Argentina, militated against its cultural transfer beyond Basque immigrants. Reputedly, President Julio Roca and Buenos Aires Mayor, Torcuato de Alvear, watched matches in 'puzzlement' at the inauguration of Plaza Euskara.[70]

The ethnic heterogeneity within neighbourhoods in Argentine cities meant that the tendency to form football clubs along national immigrant lines was far less prevalent than in neighbouring nations like Chile and Brazil. In those two countries, clubs such as Unión Española, Audax Italia and CD Palestino in Chile, and Palestra Italia (later Palmeiras) and

---

[68] Gaffney (2009, 160–164).
[69] Scher et al. (2010, 86–88).
[70] Torres (2010, 557).

Vasco da Gama (founded by Portuguese) in Brazil, were formed by, and represented distinct immigrant groups.[71]

The lack of ghettoisation meant that this process scarcely occurred in Argentina. Even amongst clubs of the British community, those such as Old Caledonians and St. Andrew's Athletic Club, which were overtly ethnically Scottish, had only a limited longevity. Clubs formed explicitly along ethnic lines were not established until the 1950s, with the arrival of Sportivo Italiano (1955) and later followed by Deportivo Español (1956) and Deportivo Armenio (1962), by which time the assimilation of immigrants into Argentina was an accomplished fact.[72]

If clubs were not formed exclusively along ethnic lines, then conversely, many chose names that exacerbated a sense of *argentinidad* ('Argentine-ness'). For example, the use of the suffix Argentino was common, as in the case of Argentino de Quilmes formed in 1899 in the largely British suburb, south of the capital. Vic Duke and Liz Crolley have suggested that this was done as a rebuke to the elitism of British community clubs who would not let them join.[73] Yet there was room in their ranks for Anglo-Criollos, which obscures such anti-British rhetoric. As *La Nación* recorded in April 1904, amongst Argentino's line-up for the derby match against Quilmes were two players of British origin, W. McIntyre and G. Morgan.[74] Another way of expressing patriotism was to name the club after Argentine independence heroes like José San Martín, Guillermo Brown, Hipólito Vieytes and Manuel Belgrano, as well as the pantheon of post-independence liberal nation builders like Bernardino Rivadavia, Domingo Sarmiento and Mitre.[75] Patriotic affectations extended beyond the naming of clubs, to also include the shirt colour and official date of foundation. When Club Atlético General Belgrano was founded in Córdoba in 1905, the club's youthful 14-year-old President Arturo Orgaz also proposed that the sky-blue colour of the national flag, which had been designed by Belgrano, should be adopted for the club's shirts. Even Alexander Watson Hutton wanted his famous Alumni team to wear sky-blue and white striped shirts by way of 'respecting the national colour,'

---

[71] Elsey (2011, 138–140) and Bocketti (2008, 275–283).

[72] Molinari and Martínez (2013, 147–148).

[73] Duke and Crolley (2001, 94–98).

[74] *La Nación*, 10 April 1904, 7.

[75] Scher et al. (2010, 25–29) and Asociación Argentina de Football (1918, 22–40).

before conceding that the decision to wear red and white stripes for which the team was famous was made by his students.[76] Dates also held national significance. For example, Primero Agosto, formed in Buenos Aires in 1904, were named after the date that the Viceroyalty of the Río de le Plata was established in 1776. The 25 May commemoration of Argentina's self-government from Spain in 1810 has regularly been registered by clubs as their official foundation date, most famously by River Plate.[77] These moves synchronised with the wider Argentine historiographical movement of *mitrismo*, which was hegemonic in state schooling at the start of the twentieth century.

This form of sporting nationalism mirrored currents being expressed elsewhere, most notably in Ireland where the formation of the GAA in 1884 to promote an indigenous form of football and the sport of hurling routinely used such markers in its cultural separatism from British influence. This was most clearly seen in the naming of grounds after nationalist heroes, as in the examples of Croke Park, Parc Mhic Dhiarmida and Casement Park. As Mike Cronin has noted, 'their very names celebrate the shared history of the Irish as a whole, not solely those attending the ground.'[78]

Football club formation therefore became an integral part of *barrio* miscegenation in the 1900s and 1910s, especially amongst the young, who eagerly took to the game. Adolescent and teenage boys were the motor for team and club formation, banding together either at school or through playing informal games in their local *barrio*. The example of the 1907 formation of Huracán in the southern neighbourhood of Nueva Pompeya by a group of fellow students at the Colegio Luppi, led by Tomás Jeansalles, is informative. The breadth of national backgrounds of the boys: French, Italian, Spanish and Argentine, exemplified the miscegenation going on across the city. Importantly, these youngster-led neighbourhood clubs differed from existing football clubs in that they developed from the grassroots up. Not constrained by managers or teachers, these youths had the freedom to operate the clubs as they wished. In the first instance, the founding members were often just those that had gathered to form a team, deciding on the accoutrements of the

[76] *El Gráfico*, 3 June 1933, 12–13.
[77] *La Nación*, 3 August 1904, 7 and Bertolotto (2016, 20).
[78] Cronin (1998, 93).

club, such as the name, colour of the shirts and design of the badge. Dozens, if not hundreds, of clubs were formed by such groups of young men, with *La Argentina* claiming the existence of three hundred clubs in the Greater Buenos Aires area by August 1904. In the same article, the newspaper also observed, 'No team should be allowed entry to the league that does not have organisation, a committee, books and pitch etcetera.'[79]

This point raised by *La Argentina* is important, as it highlights how football clubs mutated from ad hoc groupings of young friends into organised civic associations which intersected with Argentine society in a broader sense. These young men, some as young as twelve years old, through their desire to play football, developed civic skills such as forming committees, collecting subscriptions, keeping accounts and dealing with officialdom in terms of securing access to pitches. Petitions to state bodies, whether for land access or subsidies, were couched in terms of building 'sensible and decent citizens,' with the youngsters' responsibility to looking after any public property bequeathed to them sealing the symbiosis between the state and emerging citizenry.[80] In this, clubs solicited the help of local patrons to intercede with state and administrative bodies. The most prominent example was Jorge Newbery, the famous aviator, who assisted Huracán in their attempts to secure a ground and enter league football.[81] Many of these youngster-led clubs fell by the wayside, but a sizeable number still survive. All Boys from Floresta are, as the name suggests, the most obvious, but others include Boca Juniors, Excursionistas and Vélez Sarsfield.

Duke and Crolley suggest that, whilst these local identities emerged on the basis of *barrio* solidarity rather than ethnic background, this model of urban development gave rise to a rivalry with British community clubs in Argentina based on the different ways in which the game was diffused and differing 'values on and off the pitch.'[82] There is little evidence to support this given the level of crossover between social groups and modes of diffusion. Some *criollos* and immigrants of European origin also learned football in British and other private schools, whilst Anglo-Criollos also participated in these *peladas*, street football kickabouts where young

---

[79] *La Argentina*, 14 August 1904.
[80] Scher et al. (2010, 117–120) and Frydenberg et al. (2013, 1671–1672).
[81] Frydenberg (2011, 65) and Walter (2002, 27).
[82] Duke and Crolley (2001, 97–98).

working-class lads met and played football, like what was going on in the north and midlands of England and central lowlands of Scotland. As Holt observes of the British case, 'the spirit of "fair play" as advocated in the public schools had little influence on the way the working class played or watched their sport.'[83]

The increased cultural influence of football following its popular diffusion in Argentina was reflected in the media. After the first football match report was published in Spanish by *El Pais* in January 1901, the sport took an increasingly prominent place in the sports pages of the *criollo* press.[84] Argentina's most influential newspaper, *La Nación*, devoted more column inches to football in addition to coverage of horse racing, cycling, fencing, golf, pelota, athletics and tennis.[85] Match reports from the Sunday fixtures added extra pages to the sports section of the paper, as football assumed greater importance than these other sports during the 1900s. By 1906, *La Nación* moved beyond match reports and previews and began involving itself in polemical footballing issues of the day, making the press an active participant in the sport. That April, an editorial spoke of the lack of grounds able to provide spectators with the amenities needed for big games.[86] Meanwhile, the weekly magazine *Caras y Caretas*, which acted as a barometer of Buenos Aires society, first pictured a footballer, Arturo Forrester, in 1904 in recognition of being the first Argentine player to score against a foreign touring team when he netted for Belgrano Athletic against Southampton.[87]

The importance of football as a metaphor for the projection of Argentine identity became more pronounced during the consolidation period from the 1910s onwards as the game assumed a greater prominence in the popular press, something that was not reflected in coverage of other sports. Newspapers such as *Última Hora*, *La Argentina*, *El Telégrafo de la Tarde* and most importantly *Crítica*—the champion of the popular classes—played a crucial role in the popularisation of football. Through their pages, clubs and players became known to a wider public,

---

[83] Holt (1989, 148).

[84] Macchi (1981, 5–6); *La Nación*, 1 July 1902, 7; *La Nación*, 2 July 1902, 7; *La Nación*, 7 July 1902.

[85] *La Nación*, 2 June 1902 and *La Nación*, 7 July 1902.

[86] *La Nación*, 4 June 1906, 7.

[87] Macias (2011, 279).

who followed their results with increasing fascination. In the first decade of the twentieth century, a new generation of specialist sportswriters: Roberto Levillier, Ángel Bohigas, Escobar Bavio, Zalazar Alamira writing under the pseudonym 'Dinty Moore,' Rojas Paz who was better known as 'El Negro de la Tribuna,' José Gabriel writing under the guise of 'Last Reason,' Augusto Mario Delfino and Palacio Zini, broadened football's profile to the Spanish-speaking population of Argentina.[88]

The popularisation of football in Argentina was intensified by the introduction of an international dimension. Whilst cross-border matches had occurred for several years between Argentine and Uruguayan teams, the annual arrival of English touring teams, starting with Southampton FC in 1904, had a galvanising effect in promoting football in Argentina. According to *La Nación*, 'The arrival of Southampton can count itself as one of the biggest sporting events that has been held in our country, extending beyond the narrow confines of football to attract the afficionados of all sports.'[89] At a welcome banquet for the Englishmen, the tour's promotor, Baron De Marchi said that he knew that in the face of Southampton's power, the Argentine teams could not hope to triumph, but anticipated that the Englishmen would act as teachers, serving lessons for the Argentine players as they sought to perfect their game.[90]

The arrival of the 'Saints' was also recognition of Argentina by football's English originators as a serious footballing nation, coinciding with the affiliation of the AAFL to the Football Association, eleven years after Watson Hutton first solicited it. *La Nación* noted with pride that the only other association granted that honour from outside the UK was from Australia.[91] It was recognition of Argentina as an emerging international power in the game.

Southampton's opening match against perennial Argentine champions Alumni drew a record crowd of 8,500 spectators, marking football's breakthrough as a key cultural phenomenon in Argentina, not least as a 'spectacle' with the commercial opportunities this could generate. As *La Nación* reflected, the 'virile English game' was now so popular that

---

[88] Macchi (1981, 5–6) and Aira (2015, 29).
[89] *La Nación*, 22 April 1904, 7 and *La Nación*, 25 June 1904, 3.
[90] *La Nación*, 26 June 1904, 6.
[91] *La Nación*, 7 June 1904, 7.

it could now definitively claim to be the 'national sport.'[92] It was a sentiment shared in the English language press too, with *The Standard* opining that Argentine football had now 'left the infant stage behind' and expressing the hope that it would not be too long before Argentine teams toured England as well.[93] Ultimately, Southampton won the match 3-0, confirming their status as a team 'of the first order,' their 'scientific football' being good enough to have won the game by a bigger margin and ending Argentine notions of footballing grandeur. Argentine football now had a benchmark against which to measure its future development.[94]

The success of Southampton's visit gave rise to further tours by overseas sides. Nottingham Forest visited in 1905 and they in turn were followed by a team of South Africans in 1906. The visit of the South Africans was epoch-making in terms of football representing Argentine national identity. On 24 June 1906, Alfredo Brown scored the winner as Alumni beat the tourists 1-0, the first time that an Argentine team had beaten overseas opposition. The symbiotic relationship between football and the state was sealed when after the match President José Alcorta sought out and embraced Brown, an act described by the novelist Osvaldo Soriano as, 'the first time that a president had used football for popular ends.'[95] It was regarded by the press as a victory for all of Argentina, not just the British community in Argentina. Argentine football had at last shown it could compete with the foreigners. As *La Nación* crowed, 'For our national football, Alumni – South Africa constituted a total triumph and it will remain long in the memory, serving as an example and stimulating the future.'[96] By the time Southern League side Swindon Town visited Argentina in 1912, the improvement in quality of the Argentine game was evident, with two of the six tour matches being drawn. After the second draw, *The Standard* recognised that Argentine football had attained a 'high degree of excellence,' acknowledging that the men in sky-blue and white striped shirts had 'played really well and there was hardly a weak spot in it.'[97]

---

[92] *La Nación*, 27 June 1904, 4.
[93] *The Standard*, 29 June 1904, 1.
[94] *La Nación*, 27 June 1904, 4.
[95] Cited in Fernández Moores (2010, 68).
[96] *La Nación*, 25 June 1906, 8.
[97] *The Standard*, 1 July 1912, 2.

In barely three decades, football in Argentina had gone from a sport played almost exclusively by the British community to Argentina's national game and a symbol of organic assimilation and a cultural signifier of Argentina internationally. As *La Nación* noted in 1916, 'The diffusion of football has reached unexpected limits. Its national character clearly defined.'[98]

The game's arrival in 1867 coincided with a period of British economic and cultural hegemony, encouraged by a group of modernising Argentine nation builders, who saw Britain as a source of emulation. This led to football being considered by historians an agent of Britain's 'informal empire' in Argentina, especially through its diffusion through British-run private schools and railway companies. Whilst this position has its merits, it is a partial interpretation, with class being a more crucial factor than nationality. Diffusion through the school system was limited to those who could afford to attend private schools. Whilst schools such as the BAEHS did act as a bridge between the various communities in Argentina, promoting a set of values considered by liberal national builders to be essential to the future good running of the country through the playing of sport, their scope was rather limited. As in the UK, those from the popular classes received no such formal tutelage in the sport or the associated acculturation in its values.

Workers in British-owned companies, particularly the railway industry, provided a more propitious vector for the diffusion of football and the assimilation of immigrants. Whilst the practice was initiated by British employees, it soon gained traction amongst their Argentine and immigrant co-workers, acting as an adhesive for integration amongst the various nationalities, leading the South American correspondent of the *Railway Gazette* to query in 1927, 'whether it would have been discovered so rapidly, or the games taken to with such interest and promptness, if they did not have the example of British engineers and contractors that arrived in the country from the middle of the century to start the construction of the railway.'[99]

There were also secondary effects for football's diffusion coming from the spread of the railway network in Argentina. The construction of commuter towns, especially to the south of the Greater Buenos Aires

---

[98] *La Nación*, 18 July 1916, 6.
[99] Cited in Scher et al. (2010, 90–92).

conurbation provided new opportunities for club formation as their populations increased. Railway companies had land available immediately adjacent to the tracks, repair yards and stations, that was not suitable for industrial and house construction, but usable for football pitches. In football's consolidation phase, this availability often meant the difference between a foundling club thriving or folding.

The popular diffusion of football in Argentina coincided with mass European immigration and concurrent debates over national identity as Argentina celebrated a centenary of independence. The absence of strictly ethnically based ghettos amongst immigrants meant that clubs representing specific national communities in Argentine football were rare compared to neighbouring countries. By contrast, football provided a valuable vehicle for miscegenation at a local neighbourhood level, demonstrating immigrants' civic attachment to Argentina by naming clubs after national icons, exemplifying the prevailing historiographical current of *mitrismo*.

References

Aira, Carlos. 2015. *Héroes de Tiento: Historias del Fútbol Argentina 1920–1930*. Buenos Aires: Ediciones Fabro.
Alabarces, Pablo. 2007. *Fútbol y patria. El fútbol y las narrativas de la Nación en la Argentina*, 4th ed. Buenos Aires: Prometeo Libros.
Alabarces, Pablo. 2018. *Historía Mínima del fútbol en América Latina*. Madrid: Turner Publicaciones.
Alberdi, Juan B. 2002. Immigration as a Means of Progress. In *The Argentina Reader*, ed. Gabriela Nouzeilles and Graciela Montaldo, 95–101. Durham, NC: Duke University Press.
Alberdi, Juan B. 2013. Bases and Starting Points for the Argentine Republic (1852) (Excerpts). In *Liberal Thought in Argentina 1837–1940*, ed. Natalio R. Botana and Ezequiel Gallo, 115–176. Indianapolis: Liberty Fund Inc.
Archetti, Eduardo. 1999. *Masculinities: Football, Polo and the Tango in Argentina*. Oxford: Berg.
Armus, Diego, and Pablo Scharagrodsky. 2014. El Fútbol en las Escuelas y Colegios Argentinos Notas Sobre un Desencuentro en el Siglo XX. In *Del football al fútbol/futebol: historias argentinas, brasileras y uruguayas en el siglo xx*, ed. Diego Armus and Stefan Rinke, 85–100. Madrid: Iberoamericana.
Asociación Argentina de Football. 1918. *Memoria y Balance General 1917*. Buenos Aires: Imp. Kidd & Cia.
Bakewell, Peter. 2004. *A History of Latin America*, 2nd ed. Oxford: Blackwell.
Belich, James. 2011. *Replenishing the Earth: The Settler Revolution and the Angloworld*. Oxford: Oxford University Press.

Bertolotto, Miguel Ángel. 2016. *River Plate. Mientras viva tu bandera*. Buenos Aires: Atlántida.

Bocketti, Greg. 2008. Italian Immigrants, Brazilian Football, and the Dilemma of National Identity. *Journal of Latin American Studies* 40: 275–302.

Brown, Matthew. 2014. *From Frontiers to Football: An Alternative History of Latin America Since 1800*. London: Reaktion Books.

Brown, Matthew, and Gloria Lanci. 2016. Football and Urban Expansion in São Paulo, Brazil 1880–1920. *Sport in History* 36 (2): 162–189.

Buján, Jorge. 2015. Neo-gothic Style in Argentina: Shaping British National Identity in Exile. *Postmedieval* 6 (3) (Fall): 324–339.

Cashmore, Ellis. 2000. *Sports Culture: An A-Z Guide*. London: Routledge.

Clarin.com. 2003. Alumni: en el nombre de fútbol. 24 April. https://www.clarin.com/deportes/alumni-nombre-futbol_0_Syv-vh-xAKg.html#:~:text=Se%20llam%C3%B3%20as%C3%AD%20porque%20un,camiseta%20blanca%20a%20bastones%20rojos. Accessed 19 February 2015.

Congreso de la Nación Cámara de Diputados. 1915. *Diario de Sesiones, 18 August 1915*. Buenos Aires.

Cronin, Mike. 1998. Enshrined in Blood: The Naming of Gaelic Athletic Association Grounds and Clubs. *Sports Historian* 18 (1): 90–104.

Davies, Steph. 2015. *Hiraeth: Stories from Welsh Patagonia*. Wales: Parthian.

Dodds, James. 1897. *Records of the Scottish Settlers and Their Churches*. Buenos Aires: Grant and Sylvester.

Duke, Vic, and Liz Crolley. 2001. Fútbol, Politicians and the People: Populism and Politics in Argentina. *The International Journal of the History of Sport* 18 (3): 93–116.

Elsey, Brenda. 2011. *Citizens & Sportsmen: Fútbol & Politics in 20th Century Chile*. Austin: University of Texas Press.

Fabbri, Alejandro. 2012. *El Nacimiento de una Pasión Continental*. Buenos Aires: Capital Intelectual,

Ferguson, Niall. 2004. *Empire: How Britain Made the Modern World*. London: Penguin Books.

Fernández Moores, Ezequiel. 2010. *Breve historia del deporte argentino*. Buenos Aires: El Ateneo.

Frydenberg, Julio. 2011. *Historia Social del Fútbol: Del amateurismo a la profesionalización*. Buenos Aires: Siglo Veintiuno Editores.

Frydenberg, Julio, Rodrigo Daskal, and César R. Torres. 2013. Sports Clubs with Football in Argentina: Conflicts, Debates and Continuities. *The International Journal of the History of Sport* 30 (14): 1670–1686.

Gabaccia, Donna R., and Fraser M. Ottanelli, eds. 2001. *Italian Workers of the World: Labour Migration and the Formation of Multiethnic States*. Chicago: University of Illinois Press.

Gaffney, Chris. 2009. Stadiums and Society in Twenty-First Century Buenos Aires. *Soccer and Society* 10 (2): 160–182.

Gálvez, Manuel. 1910. *El diario de Gabriel Quiroga: Opiniones sobre la vida argentina*. Buenos Aires: Arnoldo Moen & Hno.
Goebel, Michael. 2011. *Argentina's Partisan Past*. Liverpool: Liverpool University Press.
Goldblatt, David. 2007. *The Ball Is Round: A Global History of Football*. London: Penguin.
Gutiérrez, Diego M., Marco Bettine, and Borja García. 2021. The Railway and the Ball, the Spread of Football in São Paulo State. *Sport in History* 41 (3): 309–332.
Harvey, Robert. 2002. *Liberators: South America's Savage Wars of Freedom 1810–30*. London: Robinson.
Heald, Walter. 1867. *Diary of Walter Heald, Volume 1, 7 March 1866–13 September 1867*. John Rylands Library, University of Manchester.
Hobsbawm, Eric. 1994. *The Age of Empire 1875–1914*. London: Abacus.
Holt, Richard. 1989. *Sport and the British: A Modern History*. Oxford: Clarendon Paperbacks.
Huggins, Mike, and John Tolson. 2001. The Railways and Sport in Victorian Britain: A Critical Reassessment. *The Journal of Transport History* 22 (2) (September): 99–115.
Kelly, Helen. 2009. *Irish "Ingleses." The Irish Experience in Argentina 1840–1920*. Dublin: Irish Academic Press.
Knight, Alan. 2008. Rethinking British Informal Empire in Latin America (Especially Argentina). In *Informal Empire in Latin America: Culture, Commerce and Capital*, ed. Matthew Brown, 23–48. Oxford: Blackwell.
Lewis, Colin M. 2007. «Anglo-Criollo» Rather than British: Early Investments in Argentinian Railways and Utilities. In *Estudios sobre la Historia de los Ferrocarriles Argentinos (1857–1940)*, ed. Jorge Schvarzer and Andrés Martín Regalsky, 223–270. Buenos Aires: Universidad de Buenos Aires.
Macchi, Rubén René. 1981. *Desde 1893 Hasta 1981 Toda la Historia de la Selección Argentina*. Buenos Aires: GAM Ediciones.
Macias, Julio. 2011. *Quién es quién de la Selección Argentina: diccionario sobre los futbolistas internacionales: 1902–2010*. Buenos Aires: Corregidor.
Maglione, Eduardo F. 1909. Cosmopolitismo y espíritu nacional. *Renacimiento* II (November): 320–326.
Martínez Estrada, Ezequiel. 2002. X-Ray of the Pampa. In *The Argentina Reader*, ed. Gabriela Nouzeilles and Graciela Montaldo, 259–262. Durham, NC: Duke University Press.
Mason, Tony. 1980. *Association Football & English Society 1863–1915*. Brighton: Branch Line.
Mason, Tony. 1995. *Passion of the People? Football in South America*. London: Verso.
Mason, Tony, and Eliza Riedi. 2010. *Sport and the Military: The British Armed Forces, 1880–1960*. Cambridge: Cambridge University Press.
Mazzitelli, Hugo Daniel. 2011. *Ferro y Su Gente*. Buenos Aires: Nueva Libreria.

McKenna, Patrick. 1997. Irish Migration to Argentina. In *Patterns of Migration*, ed. Patrick O'Sullivan, 63–83. Leicester: Leicester University Press.

Molinari, Alejandro, and Roberto L. Martínez. 2013. *El Fútbol. La conquista popular de una pasión argentina.* Avellaneda: Editorial de la Cultura Urbana.

Orton, Mark. 2022. The Game of the Italians: Football and Dual Identity in Argentina 1910–1935. *Studia Universitatis Babes-Bolyai, Historia* 67 (2): (in press).

Raffo, Víctor. 2008. Irish Association Football in Argentina. *Irish Migration Studies in Latin America* 6 (1) (March): 15–20.

República Argentina. 1916. *Tercer censo nacional, leventado el 1° de junio de 1914.* Buenos Aires.

Rock. David. 2017. Anglicanism in Latin America, 1810–1918. In *The Oxford History of Anglicanism, Volume III*, Chapter 18. Oxford: Oxford University Press.

Rock, David. 2019. *The British in Argentina: Commerce, Settlers & Power, 1800–2000*. Cham: Palgrave Macmillan.

Rogers, Geraldine. 2008. *Caras y Caretas, Cultura, Política y Espectáculo en los Inicios del Siglo XX Argentina*. La Plata: EDULP.

Romero Brest, Enrique. 1905. *Curso superior de educación física. Tomo II: pedagogía y práctica de la educación física*. Buenos Aires: Las Ciencias.

Sáenz Quesada, María. 2012. *La Argentina. Historia del País y de su Gente*. Buenos Aires: Editorial Sudamericana.

Scher, Ariel, Guillermo Blanco, and Jorge Búsico. 2010. *Deporte Nacional*. Buenos Aires: Emecé.

Scobie, James. 1971. *Argentina, a City and a Nation*. Oxford: Oxford University Press.

Solberg, Carl. 1970. *Immigration and Nationalism*. Austin: University of Texas Press.

Taylor, Chris. 1998. *The Beautiful Game—A Journey Through Latin American Football*. London: Victor Gollancz.

Taylor, Matthew. 2011. *Football: A Short History*. Oxford: Shire Publications.

Torres, César R. 2010. South America. In *Routledge Companion to Sports History*, ed. S. W. Pope and John Nauright, 553–570. Abingdon: Routledge.

Walter, Richard J. 2002. *Politics and Urban Growth in Buenos Aires 1910–1942*. Cambridge: Cambridge University Press.

Williamson, Edwin. 1992. *The Penguin History of Latin America*. London: Penguin Books.

Zalduendo, Eduardo. 1968. *Las inversiones británicos para la promoción y desarrollo de ferrocarriles el siglo X IX: el caso de Argentina, Brasil, Canadá e India*. Buenos Aires: Instituto Torcuato Di Tella.

CHAPTER 3

Creating Argentinidad Through Football 1913–1930

This chapter focuses on how football reflected socio-political debates that shaped the period between 1913 and 1930, which marked the democratic opening of Argentina following the passing of the Sáenz Peña electoral reforms of 1912 and its abrupt ending with the military overthrow of President Yrigoyen. Chief amongst these debates was the 'social question' of how best to assimilate millions of European and Middle Eastern immigrants into a cohesive Argentine identity. One way in which this identity was articulated was through the development in the press of an idiosyncratic Argentine footballing style called *la nuestra* during the 1920s. Predicated on perceived differences with that played by the game's British originators, *la nuestra* offered a way for Argentines to 'decolonise' football and claim it as their own, as a narrative for assimilation. This chapter demonstrates that this mythical construction needs revision, especially the discourse surrounding the '*criollo* rebirth' in 1913 which denied any continued Anglo-Argentine involvement in the game. Other prominent issues of national identity were either repressed, marginalised or excluded completely. Amongst these issues were the role of women, notions of dual-identity which complicated the process of full assimilation of immigrants, race, and the position of Afro-Argentines and Indigenous people in Argentine society as well as the relationship between the central power of Buenos Aires and the interior of Argentina. This chapter assesses

© The Author(s), under exclusive license to Springer Nature Switzerland AG 2023
M. Orton, *Football and National Identity in Twentieth-Century Argentina*, Palgrave Studies in Sport and Politics,
https://doi.org/10.1007/978-3-031-20589-7_3

the extent to which football offered these under-represented sectors a visibility not otherwise available within Argentine society in an area that has been overlooked by scholars.

The mythical discourse surrounding Argentine football casting off its British roots with the concept of a '*criollo* rebirth,' symbolised by Racing Club de Avellaneda winning the 1913 Asociación Argentina de Football version of the league title with a team mainly composed of non-British origin players, has remained durable in the work of academics like Pablo Alabarces, Eduardo Archetti and Osvaldo Bayer. This chapter argues that the process of *criolliziación* was less linear and did not signify the end of British influence on Argentine football in the way they have suggested.[1]

The literature on Argentina has tended to be silent about the level of dual identity in the country during the early twentieth century, focusing instead on the assimilation experience. As Fernando Devoto has noted, in Argentine historiography, unlike that in the United States, scholars have been reluctant to describe the nation as a multi-ethnic society.[2] This chapter explores how football offered a way for the Italian community to exert a greater influence in Argentine society than their absolute numbers would otherwise suggest, investigating the agency of the collective as administrators, players and supporters. Furthermore, by investigating the case study of Genoa's 1923 tour to Argentina, it shows how football gave the Italo-Argentine community opportunity to also express its Italian identity.

Having focused on how football came to reflect changes in Argentine economic hierarchies, the chapter moves on to examine the role the sport played in giving voice to under-represented sectors of Argentine society, starting with women. Using contemporary press coverage, it builds on preliminary work done by Brenda Elsey and Joshua Nadel on the origins of women's participation as players in Argentine football before exploring the wider juxtaposition of women in the footballing sphere in the early part of the twentieth century.[3]

Whilst discourses surrounding ethnicity and the assimilation of white immigrants have dominated the historiography of Argentine national

---

[1] Bayer (2016, 15–19), Alabarces (2007, 39–46), and Archetti (1999, 58–65).

[2] Devoto (2001, 41).

[3] Elsey and Nadel (2019).

identity, the issue of race and racism has received less academic attention, although Erika Edwards' 2019 work about the African-descended population in Argentina, 'Hiding in Plain Sight' has led efforts to counter this.[4] It is a narrative dominated since the nineteenth century by exclusion, as liberal nation builders geared immigration to make Argentina a white, Europeanised and 'civilised' nation, whilst concurrently trying to erase the Indigenous population and eject them from their land. The *crisol de razas* designed to incorporate immigrants into a single national identity, explicitly excluded Afro-descendants and Indigenous Argentines. As Barbara Sutton observes, Afro-Argentines were 'rendered invisible,' with their absence in society attributed to attrition in Argentina's civil wars of the nineteenth century and the War of the Triple Alliance against Paraguay, which saw a disproportionate number of Black people do the fighting.[5] This negation also features in the historiography of Argentine football. Archetti wrote 'The Argentinians never imagined that they could play like Brazilians because they never had black players on the most successful national teams.'[6] Grant Farred contends 'It is not simply that Argentine society is so adept at marking and demeaning "foreign" blackness, but that Veron-ismo – Farred's argument that the Argentine player of the 1990s and 2000s, Juan Sebastián Verón was black but never represented as such – is resilient in its refusal to see difference amongst its own national subjects.'[7] This chapter highlights that this is not entirely the case, as there was an Afro-Argentine presence in Argentine football, albeit with very few examples. Furthermore, it examines how in this perceived absence, a racial discourse was projected onto those footballers visiting Argentina as a way of buttressing the country's self-perception as a 'civilised European' country, in contrast to neighbouring Brazil in which constructions of national identity have been highly inclusionary of its mulatto and African heritage, leading Roger Kittleson to conclude that, 'Conceptions of *brasildade* in soccer depended on theories that Brazil had a mixed-race culture.'[8]

---

[4] Edwards (2019).
[5] Sutton (2008, 107–108), and Farred (2005, 99).
[6] Archetti (1999, 75–76).
[7] Farred (2004, 56).
[8] Kittleson (2014, 6–8).

The chapter concludes by examining the relationship between Argentina's capital, Buenos Aires, and the interior of the country. It is a discourse that has also been overlooked in the existing football literature save for the scholarship of Jeffrey Richey, whose work this chapter builds on through a thorough investigation of the role of the Campeonato Argentina in this relationship and representations of the interior in Argentine football.[9]

Conceptualising National Identity: La Nuestra and the Myth of the Criollo Rebirth

The consolidation of Argentine football coincided with centenary celebrations of self-government in 1910, and independence in 1916, giving rise to a period of reflection about where Argentina stood as a nation. This rumination produced revisionist conclusions amongst some intellectuals as to the role of the British, and liberal Argentine nation builders in that progress. From the mid-1910s and into the 1920s and 1930s, there was significant resentment against the grip that British capital held over Argentina, and the negative effect it had over the country's de facto independence as part of Britain's perceived 'informal empire'. Out of this atmosphere came a reimagination of Argentina's footballing history in the pages of *El Gráfico* during the 1920s, in which the contribution made by Anglo-Criollos to this development was undermined. Not only this, Racing's league victory in 1913 was posited as demarcating the 'independence' of Argentine football from British neo-colonial influence, a position that has been validated by later scholars like Alabarces, Archetti and Martín Caparrós.[10] By contrast, this section challenges the premises of such revisionist mythology.

Anti-British feeling and concerns over the 'social question' of immigration with its associated 'rootlessness' were exteriorised by nationalist *criollo* intellectuals such as Manuel Gálvez, Ricardo Rojas and Leopoldo Lugones, who became known as the 'Centenary Generation'. Originating from the provinces, these writers lamented the centralised control exerted by urban and cosmopolitan Buenos Aires. Feeling disenfranchised, they argued that Argentina was losing its 'traditional' identity of the immediate post-independence period when provincial *caudillos* held power

---

[9] Richey (2013).
[10] Archetti (1999, 53–56), Alabarces (2007, 46–47), and Caparrós (2004, 35).

and sought to reassert a sense of *argentinidad* which had its locus in the countryside. These writers also proposed the revision of Argentina's 'Official History' in the light of the perceived failure of liberal hegemony represented by the likes of Bartolomé Mitre, Domingo Sarmiento and Carlos Pellegrini. Crucial to this discourse surrounding the *criollo* prototype was the rehabilitation of previously excluded pre-immigrant groups, such as the *gauchos*, who had mixed Spanish, Indigenous and Afro-Argentine blood. In 1913, Lugones gave a series of popular lectures at the Teatro Odeon in Buenos Aires, in which he venerated the *gaucho* as the archetypal Argentine, claiming that despite attempts to eradicate Argentina's indigenous presence, 'strong traces of the gaucho remain in the Argentine of today.'[11] Promotion of the *gaucho* was similar in character to the reverence given to the cowboy in the United States during the same period, acting as a cultural restoring point in a period of great social and economic change. The *gaucho* reflected the contrast between cosmopolitan and urban Buenos Aires, and the rural idyll of the pampas, considered by revisionists, with its customs and traditions as the real essence of Argentina. For these incipient revisionists, ethnic rather than civic identity was the basis of *argentinidad*.

Rojas outlined his cure for the 'rootlessness' brought on by mass immigration in his seminal 1909 work, *La restauración nacionalista*. He wrote that the public education system had a key role to play in the development of 'true' Argentine citizens, 'to renew our history, cultivate our own legends, revive an awareness of tradition,' arguing 'It is now time to impose a nationalist character' to Argentina's future.[12]

If by 1904 football was considered by the press as Argentina's national sport and its sides capable of challenging English professional teams, within a decade it also better reflected the demographic reality of Argentina than before. The specific influence of the British community over the game inevitably waned over time in the face of these demographic changes, giving rise to a narrative of *criollización* or nativising of Argentine football. Whilst football offered a way of creating identity through shared common experience at a local level, at a national level identity was expressed in a more intellectual way through the pages of the influential sports magazine *El Gráfico*, founded in 1919 by Constancio C.

[11] Lugones (2002, 211–212).
[12] Rojas (1909, 63–64).

Vigil. Over the next two decades, the magazine's columnists attempted to impose a nationalist character on Argentina's footballing history through its pages. It was a narrative couched in quasi-colonial terms, in which Argentine football was 'freed' from British influence to pursue its own course, one that was expressed by a differentiated Argentine playing style, described as *la nuestra* ('our way'). *La nuestra* was imbued with a revisionist mythology which embraced the input of Italian and Spanish immigrants whilst simultaneously rejecting that coming from immigrants originating from the British Isles in creating a footballing *argentinidad*. Instead, British 'style' was projected by journalists as the counterpoint against which *criollo* exceptionalism was confirmed.

In constructing this ethnic dimension in which the British are excluded, *El Gráfico*'s writers reflected wider conflicts between civic and ethnic ideas of nationalism and what Michael Goebel describes as, 'opposition between a "liberal" and "revisionist" pantheon of national heroes,'[13] in which players such as Arnoldo Watson Hutton represent the former, and Alberto Ohaco the latter as Argentine football was rebranded with the decline of liberalism, whose economic policies had paved the way for the game's diffusion.

Uruguayan-born journalist Jorge Lorenzo, witing in *El Gráfico* under the pen-name, Borocotó was fundamental to the development of this discourse. In 1928, he argued that British influence had given way to the 'less phlegmatic and more restless spirit of the Latin.' Furthermore, in his opinion, immigrants of Latin origin 'were very soon modifying the science of the game and making one of their own, which is now widely recognised,' and was 'more agile and attractive football' to that played by the teams of the British community.[14] Yet, from the outset of organised football in Argentina there have been plentiful examples of British origin players playing in a style that would be considered *criollo*. Interviewed years later by *El Gráfico*, the St. Andrew's player, Charles Douglas Moffat, highlighted Jack Sutherland of Old Caledonians as the stand-out performer in the League's 1891 debut season, 'Jack, now in Scotland was a crack player and here nobody could stop him: he had a complete game, highlighted above all by the dribble.'[15]

---

[13] Goebel (2011, 14–16).

[14] *El Gráfico*, 7 July 1928, 38.

[15] Cited in Scher et al. (2010, 95–96).

In his conceptualisation of *la nuestra*, Borocotó rejected all notions of hybridisation or the *crisol de razas* ('melting pot'), claiming that Italians or Spaniards in Europe could not play in the same way as their compatriots born and raised in Argentina. Instead, Borocotó argued that certain facets were inalienable, arising from environmental factors he considered unique to Argentina such as the consumption of *mate* (a local herbal infusion) and barbecued Argentine beef.[16] Similar attempts to infuse local colour and imagery into the wider Argentine literary tradition also met with local resistance. In his essay *The Argentine Writer and Tradition*, Jorge Luis Borges argued 'The Argentine cult of local colour is a recent European cult which the nationalists ought to reject as foreign.'[17] Borges went on to suggest that 'we cannot limit ourselves to purely Argentine subjects in order to be Argentine; for either being Argentine is an inescapable act of fate – or being Argentine is a mere affectation, a mask.'[18] The writings of Borocotó can be seen in a similar light, a caricature of *argentinidad* rather than a well-crafted observation of the evolution of Argentina's footballing identity.

Key to *la nuestra* was spontaneity, the ability to use individual skill and out-think the opposition that stemmed from players not being formally coached how to play. Working-class boys escaping the crowded *conventillos* and freed from adult supervision were innovators of a differentiated style of play which militated towards close ball control on capricious surfaces and the use of *viveza criolla* or 'native cunning' to outwit opponents in one-to-one situations. The *potrero* or improvised wasteland pitch was the space in which boys honed these skills, and sacred to the myth of *la nuestra*, like how the beaches of Rio became synonymous with the construction of the Brazilian *jogo bonito* ('beautiful game') in its own nationalisation myth.

Borocotó stressed that these factors made *criollo* football different from that practiced by the 'English' in Argentina. However, comparisons can be made with the situation in the poorer neighbourhoods of Edwardian England. According to Richard Holt, young boys chased off by police from playing in the street would play, 'in courts and alleys, on vacant plots

---

[16] *El Gráfico*, 11 August 1950, 46–48.
[17] Borges (2000, 215).
[18] Ibid., 219.

of land, on brick-fields, indeed on any space at all that may be found.'[19] It is a narrative that could equally have been written in Buenos Aires, simply a case of changing the terminology: the *pelota de trapo* 'rag ball' being substituted for 'jumpers for goalposts', and *conventillo* replacing tenement, meaning that such differences were more rooted in class than ethnicity, giving the popular classes of both nations more that united them than separated them.

The lessening of British influence on Argentine football had a resonance that went beyond the sporting environment. For Argentine scholars such as Archetti, Alabarces and Caparrós, the concept of the *criollo* rebirth of Argentine football starting with Racing Club de Avellaneda's victory in the Asociación Argentina de Football's version of the 1913 league championship—the first by a non-British community club—assumes a national importance almost on a par with the securing of independence from Spain in 1816, in marking an end to football's perceived 'colonial' period in Argentina.[20] As Osvaldo Bayer adds, 'The prologue of *criollo* football was written by the English. But now in the first chapter names of different origin would be mixed in.'[21] Numerous factors complicate the idea that Racing's triumphs—they subsequently won the next five championships—signified a *criollo* rebirth. Most significantly, the presence of three Anglo-Criollo players in Racing's 1913 championship-winning team, in the shape of Loncan, Prince and Wine, confirms the continuation of a certain amount of British influence, despite Archetti's contention that they were 'marginal' players. Indeed, Prince and Loncan were still part of Racing's squad in 1918.[22]

Historians have also cited the demise of the hitherto all-powerful Alumni in 1913 as an important counterpoint against which to position Racing's success as a turning point. Despite being described by Molinari and Martínez as the archetypal 'British' club, Alumni were in the main a team of Anglo-Criollos, so should be treated as Campomar suggests, as being just as *criollo* as Racing.[23] Alumni's disappearance,

---

[19] Holt (1989, 135–142).

[20] Archetti (1999), Alabarces (2007, 46–47), Caparrós (2004, 35), and Goebel (2011, 15).

[21] Bayer (2016, 18).

[22] Archetti (1999, 58–61), and *Mundo Deportivo*, 8 December 1949, 47–54.

[23] Molinari and Martínez (2013, 66), and Campomar (2014, 68–71).

whilst reflecting the changing demography of Argentine football, was also the product of several circumstances unique to the institution. Whilst other clubs were adapting to the increasing popularity of the game off the field by constructing bigger and more comfortable spectating facilities, Alumni never kept pace. They continued to rent stadia instead of investing in their own ground at Coghlan which was incapable of staging the ever-increasing crowds, steadfastly maintaining their amateur ethos by donating gate receipts to charitable institutions like the Hospital Británico instead. The closed nature of the club, only extending membership to existing and former students and teachers, reduced Alumni's playing pool as others were widening theirs to the local community. Alumni's founder, Alexander Watson Hutton, was also getting older; aged fifty-eight, he was no longer keen to continue the running of the club. After failing to field a team in the 1912 league championship, Alumni were finally wound up by their membership on 24 April 1913, with its retained balance of 12,322.29 pesos being distributed between eight charities.[24] Alumni remained in the public imagination as genuine Argentine footballing legends. In 1923, they reformed for a charity match against a team of veterans from the Argentine League. Previewing the game, *La Nación* claimed that Alumni's reappearance 'awakened the interest of a great number of supporters who longed to see them play again after many years of retirement.'[25]

In 1928, *El Gráfico* asserted that the *criollo* rebirth came when British names were replaced by those with, 'Italian and Spanish surnames like García, Martínez, Ohaco, Olazar, Chiappe, Calomino, Laforia, Isola etc.'[26] Furthermore, Archetti claimed that 'British community players "disappeared" from the national team.'[27] Yet such claims are misleading. In 1914, the Italian club Torino played a series of tour matches against Argentine representative sides. Whilst it is true that the likes of Ohaco, Olazar and others from Racing's all-conquering team were representing Argentina, these were supplemented by five Anglo-Criollo players— Carlos Wilson, Jorge Brown, Eliseo Brown, Arnoldo Watson Hutton and Heriberto Simmons—who figured prominently in the series, reinforcing

---

[24] Molinari and Martínez (2013, 67–73), and Campomar (2014, 33–36).
[25] *La Nación*, 16 July 1923, 7.
[26] *El Gráfico*, 7 July 1928, 5.
[27] Archetti (1999, 58–61).

the significant role that Anglo-Criollos continued to play in Argentine football. It was not until 1920 that Argentina played for a year without an Anglo-Criollo player in its national team.[28] The exclusion of Anglo-Criollos from the Argentine citizenry is further evidence of nationalist revisionism guiding the historiography surrounding the role of football in Argentine national identity construction. Molinari and Martínez contend that although many of the British community involved in the establishment of football in the country were born in Argentina, they were not counted as *criollo* because their parents never considered themselves immigrants in the same way as those coming from Italy and Spain. As Archetti noted, 'The sons of "English" immigrants were never conceived of as *criollos*, and could not become *criollo* by playing football,' although without illuminating why.[29]

The continued negation by scholars of the role played by Anglo-Criollos, especially the working-class and lower middle-class sons of British workers, belies the fact that in this melting-pot of races, Anglo-Criollos were both active in Argentine society more widely, and in football's popular diffusion. Marriage within Argentina was actively encouraged amongst young British workers by managers of the British-owned railway companies, as it induced them to remain in the country and spend their working lives with the company, as well as integrating better into Argentine society, thus producing the next generation of workers. As the *Central Argentine Railway Magazine* wrote in 1913, 'We are very pleased to see our young colleagues sowing their wild oats.'[30] Whilst the children of British managers were sent by their parents to British boarding schools, returning to Argentina fluent only in English, their more numerous counterparts from the lower classes remained in Argentina for their education, becoming fully bilingual and better prepared to integrate with *criollo* children and those from other immigrant communities.[31]

For example, in the foundation of Boca Juniors, alongside the Italians, Basques and *criollos*, Arturo Penney and Guillermo Ryan were amongst the first members. It was confirmation that working-class British settlers

---

[28] *La Nación*, 28 August 1914, 9; *La Nación*, 31 August 1914, 8; *La Nación*, 7 September 1914, 9.

[29] Molinari and Martínez (2013, 66), and Archetti (1999, 59).

[30] *Central Argentine Railway Magazine*, May 1913.

[31] *The Standard*, 6 March 1914.

in Argentina assimilated and mixed not just in works' teams, but in *barrio* clubs as well. Boca's debut season of 1905 saw several Anglo-Criollos play for the club. Appearing alongside Penney, were his brother Alberto, Benito and Guillermo Tyler, Rafael Pratt and Mullen.[32] Boca were not a lone example, in the 1900s, there were plenty of examples of Anglo-Criollos being at the heart of popular club formation, together with immigrants of other backgrounds, albeit the latter were in greater numbers given their demographic superiority. The sports pages of *La Nación* regularly carried notices proclaiming the formation of new clubs, with address details and the names of players and key officials. One such announcement in 1902 regarding the foundation of Club Maldonado noted the presence of E. O. Jacobs and J. Collingwood amongst the players.[33] This was further exemplified in 1904 with the election of C. Boogey as president of General Arenales and that of J. P. Murray as treasurer of Jorge Brown.[34] The views of Borocotó's fellow *El Gráfico* writer, Chantecler, should be noted in this light, writing in 1932 of the accumulation of influences from all the immigrant communities that gave Argentine football 'its own stamp'.[35] Anglo-Criollos were explicitly *not* excluded from contributing to a national style just as those originating from Italy, Spain or elsewhere were included.

Alabarces and Juan Manuel Sodo have suggested that whilst British social clubs served as a model for the formation of football clubs by *criollos*, the popular diffusion of football left the British community behind as it progressed from this initial evolutionary stage, arguing that these clubs instead found refuge in rugby, but this is an incomplete assumption.[36] Whilst it is true that a number of British community clubs associated with the middle class, such as Lomas Athletic (1909), Rosario Athletic (1916), Belgrano Athletic (1916) and San Isidro (1931) progressively abandoned football in the face of 'plebianisation', in favour of rugby union—a sport which maintained an amateur ethos until the twenty-first century—it was by no means a universal move. A greater number of clubs, such as Quilmes, Banfield and the railway clubs, adapted to the

---

[32] Rosatti (2009, 29).
[33] *La Nación*, 13 September 1902.
[34] *La Nación*, 3 August 1904, 7.
[35] *El Gráfico*, 23 January 1932, 21.
[36] Alabarces (2007, 52), and Sodo (2010/2011, 8–9).

new demographic realities by extending their fanbase, playing staff and membership to wider sectors of society as their British origins became diluted over time. Census figures from 1914 showed that the 27,692 British-born residents made up just 1.2% of foreigners in Argentina, whilst the near one million Italians represented 40% of Argentina's foreign population.[37]

The biggest factor for this opening up of erstwhile British community clubs was not anything happening in Argentina, but instead several thousand miles away across the Atlantic: The First World War of 1914–1918. From Argentina, 4852 Britons and Anglo-Criollos volunteered to fight for their mother country in the conflict, representing a quarter of the male population of the British collective over the age of fifteen. As the first boat-train left Buenos Aires in August 1914, there were hopeful predictions by volunteers that that they would be back in Argentina within a year.[38] Over 1000 of the volunteers were railway workers, a core constituency for footballers in Argentina during the 1910s, something that had major consequences for clubs like Banfield and Quilmes who were heavily reliant upon them.[39] The result of this loss of manpower, in the peak of both age and fitness, was a blow for the British community clubs in terms of reducing both their player pool and their supporting administrative functions, with Rosario Athletic seeing 104 of its 326 members enlisting with His Majesty's Forces. The performance of these clubs in the Argentine League competitions certainly bears this out. Banfield, who had finished highly in both 1913 and 1914, lost many of their players to the Great War, and were relegated in 1917, a fate that befell both Belgrano Athletic and Quilmes a year earlier.[40] By 1918 it was the *criollo* and European immigrant workers who were the driving force in forming clubs amongst railway employees. An example was Ferro Carril Sud from Ayacucho founded that year under the presidency of Raúl Fernández. The line-up for the club's first fixture against Tiro Federal, in which there were no players of British origin, reflected the degree to which the First World War hastened the diffusion of football in Argentina

---

[37] República Argentina (1916, 396).

[38] Tato (2011, 279), and Holder (1920, 117–207).

[39] Tato (2011, 279), and Holder (1920, 117–207).

[40] *Ciencia Hoy*, August 2014; Estévez (2013, 53–60), Dellacasa (1939, 16, 157), and Centenario del Club Atlético del Rosario-Plaza Jewell (1967, 49–59).

beyond its original constituency.⁴¹ Whilst other immigrant communities in Argentina were similarly involved in the European conflict, most notably the German, French and Italians, none were so proportionately affected as the British.

Therefore, whilst demographic changes inevitably saw the influence of the British community decline in Argentine football, the revisionist narrative surrounding the 'nationalisation' of Argentine football which diminished the contribution of Anglo-Criollos to the development of the game in Argentina was itself in need of revision. Indeed, rather than there being a complete *criollización* of Argentine football, another immigratory community was coming to the fore: the Italo-Argentines.

La Italianización Del Fútbol Argentino

In 1923, an advertisement for Bariatti and Co furniture appeared in the pages of *La Nación*:

> "Genoa Club" Young footballers ... welcome to this great land of Argentina, where the effort and honest labour of OUR BEST have found real success.
>
> OUR COMPANY, of Italian origin, is eloquent testimony of Argentine hospitality in its consistent and incomparable progress.⁴²

It reflected a discourse present in the 1910s and 1920s around the assimilation and integration of immigrants into a unified Argentine society, one that continued to trouble politicians and intellectuals of various viewpoints. If one group magnified these debates, it was the Italian community, which accounted for almost half of the immigrant population, and who embodied both Argentine and Italian identity.

As well as control of the Argentine economy, the dominant nature of Italian cultural contribution to the *crisol de razas*, in terms of linguistics, customs and gastronomy, led *criollo* nationalists to fear that Argentina was becoming Italianised, rather than the Italian community being Argentinised. Italo-Argentines were seen as infiltrators, with Rojas arguing that they 'have become dangerous as the result of their excessive quantity.'⁴³

---

⁴¹ *El Porvenir*, 21 April 1918.
⁴² *La Nación*, 20 August 1923, 7; Orton (2022).
⁴³ Rojas (1909, 469–471), and Orton (2022).

It was a theory synthesised in Néstor Maciel's 1924 book, whose title summed up the apparent threat, *La Italianización de la Argentina*.[44] As María Sáenz Peña suggests, the nature of Italian immigration, in which the ratio of arrivals was 2:1 in favour of men, meant that marriages with *criolla* women were the norm. This combined with lower rates of marriage within the *criollo* population led intellectuals to predict that by the middle of the twentieth century, 'Argentina would be an Italo-American republic.'[45] It was a feeling exacerbated by the presence of so many Italian-only institutions across Argentina, beginning with the establishment of the Italian Hospital of Buenos Aires in 1858. By 1904, there were 121 Italian societies in the city of Buenos Aires alone, with a combined membership of 100,000. Amongst the most influential of these were the Unione e Benevolenza mutual society which had branches throughout Argentina, and the Dante Alighieri Association which sought to preserve Italian culture within the community. In the religious sphere, the Salesian order was also influential especially in the provision of education in Italian schools. These various institutions acted interconnectedly, uniting Italo-Argentines around a common idea of Italian identity.

Just as within the British community in Argentina, the First World War consolidated notions of dual identity within the Italo-Argentine collective. Whilst not in the same proportions as their British-Criollo counterparts, some 32,000 answered the call to fight for Italy when they joined the War in 1915. Although the decision to enlist was an individual one, peer pressure was brought to bear on those called up by the Italian consulate. For example, the Circulo Italiano in Buenos Aires expelled any man of fighting age who did not return to Italy and enrol in the armed forces. The Italo-Argentine community celebrated the contribution made and lives lost in support of Italy's wartime effort with the unveiling of plaques in Buenos Aires in 1920.[46]

In the socio-political field, a more militant unionisation in support of workers' rights by socialists and anarchists was often led by Italians, such the anarchist Pedro Gori. As a result, the blame for worker agitation and resulting social strife was laid squarely on the shoulders of these outsiders, leading to the introduction of the 1910 Law of Social Defence, designed

---

[44] MacLachlan (2006, 46–49), and Orton (2022).

[45] Sáenz Quesada (2012, 393–394), Latzina (1899, 167), and Orton (2022).

[46] Devoto (2006, 319); *La Nación*, 23 May 1920, 6; Orton (2022).

to deal with foreign-born political agitators. This militancy was also seen in football, as players sought to improve their working conditions. A 1931 strike held by members of the Asociación Mutualista Footballers was led by several players from the Italian community including Juan Scurzoni, Bartolucci and Hugo Settis. Denounced as anarchists by the authorities of the Asociación Amateur Argentino de Football (AAAF), these ringleaders were deemed no longer eligible to play for Argentina because of their 'subversive' activity.[47]

It was in the economic field that Italian immigrant impact on Argentina was most evident. In a more pronounced way than other settler groups, such as the Spanish, the Italo-Argentine community were driven to succeed economically—to *Fare l'America*, 'make it in America'—and attain social mobility within Argentine society.[48] This work ethic combined with a greater level of literacy resulted in Italian immigrants and their families being at the vanguard of an emergent bourgeoisie of entrepreneurial industrialists and shopkeepers, introducing new techniques from Europe and filling the void of incipient industrialists which was not filled by native Argentines. This work ethic enabled Italo-Argentines to assume the economic dominance in Argentina vacated by the British after the First World War, owning more than half of the country's industrial production.

Like their fellow entrepreneurs in the United States and other industrialising and increasingly urbanised societies, Italo-Argentine businessmen used the popularity of sports clubs for their own commercial and political ends. The 1912 Sáenz Peña electoral reforms saw an immediate impact in terms of political participation amongst the Italian community. The socialist victory in the Buenos Aires by-elections of 1913 brought Italian immigrants like Nicolás Repetto and Mario Bravo into the Chamber of Deputies for the first time.

The Argentine democratic club model in which football clubs were owned by members rather than by shareholders meant that football acted as an excellent proving ground for incipient political careers, with elected roles within clubs offering a platform for demonstrating fitness for office in a wider setting, as well as building a personal support base amongst club members. This was seen in the example of River Plate. After the

[47] Bayer (2016, 38), and Orton (2022).
[48] Foerster (1924, 423), and Orton (2022).

club's first president Leopoldo Bard completed his mandate in 1908, his seven successors up until 1931 were all Italo-Argentines, using the position as a springboard for political office, as well as utilising their commercial and professional positions to improve the club's facilities and ensure their continued success in club elections.In the 1928 club elections, 65% of those bidding for office were Italo-Argentines. Amongst them was Antonio Zolezzi, who after immigrating from Genoa, founded a business in the *barrio* of La Boca before becoming two-time president of River. As a Socialist councillor, Zolezzi used his political influence to obtain subsidies from the Buenos Aires metropolitan government for River and their erstwhile neighbours in La Boca, Boca Juniors.[49]

Another Genovese, José Bacigaluppi, helped lead the club out of a troubled financial situation, setting it on the course to become the global institution that it is today. He became president of River in 1921, who had until that point led a nomadic existence since their foundation in the *barrio* of La Boca in 1901. Recognising the need to stabilise the club in one location where it could grow a mass membership, Bacigaluppi told a meeting of the club's management committee 'River is not a club for a *barrio*, it is for a city.'[50] Bacigaluppi was symbolic of the aspirational social mobility within the Italian community. Whilst the club's founding members were largely from the working class of La Boca's dockworkers, he managed a business that dealt in the sale of land in the rapidly growing city and was well placed to find a site for a stadium big enough to match his ambitions for the club. Thanks to his contacts, Bacigaluppi was able to secure the rent of a huge site in the exclusive northern *barrio* of Recoleta from the Buenos Aires to Pacific Railway company for five years. From a base of 400 in 1920, the membership grew more than seven-fold to 3493 in 1922 thanks to the move.[51]

Whilst football teams were not exclusively Italian in composition, there is sufficient evidence to show that from the 1910s until the 1930s Italo-Argentine players rose to the top in terms of talent and influence and were widely considered to be the best players in the Argentine game. Using the cover stars of the influential sports magazine *El Gráfico* as a barometer

[49] *BoletíN Oficial de River Plate*, Año 1, No. 3, January 1929, 4; Barovero (2013, 39), and Orton (2022).

[50] Cited in Aira (2015, 115), and Orton (2022).

[51] *BoletíN Oficial de River Plate*, Año 1, No. 3, January 1929; *La Nación*, 6 December 1925; Orton (2022).

of prominence, the overwhelming presence of Italo-Argentine players is evident. The first player to appear on its cover was Américo Tesorieri on 8 July 1922, and from that point until the end of 1930, of all the players that appeared on the cover of *El Gráfico* more than once, 80% were of Italian origin, with Raimundo Orsi and Roberto Cherro each appearing on the cover at least five times. Their level of influence can also be seen in a 1941 article by Frascara. In discussing the nine players who had been the 'architects' of the *rioplatense* style of play up until that time, six of them were Italo-Argentines: Natalio Perinetti, Luis Ravaschino, Bacchi, Roberto Cherro, Chiesa and Cesáreo Onzari.[52] Another way of assessing the impact of Italo-Argentines on Argentine football is the composition of the country's national team. After Anglo-Criollo players started to leave the scene, the Italian collective began to assume their influential role, which for much of the 1920s, saw Italo-Argentines make up two-thirds of the team.

Heavy Italo-Argentine influence was also seen in the support base of some of Argentina's biggest clubs. Founded by players from a cross-section of Argentina's immigrants, Vélez Sarsfield's establishment in the Liniers district, which was heavily populated by Italo-Argentines, saw that community account for 55% of the club's membership by 1924. In 1914, the club changed the colour of its shirt to that of the Italian tricolour in homage to its support base, whilst the Italo-Argentine building magnate, José Amalfitani, president between 1923 and 1925 and from 1941 to 1969, left such an enduring legacy that the club's stadium is now named after him.[53]

Another way of assessing ideas of dual identity is to examine relationships between the point of departure and that of arrival for immigrants. The tour of Italian champions Genoa to Argentina in 1923 is therefore instructive in demonstrating how these notions of dual identity were reflected through football in the context of wider relations between the Italo-Argentine community—of which 800,000 still held Italian passports—and the Argentine state.[54] Italian immigration regained momentum after the First World War, with 100,000 arriving in 1923

---

[52] *El Gráfico*, 24 January 1941, 18–20; Orton (2022).

[53] Club Atlético Vélez Sarsfield (1925, 40–47), Club Atlético Vélez Sarsfield (1932, 42–56), Club Atlético Vélez Sarsfield (1935, 20–21), and Orton (2022).

[54] *La Nación*, 11 August 1923, 7; Orton (2022).

alone, more than double the number migrating to the United States. This meant that the 1.2 million Italians' resident in Argentina was greater than the population of Rome.[55]

Genoa was a significant connection given the iconic role played by the Ligurian city as the port of departure for many of the millions of Italian emigrants to Argentina. Thousands of Italo-Argentines lined the dockside of Buenos Aires to welcome the Genoa team as they arrived on the *Principessa Mafalda* on 16 August. The composition of this impromptu welcoming committee crossed class lines as middle-class Italian merchants and small industrialists rubbed shoulders with the proletariat from the *conventillos* in a unified demonstration of their Italian-ness.[56] The great interest of the Italo-Argentine community manifested itself in numerous ways, the extent of which was not seen before or after for any touring teams. FIAT, who established its first factory in Argentina that year, made seven of its modern 515 models available to Genoa's entourage to transport themselves around Buenos Aires for the duration of their visit.

The duality of identity was reflected in Genoa's opening match against Zona Norte at the stadium of Sportivo Barracas. In advance of kick-off there was an unscheduled fly-past in honour of the visitors by Italo-Argentine pilots led by Captain Eduardo Oliveiro who served in the Italian air force during the First World War.[57] Thirty thousand fans speaking Spanish, Italian and the hybrid Italian-inflected *lunfardo* dialect, packed the stands displaying both Argentine and Italian flags.[58] For the second of Genoa's three matches against Zona Sur, a silver trophy was donated for the winners by the Nuevo Banco Italiano, prompting *La Nación* to argue 'It is fit to assert that the banking institution was an exteriorisation of confraternity between the Italian and Argentine nations.'[59] For the final match on Argentine soil, Genoa played against the Argentine national team for a cup donated by Crown Prince Umberto of Italy.[60]

---

[55] *La Nación*, 19 October 1923, 5; Orton (2022).

[56] *El Telégrafo de la Tarde*, 16 August 1923; *La Nación*, 22 July 1923, Sec. 2, 3; Orton (2022).

[57] *La Nación*, 20 August 1923, 6; Orton (2022).

[58] Aira (2015, 140–141), and (Orton 2022).

[59] *La Nación*, 22 August 1923, 8; Orton (2022).

[60] *La Nación*, 8 September 1923, 9; Orton (2022).

Later tours by Italian clubs, such as that by Torino in 1929, engendered nothing like the same level of affection as that bestowed upon Genoa. Distaste towards the Fascist regime within the Italo-Argentine community, as well as by Argentine cultural nationalists, was manifested by the whistling of the Bologna team, intimately linked with the regime when they gave the Fascist salute ahead of one of their 1929 tour matches.[61]

'The Gallery of Beautiful Faces'

As Chapter 2 showed, physical education was taken seriously by Argentine nation builders for both boys and girls, although for more than half a century it was confined to the middle classes who attended private schools. For example, Domingo Sarmiento made provision for dance and gymnastics when becoming director of the Colegio de Niñas de Santa Rosa in 1839. In the 1870s, the national head of physical education, Dr. Francisco Berra, wrote that it was as important for girls as it was for boys, arguing that physical education for girls helped prevent women's nervous conditions—a recurring theme in debates surrounding women's sports. Such opinions reinforced what Dominic Malcolm describes as, 'images of female frailty and the dominance of white middle- and upper-class male values of physical skill and strength, mental acumen, gentlemanly conduct and fair play.'[62]

Whilst the health benefits of physical exercise were recognised for both sexes, doctors debated in the early twentieth century what types of sport and exercise were appropriate for women given their impact on 'female reproductive functions.' Some sporting practices were considered gender-specific, with football and boxing amongst those sports deemed 'masculine' and not suitable for female participation, whilst gender-neutral sports such as tennis, hockey and swimming were felt to be far more suitable.[63] In a letter to the editor of *La Nación*, one physician, Dr A. A. Fernández, outlined his 'scientific' reasons why women shouldn't play football, pointing to the danger that to do so could,

---

[61] Martin (2004, 194–197), and Epolito (2012, 236); *La Cancha*, 3 September 1929; Orton (2022).

[62] Malcolm (2008, 116–117).

[63] Anderson (2009, 642–644).

'subdue their delicate, fragile maternal apparatus'. By contrast, he argued that the Swedish gymnastics—developed by Per Henrich Ling in the first half of the nineteenth century—practiced in the state education system was the best form of physical exercise due to its suitability for preparing young women for motherhood because of its concentration on the exercise of the abdominal muscles, flexibility of the hips and development of the pectoral muscles.[64]

Female excellence in 'approved' sports was celebrated, with *El Gráfico* publishing pictures of sportswomen on its front cover. As Augusto de Muro wrote in his report on the 1920 Río de la Plata tennis championships, 'One of the stand-out things in the development of tennis has been the progress in the play of women,' before noting, 'The two semi-final matches and the final of the ladies' singles, were undoubtedly better than that of the mens.' *La Nación* continued to champion women's tennis, claiming that it was 'healthy,' and it was 'the best coefficient of their beauty.'[65]

Indeed, masculine stereotypes of the female form drove the discourse around the role of women in Argentinian sport. As the work of Gisela Kaczan highlights, mainstream magazines such as *Caras y Caretas* and *El Hogar* devoted articles in the early decades of the twentieth century to women's exercise with accompanying pictures designed to promote the development of the elegant female form, although during this period the dress appropriated for such exercise underwent great change from the bodices worn with clothing that left no exposed flesh, to more comfortable, flowing clothing that allowed for more freedom of movement in the arms and legs in making the exercise more effective and dynamic.[66]

Whilst women did participate in sports via the wider ambit of football clubs in their role as *polideportivos* (multi-sport clubs), football was not one of the activities on offer to them. In Britain, football had been played by women in charity matches since the 1890s, albeit without support from the English and Scottish governing bodies, but it was not until October 1923 that attempts were made to play women's football in Argentina under the auspices of the newly founded Liga Femenina de Football. As with the British cases, this body had no connection with the

---

[64] *La Nación*, 14 October 1923, Sports, 3.

[65] *La Nación*, 6 June 1920, Sec 2, 1.

[66] Kaczan (2016, 23–43 and 30–31).

existing organisational structure of the men's game, although there was no 'official' ban by the Argentine footballing authorities on the use of affiliated grounds for women's football like that employed by the Football Association in England in 1921.[67]

The Argentine press on the other hand were deeply sceptical. In 1921, *El Gráfico* published an article written by the England international player Andy Ducat entitled, 'Why women should not play football.' It was illustrated with several pictures depicting women that were more concerned with their appearance and exhibitions of lesbian behaviour than playing the game. Ducat considered that women naturally were 'too fragile' for such a rough game, running the risk of gaining muscle and transforming into a tomboy instead of being a woman.[68] Constant allusions to women's football being an arena for lesbianism continued to reinforce male prejudices to the female game, with Bernardo Canal Feijóo's 1924 poem, *Fútbol de mujeres* referring to the fact that, 'the clashes brought the players into an unacceptable lesbian embrace.'[69]

Previewing this foundational event, *La Nación* proffered some interesting reservations about the match taking place. In a sporting sense, the newspaper admired the enthusiasm and efforts of the women to upskill themselves with the aim of 'offering a cautious exhibition,' suggesting that the game was 'serving to combat certain prejudices about the appearance of women on the sports field, in honest competition.' The apparent desire of the Liga Femenina to create footballers in a 'professional way' dismayed *La Nación*, which it argued 'diminishes the true value of the initiative.'[70] The article concluded with the chauvinist remark that the female players 'offered the habitual feminine remarks, their coquettishness about going on the pitch maintaining the good taste of their appearance in the ladies' room'.[71]

That first game on 12 October 1923 was billed as a match between Las Argentinas, composed of Argentine sportswomen from various disciplines, and Las Cosmopolitas, a combination of South African ladies who settled in Argentina as refugees from the Boer War. The match, staged by

---

[67] Aira (2015, 142–143); *La Nación*, 3 October 1923, 7; Williams (2021, 27).
[68] *El Gráfico*, 15 January 1921.
[69] Cited in Cabrera and Hijós (2020, 42–46).
[70] *La Nación*, 7 October 1923, Sports, 3.
[71] Ibid., 3.

a local empresario, was held at the ground of Boca Juniors with tickets priced at two pesos for stand seats and one peso for the terraces, half the standard rate for watching a men's game. Las Argentinas, including Elsa Martínez, Josefina Bergeris, Emma Meyer, Nélida Martínez, Alicia Pisset, Margarita Silva and Estrella Villgrán, won 4–3. According to *La Vanguardia*'s report, the game was an 'exotic spectacle.' It was also a commercial success with a healthy attendance of 6000, formed in the majority by women.[72]

The activities of that October proved to be something of a false dawn for Argentine women's football, although in 1925 *El Gráfico* pictured on its front cover Carmen Pomies of Feminine Sport Club de Paris and Florrie Redford of Dick Kerr Ladies shaking hands ahead of a friendly between the two European sides under the banner headline, 'The Woman and Football'. Whilst sadly there was no Argentine involvement in the picture, it was at least an implicit recognition of the active existence of women's football by Argentina's biggest sports magazine.[73] Brenda Elsey and Josh Nadel suggest that the game continued to be played informally in an industrial setting by working-class women as they became increasingly represented in the factories of the Greater Buenos metropolitan area during the 1930s.[74]

The marginalisation of women in Argentine football extended beyond their participation as players due to the deeply patriarchal nature of Argentine society from Spanish colonial times. The passage of Law 11.357 introduced by the socialist deputy Mario Bravo, which gave all women of ages, except married women, the same civil rights as men in respect to ownership of property, work and custody of children, improved the position of women during the 1920s. Its scope within marriage was negated though, with the husband maintaining domination of familial decision-making.[75]

From the first representations of football in the Argentine press, the role of women has been as a decorative afterthought, rather than as direct

---

[72] *La Nación*, 3 October 1923, 7; *La Vanguardia*, 13 October 1923; *Crítica*, 13 October 1923, 2.

[73] *El Gráfico*, 13 June 1925, 1.

[74] Elsey and Nadel (2019, 29–31).

[75] Sáenz Quesada (2012, 482–483).

participants, the nature of their attendance conditioned by male expectations. For example, *Última Hora* complained that at a San Lorenzo v Racing Club match in September 1921, 'some women home fans were unbearable. They drove us mad with their shouts ... Such were the annoyances that we suffered, that in the end it occurred to us to think that if they should all be at home darning socks.'[76]

Within football clubs, the participation of women was restricted to the peripheral social and non-football sporting activities provided. This was reflected in the official *River Plate* magazine from January 1929, under the headline, 'Gallery of Beautiful Faces,' which proclaimed, 'With this section that we begin today, in the pages of this bulletin, we will honour the feminine element, making a parade that makes note of their grace and their happiness in all the sporting and social manifestations of our institution ... the numerous cluster of enthusiastic representatives of the weaker sex that populate our tennis courts and pitches.'[77] The secondary status of women was reaffirmed by a 1934 advert exhorting people to become members of River Plate in *El Gráfico*. In it a man dressed in football kit is foregrounded, whilst a woman in tennis dress holding a racket is placed firmly in the background.[78]

NEGROS Y PARDOS: AFRO-ARGENTINES IN ARGENTINE FOOTBALL

Underpinning ideas of race in Argentina in the late nineteenth century and in the early decades of the twentieth century were the social positivist theories of European thinkers such as Herbert Spencer, Count Gabineau and Gustave Le Bon. These theories posited the inferiority of non-white races and informed immigration policy, which was targeted at attracting white Europeans to 'improve' the race.'[79]

The labels applied to those of Afro-Argentine, Indigenous or *mestizo* descent were derogatory and insidious. Terms such as *negro* (black), *moreno* (dark) and *pardo* (mixed racial origin) were used to degrade and reinforce their outsider status in terms of citizenship. Furthermore, the

---

[76] *Última Hora*, 5 September 1921.
[77] *BoletíN Oficial del Club Atlético River Plate*, January 1929, 19.
[78] *El Gráfico*, 26 May 1934.
[79] Solberg (1970, 18).

word *negro* was used not only to describe Afro-Argentines, in the more obvious sense of colour, but also anyone of *mestizo*, Indigenous or even provincial background, making its negative connotation obvious as the rejection of anyone not originating from 'civilised' Buenos Aires.[80]

This denial of *argentinidad* to those of *mestizo* origin can be seen in the case of José Laguna who played for Huracán and Argentina in the 1910s and 1920s. In 1920, Palacio Zini wrote about Laguna in *Crítica*, expressing the positivist attitudes held towards race in Argentina at the time. The article entitled 'A celebrated Black player' cited Laguna as a 'living example' of 'man descended from monkey.' Further demeaning the player, Zini wrote, 'how the little *pardo* dances! He is like a monkey for his agility, and an orangutan for his little leaps! … Today, time and environment have lifted him to the atmosphere of the whites and for many, he is a young gentleman.'[81] Zini systematically dehumanises Laguna with his primate comparisons, denies his Argentine-ness by insisting he must have come from Paraguay despite Laguna having been born in the northern province of Salta, and reduces him to the status of an exotic anthropological exhibit who is only 'raised' to the level of a white man by virtue of his exceptional footballing ability.[82]

People of African descent have been present in Argentina since the time of Spanish Conquest in the mid-sixteenth century. Originally, they appeared as servants of the colonial nobility, later becoming artisans, dock workers and domestic workers after the end of the Argentine slave trade in 1813. The centrality of Buenos Aires as a distribution point for the Atlantic slave trade also contributed to their presence, although most of the slaves were moved on to other parts of Spanish America. Slaves originated from the western seaboard of Africa, in the modern nation states of Senegal, Gambia, Ivory Coast and Angola, which was the provenance of many Afro-Argentines. George Reid Andrews argues that the economic boom which followed the end of Argentina's civil wars in the second half of the nineteenth century should have been propitious for the advancement of Afro-Argentines, but that the deluge of European immigration saw their presence in Buenos Aires denuded from 25% of the population in 1838 to just 2% in 1887 as they were displaced in the

---

[80] Sutton (2008, 112), Reid Andrews (1979, 21–37), and Aira (2015, 58).
[81] *CrítIca*, 14 October 1920, 8.
[82] Ibid., 8.

labour market. Competition with immigrants for affordable housing also forced them to move further away from the centre of the capital to the peripheries. Reid Andrews argues that there was also a deliberate policy amongst Afro-Argentines not to engage with immigrant populations, further marginalising Black people within Argentine society.[83]

Whilst later representations of visiting Black footballers would be marred by a racially derogatory narrative, the first appearance of a Black player on an Argentine football field, Walter Tull of English tourists Tottenham Hotspur, seems to have been received positively. According to the *Buenos Aires Herald*, 'Early in the tour Tull has installed himself as favourite with the crowd.'[84] When Argentine teams played against Brazilian sides fielding Black players, the reception both in the press and on the terraces turned to hostility. Argentine self-perception as being European and white meant that they looked down on their multi-racial neighbours, referring to them as *macacos* or 'monkeys' in a Spencerian discourse of Argentine racial superiority. In October 1920, ahead of the visit of the Brazilian national team for a friendly on their way home from the South American Championship, a journalist writing under the pen-name Mr Bull wrote an infamous article in *Crítica* entitled 'Monkeys in Buenos Aires, a Greeting for the Illustrious Guests'. In it he maintained that the 'little *macacos* are now on Argentine soil,' before going on to claim of the Brazilians, 'These coloureds who talk like us and try to mix with the rest of the Americas. It is an illusion. Brazil is a sham.' Finally, in a nod to Argentina's perceived 'civilisation,' Mr Bull boasted, 'it is unlikely that Europeans will settle in a nation that has a black man for a coat of arms.'[85] Their description as *macacos* reflects the perception that in Argentina, Brazilians were considered further down the evolutionary scale, 'barely one remove from the Conradian jungle,' as Farred reports.[86] Ironically, there was not a single black player in the Brazilian party, but such was the level of insult felt that several of the squad refused to play, and the game ended up being played on an eight-a-side basis and the match not considered a full international. To avoid a diplomatic incident, the Argentine Foreign Office apologised to the Brazilian Embassy for

---

[83] Reid Andrews (1979, 21–25).
[84] *The Buenos Aires Herald*, 19 June 1909, 5.
[85] *Crítica*, 3 October 1920, 8.
[86] Farred (2005, 104–105).

the injudicious article, as did *Crítica*'s editor, Natalio Botana. The incident did though put off Brazilian authorities from selecting Afro-Brazilian players for the next South American Championship.[87] Black Uruguayan players were also on the receiving end of racist reporting. Describing the infamous 'Olympic' match of 1924, *The Buenos Aires Herald* wrote 'Andrade charged Onzari violently from behind and a shower of pebbles fell on the offending darkie.'[88]

By contrast to the conflation between African origin and national culture in Argentina's northern neighbour Brazil, Afro-Argentines were explicitly excluded from constructions of national identity in Argentina, something that extended to its football, which was seen as being of exclusively European origin.[89] Whilst Afro-Brazilian players such as Arthur Friedenreich, Domingos da Guia and Leônidas da Silva were made national icons in the first half of the twentieth century as celebration of a 'tropical modern Brazil' as Kittelson puts it, no Afro-Argentines gained similar recognition in the Argentine game. Indeed, it would take nearly half a century to highlight even a handful of Afro-Argentines to make an impact in Argentine football.[90] As *El Gráfico* commented in November 1928, 'Either there are hardly any blacks, or they don't play football as they do in Uruguay … The only black player that has excelled in Argentine sport is De los Santos, the great El Porvenir forward.'[91]

It was not until the emergence of Alejandro de los Santos as a major talent in the 1920s that an Afro-Argentine player was revered by Argentine spectators. Nicknamed '*El Negro*', the striker was a member of Argentina's team that won the 1925 South American Championship, becoming the first Afro-Argentine to play for his country in that year and the last until José Manuel Ramos Delgado in the 1950s. Born in 1902 in Paraná in the province of Entre Ríos, De los Santos was the descendent of Angolan slaves, speaking Portuguese—the language of Angola's colonial masters—at home. He established himself as a potent striker in non-league football, eventually earning himself a transfer to San Lorenzo de Almagro as a 19 year old.

---

[87] Aira (2015, 52), and Kittleson (2014, 33).
[88] *The Buenos Aires Herald*, 3 October 1924.
[89] Kittleson (2014, 3).
[90] Ibid., 15.
[91] *El Gráfico*, 24 November 1928, 10.

Whilst De los Santos was the most famous Afro-Argentine footballer, a handful of others made a name for themselves in succeeding decades. One of the best players to come from the province of Córdoba, Julio Benavidez, also nicknamed '*Negro*,' was the axis of the attack at Instituto de Córdoba for six years before finding further fame at Boca Juniors, with whom he was a league champion in 1934 and 1935. According to *El Gráfico*, he was an 'undoubtedly skilful' player in an era of 'artistic football.'[92]

Defenders Carlos Fariña with Ferro Carril Oeste in the 1930s, and Alberto Arcangel Britos, the son of Cape Verdean immigrants, with Independiente in the 1950s, also enjoyed fine careers. Whilst not as numerous as other migrations to Argentine, immigration from Cape Verde to Argentina began in the late nineteenth century and gathered pace in the 1920s following one of the worst famines in the islands' history. In contrast to the established Afro-Argentine community, Cape Verdean descendants integrated into Argentine society with some ease, holding ambivalent feelings regarding ethnic identity and denying their African roots to 'Argentinise' themselves.[93]

Emblematic of this Cape Verdean assimilation was José Manuel Ramos Delgado, whose father hailed from the island of São Vicente. Ramos Delgado earned twenty-five caps for Argentina between 1958 and 1965, making the Argentine squads for the 1958 and 1962 World Cups. Despite his accomplished international career, as a *mulatto* Ramos Delgado was subjected to a casual racism in the press that permeated Argentine football more widely. An example of which came in an *El Gráfico* article about Argentina's pre-World Cup tour to Italy in 1958. Described as an 'Ethiopian' with skin the colour of 'milky coffee,' when Ramos Delgado arrived at Senegal for a stopover with the rest of the squad, the magazine claimed that the rest of the Argentine team, 'told him: "Put on white trousers and start to serve," because in the airport the waiters were African and black.'[94]

One example captures the essence of racial attitudes in Argentina more clearly than any other: that of the Da Graca family, who for three generations played for Los Andes in the southern suburbs of Buenos Aires.

---

[92] El Gráfico (2018).
[93] Maffia (2008, 179), and Newitt (2015, 179).
[94] *El Gráfico*, 30 May 1958, 5.

Whilst little is known about the family's background, the Portuguese surname suggests that they were descended from Angolan slaves, with the eldest, Manuel da Graca, who debuted for the club in 1937, having direct Afro-Argentine ancestry. His son, Abel, who played for the club from 1967 was considered a *mulatto* as the result of having a black father and white mother, whilst Abel's son, Hernán, the product of further miscegenation was simply considered *criollo*, to the extent that 'it is now impossible to recognise his Afro-Argentine heritage,' becoming 'a metaphor for the direction of Afro-Americans in Argentina,' as *Un Caño* magazine described it.[95] The Da Gracas were therefore an archetype of the 'whitening' of Argentina.

But these players were exceptions rather than the rule, and Afro-Argentines were certainly not as prevalent as their Afro-Uruguayan counterparts were in Uruguay as will be seen in the next chapter. The problem for Black and Indigenous players in Argentina was the scarcity of role models or heroes to act as a vanguard as was the case with pioneers such as Isabel Gradín in Uruguay as an embedded structural racism in Argentina hindered their progress.[96] The willingness to accept racially charged nicknames on the part of some *mestizo* and Afro-Argentine players and not acknowledge their racial heritage perpetuated this sense of negation and subjugation. As Ernesto Pico, a *mestizo* from the northwestern province of San Juan, recalled of his arrival at San Lorenzo in the 1940s, 'they never called me Picot, they called me *negrito* ('little blackie'),' something that became routine in press coverage of the player. After a match-winning performance against River Plate in June 1954, *Goles* wrote that '*negro*' Picot was San Lorenzo's secret weapon.[97] As the next section investigates, those emanating from the interior were also subject to a discourse of negation that included elements based on race and ethnicity.

---

[95] Un Caño (2005).
[96] *El Gráfico*, 24 November 1928, 10.
[97] Macias (2008, 30); *Goles*, 15 June 1954, 13.

Chacareros y Peloduros: Challenging the Outsider Status of the Interior

In 1928, the Argentine writer, Bernardo Canal Feijóo, wrote an article in *El Liberal* newspaper about the victory of his northern home province, Santiago del Estero, in the Campeonato Argentino football tournament. He celebrated what he considered a victory over *porteño* triumphalism, claiming 'Each of the *santiagueño* goals yesterday delivered a blow to the hearts held captive by that naïve vanity. And I'm sure that not one *porteño* failed to depart from the River Plate stadium with a concept of the true geographic breadth of our common fatherland.'[98] The article neatly encapsulated the tensions inherent in the relationship between the metropole Buenos Aires, and the interior of Argentina.

It is impossible to discuss the role of the interior without simultaneously examining the role of Indigenous and *mestizo* populations in Argentine society since their fates have been intertwined since the current model of unitarist government was adopted in the mid-nineteenth century. If Afro-Argentines were rendered invisible through neglect, then worse was applied to the peripheral provinces of Argentina and their *mestizo* and Indigenous populations. For Indigenous Argentines, this was a result of their deliberate militarily destruction by the state during a campaign led by General Julio Roca between 1879 and 1884. Described euphemistically as the 'Conquest of the Desert,' this 'civilising' expropriation of land in the Pampas, Patagonia and the Gran Chaco previously inhabited by Indigenous groups was also designed to 'modernise' it by maximising its economic productivity. The operation also confirmed the writ of the government across all the territory of Argentina, 40% of which was in the hands of Indigenous tribes resistant to domination from the capital.[99]

Within the competing *mitrista* and revisionist notions of national identity, there was no room for representations of Argentina's Indigenous populations. According to the sociologist, Lucas Ayagarray, the *mestizo* (of mixed Indigenous and *criollo* blood) was incapable of achieving civilisation. As he wrote in 1904, the *mestizo* is a 'dull creature: "incapable

---

[98] Wood (2017, 29); *El Liberal*, 8 October 1928.

[99] Sáenz Quesada (2012, 361), and Brown (2014, 50–51).

of grasping synthetic concepts and advanced methods of reasoning".'[100] Even the rehabilitation of the *gaucho*, the *mestizo* horsemen of the *pampas*, by revisionists confined national identity to the economically productive Pampean provinces of the central belt of Buenos Aires, Santa Fe and La Pampa. This exclusion of non-Pampean provinces whose greater Indigenous heritage in contrast to the cosmopolitanism of Buenos Aires arguably made them more authentic as archetypes of the 'real' Argentina, created great resentment in marginal provinces.[101] Argentina's negation of its aboriginal heritage contrasted with countries such as Mexico and Peru where indigenous populations were seen as essential components of national identity. Elsewhere in Latin America, the concept of *mestizaje* meant the mixing of the Indigenous with the European. But that idea was non-existent in Argentina as the *crisol de razas* discourse of uniting white European immigrants into a single national identity held sway, despite indigenous Argentines accounting for 1.4% of the country's population.[102]

Despite being effectively de-nationalised by state violence, the presence of Indigenous and *mestizo* populations remained important to the economic development of Argentina's outlying provinces, particularly in the north which were culturally and ethnically closer to Bolivia and Paraguay than to Buenos Aires. These more climatically extreme provinces, such as Jujuy, Santiago del Estero and Salta, proved less attractive to European settlers, who preferred the temperate lands of the Argentine Littoral, closer to their disembarkation zones, leaving a need for agricultural and day labourers that was fulfilled by these Indigenous groups.[103]

As seen in Chapter 2, the catalyst for football's diffusion into the Argentine interior was the expansion of the railway network. However, provincial football was left to its own devices. Physical distance and a lack of appetite on the part of the Buenos Aires-centric footballing establishment for fully integrating the sport nationally in Argentina deterred regular games with teams from the capital save for brief tours over national holidays. *La Nación* bemoaned this lack of progress in a 1923

---

[100] Ayarragaray (1925, 244).
[101] Coni (1969, 24).
[102] Gordillo and Hirsch (2003, 4–8).
[103] Ibid., 110–112; Sáenz Quesada (2012, 396).

article, in which it blamed, 'the shortage of a more frequent interchange with the most powerful teams that bring good teachings.'[104]

Negligence on the part of central authorities began to be addressed with the inauguration of the Campeonato Argentino in 1920 by the Asociación Amateur de Football (AAmF), the dissident rival of the 'official' Asociación Argentino de Football (AAF), which held Argentina's international membership with FIFA (the two were reconciled with the formation of the AAAF in 1926).[105] Richey claims that the foundational idea for the competition by AAmF president, Adrián Beccar Varela, was driven more by quasi-state building ambitions than by commercial necessity, but it can alternatively be argued that rivalry with the AAF was the chief motive.[106] With the AAF offering players of its affiliated clubs the opportunity to represent Argentina in international competition, the AAmF felt compelled to offer players from its membership a similar representative route to boost its credibility. With international football denied to it, save for quasi-internationals against similar dissident associations in Uruguay and Chile, the answer was found in a novel pan-Argentine tournament instead.[107] The Campeonato Argentino was an interprovincial competition in which the best players from all over Argentina were invited to Buenos Aires to play for the Copa Presidente de la Nación, donated by President Hipólito Yrigoyen.[108] The competition also received moral and financial support from the Mayor of Buenos Aires, Dr. José Luis Cantilo, whose municipal authority donated 2000 pesos, as did the provincial government of Corrientes, towards the costs of travel and accommodation for teams from the periphery of Argentina.[109]

The 1920 annual report of the AAmF made some bold claims as to the impact of the tournament, hailing its transformative effect on the outlying provinces of Tucumán, Corrientes and Santiago del Estero, before boasting 'We have awoken interest in all the Republic through this competition … The patriotism and *argentinidad* awoken by this

---

[104] *La Nación*, 19 August 1923, Sec 2, 2.
[105] Levinsky (2016, 411).
[106] Richey (2013, 117–119).
[107] AsociacióN Amateurs de Football (1924, 19–20).
[108] AsociacióN Amateurs de Football (1921, 22–23).
[109] Ibid., 22–23.

competition equally stand out.'[110] Other observations smacked of the condescension that marked relations between the capital and the interior from the mid-nineteenth century, 'As a support to culture and social action, the Championship has been no less efficient ... most of the players were visiting the capital for the first time. They have been able to admire its beauty, its buildings, its theatres, public promenades, and important establishments.'[111] It was a 1920s way of inculcating cosmopolitan 'civilisation' amongst the 'barbarians' of the interior in a modern version of the former president Domingo Sarmiento's nineteenth-century trope that the indigenous populations of Argentina were 'nothing more than stubborn animals with no capacity for civilisation.'[112]

Richey has accorded the competition a greater national political relevance than is evident in primary sources. In suggesting that the Campeonato Argentino was 'a prominent facet of an early twentieth-century push to unify Argentina geographically and socio-politically,' he overlooks the fact that President Yrigoyen's interest in provincial affairs came principally in shutting down opposition to his government.[113] On nineteen occasions between 1916 and 1922, Yrigoyen used his presidential power of interdiction over provincial governments to 'rectify' the running of provinces where this ran counter to central authority.[114]

If one of the benefits of the Campeonato Argentino was to raise the standard of football in the interior relative to the footballing strongholds of the Federal Capital, Buenos Aires and Santa Fe, the early editions were a failure as all the tournaments between 1920 and 1927 were won by either the Federal Capital or the province of Buenos Aires. This led *La Nácion* in 1923 to suggest supplementary 'missionary' work be undertaken by the footballing authorities in Buenos Aires, arguing that, 'They have lacked in the provinces the great teams of English professionals that were such fertile ground for the learnings left in our country.'[115] The article suggested that the footballers from Rosario were not typical of the rest of the interior owing to the fact that they were 'from the start

[110] Ibid., 24.
[111] Ibid., 25.
[112] Helg (1990, 40).
[113] Richey (2013, 117–119).
[114] Romero (2004, 51).
[115] *La Nación*, 19 August 1923, Sec 2, 2.

playing on the same fields as the Buenos Aires teams.'[116] Whilst recognising the merit of the Campeonato Argentino in integrating provincial teams into the national whole, the piece derided the utility of average teams touring the interior, 'which fail to deliver any learnings and only serve as a false mirage to the clubs of the interior, impeding an improvement that would be pleasing to all Argentines.'[117] Conveying a discourse of *porteño* superiority, *La Nación* suggested that it was not just in terms of skills and tactics that the best teams from Buenos Aires were needed, but also in *how* to play the game in terms of behaviour, 'to show the provinces that although they are not going to win, there are also other objectives [fair play],' reflecting notions of the capital civilising the interior that had existed for half a century or more.[118]

Following the 1926 merger of the rival governing bodies into the AAAF, this new entity now had responsibility for the tournament. Santiago del Estero's 1928 victory in the Campeonato Argentino was paradigm-shifting, as a rare opportunity for the Argentine periphery to project itself into the national imaginary. By picturing the players of the tournament finalists Santiago del Estero and Paraná, *La Nación* showed that Indigenous and *mestizo* players were successful in the Argentine game, and as such heroes of a national dimension. Victory allowed for the projection of regional identity on the provincials' own terms, rather than the stereotypes imposed by the capital, *La Argentina* having portrayed Santiago del Estero dismissively as *chacareros* or 'little farmers'.[119] As the *santiagueño* team's star, Segundo Luna related after the final, 'The triumph of today is that of my little country.'[120] *'El Indio'* Luna was joined in the side by his half brothers, Ramón, Juan and Nazareno, giving a discernible indigenous presence in the team that earned the *santiagueños* the racially derogatory nickname of *peloduros* on the account of their supposedly brush-like hair.[121]

Some sections of the *porteño* press were unable to countenance the legitimacy of a provincial victory after the capital's team was eliminated,

---

[116] Ibid., 2.
[117] Ibid., 2.
[118] Ibid., 2.
[119] *La Argentina*, 8 October 1928.
[120] *Crítica*, 13 October 1928.
[121] Aira (2015, 442–443).

with *Última Hora* arguing that Santiago's victory was 'an irony of destiny' and that in terms of technique, 'Football in the interior has much to learn to be able to impose itself on a team from the Capital or Province [of Buenos Aires].'[122] By contrast, other newspapers from the capital at least accorded the interior some respect, with José Gabriel writing in *Crítica*, 'The Campeonato Argentino, wanting to evolve, took a little journey into the interior. When it returns it will be more Argentine.'[123]

The *santiagueño* victory sparked wider debates about giving the interior provinces a greater say in the governance of Argentine football and the need to construct a more representative national team. Journalist Jack Day wrote 'When we say Argentines, we don't only refer to those from the Capital or those from Rosario,' before asking rhetorically 'who organises the representative teams?' before emphasising the need for restructuring within the AAAF to include the interior in the decision-making process.[124] *La Nación* proposed 'Now the prestige of provincial combinations is incontestable and it is now time to incorporate their outstanding values into the national team'.[125] A case in point was Segundo Luna, who was not only iconic for helping Santiago del Estero to win the Campeonato Argentino, but also for being a rare beacon of interior and Indigenous representation in the Argentine national team. In the shirt of the *albiceleste*, Luna helped Argentina win the 1927 South American Championship as well as being in the squad for the 1928 Amsterdam Olympics alongside fellow *santiagueño* Alberto Helmann. Luna's absence from the starting line-up in Holland aroused claims of discrimination in his native Santiago del Estero. On 19 June, *El Liberal* lamented, 'Why exclude one of the stars of the interior, even when as everyone knows his capacities are superior to those [players] from the capital? The response for the most obtuse is easy: because of the simple preferences and personal sympathies of the delegates.'[126] Luna's membership of the 1928 Olympic squad was recognised on the team's return to Montevideo harbour after Argentina had won the silver medal, with the

---

[122] *Última Hora*, 8 October 1928.

[123] *CrítIca*, 13 October 1928.

[124] *La Nación*, 21 October 1928, Sec 2, 5.

[125] *La Nación*, 13 October 1928, 16.

[126] *El Liberal*, 19 June 1928.

welcoming delegation giving three cheers in his native Guaraní language as well as Spanish in his honour.[127]

Less than a year after Santiago del Estero's victory in the Campeonato Argentino, it was clear that *porteño* attitudes to provincial football had changed little regarding incorporating the interior into national football. The defeats of Racing Club by a Tucumán selection, and Huracán in Córdoba on the 9 July national holiday were attributed to travel fatigue and the mindset of players on vacation, rather than the superior qualities of the provincial sides. Journalist, Dinty Moore, bemoaned the disdain with which those from the interior were demeaned as *chacareros*, suggesting instead there was merit in replacing the tours of foreign clubs to the capital with those by emerging teams from the interior to further aid their development, adding that interest in these tours was waning as the result of the visits of Motherwell and Chelsea over the previous twelve months. Moore's solution was 'to bring to Buenos Aires the best provincial teams [so that] the *chacareros* could challenge the ignorance from the contempt with which they are seen.'[128]

Another feature of the Campeonato Argentino was that it brought other styles of play within Argentina to wider attention, as teams from the capital encountered those from the interior. Whilst *la nuestra* was promoted as a national playing style, it was a *porteño* construct, although perceived as Argentine in character. Regional variation was very noticeable during this period, the result of differing environmental and social characteristics across the country. The first discernible regional variant to establish itself, although closely related to *la nuestra*, was the *Escuela Rosarina* or Rosario School, developed as its name suggests in the city of Rosario, which from the earliest days of organised football in Argentina had well developed links with the capital in various cup competitions. A short-passing style of football, the *Escuela Rosarina* produced numerous skilful adherents who earned selection for the Argentine national team in the early decades of the twentieth century such as Adolfo Celli, Atilio Badalini, Gabino Sosa and Zenón Díaz.

After captaining Santiago del Estero to victory in 1928, José Díaz argued in an interview with *Crítica*, that their opponents from the Federal Capital were 'ostentatious', with an overuse of the dribble and individual

[127] *La Nación*, 17 July 1928, 14.
[128] *La Nación*, 11 July 1929, 14.

skills. By contrast, he claimed of his own side, 'When we have possession, we continue to run, not stopping to show off some suicidal trick, that distracts from the primary aim of scoring a goal.' From the northerner's perspective, the aesthetic aspect was secondary to the main objective of scoring goals.[129] The Campeonato reinforced regional stereotypes, both in terms of ethnicity, and in styles of play that were conditioned by the climate and topography. Moore considered in an article in *River Plate* magazine in September 1929, 'The public of Buenos Aires will see this year a complete exhibition of ways and styles that have been created in the country because of the multiple factors that condition human life throughout the immensity of the [Argentine] territory.' Amongst those factors identified was the economy of effort employed by players from Jujuy, Salta and Catamarca used to confronting the challenges of altitude in the foothills of the Andes.[130] In his report, Moore reprises the essentialism of Borocotó's construction of *la nuestra*, although at a regional rather than national level.

Santiago del Estero's success marked the highpoint of provincial exposure in Argentine football for nearly four decades. The Campeonato lost interest and financial backing, ceasing to be played annually from 1932 as football in the interior was relegated to the shadows until the inclusion of provincial clubs in the Campeonato Nacional from 1967. The inclusion of *mestizo* and Indigenous people into Argentine society was sidelined until Juan Domingo Perón's rise to power in the 1940s.

Football's use in the construction of narratives around national identity at an intellectual level was driven by revisionist discourses formulated almost two decades after the event. British influences implicit in football's arrival to Argentina were reassessed by writers such as Borocotó as neo-colonial, necessitating the need for a mythical point of independence or rebirth of Argentine football from the stimulus of Britain's perceived 'informal empire,' first achieved in 1913 with Racing Club de Avellaneda's championship win without a preponderance of Anglo-Argentine players. It was an act that was supplemented by a discourse in influential magazines such as *El Gráfico* in the 1920s and 1930s that elevated *la nuestra*, shorn of British influence, to its current status as a pillar of Argentine identity. This construction negated the positive contribution of

---

[129] *Crítica*, 8 October 1928, 8.
[130] *River Plate*, September 1929, 6.

Anglo-Criollos, despite being as *criollo* as any other immigrant grouping. As such, this discourse fundamentally missed the point that Argentina's footballing development was marked by class differences and not ethnic ones, reflecting wider problems in constructing national consensus within Argentina.

By the time Argentina played in the 1930 World Cup, it was clear that Argentina was still some way from exhibiting a national identity that was inclusive of all its citizens. These case studies have shown that amongst the biggest immigrant grouping in Argentina, the Italo-Argentines, dual identity remained an important factor in Argentine society. Despite being active agents in the Argentine economy and civil society, feelings of *argentinidad* did not preclude simultaneous emotions of Italian-ness. This was highlighted during Genoa's 1923 tour of Argentina when the Italo-Argentine community felt able to celebrate both their Italian heritage and identification with their Argentine homeland. The dominance of Italo-Argentines at all levels of Argentine football from the early 1920s reflected what could be described as an Italianisation rather than a *criollización* of Argentine football, mirroring the concerns of Argentine nationalists that Argentina was in danger of becoming an Italian colony.

Whilst Argentine women were slowly beginning to achieve some civic rights, they were still denied the franchise as masculine hegemony very much held sway. Football equally remained a male-dominated arena, although present in football stadia women were expected to be seen and not heard, attracting opprobrium if they dared to vent their own opinions. Whilst women were club members and participated in non-footballing activities, they played no executive role within them, and were actively discouraged from playing the game themselves for fear of damaging their femininity and falling to the 'apparent' vice of lesbianism.

Afro-Argentine, Indigenous and mestizo minorities were as systematically excluded from Argentine representative football in this period as they were from national narratives of identity. Whilst players such as Alejandro de los Santos, José Laguna and Segundo Luna made isolated breakthroughs, the racial composition of the Argentine national team remained almost uniformly white, reflecting the dominant racial discourse of Argentina being a 'civilised' European country. A discourse of racial superiority that was also projected by the Argentine press against players from neighbouring countries, most notably Brazil, as the 1920 '*macacos*' controversy in *Crítica* demonstrates.

In the 1920s, the interior managed briefly to project itself into the national narrative through football for the first time since the civil wars of the mid-nineteenth century placed power in the hands of the capital, Buenos Aires. The introduction of the Campeonato Argentino in 1920 offered provincial teams a fleeting period in the limelight each year. Seen as a novelty and subjected to mockery in the *porteño* press which continued to view Indigenous and *mestizo*-composed sides from the interior in the same condescending way as the nation builders who had dismissed them as 'barbarians' in the late 1800s, the improving standard of provincial teams saw them competing with the more powerful sides from the capital within a decade. Santiago del Estero's 1928 victory, featuring numerous *mestizo* players, appeared briefly to offer the genuine prospect of the integration of the interior into the national project. These hopes proved short-lived as the Buenos Aires-led authorities proved reluctant to cede any central control. Argentina's minorities remained excluded from narratives of Argentine identity until Juan Perón's ascent to power in 1946 transformed Argentina's society.

References

Aira, Carlos. 2015. *Héroes de Tiento: Historias del Fútbol Argentina 1920–1930*. Buenos Aires: Ediciones Fabro.

Alabarces, Pablo. 2007. *Fútbol y patria. El fútbol y las narrativas de la Nación en la Argentina*, 4th ed. Buenos Aires: Prometeo Libros.

Anderson, Patricia. 2009. Mens Sana in Corpore Sano: Debating Female Sport in Argentina: 1900–46. *The International Journal of the History of Sport* 26 (5): 640–653.

Archetti, Eduardo. 1999. *Masculinities: Football, Polo and the Tango in Argentina*. Oxford: Berg.

Asociación Amateurs de Football. 1924. *Memoria y Balance General 1923*. Buenos Aires: Talleres Gráficos Argentinos de L. J. Rosso y Cia.

Asociación Amateurs de Football. 1921. *Memoria Correspondiente de Ejercicio de 1920*. Buenos Aires: R. Herrando & Cia. Impresores.

Ayarragaray, Lucas. 1925. *La anarquía argentina y el caudillismo*. Buenos Aires: J. Lajouane & Cía.

Barovero, Diego Alberto. 2013. *Caudillos and protagonista políticos en La Boca del Riachuelo*. Buenos Aires: Editorial Dunken.

Bayer, Osvaldo. 2016. *Fútbol Argentino*. Buenos Aires: Sudamericana.

Borges, Jorge Luis. 2000. *Labyrinths: Selected Stories and Other Writings*. London: Penguin Classics.

Brown, Matthew. 2014. *From Frontiers to Football: An Alternative History of Latin America Since 1800*. London: Reaktion Books.

Cabrera, Nicolás, and Nemesia Hijós. 2020. Juegos de espejos: una historia mínima del fútbol femenino en Argentina y Brasil. In *Los días del Mundial: miradas críticas y globales sobre Francia 2019*, eds. Nemesia Hijós, Verónica Moreira and Rodrigo Soto-Lagos, 42–45. Buenos Aires: CLACSO.

Campomar, Andreas. 2014. *¡Golazo!* London: Quercus.

Caparrós, Martín. 2004. *Boquita*. Buenos Aires: Booklet.

Centenario del Club Atlético del Rosario-Plaza Jewell. 1967. *Historia de 100 años de deporte amateur*. Rosario: Amalevi.

Club Atlético Vélez Sársfield. 1925. *Memoria y Ejercicio 1924*. Buenos Aires.

Club Atlético Vélez Sársfield. 1932. *Memoria y Ejercicio 1931*. Buenos Aires.

Club Atlético Vélez Sársfield. 1935. *Memoria y Ejercicio 1934*. Buenos Aires.

Coni, Emilio A. 1969. *El gaucho: Argentina - Brasil - Uruguay*. Buenos Aires: Solar/Hachette.

Dellacasa, Juan. 1939. *Puntapié penal*. Rosario.

Devoto, Fernando J. 2001. Programs and Politics of the First Italian Elite of Buenos Aires, 1852–80. In *Italian Workers of the World*, ed. Donna R. Gabaccia and Fraser M. Ottanelli, 41–59. Chicago: University of Illinois Press.

Devoto, Fernando J. 2006. *Historia de los italianos en la Argentina*. Buenos Aires: Editorial Biblos.

Edwards, Erika Denise. 2019. *Hiding in Plain Sight: Black Women, the Law, and the Making of a White Argentine Republic*. Tuscaloosa: University of Alabama Press.

El Gráfico. 2018. Julio Benavidez, jugaba a jugar. 25 April. https://www.elgrafico.com.ar/articulo/1088/31732/julio-benavidez-jugaba-a-jugar. Accessed 26 June 2021.

Elsey, Brenda, and Joshua Nadel. 2019. *Futbolera*. Austin: University of Texas Press.

Epolito, George. 2012. Golondrinas: Passages of influence: The construction of national/cultural identities in Italy and the Río de la Plata Basin of South America. *National Identities* 14 (3), September: 227–241.

Estévez, Diego. 2013. *38 Campeones del Fútbol Argentino 1891–2013*. Buenos Aires: Ediciones Continente.

Farred, Grant. 2005. Race and Silence in Argentine Football. In *In the Game*, ed. Amy Bass, 95–115. New York: AIAA.

Farred, Grant. 2004. Fiaca and Veron-ismo: Race and Silence in Argentine Football. *Leisure Studies* 23 (1): 47–61.

Foerster, Robert F. 1924. *The Italian Emigration of Our Time*. Cambridge, Mass: Harvard University Press.

Goebel, Michael. 2011. *Argentina's Partisan Past*. Liverpool: Liverpool University Press.

Gordillo, Gastón, and Silvia Hirsch. 2003. Indigenous Struggles and Contested Identities in Argentina Histories of Invisibilization and Reemergence. *Journal of Latin American Anthropology* 8(3), September: 4–30.

Helg, Aline. 1990. Race in Argentina and Cuba, 1880–1930: Theory, Policies and Popular Reaction. In *The Idea of Race in Latin America, 1870–1940*, ed. Richard Graham, 39–43. Austin: University of Texas Press.

Holder, Arthur L. 1920. *Activities of the British Community in Argentina during the Great War 1914–1919*. Buenos Aires: Buenos Aires Herald.

Holt, Richard. 1989. *Sport and the British: A Modern History*. Oxford: Clarendon Paperbacks.

Kaczan, Gisela P. 2016. La práctica gimnástica y el deporte, la cultura física y el cuerpo bello en la historia de las mujeres. Argentina 1900–1930. *Hist. Crit.* No. 61. Julio–septiembre: 23–43.

Kittleson, Roger. 2014. *The Country of Football: Soccer and the Making of Modern Brazil*. Berkeley: University of California Press.

Latzina, Francisco. 1899. *Diccionario geográfico argentino*. Buenos Aires: Jacobo Peuser.

Levinsky, Sergio. 2016. *AFA. El fútbol pasa, los negocios quedan: Una historia política y deportiva*. Buenos Aires: Autoria Editorial.

Lugones, Leopoldo. 2002. National Identity in a Cosmopolitan Society. In *The Argentina Reader*, ed. Gabriela Nouzeilles and Graciela Montaldo, 209–213. Durham, NC: Duke University Press.

Macias, Diego, ed. 2008. *El santonario*. Buenos Aires: Arte Gráfico Editorial Argentino.

MacLachlan, Colin M. 2006. *Argentina: What Went Wrong*. Westport: Praeger.

Maffia, Marta. 2008. Cape Verdeana in Argentina. In *Transnational Archipelago: Perspectives on Cape Verdean Migration and Diaspora*, ed. Luís. Batalha and Jørgen. Carling, 47–54. Amsterdam: Amsterdam University Press.

Malcom, Dominic. 2008. *The Sage Dictionary of Sports Studies*. London: Sage.

Martin, Simon. 2004. *Football and Fascism: The National Game under Mussolini*. Oxford: Berg.

Molinari, Alejandro, and Roberto L. Martínez. 2013. *El Fútbol. La conquista popular de una pasión argentina*. Avellaneda: Editorial de la Cultura Urbana.

Newitt, Malyn. 2015. *Emigration and the Sea: An Alternative History of Portugal and the Portuguese*. Oxford: Oxford University Press.

Orton, Mark. 2022. The Game of the Italians: Football and Dual Identity in Argentina 1910–1935. *Studia Universitatis Babes-Bolyai* 67 (2): (in press).

República Argentina. 1916. *Tercer censo nacional, leventado el 1° de junio de 1914*. Buenos Aires.

Reid Andrews, George. 1979. Race Versus Class Association: The Afro-Argentines of Buenos Aires, 1850–1900. *Journal of Latin American Studies* 11 (1): 21–37.

Richey, Jeffrey W. 2013. *Playing at Nation: Soccer Institutions, Racial Ideology and National Integration in Argentina 1912–31*. Unpublished PhD thesis. Chapel Hill: University of North Carolina.

Rojas, Ricardo. 1909. *La restauración nacionalista*. Buenos Aires: Ministerio de Justicia e Instrucción Pública.

Romero, Luis Alberto. 2004. *A History of Argentina in the Twentieth Century*. University Park, Pennsylvania: Penn State University Press.

Rosatti, Horacio. 2009. *Cien años de multitud: historia de Boca Juniors, una pasión argentina: I. El period amateur: 1905–1930*. Buenos Aires: Galerna.

Sáenz Quesada, María. 2012. *La Argentina. Historia del País y de su Gente*. Buenos Aires: Editorial Sudamericana.

Scher, Ariel, Guillermo Blanco, and Jorge Búsico. 2010. *Deporte Nacional*. Buenos Aires: Emecé.

Sodo, Juan Manuel. 2010/2011. Apuntes para una historia del fútbol argentino en clave "violencia". *Esporte e Sociedade* 6 (16), November/February: 1–15.

Solberg, Carl. 1970. *Immigration and Nationalism*. Austin: University of Texas Press.

Sutton, Barbara. 2008. Contesting Racism, Democratic Citizenship, Human Rights and Antiracist Politics in Argentina. *Latin American Perspectives* 35 (6), November: 106–121.

Tato, María Inés. 2011. El llamado de la patria. Británicos e italianos residentes en la Argentina frente la Primera Guerra Mundial. *Estudios Migratorios Latinoamericanos* 71: 273–292.

Un Caño. 2005. El ascenso en el ADN. 9 April. www.revistauncanio.com.ar/picado/el-ascenso-en-el-adn/. Accessed 31 March 2018.

Williams, Jean. 2021. *The History of Women's Football*. Barnsley: Pen and Sword.

Wood, David. 2017. *Football and Literature in South America*. Abingdon: Routledge.

CHAPTER 4

Flying the Flag: Football and the International Projection of Argentinidad 1913–1930

As transatlantic trade and sporting relations resumed in the 1920s after the dislocation of the First World War, this chapter interrogates how football offered Argentina a way of projecting itself internationally during this period through participation in global competitions such as the 1928 Olympic Games and the inaugural World Cup of 1930, as well as through tours to and from Argentina by Argentine and European clubs. It focuses on how the press used these encounters to not only project a differentiated Argentine playing style but represent Argentine 'civilisation' through the portrayal of 'essential' values. In exploring these bilateral encounters, this chapter contends that the transnational exchange of ideas enriched Argentine football's development. By projecting Argentine football in the 'mirror' of neighbouring Uruguay, it identifies the contradictions arising from having a shared *rioplatense* identity and the need for new differentiated identities as the two nations vied for world football supremacy at the end of the 1920s, confirming that Uruguay was the natural 'other' against which to transpose Argentina's early footballing identity instead of English football as Eduardo Archetti suggests.[1] The chapter concludes by looking at the first great migration of Argentine footballers: to Italy from the 1910s and how this called into question the national identity of

---

[1] Archetti (1999, 71).

those who crossed the Atlantic depending on the rival viewpoints of the Argentine and Italian press.

Pablo Alabarces and Mariela Rodríguez argue that for football to become an effective agent of Argentine identity, it needed international successes to cement that process, pointing to Boca Juniors' 1925 European tour and Argentina's silver medals at the 1928 Olympic Games and 1930 World Cup, as examples of such success.[2] This chapter builds on these interpretations by assessing the extent to which football acted as a metaphor for the international projection of Argentine identity through the examination of tours by European clubs to Argentina and reciprocal tours made by Argentine clubs to Europe, through the case studies of two largely overlooked 1929 tours, those of Ferencváros to Argentina, and Sportivo Barracas to Europe. Whilst Archetti recognises that following Ferencváros' visit, 'Argentinians believed that their style of playing was very much like the football played in Austria and Hungary,' this chapter examines this transnational exchange far more deeply.[3] It also argues that Boca's 1925 tour was more of a mercantile endeavour, with *Crítica*'s nationalistic rhetoric designed to sell newspapers, and that by contrast Sportivo Barracas' 1929 tour was more representative of both the Argentine nation and its football.

The classical interpretation of *la nuestra* in the 1920s by writers such as Borocotó was to compare Argentine football with that of its British originators from which it evolved. César Torres suggests that a discernible *rioplatense* style of playing football representative of a 'pluralistic, modern, urbanized, and westernized Argentine society' had become established by the 1920s.[4] This chapter argues it is instructive to cast Uruguayan football as the mirror against which to compare the early Argentine game. Whilst Archetti has argued, 'In this transformation the gaze of the "distant other", the Europeans, and the "near other", the Uruguayans, would be important,' this section goes far deeper.[5] It examines how out of shared British roots a *rioplatense* style common to both sides of the River Plate developed, before diverging between the aesthetically pleasing *la nuestra* of Argentina and the more robust *garra charrúa* of Uruguay.

---

[2] Alabarces and Rodríguez (1999, 119–121).
[3] Archetti (1996, 205).
[4] Torres (2003, 5).
[5] Archetti (1999, 61).

Whilst the presence of dual Italo-Argentine identity within Argentine football reflected wider complications surrounding Argentine national identity, the same was true of narratives of Italian identity. The fluid nature of national identity amongst Italo-Argentines was reflected by the migration to Italy of dozens of Argentine footballers from the 1910s to the 1940s, and further confused by their incidence in the Italian national team, exemplified by the presence of four Argentine-born players in Italy's 1934 World Cup-winning team. Zachary Bigalke has approached the issue through an in-depth study of the Italo-Argentine involvement in that World Cup victory, one that has also attracted the interest of Simon Martin due to the links between Italian football and the Fascist state.[6] Scholarship by Pierre Lanfranchi and Matthew Taylor has focused principally on the migratory phenomenon that they suggest began in 1925 with Torino's signing of Julio Libonatti, something that aroused 'ambiguities' enabling different interpretations of national identity to be applied in the respective countries.[7] Historians posit that this migratory flow was the result of regulatory changes within Italian football included within the 1926 Carta di Viareggio which banned foreign players, but allowed for the contracting of South American players with Italian heritage.[8] This chapter argues that footballing interactions between the two nations ran much deeper than this and began at an earlier point than previously suggested. It investigates these 'ambiguities' more deeply to reach a more comprehensive understanding of the nature and complexity of dual Argentine and Italian identity within Italy by analysing the point of view of the Italian press and some of the players themselves.

The presence of Italo-Argentines in Italian football since the 1910s has been overlooked by the existing historiography. Pre-dating the rise to power of Mussolini's Fascist regime, their existence cannot be solely attributed to nationalist policies and is resonant of the more personal and familial debates surrounding identity on the part of individual Italo-Argentine families. These footballers were the offspring of the 750,000 Italian returnees from Argentine migration between 1871 and 1950. Whilst Bigalke identifies that the return of Italian families reflected general patterns of transitory transatlantic migration, this section goes further in

---

[6] Bigalke (2017); Martin (2004, 58–65).
[7] Lanfranchi and Taylor (2001, 72–81).
[8] Martin (2004, 58–65).

explaining their specific contribution to Italian football.⁹ The significance of their upbringing in Argentina was that they learned the sport in the *potreros* of Argentine cities like Buenos Aires and Rosario, where football was more developed than in Italy, honing skills that enabled them to flourish in Italian football after returning with their parents to the land of their ancestors.

INTERNATIONAL PROJECTION AND TRANSNATIONAL EXCHANGES IN ARGENTINE FOOTBALL

Transatlantic footballing relations resumed in the 1920s after the interruption caused by the First World War, with fourteen European touring teams visiting Argentina during the decade. Whilst pre-war visits of British touring teams were seen in the press as essential to the improvement and development of Argentine football, the ability to continue its self-development unmolested by war in the intervening period meant that the pedagogical motives for such tours were now redundant. Early post-war tours by the British sides, Third Lanark and Plymouth Argyle were not particularly well received by either the Argentine public or its press. Coming from the Scottish League and Southern League, respectively, these clubs were of a lower standard than those such as Southampton and Nottingham Forest that Argentines had received a decade or more earlier.

Plymouth's 1924 visit was illustrative. Despite winning their opening match 1–0 against a Buenos Aires Select XI, the Devon side was described in *La Argentina* as, 'showing nothing new in relation to previous visits,' before going on to condemn Plymouth as 'the poorest professional team that has visited us.'¹⁰ The conclusion of the tour, which left a 15,000-peso deficit in the coffers of the AAF due to a lack of box office interest, led to further backlash in the Argentine press about the utility of British tours to Argentina. In an article entitled, 'The professionals no longer interest us,' *Crítica* complained that once Plymouth's style of play became known, the interest of fans disappeared. The newspaper argued the same of Third Lanark's visit a year earlier, asking what lessons had been left by

---

⁹ Bigalke (2017, 93–94).
¹⁰ *La Argentina*, 23 June 1924.

the touring sides for the £4,000 they had each received from the AAF.[11] As *La Nación* observed in 1925, Swindon were the last British tourists to return home unbeaten in 1912; now a dozen years later, the pendulum was firmly in favour of Argentine sides as Plymouth Argyle ended their tour with a record of won two, drawn two and lost three.[12]

Things did not improve when Motherwell, the next British visitors, arrived four years later. The Scottish team's manager, John Hunter failed to impress his hosts with his opening remarks, 'As teachers we come to teach [the Argentines] how to play.'[13] After Motherwell were beaten by a Buenos Aires select team, the Argentine football administrator, Adrián Beccar Varela, noted, 'These don't have anything to teach, it is another modest team like Lanark.'[14] There were similar reservations ahead of English Second Division Chelsea's visit in 1929, with *River Plate* magazine complaining: 'currently there does not exist a defined superiority between English and South American football.'[15]

It was not just British tourists that dissatisfied Argentine spectators. In 1928, a much-vaunted Barcelona team was beaten 3–1 and held to a 0–0 draw by the national team, emboldening *Crítica* to claim, 'The superiority shown over Barcelona ratified the quality of Argentine football.'[16] Not that Torino fared any better a year later. Despite fielding three Argentine-born players: Julio Libonatti, Arturo Ludueña and Adolfo Baloncieri, Torino failed to win over the Argentine public, prompting *La Nación* to lament that, 'The latest visits of foreign teams have not achieved anything in terms of generating memories or satisfying the expectation that the announcement of their presence [Barcelona, Chelsea and Torino] to our fields had excited among supporters.'[17]

One successful element of these tours was the transnational transfer of ideas between Argentina and the Danubian school of football exemplified in Austria, Czechoslovakia and Hungary. The 1922 tour of Czech club, Teplizer, who had been unbeaten in the Bohemian League since 1919,

---

[11] *Crítica*, 21 July 1924.
[12] *La Nación*, 13 May 1928.
[13] *La Argentina*, 11 May 1928.
[14] *La Argentina*, 14 May 1928.
[15] *River Plate*, Año 2, No.6, April 1929, 4.
[16] *Crítica*, 6 August 1928.
[17] *La Nación*, 29 July 1929, 13.

was the first interaction between the two footballing traditions. Each of Teplizer's five matches was played in front of capacity crowds at Sportivo Barracas' stadium, with the attractive play of the tourists appealing to Argentine tastes. The link was further embedded by an observation made by the Genoa captain, Ettore Leale, during his side's Argentine tour in 1923. Leale suggested that Argentine footballers' speed and quick passing made them 'analogous to the players of Central Europe,' in contrast to the slower play exhibited in northern Europe, 'as the enthusiasts of this country can appreciate from the matches against the Czechs [Teplizer].'[18]

The Argentine press maintained a keen interest in Danubian football throughout the 1920s. Commenting on the migratory wave of Hungarian players to the Italian League in 1925, *La Nación* noted the comments of Italian journalist, Bruno Roghi, 'The benefits stamp themselves with teams adopting a more elevated technique [from the Hungarians].'[19] Articles published in *La Nación* by Vienna-based journalist, Adolfo Engels, kept Argentine readers abreast of developments in Central European football. In 1928, he noted the desire of Austrian coach, Hugo Meisl, that an Argentine or Uruguayan team could visit Vienna having watched them both with admiration at the Amsterdam Olympics.[20]

The mutual appreciation between the Argentine and Danubian styles was sealed in 1929 with Ferencváros' tour to Argentina. Runners-up in the Hungarian League, the Budapest side came to the Río de la Plata replete with Hungarian internationals such as József Takács, Gabór Obitz and Martón Bukovi, and were worthy exponents of the Danubian school of football, having pounded Rapid Vienna 7–1 at home in the Mitropa Cup final just months earlier.[21] The appreciation of Argentine crowds for Ferencváros was evident from the start and increased with each game they played. In their opening 4–3 victory over River Plate, Ferencváros' attacking play led *La Nación* to note that Ferencváros 'conquered the unanimous sympathy of the crowd.'[22] Whilst the previous visits of European teams during the 1920s had highlighted the speed of the Argentine

[18] *La Nación*, 20 August 1923, 7.
[19] *La Nación*, 1 November 1925, Sec 2, 1.
[20] *La Nación*, 19 August 1928.
[21] *La Nación*, 30 July 1929, 15.
[22] *La Nación*, 2 August 1929, 15.

game, the Hungarians were lauded for the fact that their players were often quicker in their passing than their Argentine opponents. In the game against the Argentine national team in which Ferencváros lost to two goals in the final ten minutes, *La Nación* observed, 'the majority of attacks of one or other side was made on the basis of quick passes to the centre.' The entertainment level was contrasted against another fixture that same afternoon between Independiente and Italian side, Torino, which was alternatively described as 'mediocre.'[23] Ferencváros won their final game in Argentina, 2–1 against Racing Club, again earning the plaudits of *La Nación* who eulogised the Hungarians' 'singular mobility of play,' contrasting it with the relative slowness of the Argentine team, claiming that Racing 'dressed themselves up as Saxons,' continuing the trope of English football being slow and boring.[24]

The impact of Ferencváros' visit to Argentina was reflected in an article by Dinty Moore. He noted with interest 'the desire' of Danubian teams to evaluate themselves against the best of the Río de la Plata, 'that play in the same style as the Hungarians,' having grown tired of playing—and beating—the English professionals. Moore welcomed the presence of Ferencváros, whose play was 'not coldly efficient like the English, nor impetuous and disorderly like the Spanish … but instead something that is more agreeable to us … something of ours comes in the game of the Hungarians.'[25]

Though Argentine clubs had made lucrative foreign tours within South America, most notably to Brazil, offering Argentines the opportunity to reinforce its regional footballing hegemony, none had yet challenged themselves against Europeans on their own continent. In 1925, that changed with huge repercussions for the Argentine game. Boca Juniors' tour of Europe served to redress the Argentine absence from the Paris Olympics the previous year in which internal administrative wrangling stopped Argentina accepting an invitation to compete.

The tour has been studied by a number of scholars, not least Julio Frydenberg and Matthew Karush in terms of how Argentina was projected in the press to cement notions of Argentine national identity

---

[23] *La Nación*, 11 August 1929, Sports, 3.
[24] *La Nación*, 14 August 1929, 5.
[25] *La Nación*, 8 August 1929, 15.

and a distinct Argentine way of playing in the minds of Europeans.[26] It can be alternatively argued that the resonance of the tour had more to do with a skilfully executed piece of populist jingoism on the part of *Crítica* newspaper to increase its readership in the competitive Buenos Aires media market, with one of its journalists accompanying the tour party. At the outset, *Crítica* outlined its agenda, arguing the 'patriotic importance' of the tour, going on to elaborate that, 'Argentine football needs to be known abroad.' It concluded that, 'The journey … is taken to obtain abroad the biggest of successes for the institution, for sport and for our country.'[27] Yet, as Frydenberg has identified, Boca was simply a club, whilst *Crítica* critically conflated the club as representative of all Argentine football.[28] This was not a viewpoint shared by *La Razón* which claimed, 'Boca is not the highest expression of Argentinian soccer … What does the prestigious club represent, at the end of the day? At most *porteño* soccer, not an Argentine one, because Buenos Aires is not the nation.'[29]

A more compelling case study is the previously unreported 1929 European tour of Sportivo Barracas. In February 1929, the club, supplemented by several provincial players, including Felipe Cherro, Luis Célico and Segundo Luna, undertook a European tour that was more representative of Argentina than that of Boca in 1925. They played twenty-five matches in a range of unaccustomed weather conditions, especially snow.[30] Not one of Argentina's more prestigious clubs, Sportivo surprised the media with the ambitious scope of the tour, taking on the best sides in Italy and some of the top Spanish teams. After a series of early defeats, most notably to a Raimundo Orsi-inspired Juventus, *La Nación* wrote, 'When the expeditioners disembarked in the first European port, it was said that they would need umbrellas and a picnic basket. They need to open the umbrellas to withstand the downpour of criticism and prepare the basket for the harvest of goals [conceded].'[31]

---

[26] Frydenberg (2003, 91–120); Karush (2003, 11–32); Aira (2015, 236); Saavedra (2009a, 8); Rosatti (2009, 100–114).

[27] *Crítica*, January 1925, 14.

[28] Frydenberg (2003, 94–95).

[29] Cited in Campomar (2014, 112).

[30] Asociación Amateurs Argentino de Football (1930, 100).

[31] *La Nación*, 14 February 1929, 14.

Sportivo's fortunes changed for the better on the remainder of the Italian leg, earning rave reviews in the local press regarding their representation of *la nuestra*. An impressive victory over AC Milan in wintry conditions earned this eulogy from the *Gazzetta dello Sport*, later reprinted in *La Nación*, 'Sportivo Barracas showed themselves to be a great team and left the impression that they could play even better in normal conditions. The public admired the style and play of the Argentines ... However, the Argentines soon adapted to the state of the pitch and made skilful passes and developed a harmonic, precise, speedy and brilliant play.'[32] After beating Fiorentina 4–1, an Italian journalist noted that *rioplatense* football was the best in the world, a point reached by learning lessons from 'European teachers' before 'taking forward this knowledge in prodigious form until arriving at a true sporting masterpiece.' Then turning to Sportivo Barracas specifically, he acknowledged, 'The results obtained on foreign pitches in front of foreign crowds speak in an eloquent way of the valour and prestige of this formidable adversary.'[33]

At the conclusion of the tour, Sportivo's president, Beltrán, subtly criticised Boca's 1925 expedition with its 'easy' opponents in his summary of Sportivo's tour in the pages of *Crítica*. Describing his team as, 'an admirable representation which has maintained the honour and conditions of the country,' Beltrán went on to say that if the aim were to simply win games, 'we would have arranged games with easy teams, in Corsica, Sardinia or Las Palmas ... In Italy was the most brilliant part of the tour. We triumphed in Milan where Sparta Prague, Slavia Prague, the English professionals, Germans, and Austrians had lost.'[34]

For its part, Argentine football's governing body highlighted the benefit of the Sportivo Barracas tour as serving as a 'guideline to the valuation of the football played by Argentine players.'[35] The team's record of eleven wins, four draws and ten defeats acted as a reliable barometer of Argentina's football, showing that even the country's more modest clubs could compete favourably with the best clubs in continental Europe. *La Nación* considered that the best feature of Sportivo Barracas' tour was the resilience displayed by the Argentine side in overcoming so many defeats

---

[32] *La Nación*, 26 February 1929, 3.
[33] *La Nación*, 3 March 1929, 4.
[34] *Crítica*, 5 May 1929.
[35] Asociación Amateurs Argentino de Football (1930, 100).

to end the tour on a high note when they were physically and emotionally exhausted, something described as the 'most supreme virtue in sport,' and a trait not traditionally associated with Argentine football.[36]

Such tours reinforced ideas of Argentine national footballing characteristics. Whilst the emphasis on individual skill and technique faithfully reflected the ideals of *la nuestra*, the prominence of organised team-play or 'homogeneity' as it was described, and sportsmanship alternatively exploded other elements of the myth of Argentine exceptionalism. Press reportage throughout the 1920s made a point of advocating the importance of sportsmanship in sides representing Argentina. After Argentina's victory over Genoa in 1923, *La Nación* wrote, 'what most impressed us was the gentlemanliness and clean play, since this is a moral quality, which is more valuable than the physical condition of the players.'[37] It was as though the newspaper was reporting on an Alumni performance twenty years earlier, such was the emphasis on fair play. Even within *Crítica*'s coverage of the 1925 Boca tour, aside from boasts that club had raised high 'the Argentine sporting flag,' there was satisfaction that the club had left in Europe 'a great sensation of skill and chivalry.'[38] The point was further emphasised at the end of the decade with *La Nación* noting with pride that German journalists had described the Argentine team at the 1928 Olympics as 'the gentlemen of the pitch.'[39] As such, Argentina were demonstrating to the 'civilised' Europeans that they were just like them.

The similarity to these values practised by Ferencváros on their 1929 tour helped secure the symbiosis between Argentine football and the Danubian school. The Hungarians' sense of fair play was keenly noted by *La Nación*, 'The players of Ferencváros are essentially disciplined and respected all of the referee's mistakes with their dignified respect serving as an example.'[40] The organisation of the Ferencváros' play was also revered in the Argentine press, 'It is a homogenous team, and its components are known for their technique ... Individually they don't possess men capable of provoking the enthusiasm of supporters, since the

[36] *La Nación*, 18 March 1929, 3.
[37] *La Nación*, 20 August 1923, 7.
[38] *Crítica*, 12 June 1925, 14.
[39] *La Nación*, 7 August 1929, 15.
[40] Ibid, 15.

strength of the team resides in the harmony of the side.'[41] The transnational exchange of footballing ideas between Argentina and Hungary reached its apogee less than a decade later with the arrival of Hungarian coach, Imre Hirschl at Gimnasia y Esgrima de La Plata, as will be seen in Chapter 5.

Brothers in Arms: Argentine Football and the Uruguayan 'Other'

The proximity of Uruguay, with its shared colonial, demographic and cultural history as part of the Spanish Viceroyalty of the Río de la Plata until its independence in 1827, and with its capital Montevideo separated from Buenos Aires only by the Río de la Plata estuary, makes it a natural counterpoint against which to compare the development of an idiosyncratic football playing style with Argentina. Football became a cultural means for creating an artificial semblance of difference between the two, facilitating in the Uruguayan case especially, a way of being perceived differently from Argentina. These differences were diffused to a wider a public was through the pages of the media on either side of the Río de la Plata in the early decades of the twentieth century.[42]

Uruguayan football initially developed along similar lines to Argentina, introduced by British immigrants and propagated through British cricket clubs, private schools and railway companies. A *criollo* Uruguayan team, Nacional, was founded by students of the Universidad de la República in 1899 as a bulwark against the hegemony of the British teams. Whilst distance, lack of transnational transport infrastructure and natural barriers like the Andes precluded early footballing contact with the other countries of South America, Montevideo—just a short boat ride away—offered the easiest opportunity for the establishment of cross-border sporting relations for Argentina. Inter-city matches between teams from the British communities of Buenos Aires and Montevideo had been held annually between 1889 and 1894 to celebrate the birthday of Queen Victoria.[43] From there, it was not long before full internationals between the two countries began in 1902, with Argentina winning the inaugural encounter

---

[41] *La Nación*, 1 July 1929, 3.
[42] Giulianotti (1999, 134–154); Orton (2017, 2).
[43] Prats (2014, 18–20).

6–0.⁴⁴ These games were played with such regularity that they soon usurped England v Scotland matches as the most played fixture in international football.

Despite the two nations having remarkably similar demographic profiles, the difference in racial composition of the opposing teams was striking from the outset. Apart from José Laguna, Alejandro de los Santos and Segundo Luna in the 1910s and 1920s, the Argentine national side was predominantly white. By contrast the Uruguayans embraced their Black footballers, fielding two, Juan Delgado and Isabelino Gradín, at the South American Championship as early as 1916, the first international team to do so. The undoubted star of Uruguay's victorious 1924 Olympic campaign was José Leandro Andrade, nicknamed 'The Black Marvel' by the French press. His elasticity in appearing to change direction in one movement whilst on the ball owed much to his training as a professional tango dancer.⁴⁵

The introduction of the South American Championship in 1916 added extra significance to fixtures between the two nations, as the winners invariably went on to win the competition until 1939 (the only exceptions coming in 1919 and 1922 when it was won by Brazil). Indeed, Uruguay began to assert itself as the best team on the continent. Their gold medal win at the 1924 Olympics highlighted Southern Cone football to a global audience for the first time and their further victories at the 1928 Olympics and the inaugural World Cup in 1930, in which Argentina were runners-up on each occasion, meant that *rioplatense* football was now a leading global power and no longer seen as subservient to the European game.

The 1924 Olympics were critical in terms of global understanding of Uruguay as a separate independent country to Argentina. Lorenzo Batlles Berres conflated the team with the Uruguayan nation in *El Día*, 'You are Uruguay. You are now the motherland boys …the symbol of that little dot, nearly invisible on the map … which has been getting larger, larger, larger.'⁴⁶ Paradoxically, Uruguay's victory was also used to celebrate a joint *Rioplatense* identity, one forged in the battle for independence from Spanish colonial rule. This fraternity was expressed on both sides of the Río de la Plata. An editorial by the Montevideo newspaper *El Día* and

---

⁴⁴ *La Nación*, 21 July 1902, 7.
⁴⁵ Galeano (1997, 42–43).
⁴⁶ Cited in Campomar (2014, 102–105); Orton (2017, 5).

that was republished in Argentina by *La Nación* rejoiced, 'The Argentine soul and the Uruguayan soul have vibrated in unison in these times of clamorous jubilation ... we want to show the world that the two countries on the shores of the River Plate are brothers, not in a trivialised way, but in the profound and cordial flavour of unbridled affection.'[47] On the Argentine side, *La Vanguardia* attributed victory to 'twenty-two men who ethnically, geographically, and psychologically constitute a unity, a unity universally described as *rioplatense*.'[48] In both the global and Argentine imaginary, Uruguay's victory was a primarily regional one, the conflation as a joint effort with Argentina apparent, even with the Argentines absent. The inference was that had Argentina competed, they too would have been on the podium with their 'brother' Uruguayans.

When Uruguay defended their Olympic title in Amsterdam in 1928, they were joined this time by Argentina, with the draw keeping the pair apart until the final. Their presence at the pinnacle of world football again raised the issue of joint *rioplatense* identity. A lengthy piece in *Última Hora* before the final expanded on this narrative, reflecting on the pre-independence unity of the two countries within the Viceroyalty of the Río de la Plata. It argued that the *rioplatense* pair competing against other was strange as 'Basques and Catalans playing against each other,' in the sense that, 'in reality we Argentines and Uruguayans are as one.' The article concluded, 'That is why, in honour of these essential defining factors of the *rioplatense* community, a combined national team should play in these world championships. For even though it is no longer politically feasible to make the Río de la Plata into a single nation, nothing can stop us from being one in spiritual activities, in sports—just like we were on 25 May 1810 and 9 July 1816.'[49] Uruguay won the final after a replay, but after both teams returned to South America aboard the *Alcantara*, they were received in Montevideo by the head of the city's council, César Batlle Pacheco, who addressed the Argentine players with great magnanimity, 'This trophy is brought to the Fatherland of the Río [de la Plata]; it is an accomplishment of both parties.'[50]

---

[47] *La Nación*, 12 June 1924, 2; Orton (2017, 6).
[48] *La Vanguardia*, 19 July 1930, 6.
[49] *Última Hora*, 14 June 1928.
[50] *La Nación*, 17 July 1928, 14.

When the two nations met again two years later in the inaugural World Cup Final in Montevideo, *rioplatense* brotherhood disappeared to be replaced by a mutual neighbourly dislike. It was as if when competing in Europe, *rioplatense* unity invoked the common fight against European colonialism, but when back on South American soil this was replaced by fratricidal jealousy and an aspiration to regional dominance. Uruguay's perceived gamesmanship towards Argentina during the competition resulted in a rupture between the nations' respective footballing administrations. The AAAF wrote in its 1930 annual report: 'For reasons that are in the public domain, the ruling council decreed the breaking of relations with the Uruguayan Association.' Among the reasons given were 'the aggressive onset of the Uruguayan players against ours,' 'a manifest and dangerously hostile atmosphere,' before going on to decry that, 'said insults and provocations came from people of all social classes and without distinction of sexes.'[51] *El Gráfico* considered the AAAF's stance in breaking-off relations to be an overreaction, calling instead for a pausing of encounters between the *rioplatense* rivals until cool heads could be restored.[52] In the view of visiting British writer Rosita Forbes, the bad blood could be 'traced to the bitterness on one side and the impolitic rejoicing on the other which followed the defeat of the larger republic in the stadiums of Montevideo.'[53] The spat had wider continental ramifications, leading to a suspension of the South American Championship until 1935, by which time the two governing bodies had been reconciled.[54]

The bad blood between the rival nations also impacted on Uruguayan footballers, who played for Argentine clubs in greater numbers following the introduction of professionalism in 1931. Independiente reinforced their ranks with four Uruguayans, including the star right-winger Roberto Porta, but the signing of foreign players was not universally popular amongst opposition fans. Porta was initially unsettled by the different atmosphere, made uncomfortable by the supporters of rivals that were hostile towards him because of his Uruguayan nationality.[55]

---

[51] Asociación Amateurs Argentino de Football (1931, 40–45).
[52] *El Gráfico*, 9 August 1930.
[53] Forbes (1933, 5).
[54] Wernicke (2016, 65–66).
[55] *El Gráfico*, 3 December 1932, 12.

Some in the press attributed Argentina's 1930 defeat to a lack of moral courage, and reporting dripped with machismo with *La Prensa* denouncing the team as 'lady-players.'[56] As Argentine striker Francisco Varallo later admitted, 'We could not beat the Uruguayans because we were cowards. The majority of the players had fear, and they always beat us because they were more resolute.'[57] Osvaldo Bayer argues that the 1930 World Cup was a watershed, in that had Argentina won it would have enabled them to shed 'the complex of paternity' that appeared to inhibit the team when they played their great rivals, but Uruguay's ultimate victory meant that, 'we continue being their sons.'[58] This perception of neurosis has some traction in Argentina, where psychoanalysis has been utilised since the 1910s, gaining a mass middle-class popularity rarely seen elsewhere in the developed world.

Some differentiation in playing style between the two nations was revealed as early as 1924. The Uruguayans' short-passing game was seen as the legacy of the former Scottish international Joe Harley, who migrated to the River Plate to work on the railways, and who played for Peñarol. This style was revered in Uruguay as '*a la escocesa*' in recognition of its Scottish roots, in stark contrast to the negation of British influence on the development of footballing style in Argentina.[59] According to Uruguayan commentator Andrés Morales, from 1924 Uruguay, 'Started to forge a style that felt itself superior to the Europeans and different to the Argentines. The skill … combines itself with a profound courage in the face of difficult moments … It is in the 1920s, then, that it started to generate a self-image that would start to disturb Argentina.'[60] In the same way as the writers of *El Gráfico* sought to establish a narrative which captured the essence of Argentine national football, a similar process was underway in Uruguay to define their football. The result was the notion of '*garra charrúa*,' which embraced Uruguay's indigenous identity rather than negating it as the Argentines had done. The term was first coined at the 1935 South American Extra Championship in Lima, in which an ageing Uruguayan team were unexpectedly successful, beating Argentina

---

[56] Cited in Mason (1995, 40–43).

[57] *La Prensa*, 31 May 2001.

[58] Bayer (2016, 32–33); Orton (2017, 10).

[59] Prats (2014, 34–36); Giulianotti (1999, 138–139).

[60] Osaba (2012, 59); Orton (2017, 9).

3–0 in the process. Their obdurate progress through the tournament was likened to the resistance of the indigenous Charrúa during the Spanish colonial period, known as *garra charrúa*.[61] That the Uruguayans should glorify its indigenous past is somewhat ironic, given that in a similar way to Argentina they had systematically decimated the Charrúa and other indigenous populations like the more populous Guaraní, who had been 'civilised' by Jesuit missionaries, leaving Uruguay without a discernible indigenous identity. By the 1940s, one historian had encapsulated it as a 'synthesis of racial fortitude, a tangible and spiritual manifestation of Latin mental agility and physical virility.'[62] In doing so, it was as a revisionist acceptance of the place in the nation's cultural history for Uruguay's indigenous population, in a similar way to which the *gauchos* were venerated by Argentine revisionists, as Rafael Bayce says, 'washing their hands of the blame for the genocide.'[63] In the Uruguayan newspaper *El País*, this perceived mental toughness was described as follows, 'The referee's whistle signalled the end of a titanic fight between the two colossus,' and, with it, Uruguay were flourished with deserved success, this tiny Uruguay in territorial extension, but great, immeasurably great through its moral values, through the proud strength of its race of fierce blood, like good *charrúa* blood.'[64]

The meeting of the two *rioplatense* nations in the finals of the 1928 Olympics and the 1930 World Cup confirmed the need to differentiate between the two. The stereotypes of Uruguayans as workers and Argentines as aesthetes were eloquently expressed by Italian journalist, Gianni Brera, after the 1930 World Cup, 'Argentina play football with a lot of imagination and elegance, but technical superiority cannot compensate for the abandonment of tactics. Between the two *rioplatense* national teams, the ants are the Uruguayans, the cicadas are the Argentinians.'[65]

---

[61] Ibid, 59–60.
[62] Giménez (2007, 9).
[63] Bayce (2014, 57).
[64] *El País* (Montevideo), 31 July 1930, 10; Orton (2017, 12).
[65] Archetti (1996, 205); Orton (2022).

Rimpatriati: Italo-Argentines in Italian Football

The first Italo-Argentine to make an impact in Italian football was Cesare Lovati. Born in Buenos Aires on Christmas Day 1891, midfielder Lovati made his debut for AC Milan in 1910 before going on to play six times for the Italian national team.[66] One feature of these early Italo-Argentine returning migrants was the incidence of siblings in the same teams. Although a year or two apart in age, they were often selected *en bloc* because they were collectively better than their Italian-born peers. The four Mosso brothers—Eugenio, Francisco, Julio and Benito—left Mendoza for Turin as teenagers in 1912 to return to their parents' native Piedmont. All played for Torino, with Eugenio representing Italy.[67] The three Boglietti brothers—Ernesto, Romulo and Octavio—also migrated to Turin in the early 1910s, aged 14, 13 and 12, respectively. Romulo debuted as a teenager for Juventus in 1913, having already played for Gimnasia y Esgrima de General Paz in his native Córdoba, shortly to be followed into the Juve side by his brothers.[68] This phenomenon was further exemplified by the Badini brothers, born and raised in Rosario who returned as teenagers to their parents' native Bologna, with Angelo and Emilio starting to play for the club in 1913, soon to be followed by their two younger brothers. The integration of the Badinis, Bogliettis, Mossos and others into Italian football were early examples of how players who learned their football in Argentina, offering something different in terms of ability and playing style, alerted Italian clubs to the possibilities offered by Italo-Argentine players. As such, these footballing representatives of dual identity cannot simply be dismissed as the offspring of *golondrinas* who just happened to be born in Argentina. As Table 4.1 shows, four of the eleven Italo-Argentines to have worn the *azzurri* of the Italian national team up until 1935 came from this first wave of *rimpatriati* or 'repatriated' players.

The first player to cross the Atlantic for purely economic reasons was Julio Libonatti who joined *I Granata* from Newell's Old Boys in 1925 after being talent spotted by Torino's president, Enrico Marone, whilst in Buenos Aires on business as owner of the Cinzano drinks company. But it was the nationalist reforms of the Italian game enshrined in the 1926

---

[66] *Gazzetta dello Sport*, 23 July 1961; Orton (2022).
[67] Lo Presti (2017, 8); Orton (2022).
[68] Ibid, 8–15; Orton (2022).

Table 4.1 Italo-Argentines in the Italian National Team 1914–1935[69]

Player	Year of Birth	Date of Debut	Italy Caps
Eugenio Mosso	1895	05/04/1914	1
Cesare Lovati	1894	18/01/1920	6
Adolfo Baloncieri	1897	13/05/1920	47
Emilio Badini	1897	31/08/1920	2
Julio Libonatti	1901	28/10/1926	17
Raimundo Orsi	1901	01/12/1929	35
Renato Cesarini	1906	25/01/1931	11
Attilio De María	1909	27/11/1932	13
Luis Monti	1901	27/11/1932	18
Enrique Guaita	1910	11/02/1934	10
Alejandro Scopelli	1908	12/05/1935	1

Carta di Viareggio that led to the real talent drain of Italo-Argentine players to Italy. These signings were an imaginative response on the part of Italian clubs to the Charter, which scaled back the signing of foreign players from powerful neighbouring Danubian countries like Austria, Yugoslavia and Hungary, from two per team in 1926 to none by 1928. The rationale behind this policy being that the Italian league championship should not become an extension of the Austrian and Hungarian competitions, thus aiding the development of young Italian players. The pretext that the Argentine players were brought back because of their Italian cultural roots was something of an oxymoron; they were in fact repatriated *exactly* because they offered something different to what already was on offer in Italy. Paradoxically, they became direct replacements for the now excluded Austrians and Hungarians, perverting the Charter's original intentions.

This second migratory trend, including the cream of Argentine footballers such as Orsi, Renato Cesarini and Guillermo Stábile occurred as the Fascist regime of Benito Mussolini used football to create a feeling of unity and national sense of purpose, one that had been undermined by mass emigration from the economically underdeveloped country. This saw an international Italian diaspora of six million people living outside the peninsula by 1914, a sizeable proportion of which lived on the banks

---

[69] Melegari (2018, 611–639).

of the Río de la Plata. Considered part of the Italian race, these descendants of emigrants were welcomed 'home' with open arms as being members of a 'Greater Italy,' whose extremity went beyond the geographical confines of the Italian Peninsula, with citizenship granted on the basis of *jus sanguini*.[70] It was a refrain taken up in a 1931 article published in *La Gazzetta dello Sport* and reprinted in its entirety in Argentina by *La Nación*. According to the Italian newspaper, 'The repatriated are authentic Italians,' Italian by blood ties even if they were also Argentine by birth, arguing that, 'when these elements return to the Fatherland it is not that they reassume Italian citizenship because one does not acquire that which he has not renounced.'[71]

What was seen in Italy as an 'inevitable repatriation of Italian citizens' was regarded differently in Argentina. The exodus of Argentina's top players enabled *El Gráfico* to expound a nationalist narrative, in which Italian immigrants were perceived to have been 'improved' by *criollo* ways and went home as 'Super-Italians' and *criollo* footballing missionaries. As the magazine explained when Guillermo Stábile left in 1930 after top-scoring for Argentina at the World Cup, claiming that like Orsi and Cesarini he was leaving to give a 'good football lesson' and that collectively, 'it is necessary to go abroad, the good players that do us proud abroad are working patriotically.'[72]

The departure of the *rimpatriati* was mourned in sections of the Argentine press. *La Nación* described the migration as, 'a phenomenon of which nobody could predicted the intensity and the extension. Today they constitute a well-fed battalion.'[73] Even *El Gráfico*'s attitude soon turned sour. After Orsi's bravura performance in Italy's 3–2 victory over Hungary in 1931, an editorial commented acerbically, 'Remembering the last performances of Orsi in Buenos Aires, the question arises forcefully: what miracle is this? Maybe the miracle of the liras.'[74] According to Bayer,

---

[70] Lanfranchi and Taylor (2001, 72–73); Martin (2004, 63–65); Foot (2007, 429–431); Orton (2022).

[71] *La Nación*, 15 March 1931, Sec. 2, 6; Orton (2022).

[72] *El Gráfico*, 25 October 1930, 37; Orton (2022).

[73] *La Nación*, 15 March 1931, Sec. 2, 6; Orton (2022).

[74] *El Gráfico*, 2 December 1932, 7.

this was the start of 'a colonial bleeding that remains even today—and more than ever—is suffered by *criollo* football.'[75]

The Italian response was unequivocal. *La Gazzetta dello Sport* dismissed Argentine complaints about the loss of their best players, arguing that, 'Argentines don't leave for Italy; Italians return to Italy.' The newspaper made the case that economics was the main driver and that Italo-Argentines crossing the Atlantic were no different to a player moving from southern Italy to a club in the north to earn more money, claiming, 'It is a question of distance and not of principle.'[76]

Italian citizenship had associated civic duties like military service, a serious consideration given Italy's colonial forays into the Horn of Africa in the late 1920s and early 1930s. Italy coach Vittorio Pozzo justified the selection of Italo-Argentines for the national team on this basis, famously claiming, 'If they can die for Italy, they can play for Italy!'[77] The first to do so in the Fascist era was Libonatti, adding 17 appearances for the *Azzurri* to the 15 international caps he earned for Argentina. The presence of Italo-Argentines in the blue jersey represented a reversal of the detrimental effect of Italian emigration, as members of the diaspora contributed to the greater national good by playing for Italy. There were dissenting voices though. Italy's coach Augusto Rangone resigned in June 1928 in protest at the fast-tracking of Orsi into the national side. *La Gazzetta dello Sport* cautioned, 'the danger is the numerous Italo-Argentine imports will lead to the biggest clubs showing disinterest in the formation of players from their own junior ranks.' Something that could have the unintended consequence of young locally born Italian players turning away from the sport due to the dearth of opportunities, 'transforming himself into a spectator in the stands instead.'[78]

There was a significant precedent for utilising Italo-Argentine sportsmen to showcase the Fascist regime. Although born in Italy, the swimmer, Enrique Tiraboschi, was raised in Argentina and reached international prominence in August 1923 when he swam the English Channel in a record time. In an open letter to the Argentine people published in *La Nación*, Italian prime minister, Benito Mussolini wrote, 'Today an Italian

[75] Bayer (2016, 25); Orton (2022).
[76] *La Nación* 15 March 1931, Sec.2, 6; Orton (2022).
[77] Cited in Glanville (2005, 25); Orton (2022).
[78] *La Nación* 15 March 1931, Sec.2, 6; Orton (2022).

unites the glory of his native country to the land that gave him hospitality, Italy sends an enthusiastic greeting to the great Argentine people, who represent so nobly and with such energy the immortal Latin gaze.'[79]

Italy's victory at the 1934 World Cup with four Italo-Argentines—Monti, Demaría, Orsi and Guaita—in the squad, highlighted this duality of identity, with *El Gráfico* contradicting the ethnocentric theories of its writers by reporting, 'the numerous Italian community from our country have celebrated this triumph with a rejoicing that they have perfect right to.'[80] *La Nación* reflected the almost interchangeable notions of identity amongst Italo-Argentines, 'For us the Italian triumph has two aspects equally full of spontaneous sympathy; that which Italy deserves from us as a nation intertwined with our nationality in permanent character through blood, love and recognition, and the other flowing from the injection made by the inclusion of four Argentine lads that were key to the fight for the trophy.'[81]

Had the Argentine team progressed further than the first round in the competition, it would have been interesting to see exactly how these loyalties would have been reconciled, especially in the event of the two nations playing each other directly. Bigalke suggests that lack of contact at international level meant that elite players were not forced into emotional or moral decisions about who to represent internationally, and as such acted in a mercenary way by playing for which country was most beneficial to their financial situation.[82] The case can be made that such decisions were more complex for Italo-Argentine footballers. It was a complexity summed up by a later *rimpatriato*, Omar Sívori, 'I am the grandson of an Italian from Chiavari (near Genoa), something which allows me to be Argentine and Italian at the same time.'[83] The choice of national jersey was an overt way of deciding on national identity, given that in international football players could only represent one country at a given time. Emotional considerations also came into making such decisions. For example, Luis Monti chose the *Azzurri* of Italy after being scapegoated for Argentina's defeat in the 1930 World Cup Final against Uruguay.

---

[79] *La Nación*, 21 August 1923, 1; Orton (2022).
[80] Saavedra (2009b, 56–57); Orton (2022).
[81] *La Nación*, 14 June 1934, 1; Orton (2022).
[82] Bigalke (2017, 77); Orton (2022).
[83] *Mundo Deportivo*, 8 May 1962, 23; (Orton 2022).

He had claimed, 'All the Argentinians had made me feel like rubbish, a maggot, branding me a coward and blaming me exclusively for the loss against the Uruguayans.'[84] Not every player who migrated to Italian football could be lured into wearing the Italian jersey. Argentina's 1930 World Cup goalscoring hero, Stábile joined Italian club Genoa shortly afterwards, with *El Gráfico* noting, 'Stábile goes to Italy, not to defend football in the peninsula, but to defend *criollo* football, since he is a *criollo* player.'[85] In Stábile's case, this was not an exaggeration. Alone of the *rimpatriati*, Stábile refused to accept Italian citizenship or selection for the Italian national team, seeing the move to Genoa as purely an economic one, like the old *golondrinas*, to help his young family. After later returning to Argentina, Stábile had a long and successful period as coach of the national team that only ended with the tumultuous defeat to Czechoslovakia at the 1958 World Cup.

The alacrity with which some of the early *rimpatriati* served their mother country in the First World War ensured their commitment to Italy was not questioned in the same way as later arrivals. Francisco Mosso and Ernesto Boglietto both fought in the army, whilst Romulo Boglietto served in the nascent Italian air force. Pozzo's criteria of selecting players for national team duty based on their willingness to die for Italy, soon looked empty, however, when just four months after making his debut for Italy in May 1935, Alejandro Scopelli, along with fellow Italo-Argentine players, Guaita and Andrés Stagnaro, escaped across the French border to avoid fulfilling their call-up to fight in Abyssinia. The incident changed the tone of the relationship between Italo-Argentine footballers and the Italian press, who now considered them mercenaries with no emotional bond to the land of their ancestors.[86]

Whilst Bigalke and others have argued that the introduction of professionalism in Argentina in 1931 and Italy's military involvement in Abyssinia, and later in the Second World War led to the wholesale return of Italo-Argentines to Argentina, this was not the case.[87] A good number including the likes of Monti stayed until well into the 1940s, and it was

---

[84] Cited in Campomar (2014, 145); Orton (2022).
[85] *El Gráfico*, 25 October 1930, 37; Orton (2022).
[86] Lanfranchi and Taylor (2001, 72–81); Orton (2022).
[87] Bigalke (2017, 96); Orton (2022).

the ruination of Italy's economy by the War that was the most decisive factor in their ultimate return.

The presence of Argentine football teams on European soil from the mid-1920s projected an archetypal playing style to international audiences, with performances by Boca Juniors and Sportivo Barracas drawing admiring reports from the press in the Old Continent. Despite there being a hubristic discourse of Argentine football having nothing to learn from other footballing countries, most notably the British, new cultural interactions, particularly with Danubian football, facilitated transnational exchanges that had a demonstrable effect on Argentina's footballing style during the 1930s and 1940s. Paradoxically, rather than being solely known for the mythical style of *la nuestra*, other values were attributed to the Argentine game such as organisation, chivalry and sportsmanship. These were principles that had been discarded by the likes of Borocotó during the construction of *la nuestra* as being too British, but ironically were seen in Europe as positioning Argentina as a modern and serious country.

The discourse of national identity was further complicated by the reverse migration of the top Italo-Argentine players in the 1920s and 1930s who were central to Argentine success at the 1928 Olympic Games and 1930 World Cup. Their departure was perceived in the Argentine press in colonial terms. Whilst reaching those finals reflected Argentine prestige at a world level, the subsequent departure of Argentina's elite players and the presence of Orsi, Guaita, Monti and Demaría in Italy's World Cup win in 1934 World Cup-winning side reflected Argentina's economic weakness in the global footballing marketplace.

References

Aira, Carlos. 2015. *Héroes de Tiento: Historias del Fútbol Argentina 1920–1930*. Buenos Aires: Ediciones Fabro.

Alabarces, Pablo, and María Graciela. Rodríguez. 1999. Football and Fatherland: The Crisis of Representation in Argentinian Soccer. *Culture, Sport, Society* 2 (3): 118–133.

Archetti, Eduardo. 1999. *Masculinities: Football, Polo and the Tango in Argentina*. Oxford: Berg.

Archetti, Eduardo. 1996. In search of national identity: Argentinian Football and Europe. In *Tribal Identities, Nationalism, Europe, Sport*, ed. J.A. Mangan, 201–219. London: Taylor & Francis Ltd.

Asociación Amateurs Argentina de Football. 1930. *Memoria y Balance General 1929.* Buenos Aires: Geronimo J. Pesce y Cia. Impresores.

Asociación Amateurs Argentina de Football. 1931. *Memoria y Balance General 1930.* Buenos Aires: Geronimo J. Pesce y Cia. Impresores.

Bayce, Rafael. 2014. El sinuoso proceso de constitución de la identidad nacional y futbolística. In *Cuaderno de Historia 14, A romper la red Miradas sobre fútbol, cultura y sociedad*, eds. Juan Carlos Luzuriaga, Andrés Morales & Julio Osaba, 47–62. Montevideo: Biblioteca Nacional Uruguay.

Bayer, Osvaldo. 2016. *Fútbol Argentino*, Buenos Aires: Sudamericana.

Bigalke, Zachary R. 2017. *"If They Can Die for Italy, They Can Play for Italy!" Immigration, Italo-Argentine Identity, and the 1934 World Cup Team.* Unpublished MA Thesis, University of Oregon, Eugene.

Campomar, Andreas. 2014. *¡Golazo!* London: Quercus.

Foot, John. 2007. *Calcio: A History of Italian Football.* London: Harper Perennial.

Forbes, Rosita. 1933. *Eight Republics in Search of a Future? Evolution and Revolution in South America.* London: Cassell.

Frydenberg, Julio. 2003. Boca Juniors en Europa: El Diario *Crítica* y el Primer Nacionalismo Deportivo Argentina. *Historia: Questōes & Debates* 39: 91–120.

Galeano, Eduardo. 1997. *Football in Sun and Shadow.* London: Fourth Estate.

Giménez, A. 2007. *La pasión laica: una breve historia del fútbol uruguayo.* Montevideo: Rumbo.

Giulianotti, Richard. 1999. Built by the Two Varelas: The Rise and Fall of Football Culture and National Identity in Uruguay. *Sport in Society* 2-3: 134–154.

Glanville, Brian. 2005. *The Story of the World Cup.* London: Faber and Faber.

Karush, Matthew B. 2003. National Identity in the Sports Pages: Football and the Mass Media in 1920s Buenos Aires. *The Americas* 60 (1): 11–32.

Lanfranchi, Pierre, and Matthew Taylor. 2001. *Moving with the Ball: The Migration of Professional Footballers.* Oxford: Berg.

Lo Presti, Silvio. 2017. *Tango Bianconero.* Turin: Bradipolibri.

Martin, Simon. 2004. *Football and Fascism: The National Game under Mussolini.* Oxford: Berg.

Mason, Tony. 1995. *Passion of the People? Football in South America.* London: Verso.

Melegari, Fabrizio. 2018. *Almanacco Illustrato del Calcio* 2019. Modena: Panini.

Orton, Mark. 2022. The Game of the Italians: Football and Dual Identity in Argentina 1910–1935. *Studia Universitatis Babeș-Bolyai, Historia* 67 (2): (in press).

Orton, Mark. 2017. Ants and Cicadas: South American Football and National Identity. *Midlands Historical Review* 1: 1–22.

Osaba, Julio. 2012. Más allá de la garra. El estilo del fútbol uruguayo a través de *El Gráfico* y Nilo J. Suburú. In *Cuaderno de Historia 8, A romper la red. Aboradajes en torno al fútbol uruguayo*, ed. Pierre Arrighi, 57–69. Montevideo: Biblioteca Nacional de Uruguay.

Prats, Luis. 2014. *La Crónica Celeste. Historia de la Selección Uruguaya de Fútbol: triunfos, derrotas, mitos y polémicas [1901–2014]*. Montevideo: Fin de Siglo.

Rosatti, Horacio. 2009. *Cien años de multitud: historia de Boca Juniors, una pasión argentina: I. El period amateur: 1905–1930*. Buenos Aires: Galerna.

Saavedra, Néstor. 2009a. El Boca que se hizo aplaudir en Europa. In *Glorias Eternas: 1ra Entrega 1919–1948*, ed. Carlos Poggi, 8–11. Buenos Aires: Atlántida.

Saavedra, Néstor. 2009b. El poeta de la zurda. In *Glorias Eternas: 1ra Entrega 1919–1948*, ed. Carlos Poggi, 56–57. Buenos Aires: Atlántida.

Torres, César R. 2003, Spring. "If We Had Our Argentine Team Here!": Football and the 1924 Olympic Team. *Journal of Sport History* 30 (1): 1–21.

Wernicke, Luciano. 2016. *Historias insólitas de la Copa América*. New York: Sudaquia Editores.

CHAPTER 5

Political Football: The Age of Decline? 1931–1958

In 1974, the journalist, Dante Panzeri, wrote 'The downhill slope of football would seem to have many points of coincidence with the downhill slope of the country and this coincidence produces itself in the great link between sport and the oscillations of the national economy.'[1] This chapter investigates this symbiotic relationship, arguing that the theme of economic and footballing decline in Argentina was a tripartite one that also included the political sphere. The turbulent period between the 1930 overthrow of President Hipólito Yrigoyen by the military, through the transformative 1946–1955 presidency of Juan Perón, to the restoration of democracy with 1958 election of Arturo Frondizi, saw politics leave an indelible imprint on Argentine football. In exploring how Argentine football was used to mirror national identity more widely, this chapter assesses the extent to which the 1940s really was the apogee of *la nuestra* and a 'Golden Age' as suggested by historians, demonstrating that the answer is more nuanced and complex, and that the seeds of Argentina's later footballing decline that came to head with a humiliating first-round exit at the 1958 World Cup could be seen in the country's apparent 'time of plenty'.

---

[1] *La Opinión Suplemento Cultura*, 12 May 1974.

© The Author(s), under exclusive license to Springer Nature Switzerland AG 2023
M. Orton, *Football and National Identity in Twentieth-Century Argentina*, Palgrave Studies in Sport and Politics,
https://doi.org/10.1007/978-3-031-20589-7_5

Argentine football administrator, Armando Ramos Ruiz, argued that the Liga Argentina de Football's Act of Foundation which introduced professionalism in 1931 was the most important Argentine football document of all-time, 'in the sense that it marked a breaking point with Argentine football's "pre-history" and gives us an unbroken link to the present.'[2] Meanwhile, Panzeri suggested that the 1930 coup which temporarily closed down constitutional electoral politics meant that politicians were forced into other avenues in which to perpetuate their influence, of which football was an important one.[3] Taken together, these arguments show that the beginning of the 1930s was a key point of departure for the symbiotic relationship between football and politics, forming the theme for investigation in this section, probing the nature and effects of this association rooted in professionalism and political dysfunction.

Martín Caparrós suggests that the transition to professionalism in 1931 marked a 'democratisation' of football in Argentina, in the sense that a player no longer needed to have independent means to dedicate himself to the game, opening up the possibility of being paid to do so to anyone who had sufficient skill and desire regardless of social class.[4] Pablo Alabarces also supports this democratisation argument, adding that the displacement of the dominant classes from the pitches saw them instead take refuge in club boardrooms and the committee rooms of the game's governing bodies.[5]

Professionalism emerged though during a period of democratic deficit in Argentine politics following President Yrigoyén's overthrow, described by journalist, José Luis Torres as '*la década infame*' ('Infamous Decade').[6] According to Sergio Levinsky, it was then that the explicit link between football and political patronage emerged, as political actors finding traditional politics closed off to them sought alternative arenas to operate in.[7] Ariel Scher further suggests that the nexus between football and politics during *la década infame* came in 1937 when Eduardo Sánchez Terrero—the son-in-law of the fraudulently elected president,

[2] Ramos Ruiz (1974, 64).
[3] *Satiricón*, July 1974.
[4] Caparrós (2004, 75–78).
[5] Alabarces (2007, 55–57).
[6] Goebel (2011, 46).
[7] Levinsky (2016, 45–48).

Agustín Justo—was elected president of the AFA by member clubs.[8] Building on this scholarship, this chapter explores how professionalism's introduction led to a concentration of financial resources and political power in the hands of a small number of clubs which mirrored the democratic deficit in Argentine politics over the succeeding decade. It also considers how professionalism changed the way that football was played in Argentina, challenging ideas of *la nuestra* constructed during the 1920s.

Whilst watching River thrash Boca Juniors to all but wrap up the 1941 championship, the British ambassador to Argentina, Sir Edmond Ovey, when interviewed by *El Gráfico* observed 'In my country, creator of football, if they were to play a good Argentine team, I am sure that they would like it. The fathers of football would see then that they have outstanding sons.'[9] Combined with Argentina's domination of the South American Championship between 1941 and 1947, the ambassador's assessment appeared to validate what historians such as Ariel Scher, Guillermo Blanco and Jorge Búsico, and Oscar Barnade and Waldemar Iglesias have described as Argentine football's 'Golden Age'.[10] Yet the title of Panzeri's 1974 article in *La Opinión*, 'The 40s: Football of Gold, Lost Glory', is perhaps a more telling interpretation.[11] This chapter challenges the extent to which the 1940s was *la nuestra*'s apogee as a representation of Argentine identity, and whether Argentine football was truly as hegemonic during this period as claimed by historians.

By the early 1940s, Argentina's urban demographic makeup was changing rapidly. The extraordinary level of immigration that had driven Argentina's economic growth in the first three decades of the twentieth century now slowed to just 25,000 arrivals per year. To maintain industrial growth, Argentina utilised hitherto underused human resources, the population of the interior, prompting the large-scale migration of workers from the impoverished provinces of the Argentine periphery to Buenos Aires and other major cities, which became less cosmopolitan as a result in what Eric Hobsbawm described as 'an influx of peasants without parallel in the demographic history of the world.'[12] This change

---

[8] Scher (1996, 127–128).
[9] *El Gráfico*, 24 October 1941, 25.
[10] Scher et al. (2010, 281–285) and Barnade and Iglesias (2014, 68–69).
[11] *La Opinión Suplemento Cultura*, 12 May 1974.
[12] Hobsbawm (2017, 243).

and the challenges facing Argentina were reflected upon in 1940 by the sociologist, Alejandro Bunge, in the book, *Una Nueva Argentina* ('A New Argentina').[13] It was a slogan adopted by Juan Perón, the man who transformed Argentine politics and society during his 1946–1955 presidency.

Alabarces, Ranaan Rein and Levinsky have focused in depth on the political aspects of the link between Peronism and football, highlighting how crucial stakeholders within the sport were informally drawn into the corporatist Peronist state, with key supporters holding positions of influence in clubs and the AFA.[14] By associating his regime with sport, and football especially as the 'passion of the people', Perón followed the path taken by fellow populist leader Getulio Vargas in neighbouring Brazil over the preceding decade. Football was just as valuable to Vargas' 1937–1945 Estado Novo as it would become to Perón's New Argentina acting as an agent for 'national integration', although better lived in the imagination than reality in the Argentine case. Like Vargas, Perón was not intrinsically a football fan, preferring to practice fencing and watch boxing and motor-racing instead, but he was intimately aware of how the popularity of the game could be harnessed to progress the aims of Peronism. This was especially true in the case of Oscar Nicolini's appointment as president of the AFA and with other members of the Peronist hierarchy occupying positions of influence at Argentine clubs, notably Ramón Cereijo at Racing Club, mirroring similar moves by the Vargas regime which saw his daughter Alzira act as 'godmother' of Brazil's 1938 World Cup squad, whilst another ally Luiz Aranha ran the Confederação Brasileira de Desportos (CBD), the governing body of Brazilian football.[15]

Complementing the scholarship of Guillermo Blanco and Mariano Ben Plotkin who have looked exhaustively at the role played by the Evita Championship in using football to bring Argentine children into the Peronist national project, this chapter focuses on the pedagogical way that sport and football was used by the Peronist regime to project its vision of the 'New Argentina.'[16] Focusing on the sports magazine, *Mundo Deportivo*, which functioned as a government propaganda vehicle,

---

[13] Bunge (1940).

[14] Rein (1998, 54–76), Levinsky (2016, 71–90), and Alabarces (2007, 65–78).

[15] Kittleson (2014, 36).

[16] Blanco (2016) and Ben Plotkin (2003).

it shows how football was used for domestic consumption at a societal level to mould the kind of Argentine national identity that Peronism sought to promote.

The juxtaposition of football with workers' organisations which concluded in the players' strike of 1948–1949 raised contradictions about the relationship between Peronism and the working class. The most comprehensive exploration of the theme to date by Julio Frydenberg and Daniel Sazbon claims that the dispute's settlement 'has an ambiguous aspect.'[17] Enrico Montenari has analysed the dispute from the supporter's point of view as expounded in the working-class press, referring to the poems of Víctor Diez published in *Democracia* which implored the players not to 'leave us without football on Sunday' given its part of the Argentine routine that was as intrinsic as '[drinking] *mate* and [eating] bread and dripping.'[18] By interrogating the actions of the key actors, this chapter reaches a more encompassing analysis of the strike and its effect on football's role in Argentine identity construction.

When Juan Perón was elected president in 1946, he did so on an antiimperialist foreign policy platform targeted against the United States, who emerged from the Second World War as the global hegemon instead of the United Kingdom. Perón campaigned for the presidency under the slogan: 'Braden or Perón,' arguing that real political power in Argentina would reside in the hands of US Ambassador, Spruille Braden, if any other candidate were elected.[19] As the Cold War between the Soviet Union and the United States developed, Perón declared that Argentina was not ideologically supportive of either party, and would instead seek a 'Third Way' in international relations at the head of non-aligned nations within the Americas and those recently decolonised by the European powers.[20]

It was in this context of Perón's push for regional leadership—and competition for this role with Brazil—that the AFA took decisions not to compete at the 1950 and 1954 World Cups, and the South American Championships of 1949 and 1953. Levinsky and Scher et al. have argued that in the wake of the large-scale migration of Argentina's top players seen in the previous section, Perón directly ordered the withdrawal

---

[17] Frydenberg and Sazbon (2015, 79–80).
[18] *Democracia*, 1 July 1948, 16, Montenari (2018, 191–204).
[19] Hedges (2021, 91–94).
[20] Sáenz Quesada (2012, 546).

so as not to risk Argentina's international prestige.[21] Mason also offers this conclusion, although he expresses surprise given Peronist support for global visibility in other sporting scenarios, such as the hosting of the inaugural Pan American Games in Buenos Aires in 1951.[22] In the Argentine press, *El Gráfico* later described this period sorrowfully, 'It was a period of absurd ostracism. In which we did not know our place in the world.'[23] Whilst these were certainly factors in Argentina's international isolation during Perón's presidency, this chapter proposes that diplomatic strategies on the part of his regime also played an important part.

The Introduction of Professionalism
and *la década infame*

Socially, Argentine football changed during the opening decades of the twentieth century as the amateur ethos espoused by clubs like Alumni was displaced by the overwhelming presence of players from the popular classes. Players mutated from being club members who played with like-minded friends for fun and the civic pride of their neighbourhood, to become human capital. Footballers were now recruited by clubs on ability, and induced to move from one to another, incentivised by the possibility of playing in a better team and/or for financial gain as football became a business. Playing for 'the love of the shirt' disappeared as the primary motivation for players. Similarly, clubs were no longer the realm of founding playing members, but represented a much bigger and broad-based membership, who had multiple expectations in terms of social facilities and as consumers. The desire of fans and members to see winning football opened the way to professionalism. Years of 'covered professionalism' followed, in which players were either paid 'under the counter,' or given nominal jobs with companies or public bodies linked to clubs. Indeed, part of Racing Club's rise to prominence during the 1910s can be attributed to being able to recruit talent with the lure of jobs with the municipality of Avellaneda. Ingenious ways were found by clubs to hide these payments on their balance sheets, for example absurd amounts of money being paid for grass seed and sawdust. Argentine football was

---

[21] Levinsky (2016, 83–87) and Scher et al. (2010, 281–285).
[22] Mason (1995, 66–67).
[23] *El Gráfico Edición Especial No. 11*, September 1965, 76–77.

effectively already professional by 1927 according to *Última Hora*, with many 'amateur' players taking 'partial or total benefits from the sport' in terms of remuneration. This replicated moves towards professionalism in Britain and western Europe. As Steven Tischler wrote of the English example, 'the debate over professionalization was a by-product of the commercialization of football.'[24]

The reality of this 'democratisation' was different. Although players were now paid, in common with professional footballers in England and elsewhere they had no freedom of movement and were effectively treated as chattels by clubs, to be signed or disposed of exclusively at the whim of their employers. Player dissatisfaction with this serf-like relationship with the clubs came to a head in 1931, resulting in the formalising of professionalism in Argentina. The so-called Padlock Clause which meant that players could only change club of their own volition with the express agreement of their existing club was one cause of disagreement. Until then clubs could retain a player's registration with the League to prevent them signing for another club. Another issue was player welfare. Because of previous league schisms and reconciliations, the First Division had reached an unwieldy complement of thirty-six teams by 1931, meaning that the season often overran into the early months of the following year, the height of the Argentine summer. On 1 March 1931, Gimnasia y Esgrima de La Plata and Sportivo Barracas played a match that was still part of the 1930 season. The temperatures that afternoon reached 38 °C causing Héctor Arispe of Gimnasia to collapse with sunstroke and die later in hospital. A league commission later decided that matches played in the summer months must kick off after 5 pm when temperatures were lower.

It was in this context that on 12 April 1931, players went on a strike called by the Asociación Mutualista de Footballers, demanding freedom of contract, if not outright professionalism—'the freedom to be humans' as Hugo Settis, one of the strike leaders, put it.[25] Players' representatives marched on the Casa Rosada (Argentina's presidential palace) to present President Félix Uriburu with a petition of their demands. Uriburu passed the issue onto the Mayor of Buenos Aires, José Guerrico, who judged that since there was no implied contract in terms of wages, players were free to play for whoever they liked. For club directors, the solution was to

---

[24] *Última Hora*, 24 April 1927; Tischler (1981, 41).
[25] Cited in Pandolfi and Rivello (2015, 13).

formalise the payment of players with official salaries enabling the professional clubs to legitimately continue with the 'Padlock Clause.' Players effectively gained nothing except official recognition of what they are already receiving, in what Boca's vice-president, Luis Salessi, described as a 'whitening of the finances.'[26] Professionalism followed the British model in which players were bound to one club, who were keen to exercise a close control over their 'assets.'

The formalisation of professionalism generated a schism between those clubs with greater financial resources such as Boca Juniors, River Plate, Racing Club de Avellaneda, San Lorenzo de Almagro and Huracán, who wanted to press on with this new era, and those with lesser income for whom professionalism was not economically viable. On 18 May 1931, several of the more powerful clubs broke away from the Asociación Amateur Argentina de Football (AAAF) to form the professional Liga Argentina de Football, leaving a rump AAAF with those clubs wishing to remain amateur for financial reasons. These defections were lamented in the rump organisation's 1931 annual report which argued that, 'the big clubs prejudiced the interests of the smaller clubs in favour of the privilege of a few and basing their greatness on their economic capacity in place of sporting merits.'[27] The Liga Argentina, meanwhile, reasoned that the implementation of professionalism was based on 'improving the quality of football, legalising the situation of players and raising [the standard of] the institutions.'[28] River Plate in particular embraced the opportunities offered by professionalism. After a disappointing opening season in the Liga Argentina, River earned the sobriquet, *los millonarios* by spending the enormous sum of 150,000 pesos (£12,000) in the 1932 season on star signings like Bernabé Ferreyra from Tigre as well as Alberto Cuello, Juan Arrillaga, Carlos Santamaría, Roberto Basilico and Oscar Sciarra. The spending spree brought immediate success when River beat Independiente 3–0 in a play-off to be crowned champions—the earliest example of 'buying' success in Argentina.

Financial largesse on the part of Liga Argentina clubs drew warnings from their rival organisation, the now renamed Asociación Argentina

---

[26] Cited in Levinsky (2016, 45–48).
[27] Asociación Argentina de Football (Amateur y Profesionales) (1932, 10–20).
[28] Cited in Molinari and Martínez (2013, 153–159).

de Football (Amateur y Profesionales) (AAFAP), after finally permitting professionalism. The AAFAP urged the Liga Argentina to follow its example of a maximum salary to 'ward off the possibility of exaggerations in salaries' and maintain '[football's] moral greatness and that of its moral institutions.'[29] The AAFAP abolished the 'Padlock Clause' that Guerrico had ruled unsustainable in the amateur sphere, only to see its member clubs' best players picked off by the teams of the Liga Argentina—who as a rebel league not affiliated to FIFA could act without sanction—without payment of a transfer fee. One example was River Plate's 1931 acquisition of Carlos Peucelle from Sportivo Buenos Aires. River paid just a 10,000-peso signing-on fee for the player, although Peucelle himself did 'donate' part of his fee to his former club.[30]

The rival AAFAP and Liga Argentina eventually reconciled and merged in 1934 to form the Asociación del Football Argentino (AFA). It was at this point that power began to consolidate itself in the hands of the clubs with the biggest membership bases, the so-called *cinco grandes*: River Plate, Boca Juniors and San Lorenzo from Buenos Aires, and Independiente and Racing Club from the capital's southern suburb of Avellaneda. The bigger stadium capacities and revenue streams from membership subscriptions enabled these clubs to become dominant in the nascent transfer market and attract the best talent in the league. The remaining clubs in the league were therefore left poorer as a result. A change in the AFA's voting system to a proportional one following a league meeting in 1937, which granted two votes to clubs having a membership of between 10 and 15,000 or more, and twenty years of consecutive participation in the First Division, had major repercussions. The only clubs to meet these criteria for enhanced voting rights were the *cinco grandes*, giving them a perpetual majority with twenty-five votes against the sixteen of the rest.[31] Proportional voting contrasted with what was happening in England, home to the world's first professional league, founded in 1888. There, the Football League operated as what Richard Holt describes as 'a kind of non-profit-making cartel in which the power of the largest clubs was limited by the smallest.'[32]

---

[29] Asociación Argentina de Football (Amateur y Profesionales) (1933, 19–20).
[30] *Mundo Deportivo*, 9 August 1951, 41–48.
[31] Asociación del Football Argentino (1938, 28); *El Gráfico*, 27 March 1937.
[32] Holt (1989, 285).

The *grandes* effectively had *carte blanche* to amend AFA rules to suit themselves and veto suggestions made by other parties with which they did not agree. An early example of the voting power of the *grandes* came with the choice of Eduardo Sánchez Terrero of Boca Juniors as AFA president in 1937. Sánchez Terrero's appointment was opposed by the remaining thirteen smaller clubs, not because of his unsuitability for the role, but because his selection was decided in advance by the big clubs, without prior consultation with themselves.[33] It was the first of many occasions that the *grandes* got their own way despite being a minority. Through their domination of the proportional voting system within the AFA, the *grandes* became an oligarchy that reflected the wider democratic deficit in Argentine during the *década infame*. After the military stepped back from power in 1932, the conservative oligarchic elites kept themselves in presidential power through a series of fraudulently conducted elections boycotted by the Radical opposition. It is perhaps no coincidence that qualified voting was revoked with Peronist influence over the AFA in 1949 following the restoration of democracy three years earlier, reinstating 'one club, one vote'.

The introduction of professionalism which legally made footballers club employees meant they now had contractual obligations to maintain better fitness and to train daily, with the engagement of physical trainers by clubs now de rigueur. The changed landscape brought about by professionalism provoked questions within the press around Argentine footballing identity. Some in the media felt that professionalism had estranged Argentine football from its traditions of *la nuestra* in terms of a loss of spontaneity of play. Reflecting on the first anniversary of professionalism in June 1932, *El Gráfico* believed that the strict regimes and increasing influence of coaches would see 'the tendency to approximate our tactics to those of the English.'[34] *Mundo Deportivo* argued that the amateur era could be denominated as the 'era of the dribble,' in which a player's skill was exploited principally for personal pleasure, a time when 'triumphs were almost secondary to the consecration of "good football".' The magazine contrasted this with the 'era of the goal' ushered in by professionalism in which victory was the primary requisite of the game. Lamenting the loss of a 'little spirituality,' *Mundo Deportivo* concluded

[33] *El Gráfico*, 20 March 1937.
[34] *El Gráfico*, 25 June 1932, 13.

that, 'The old beauty implied slowness. The urgency of triumph signifies speed.'[35] It was felt that Argentine football had become more regimented and mechanical, therefore less attractive to watch. But as the next section examines, such projections were not entirely justified. Argentine football merely calibrated itself to the possibilities afforded by the increased fitness resulting from more training time in the professional era.

Argentine Football's 'Golden Age'?

Domestically, the first half of the 1940s saw the emergence of River Plate's famous *la máquina* side, considered by Panzeri to embody the essence of *la nuestra* and function as the synthesis of Argentine footballing identity. Between 1941 and 1946, the team won the league three times, finished second twice and third once, and despite the focus on their attacking prowess, for five of those seasons they conceded the fewest number of goals in the league.[36] The nickname '*la máquina*' was ascribed to River by Borocotó in *El Gráfico* after the team's 6–2 destruction of Chacarita Juniors in June 1942. Schooled in the Danubian passing game under Hungarian coach Imre Hirschl in the 1930s, it was with the appointment of Renato Cesarini as coach in 1940, replacing another Hungarian, Ferenc Platkó, that River reached their peak. Their much-fabled forward line of Juan Carlos Muñoz, José Manuel Moreno, Adolfo Pedernera, Ángel Labruna and Félix Loustau only played together eighteen times in the 157 matches played in those six seasons, but their names continued to resonate with Argentine fans in the decades since. River's constant prompting and probing led to them being known to their supporters as the 'Knights of Anguish' as it often took an interminable time for the team to score a goal.[37]

As Panzeri suggests, *la máquina* were more than a continuation of *la nuestra*; they were also genuine footballing innovators. Their 'circular football,' with Adolfo Pedernera at its epicentre, was born in 1941 at the suggestion of Carlos Peucelle, after injury ruled out first-choice forward Roberto D'Alessandro. The spearhead of the attack was withdrawn as midfielders and forwards rotated positions to throw off

---

[35] *Mundo Deportivo*, 9 August 1951, 41–48.
[36] *La Opinión Suplemento Cultura*, 12 May 1974.
[37] Bertolotto (2016, 68).

opposition markers, replicating basketball players.[38] In this sense, the sobriquet was apposite, based on a well-drilled collective play, rather than just individual inspiration, and symbolic of where Argentina perceived itself at the time, as a cutting edge, industrialised nation. It was the continuation of transnational exchanges between Argentine and Danubian football that began in the 1920s seen in Chapter 4. Players were particularly receptive to Hirschl's ideas, firstly at Gimnasia y Esgrima de La Plata, and then River Plate, ideas that were later elaborated on by Argentine coaches such as Cesarini. The team's mythical reputation was maintained because it was never challenged outside Argentina, playing in the era before the establishment of the continental Copa Libertadores, whilst European tours beyond Spain and Portugal were off the agenda due to the Second World War.

Despite their iconic status, *la máquina* were not the all-conquering team of legend: Boca Juniors were equally as successful during this period (champions in 1940, 1943 and 1944). Yet, Boca never achieved the same level of idolatry in the public imagination as their great rivals due to the less attractive way they were perceived by the media to have achieved their success. This was especially true in the pages of *El Gráfico*, who's well educated, middle-class journalists were self-appointed guardians of the myth of *la nuestra*.

Class identification lay at the heart of this differentiation. Despite both clubs originating from the same humble *barrio* of *La Boca*, from the 1920s River migrated to the middle-class *barrios* of Recoleta and then Núñez in search of a site for a new stadium, and to grow its membership base. This social mobility combined with a spendthrift approach to player recruitment in the early years of professionalism earned River a middle-class cachet. As Panzeri wrote, 'The new stadium of River in 1938 meant a certain social change for football. The luxury stadium, in a certain way demanded that the football played within it would also be luxury as was represented by *la máquina*.'[39]

The identity Boca represented on the pitch, hard work and resistance to 'art for art's sake,' reflected that of its working-class support base not just in La Boca, but across Argentina, making them the 'Team of the

---

[38] *La Opinión Suplemento Cultura*, 12 May 1974.
[39] Ibid.

People' according to the contemporary journalist Félix Frascara.[40] Boca suffered for being stereotyped as workman-like and renowned for their *garra* (indigenous fighting spirit) rather than for attractive play, especially when contrasted with the 'refined technique' of River. As Frascara wrote when Boca won the title in 1943, 'Discreet in terms of the quality of their side, the Boca Juniors team have had a campaign that was validated precisely because it beat perfection and imposed its *garra*, its courage for the fight.' Frascara also noted the role of the club's fans in their success as their 'Twelfth Man', writing, 'It is as if the passion of thousands of people share themselves in eleven equal parts to shelter themselves in the chests of the players to make themselves more robust in their faith and increase their courage.'[41] Yet, in the same edition of *El Gráfico*, there was gushing praise for runners-up, River Plate, 'To lose by a point with hope fading away in the last round of the competition is a campaign that honours River Plate. River offered up fiestas of good football thanks to the mastery of their forwards.'[42]

Boca were similarly damned with faint praise when they retained the championship twelve months later, with *El Gráfico* opining that their success was 'characteristic of a hardened team, of a team with courage, of collective spirit that doesn't wilt in adversity.'[43] Frascara wrote that, 'The Boca fans celebrated 25 victories by their team but very few times left the stadium saying, "What a beautiful game" or "How well the team played." The goals were enough, the triumph was enough.'[44] According to Panzeri, in the back-to-back championship wins of 1943 and 1944, Boca employed a perfect equilibrium between fight and play, with the gifted Mario Boyé replicating the maverick virtuoso role that Moreno fulfilled for *la máquina*. Whilst not as aesthetically pleasing as River, the more simply played, direct style of Boca was still excellent football.[45]

Whilst Boca were the epitome of professionalism in terms of the optimum combination of teamwork and individual skill, the less consistent

---

[40] *El Gráfico*, 10 December 1943, 18–25.
[41] Ibid., 18–25.
[42] Ibid., 9.
[43] *El Gráfico*, 19 December 1944, 33.
[44] *El Gráfico*, 8 December 1944, 5–7.
[45] *La Opinión Suplemento Cultura*, 12 May 1974.

play of River Plate was held up by dominant sectors of the media—particularly *El Gráfico*—as a more faithful representation of Argentina's footballing identity. The reproduction of this criteria by historians in framing ideas of an Argentine 'Golden Age' reflects the triumph of the aesthetic over results in determining relative success and River's usurpation of Boca in the public imaginary as the archetype of Argentine football during the 1940s. Put simply, Boca may have been considered the *team* of the people, but River's side was more to the *taste* of the people according to the educated writers of *El Gráfico*, reflecting a difference in cultural identity according to class.

Another feature of Argentina's 'Golden Age' was the outstanding performance of its national team which established continental hegemony during the 1940s. It was a dominance presaged in 1939 with a series of heavy victories over a Brazilian team that finished third at the World Cup just a year earlier. A 5–1 win that January was described by the Rio daily, *O Globo Sportivo* as 'The biggest setback of Brazilian Football.'[46] Argentine domination of the South American Championship under coach Guillermo Stábile during the 1940s was remarkable. Argentina won the competition on four occasions, in 1941, 1945, 1946 and 1947. The first triumph in 1941 was achieved with one of Argentina's greatest ever teams, including Adolfo Pedernera, José Manuel Moreno, Antonio Sastre and Enrique García. As *El Gráfico* summarised, 'All through the tournament, the Argentine team was the most complete and highest quality [team].'[47] Argentina's series of victories has led historians like Tony Mason to suggest that had the rest of the world not been engulfed by the Second World War resulting in the cancellations of the 1942 and 1946 World Cups, they would have had an excellent chance of being world champions.[48]

Contemporary press coverage indicates that Argentina's hegemony was not as complete as scholars have suggested. In the 1942 South American Championship, after Argentina thrashed Ecuador 12–0, there was great expectation from the media and supporters that Argentina would retain the title with essentially the same team that won the tournament

---

[46] *O Globo Sportivo*, 17 January 1939, 2.

[47] *El Gráfico*, 7 March 1941, 28; *El Gráfico Edición Especial No.11*, September 1965, 51.

[48] Mason (1995, 198–200).

a year before. However, defeat in the final against hosts Uruguay led to accusations of complacency, with Carlos Fontanarrosa noting that 'the Argentine training camp was not an example of discipline.'[49] When the competition resumed in 1945 after a three-year hiatus, it was approached with a great deal of trepidation by the Argentine press. The Argentine team was in a process of renewal, with many players of the great 1941 side, such as Pedernera and García, past their peak. New stars like Ángel Labruna and Ezra Sued were injured, and in a foretelling of future issues, Moreno was unavailable following his transfer to Mexican football, as was Antonio Sastre who moved to Brazil. *El Gráfico* even suggested that the Argentine team be withdrawn, 'We cannot risk our prestige. We run the risk of making a spectacle of ourselves. Caution advises us not to go.'[50] Ultimately, this lack of self-confidence was unfounded, and a missed opportunity averted as Argentina went on to win the tournament. It was at this point that Argentine football's 'Golden Age' reached its peak, with *El Gráfico* recording, 'The production [of Argentine players] was of an exceptional richness. In quality and quantity.'[51] By the time Argentina successfully defended the South American Championship in 1946 on home soil, the question was less who should play, but more who to leave out as the country had a surfeit of quality players. Frascara later wrote 'From 1941 to 1948 when we had to choose between Pontoni and Pedernera, between Moreno and Martino, between 'Chueco' García and Loustau. They did not always win, but how they played!'[52] It was an abundance that reflected Argentina's economic situation at the time, as its economy boomed off the back of agricultural exports to Europe although societal tensions rose about the fair distribution of this wealth, helping sweep Perón into power.

Each successive victory became more difficult to achieve as the standard of the other South American nations caught up, and Argentina laboured under the weight of expectation. *El Gráfico* noted after their final triumph in 1947 in Guayaquil, 'To play a South American Championship when one occupies the position that Argentine football has reached at a world level is not an easy sporting effort. There was history

---

[49] *El Gráfico Edición Especial No.11*, September 1965, 48.
[50] *El Gráfico Edición Especial No.11*, September 1965, 55.
[51] Ibid., 55.
[52] *El Gráfico*, 16 May 1958.

at play, the prestige, the weight of all the titles won before.'[53] As one Ecuadorian supporter remarked of Argentina's South American hegemony in Guayaquil, 'A victory against Argentina is equivalent to 15 years of glory.'[54] Due to the 1948–1949 players' strike and the subsequent exodus abroad of dozens of the country's top players, the 1947 South American Championship triumph effectively marked the end of Argentine football's 'Golden Age', as the production line of top players within Argentine abruptly came to an end.

By this time, clubs had neglected issues which could have helped Argentine football's longer-term progress, such as player welfare in terms of medical support, and the development of young players. It was a theme essayed by Mario Fortunato in *El Gráfico* as early as 1944, in which he advocated the creation of football schools. Fortunato suggested using the latest scientific knowledge to help manage the physical development of young players and rectify defects such as rickets and flat feet. He also argued that a proper footballing tutelage would generate a conveyor belt of talent which could save clubs a fortune in the transfer market. Fortunato was clear in his understanding of why this was not happening, 'It is such a *criollo* defect. We are impatient, we want to sell tomatoes before we plant them. We always look for immediate solutions and we forget ourselves in the project.'[55] The strike highlighted this lack of development and a change in emphasis at junior level as youngsters were thrust into clubs' first teams in the league. As *El Gráfico* noted of the mass promotion of these juniors in place of the striking players, 'We say that in the junior divisions they play more physically and with more bad intention than in the First Division.'[56]

There was a dissenting voice in quantifying the 1940s as Argentine football's 'Golden Age'. In his 1951 analysis of twenty years of professional football, *Mundo Deportivo*'s editor Carlos Aloé alternatively suggested that the 1924–1930 period better represented Argentine football's 'golden era'. Aloé was personally more disposed to amateurism,

---

[53] *El Gráfico*, 2 January 1948.
[54] *El Gráfico*, 19 December 1947, 27.
[55] *El Gráfico*, 24 January 1944, 16–17.
[56] *El Gráfico*, 19 November 1948.

highlighting the Boca Juniors team of 1925–1928 as the zenith of Argentine football, emphasising that the side demonstrated attributes of both individual skill and a fighting team spirit.[57]

Although he does not mention it in his article, Aloé's selection of the 1924–1930 timeframe reflected Argentina's era of being a genuine world footballing power, reaching the finals of the Olympic tournament in 1928 and World Cup in 1930. By contrast, the cancellation of the 1942 and 1946 World Cups meant that any conception of Argentina's global power in the 1940s was a matter for conjecture and speculation, leaving Argentina in the opinion of *El Gráfico* 'champions without a crown.'[58] The lack of prior planning of the type outlined by Fortunato meant that Argentine football was unprepared for structural shocks like the players' strike and its after-effects. As a result, Argentina would never exercise such continental domination again.

A 'New Argentina': Peronism and Football

Attempts to reach national consensus between workers' groups and nationalist conservatism during the *década infame* failed. In a bid to break the deadlock and set the country on a definitively nationalist course, a cabal of twenty senior members of the officer corps, the self-styled Grupo de Oficiales Unidos (GOU), fronted a military coup on 4 June 1943. They had feared the victory of a Popular coalition, including socialists and communists, in the forthcoming election would lead to social revolution against the established order.

'Social justice' now became the watchwords of nationalist policy makers as they sought popular support for their project. One of the key intellectual authors of this policy was the unknown, Colonel Juan Perón, who became an Under Secretary in the Ministry for Labour in October 1943 before later taking full control of the department. Whilst unions were prohibited from political activity by the military *junta* in 1943, they were fully supported by Perón in their primary function of championing workers' rights. Perón backed workers in workplace disputes with employers, enacted legislation improving working conditions and had the ear of key union leaders. As such, Perón was successful in uniting

---

[57] *Mundo Deportivo*, 9 August 1951, 26.
[58] *El Gráfico Edición Especial No.11*, September 1965, 70.

the working class into a single political constituency, something that Anarchists and Socialists had previously failed to do.

Discredited by its associations with Nazi Germany, and in the face of a reborn political opposition which now included Perón, the army stepped back from politics and allowed democratic elections to take place in 1946 rather than risk another coup. Perón won the presidency with 54% of the vote, the biggest mandate in Argentine electoral history, thanks to his working-class powerbase. Perón initially successfully managed to unite sectors of Argentine society as diverse as the conservative right and the urban working class, with a nationalist rhetoric based on removing foreign influence from the Argentine economy and reining in the power of the land-owning oligarchy. A new constitution, inaugurated in 1949, extended the centralisation of state authority into all spheres of national life. Building on the notions of social justice that he espoused as a member of the GOU, Perón created an ideology called *justicialismo*, which was suitably vague and lacking in intellectual depth to attract cross-sector support. As Perón liked to say, 'If I define, I exclude.'[59] Loyalty was focused on Perón by his supporters as the living embodiment of *argentinidad*, with the active backing of his charismatic wife, Eva 'Evita' Duarte de Perón. Rather than being based on some abstract concept of the *patria* (fatherland), a personality cult was created around the president, known as Peronism. Perón inherited a fortuitous economic situation as president. Argentina held large credit balances overseas, notably in the UK, as the result of agricultural products supplied during the Second World War. These balances were used for numerous populist causes, not least the nationalisation of foreign-owned railways and utilities, and the dispensing of generous social benefits to his core working-class support. As the propitious economic situation that Perón inherited worsened, principally due to the Marshall Plan diverting European demand to US agricultural producers, this cross-sector support began to dismantle and by 1949 could only be held together by increased authoritarianism.

Important to this unity of purpose was the incorporation of internal migrants into the heart of the labour movement. These immigrants, particularly from the northern provinces, were often *mestizo* and through their indigenous features were dismissed racially by *porteños* as *cabecitas negras* ('little blackheads'), just as the Santiago del Estero team in the

---

[59] Hedges (2021, 6).

Campeonato Argentino had been derided as *pelo duros* in the 1920s, whilst he poverty of these migrants was reflected in another nickname, *los descamisados* ('the shirtless ones'). The *cabecitas negras* were something of an underclass even within the workers' movement, living in the self-built *villas miserias* or shanty towns that populated the periphery of Buenos Aires and its satellite cities like Avellaneda. Attracted by the promise of jobs generated by import substitution industrialisation during the 1930s and 1940s following the crash in primary goods prices, which saw the loss of many agricultural jobs in the provinces, 1.1 million people migrated from the interior to the Greater Buenos Aires conurbation between 1935 and 1947. The *descamisados* found a champion and hope of better conditions in Perón, turning the term into a badge of honour as they provided the backbone of his popular support.[60] The presence of the *cabecitas* created class and racial tensions with the upper and middle classes, who felt that they brought ignorance and vulgarity to cultured Buenos Aires, diluting the capital's reputation as a civilised, white and European city. According to a contemporary writer they were 'the substratum of our idiosyncrasy and of our collective possibilities that were right there in their primordiality.'[61] It was a culture clash that was apparent in Perón's own family background, which was a hybrid of *criollo*, immigrant and indigenous origin adding to his self-identification as an archetype of the 'New Argentina,' claiming 'My family did not escape the norm. The Old World's ancestral culture mixes with local passions.'[62]

The arrival of internal migrants impacted the footballing arena, driving up club memberships and match attendances in the capital, as they used their improved economic circumstances to consume football as a means of integrating into their new surroundings. Many arrivals supported the *grandes* having formed affiliations based on radio commentaries broadcast nationwide from the start of the 1930s. If one team gained more *cabecita* followers than any other, it was Boca Juniors, the 'Team of the People', who had a formidable support base in the interior, confirmed by a 1932 survey undertaken by *El Gráfico* as players like Américo Tesorieri, Ludovico Bidoglio and Domingo Tarascone became stars on

---

[60] Hobsbawm (2017, 244–245), Hedges (2021, 40), and Milanesio (2010, 58–59).
[61] Cited in Goebel (2011, 82–83).
[62] Cited in Hedges (2021, 12).

a national scale through radio commentaries.[63] Whilst the terraces were becoming more indigenous and less uniformly European in appearance, it was another decade or more before the sons of *cabecitas* became a regular feature on Argentine football pitches.

Situated in the standing sections known as *populares*, the *cabecitas* were renowned for their rowdiness, bringing class differences into focus within football grounds and highlighting tensions within Perón's cross-class alliance. For the middle class, football was 'spectacle,' an entertainment akin to going to the theatre, whilst for the working classes, especially the *cabecitas*, football was an escape from the rigours of their menial work and precarious living conditions, the desire to see their side win the main driving force for their attendance.[64] Their passion often boiled over into violence, triggered by what they perceived to be partisan refereeing decisions. The *cabecitas* were at the vanguard of what Caparrós describes as Peronism's 'plebeian eruption' showing their support for the president alternate Sundays with the popular terrace chant, 'Boca, Perón, A single heart.'[65]

The response of the Peronist authorities to this increased violence was not the obvious route of repression, so beloved of Argentine leaders going back to independence, but an attempt at civic education through the propagandising of cultural norms and expectations of the citizenry in the 'New Argentina.' The regime reinforced its ideals of sporting virtue by influencing sectors of the media, taking a controlling interest in the previously Anglo-American owned Haynes publishing house, which produced the sports magazine *Mundo Deportivo* from April 1949. The magazine provided competition for *El Gráfico* which resisted the pressure to function as a Peronist mouthpiece, barely mentioning the president by name in its pages.[66]

An editorial by Carlos Aloé, a member of Perón's inner circle, in *Mundo Deportivo* in December 1949 highlighted the problem and how it could be remedied. Whilst he admired the 'vehement support for the sport' as an expression of passion, Aloé lamented 'the degeneration of this sentiment that converts noble partisan exaltation into irresponsible

---

[63] *El Gráfico*, 3 December 1932, 37.
[64] *El Gráfico*, 8 December 1944, 5–7.
[65] Caparrós (2004, 10–12).
[66] *El Gráfico*, 24 December 1948, 1; *El Gráfico*, 6 June 1943, 20; 28 June 1950, 19.

fanaticism without control,' that was causing consternation 'for those who go to matches as tranquil spectators of this sporting fiesta.'[67] He was tacitly admitting the problems in keeping all elements of Peronism's broad support happy at the same time given the class tensions within Buenos Aires arising from provincial migration. Aloé's remedy was civic education, 'The respect of our citizenry for their fellow men must be shown at the sporting stadium. This heritage of culture that gives us pride before the world cannot remain in the street, outside the stadiums.'[68] By using his *Mundo Deportivo* platform in this way, Aloé mirrored what another Peronist acolyte, Education Minister, Oscar Ivanissevich was doing as editor of *Argentina* magazine. As a lifestyle magazine, *Argentina* set the tone for what was considered cultured in society, with Ivanissevich setting himself the goal of developing a 'social conscience, an awareness of social responsibility' for all Argentines, lifting the *cabecitas* out of 'unculturedness' through his dual roles.[69]

The AFA's response to the crisis of violence at Argentine stadiums was twofold. One was to raise ticket prices to price out rowdier elements from stadiums, something derided by the populist newspaper *La Época* who complained that tickets should be, 'affordable' for the 'nucleus of supporters that belong to the authentic mass of the working population.'[70] Secondly, the AFA replaced Argentine referees with neutral ones from England. Beginning with Isaac Caswell, a number of English officials were hired to restore a sense of 'fair-play' to Argentine pitches and cool tempers on terraces by restoring confidence in refereeing decisions by dispensing on-field justice without fear or favour. As *El Gráfico* reflected in 1948, 'It has been said that the victory of the small teams over the teams of more renown, has been influenced directly by the deployment of British referees ... we did not believe that the British referees would be better than the Argentines, but it is evident that they perform better.'[71] Amongst those who gained the respect of Argentine crowds was Harry Hartles, who according to *Mundo Deportivo*, 'Although somewhat flamboyant in his gestures and attitudes, is extremely cordial and there are

[67] *Mundo Deportivo*, 8 December 1949, 22.
[68] Ibid., 22.
[69] Elena (2010, 211–213).
[70] *La Época*, 9 April 1948, 32.
[71] *El Gráfico*, 24 December 1948, 64–65.

no doubts that his knowledge in the profession is very wide.'[72] Both were policies that appeared somewhat incongruous given the pro-worker and anti-colonial rhetoric espoused by Peronists on coming to power in 1946. There were other inconsistencies involving Argentine football and Peronist anti-imperialist ideology during this period. In May 1948, the Palermo site of the first football match played at Buenos Aires Cricket Club was declared a 'National Historic Monument', whilst the Copa George VI was played for between 1946 and 1948 by Argentina's top clubs.[73]

Articles in *Mundo Deportivo* also took a tutorial tone with sporting allegories highlighting what was expected of Argentine citizens in the 'New Argentina,' a term referenced in most editorials. Healthy minds and bodies were considered essential by the Peronist regime for a happy citizenry and productive workforce, recalling notions of muscular Christianity and what had happened in Vargas' Estado Novo in Brazil. Sport was promoted as an essential element of public health, 'The cultivation of sport is not only a pastime, but also constitutes the most efficient medium to maintain and preserve a high state of healthiness.'[74] *Mundo Deportivo* articulated the importance of Argentina's sporting representation around the world, and the role played by the Peronist state in facilitating it, 'If our compatriots have been able to show all the world their quality … it is because a government understanding of their problems and concerned with the well-being of its people has been taken for the first time in the Republic [of Argentina] with the seriousness it deserves.'[75]

The construction of sporting venues was another permanent reminder of Peronism's cultural influence on Argentine society. Picturing Racing's Estadio Juan Domingo Perón, built with a state funded loan and inaugurated in 1950, *Mundo Deportivo* noted that, 'Magnificent stadiums [funded by the Peronist government] have enriched the architectural beauty of our cities and provide improved facilities for sporting jousts.'[76] The stadium, site of the football tournament of the 1951 Pan American

---

[72] *Mundo Deportivo*, 9 August 1950, 52.

[73] Lupo (2004, 25) and Estévez and Lodise (2017, 105–109).

[74] *Mundo Deportivo*, 22 January 1953, 59.

[75] Ibid., 59.

[76] Ibid., 59.

Games held in Buenos Aires, was a centrepiece of Perón's projection of Argentine modernism and regional power.

'Sundays Without Football': The Players' Strike of 1948–1949

A key feature of social change in Argentina during the 1940s was the incorporation of the working class into the national discourse, as union membership rose by nearly half a million members in the first half of the decade.[77] A climate of worker militancy, stirred by Perón during his time in the Labour Ministry, also permeated the footballing sphere with the 1944 foundation of a players' union, the Fútbolistas Argentinos Agremiados (FAA). Represented by strong dressing room shop stewards like José Eusebio Soriano at River Plate, the union advocated solidarity with players across the spectrum of professional football, not just those at the big clubs. Peronist support for worker activism was reflected by a continued growth in union membership in Argentina, which increased from 877,333 in 1946 to 1,992,404 in 1950.[78]

In 1944, the rebel Liga Mayor in Mexico, outside the control of FIFA, tempted seventeen Argentine players with promises of higher salaries. Most notable of these players was José Manuel Moreno, the maverick star of River Plate's *la máquina* team, who signed for Real España. Moreno was joined in Mexico by other stars such as Jorge Enrico and José Antonio Lazcano, who signed for Veracruz. All three players were back in Argentina by 1947 after the Liga Mayor normalised relations with the AFA in respect to transfers.[79] Although the exodus to Mexico was not as extensive as that to Italy in the 1920s and 1930s, it was a timely warning of what could happen if the maximum wages were not removed by the AFA. The mid-season loss of Moreno was particularly grievous as River dropped from top of the table, losing the title to Boca Juniors.[80]

The FAA really started flexing its muscles in April 1948, at a time when real wages for industrial workers were rising annually by 53%. The union demanded recognition from the AFA, the introduction of a minimum

---

[77] Sáenz Quesada (2012, 534–535).
[78] Smith (1989, 26–32).
[79] *El Gráfico*, 29 August 1947, 15.
[80] *El Gráfico*, 8 December 1944, 8.

wage, elimination of the 1,500 peso monthly maximum wage, payment of unpaid wages and freedom of contract at the end of each season as well as 45 days' paid holiday in the close season. The players' argument was that, as the ones generating the spectacle that fans paid to see, they should be entitled to a bigger slice of the proceeds.[81]

The clubs, especially the *grandes*, counter-argued that the players' demands were economically ruinous and threatened the very existence of professional football in Argentina. In its 1948 annual report, River Plate bemoaned that its 'generously paid' players with their 'bitterness and lack of reflection' had 'generated the profound crisis that affected everyone'.[82]

The dispute reflected employer-worker relations more widely in the football world. Concurrently in England, Wilf Mannion was in dispute with Middlesbrough, trying to secure a transfer away from the club when his contract expired, going on a one-man strike to press his case, having been unable to secure wider support from the footballer's union. It was not until 1960 that the Professional Footballers' Association (PFA) acted in a truly effective collective way, threatening strike action if the maximum wages were not scrapped by the Football Association, something secured a year later.[83] In this context, the solidarity displayed by the FAA was ground-breaking in global terms, albeit in the most labour-friendly environment yet seen in Argentina. When a positive response from the clubs and the AFA was not forthcoming, the union announced that a strike would start in April. Rapid recognition of the FAA temporarily placated the players, but when their other demands remained unmet, the strike started in July 1948. One of the most vociferous supporters of the strike was the River Plate forward Alfredo Di Stéfano, who during his time on loan at Huracán had seen teammates go unpaid for months at a time, a recurring theme at the clubs with lesser resources.

The tactic of club directors was to sow discord within the ranks of the strikers rather than negotiate in good faith with the players. As Di Stéfano recalled of the situation at River Plate, 'there were resentments between those who chose to play and those who did not.'[84] He further elaborated on his reason for striking, saying that it was not just a question of money

---

[81] James (2002, 274–278) and Levinsky (2016, 80–83).
[82] Club Atlético River Plate (1949, 64–67).
[83] Hill (2002, 28–30) and Holt (1989, 298).
[84] Cited in Hawkey (2016, 75–77).

but more about security of being paid, especially in the lower divisions where 'you play five [matches] and get paid for one.'[85]

The AFA also responded quickly and strongly, threatening legal and disciplinary action if the players did not report for duty for the round of matches due to be played on 4 July 1948.[86] Attempts at reconciliation did bring the players back on to the pitch for a few months, but there was consistent stalling on the part of the AFA and the clubs in failing to redress any part of the players' grievances. The strike resumed on 10 November, after the FAA criticised 'the lack of moral responsibility of the directors.'[87] The league championship continued a fortnight later after briefly being suspended by the AFA, but crucially without the striking players. Crowds fell as a result as strikers were replaced by junior players. The AFA ruled on 24 November 1948 that the striking players should be banned from playing for two years and have their contracts rescinded. Racing Club de Avellaneda, who were top of the league and heading for their first championship in the professional era, refused to play with juniors and forfeited several fixtures, enabling their city rivals, Independiente to claim the title instead.[88]

Scholars such as Levinsky have portrayed the strike as a traditional labour dispute, but the contemporary press was very much concerned with the effect of the strike on another actor in Argentine football: the supporter.[89] *El Gráfico*, which remained even-handed between players and administrators, editorialised that December, 'We blame neither one nor the other because each one must know it is partly their responsibility, but the undeniable thing is that the most interested party [the supporters] is not consulted and that the championship finished when the first-teamers stopped playing.'[90]

Resolution to the conflict was eventually achieved in time for the 1949 season to start belatedly. Amongst the concessions made by the clubs was that contracts could only be fixed for three years, after which a player was entitled to a free transfer, and that disciplinary action could

---

[85] Di Stéfano (2000, 88–89).
[86] *Noticias Gráficas*, 2 July 1948, 15.
[87] *La Cancha*, 17 November 1948.
[88] Asociación del Fútbol Argentino (1949).
[89] Levinsky (2016, 77–80).
[90] *El Gráfico*, 2 December 1948, 3.

not be taken against players if they were not paid on time. Crucially though, the maximum wage remained in place. Whilst Alejandro Molinari and Roberto Martínez argue that the resolution was a 'triumph for the players' and Frydenberg and Sazbon claim that the outcome meant that players 'achieved material concrete benefits, like minimum salaries,' it could be contested that the reverse was the case.[91] Di Stéfano recalled that contracts remained 'one-sided' in favour of the clubs with players still not gaining freedom of contract. He suggested that players settled under duress, 'What are you going to do? If we didn't sign, they were going to suspend us for who knows how many years.'[92]

Failure to scrap the maximum wage only added to player resentment and triggered an exodus of 105 of Argentina's top players abroad in the Argentine winter of 1949, to countries where there was no limit on earnings. The reaction of the clubs was one of contempt, with River Plate noting 'Two of our players, Néstor Rossi and Alfredo Di Stéfano, following in the footsteps of others, totally forgetting their contractual obligations, absented themselves from the country almost surreptitiously.'[93]

That the dispute dragged on for so long is puzzling given the penchant for Peronism to favour workers in industrial disputes. This was particularly true of Perón's first four-year term of office when strikes were usually short in duration. But as Ronaldo Munck, Ricardo Falcon and Bernardo Galitelli argue, 1948 marked a sea change in strikes. Industrial disputes not only increased in number but also in terms of the number of working days lost, as employers resisted workers' demands more strongly.[94] Given the network of Peronist supporters—including Oscar Nicolini at the head of the AFA—at various clubs who sought to protect their own financial interests, it was not so surprising that this dispute reflected some of the contradictions and ambiguities inherent within Peronism itself, which allied itself to different groups according to what was most opportune at the time. Indeed, it is reported that Nicolini stepped aside as AFA president after falling out with Evita, who true to her modest roots, took the

---

[91] Molinari and Martínez (2013, 181–184) and Frydenberg and Sazbon (2015, 79–80).
[92] Di Stéfano (2000, 88–89).
[93] Club Atlético River Plate (1950, 52).
[94] Munck et al. (1987, 135–137).

side of the 'workers,' players, in the dispute.[95] These contradictions were echoed two years later as *Mundo Deportivo* reflected on 20 years of professionalism, 'In 1948 football suffered a grave blow. Conflicts between directors and players provoked the strike. The proceedings are very recent, whose mention would be truly redundant, since all our friends remember them.'[96] Given the depth of analysis apparent in the rest of the article, the opaque description applied to the strike implies that the Peronist authorities were not strong on self-awareness.

A confluence of circumstances meant that Colombia was the destination of choice for more than half of the players leaving Argentina, with the establishment there of a rebel professional league, the División Mayor de la Liga, or 'Dimayor,' as it was better known. The period has been described by scholars such as Rafael Racines as 'El Dorado,' a reference to the Spanish search for gold in Colombia during colonial times, in which rapid economic growth of 5% per annum between 1945 and 1955 brought great wealth to the country, especially to entrepreneurs such as Alfredo Senior, a director of Millonarios de Bogotá, who were prepared to invest serious sums of money to make their clubs successful in this new professional era.[97]

The Dimayor was not affiliated to FIFA, and therefore not bound by its regulations when it came to international transfers. Colombian teams were therefore able to tempt foreign stars without having to pay a transfer fee to their clubs. The move made the players global pariahs and put a temporary hold on their international careers whilst they were in Colombia, but the vast increase in salary was ample compensation. For example, Millonarios de Bogotá paid their marquee acquisition Adolfo Pedernera a signing-on fee of US$5,000 and a monthly salary of US$500, which was more than three times higher than the 1,500-peso maximum wage in Argentina at the time.[98]

Pedernera's entrance to Colombia on 10 June 1949 was key to the arrival of the other Argentines. As one of the most emblematic Argentine players of the previous decade and lynchpin of River Plate's *la máquina*

---

[95] Levinsky (2016, 80–83).
[96] *Mundo Deportivo*, 9 August 1951, 64–65.
[97] Racines (2011, 114–120).
[98] Campomar (2014, 105–107).

team, Pedernera gave the fledgling competition a credibility that it previously lacked. Alongside Pedernera, Alfredo di Stéfano and Néstor Rossi departed for Colombia along with fifty-three other Argentine players. As one study claimed, 'From that moment on, migration to other latitudes – with the accompanying financial gains this implied – became the natural aspiration for a good number of Argentinian footballers.'[99] In an article entitled, 'The Cuckoo is Colombia', *El Gráfico* wrote that the exodus of the most valued players was a threat to Argentine football in which the clubs, the national team and the supporters would all lose, before making this crucial observation about the difference between transfers to Europe from which Argentine clubs received fees and those to Colombia where they received none, 'If the stars, being attentive to their position as professionals respond affirmatively to the call from a club in Colombia, there is only one way to retain them: pay them more.'[100]

Like other Argentine cultural expressions such as the tango, Argentine football was hugely popular in Colombia, providing a home from home for the Argentine exiles. As the former Argentine international, Fernando Paternoster, said of the country when working there in 1941, 'In general, there exists a very friendly sentiment for anything Argentine ... It is interesting to note the level of support for Argentine football in Colombia, so far away, who can refer to memorable players and teams and recalling performances as if they were there.'[101] A year later the exodus continued, met with disdain in sections of the press. Even foreign players leaving Argentina were treated as 'traitors.' As *Goles* reported in July 1950, 'A new desertion is to be added to the extensive list of "tourists" that could not resist the blinding shine of Colombian gold. The "seduced" of this week is the Paraguayan half, Julio Ramírez of Huracán.'[102]

Racing Club, where the Minister of Finance Ramón Cereijo held enormous influence, were the club least affected by the exodus. Certainly, their players were well looked after. In 1948, eighteen members of Racing's squad were earning the maximum wage of 1500 pesos per month, the greatest number of maximum wage earners in the League, five more than

---

[99] Cited in Lanfranchi and Taylor (2001, 88–90).
[100] Poggi (2009, 74–77).
[101] *El Gráfico*, 17 January 1941.
[102] *Goles*, 18 July 1950.

5 POLITICAL FOOTBALL: THE AGE OF DECLINE? 1931–1958

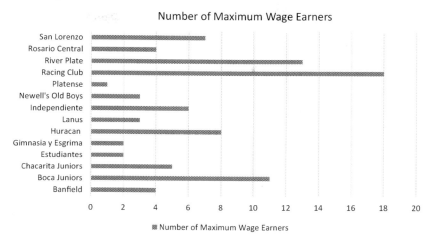

Fig. 5.1 Number of players earning the maximum wage in Argentina in 1948 by Club[105]

the next club, River Plate (see Fig. 5.1).[103] Panzeri alluded that these payments were topped up in the form of items 'made available' that were otherwise restricted imports, such as motor cars and building materials. The testimony of players such as Ezra Sued suggests that more underhand methods were also employed to stop the club's top stars from going abroad, such as the confiscation of their passports.[104] The tactics used by Racing worked as they won the league title in 1949 and 1950.

The journalist Américo Barrios considered them essential to Racing's success, 'When others get confused on the way, the champion must signal the right direction.'[106] The implication was that Racing had therefore served the national interest by not allowing its best players to go abroad and were 'justly' rewarded for their 'moral' stance, rather than meekly accept financial reality as the other clubs had done. The fact that Racing could still win the 1950 championship despite losing ten of their games

---

[103] Asociación del Fútbol Argentino (1949).
[104] Hawkey (2016, 80–81); *La Opinión Suplemento Cultura*, 12 May 1974.
[105] Asociación del Fútbol Argentino (1949).
[106] *Mundo Deportivo*, 8 December 1949, 59.

highlighted the paucity of quality in Argentine football following the departure of so many established players abroad.

Whilst the Argentine press attempted to blame the temptation of 'Colombian gold' for the country's footballing ills, it is worth bearing mind that it was Argentina that set the precedent back in 1931. As Panzeri notes, the first 'pirate league' was the Liga Argentina, whose clubs practiced the same clandestine tactics as those in Colombia's Dimayor, setting back the development of football in Brazil, Uruguay and Paraguay as their best players were signed without fees by Argentine clubs.[107] Nevertheless, as the next sections demonstrate the exodus to Colombia and elsewhere contributed to the decline of Argentine football over the succeeding decade.

The Third Way

Non-participation in global tournaments was not a new tactic on the part of Argentina's footballing authorities. Internal wrangling meant that Argentina was represented by a team of amateur and provincial players in 1934, whilst there was no Argentine team at the 1938 World Cup (similarly to the British Home Nations, although for unrelated reasons). It was Argentina's performance in the 1934 tournament, losing to Sweden in the first round, which set the precedent for the use of isolation as a protectionist and diplomatic manoeuvre by the country's footballing authorities. The team sent to Italy was not fully representative of the talent available in Argentina, given that the best players were mostly contracted to clubs in the Liga Argentina, which was unaffiliated to FIFA, and therefore ineligible for selection in the World Cup. The situation was criticised in *El Gráfico*, who complained that Argentina was not represented by its best players and that the team's performance was therefore not a true reflection of Argentine football.[108]

In retaliation for the hosting rights for that 1938 tournament being awarded to France by eighteen votes to four at FIFA's 1936 Berlin Congress—the second time in a row to a European nation rather than Argentina—the AFA requested direct qualification for the tournament. When FIFA refused this request, the AFA chose not to enter an Argentine

---

[107] *La Opinión Suplemento Cultura*, 12 May 1974.
[108] *El Gráfico*, 12 June 1934.

team. By contrast, neighbouring Brazil, with the full backing of the Vargas regime, did not pass up the opportunity to play in the 1938 World Cup, reaching the semi-final and establishing themselves for the first time as a global footballing power. As with the 1924 Olympics, Argentina's absence from the competition was perceived in the media as a missed opportunity. *El Gráfico* branded the AFA as 'Puritan' after the talented team including the likes of Moreno, Pedernera and Labruna that had helped Argentina to win the South American Championship in 1937 were denied the opportunity to demonstrate their prowess. The arrogant attitude taken by the AFA reflected the ignorance of the institution of the prevailing winds of global sporting diplomacy.

The players' strike of 1948–1949 was hugely disruptive for Argentine football internationally as well as domestically. Evidence from the AFA archives suggests that the Argentine football authorities initially underestimated the depth of support for the strike. Argentine representatives attended FIFA's London Congress in 1948 with a view to arranging friendlies against Spain, Italy, France and Portugal in preparation for the 1950 World Cup, not having faced European opposition since the 1934 tournament. These games were later cancelled by the AFA in November 1948 because of the uncertainty about being able to field a representative team caused by the ongoing industrial dispute, at a cost of 100,000 pesos in lost revenue.[109]

Similarly, with the strike still not having reached a conclusion, the AFA withdrew the Argentine team from the 1949 South American Championship due to start that April in Brazil. No official reason was given in the AFA's annual report, although Brazilian newspaper *O Globo Deportivo* suggested it was because the Argentines had scheduled a domestic tournament around the same time as the Championship.[110] It is therefore likely that as reigning South American champions, the AFA did not want Argentina to embarrass themselves by entering a much-weakened team and engineered an excuse not to participate. By contrast, neighbouring Uruguay were undergoing a similar labour dispute in their own football in 1949, which meant that their top players were also unavailable for their national team. The Uruguayans entered a team of strike-breakers and juniors, winning just two of their six games and losing 5–1 to the

---

[109] Asociación del Fútbol Argentino (1950).

[110] *O Globo Deportivo*, 24 June 1949, 1.

hosts. With several of their best players restored after their strike ended, Uruguay returned to Brazil a year later and won the 1950 World Cup.

When Valentín Suárez became president of the AFA on 21 August 1949, the most pressing issue in his in-tray now that the players' strike had ended was the issue of Argentina's participation at the 1950 World Cup in Brazil. The AFA had actually entered a team in the competition, and Argentina were paired in a qualifying group with Bolivia and Chile, the top two going through to the finals.[111] On 11 January 1950, the Argentine side was withdrawn from the competition by the AFA, after a seemingly minor dispute with the Brazilian Confederation, whose 'unjustified attitude' had prohibited its clubs from playing friendlies against Argentine teams in Santiago.[112] These developments should be seen in the wider context of contemporary sporting and diplomatic relations between the two nations as they competed for regional hegemony. The divergent paths taken during the Second World War and beyond, in which Brazil aligned itself heavily with the United States whilst Argentina stood aloof in its neutrality, also added to the mutual distrust of the two nations. Argentina had originally wanted to host the 1950 World Cup, but the Brazilians had stolen a march on them diplomatically in gathering support, emerging as unopposed candidates at FIFA's 1946 Congress in Luxembourg.

Referring to his reasons for suggesting Peronist influence lay behind Argentina's withdrawal, Levinsky has referenced the fact that the 1949 emigration of players to Colombia (who could not have played in the competition as the players were banned by FIFA) and further afield meant that it was felt Argentina would have struggled to be competitive against the top teams in the world, although this was not mentioned as a factor in the AFA's annual report.[113] It should be noted that like Uruguay, Argentina were in a position to field a competitive team. Whilst the absence of players like Mario Boyé, Julio Cozzi and Alfredo Di Stéfano would have been keenly felt, that of Adolfo Pedernera and José Manuel Moreno would have been less so as they were in their mid-thirties and past their peak. More than half the squad that won the 1947 South American Championship, including Natalio Pescia, Norberto Méndez and Ezra Sued were back playing in Argentina, enough for the AFA to enter a team

---

[111] Asociación del Fútbol Argentino (1950); *Mundo Deportivo*, 8 December 1949, 65.

[112] Asociación del Fútbol Argentino (1951).

[113] Levinsky (2016, 83–87).

that would not have disgraced itself, especially in the light of European football still being in a state of reconstruction after the cataclysm of the Second World War.

The Peronist viewpoint on Argentina's absence was corroborated very elliptically in an article by Carlos Aloé entitled 'Sporting Idols' shortly before the 1950 World Cup started. Exalting Argentina's world champions in sports such as polo, shooting and billiards, Aloé made a veiled reference to Argentina's absence from the World Cup, observing that other Argentine sportsmen/women and teams had excelled, 'In tournaments in which its representations had taken place.'[114] Alóe indicated that those players that had gone to Colombia and other destinations for financial reasons were not fit to be sporting role models for Argentine youth because they lacked 'the resignation and sacrifice' of other sportsmen such as the racing driver, Juan Manuel Fangio, who by contrast was 'a man of the people, with the absolute support of General Perón ... the perfection of the Argentine race.'[115]

Argentina's absence from the 1950 World Cup was again viewed as a missed opportunity by the country's press as the result of weak direction from its administrators. Ironically, when Uruguay emerged as the victors of the tournament ahead of overwhelming favourites Brazil, their victory, as in 1924 was treated in Argentina as a restatement of *rioplatense* supremacy in world football despite their own absence. As Borocotó wrote in *El Gráfico*, 'We didn't ask for partition in these victories of our traditional rivals and against who Argentine football of a similar physiognomy has maintained a historic equilibrium.'[116] *Goles* argued that the absence of the Argentine team took away some of the credibility of the competition. Referencing 'successful' European tours by Newell's Old Boys, Racing Club and San Lorenzo in the Argentine summer of 1949–1950, the magazine claimed that Argentina would have 'reaffirmed the technical hierarchy of our football,' and 'shown once more in the Brazilian capital that we continue being the best'.[117] Many of these victories in Europe came against relatively weak opposition in the form of lesser Spanish teams and Belgian club sides. Against the strongest sides like Real

---

[114] *Mundo Deportivo*, 25 May 1950, 26.
[115] Ibid., 26.
[116] *El Gráfico*, 11 August 1950, 46–48.
[117] *Goles*, 18 July 1950, 5.

Madrid, Barcelona and Benfica, Argentine champions Racing Club were convincingly beaten, casting doubt as to the validity of *Goles*' claims.

Argentina's isolation was broken with some high-profile friendly matches at the start of the 1950s, primarily against England, the 'motherland' of football and in the minds of scholars such as Archetti, Argentine football's 'significant other'.[118] In 1951, Argentina were given the privilege of being the first South American team to play at Wembley as part of the Festival of Britain, an invitation that was accepted with alacrity when Perón found out that England were unbeaten at 'the home of football', and who was keen that Argentina be the first to break that record. For Perón, Britain was an oppositional pole in his anti-imperialist rhetoric and he spent much of his presidency unpicking British influence over the economy by attempting to renegotiate the 1933 Roca-Runciman treaty that obligated Argentina to purchase British finished goods in exchange for Argentine agricultural products, as well as nationalising the British-owned railways, going as far as to declare Argentina's 'economic independence' in Tucumán on 9 July 1947, 121 years to the day that the country's political independence was declared in the same city.[119]

The opportunity to gain international kudos by Argentina beating its perceived nemesis was politically expedient for Perón. Although Argentina lost 2–1, thanks to the goalkeeping heroics of Miguel Rugilo, the so-called Lion of Wembley, the playing style of the Argentines was well received in the English press with The *Manchester Guardian* praising 'their close passing on the ground' and 'quickness in recovery, particularly on defence.'[120]

The AFA reciprocated the invitation by hosting the English on a two-match trip to Buenos Aires in 1953. Previewing the visit, *El Gráfico* recognised the contribution made by the English as founders and disseminators of the game, but was more grounded in terms of building them up too highly, noting that, 'Maybe we should be more exact by talking of Argentine progress than of the decline of the English game, but it is undoubtable that the British no longer exercise the footballing hegemony that it held for many years.'[121] In the first of the 1953 games,

---

[118] Archetti (1999, 73).

[119] Hedges (2021, 125).

[120] *Manchester Guardian*, 10 May 1951, 2.

[121] *El Gráfico*, 15 May 1953, 5.

Argentina beat what was officially described by both governing bodies as a Football Association XI that was essentially a team of reserves, 3–1 in a packed Estadio Monumental to hubristic acclaim. The way victory was achieved, including a wonderful individual goal from a seemingly impossible angle by Ernesto Grillo, verified assumptions about the superiority of the Argentine style over the English.[122] President Perón later declared that the date of the game, 14 May, would henceforth be known as 'Footballers' Day'. It was to be to an annual reminder that in the Argentine imaginary *la nuestra* was no longer subservient to the originators of the game. That said, there was still an element of Argentines seeking validation from their erstwhile teachers, with *El Gráfico* expressing their satisfaction after the game about the way English journalists enthused about the Argentine play that was 'so full of subtlety' and admired, 'the elasticity and mental speed that allow ours to capture, conceive and produce for them more unthought of variants.'[123]

Three days later, the game treated by the English as the official international took place, with the visitors making seven changes in what was now its first-choice team. A heavy thunderstorm threatened to prevent the game taking place, but it kicked off as scheduled. With the pitch completely saturated, it soon became unplayable, and the game was duly abandoned after 22 minutes by the referee with the score at 0–0. The draw enabled the Argentines to point to the result of the first match as evidence of their superiority over the 'masters'.

Given these successful steps towards reintegration into the international footballing community, the absence of Argentina from the 1954 World Cup in Switzerland appears baffling. Again, no reason was given by the AFA for the absence in their annual reports in either 1953 or 1954. Indeed, just a year before the tournament, national coach, Guillermo Stábile, was placed 'in charge of all facets' of the national team, including selection and training. The Argentines attended the tournament purely as observers, with Stábile compiling a report verbosely entitled, *Resumé of the diverse observations made in completion of an honourable distinction*, in which he concluded that, 'If the team had attended, it would have stood out.'[124] Failure to enter the competition was a diplomatic gaffe given

---

[122] Asociación del Fútbol Argentino (1955, 28–29).
[123] *El Gráfico*, 22 May 1953.
[124] Cited in Levinsky (2016, 103–107).

that it was in 1954 that the Peronist authorities began their campaign for Argentina to host the 1962 World Cup.

Again, Argentina's absence did not meet with universal approval. *El Gráfico* bemoaned the lack of international activity, pointing out that the Argentine team had not played since taking on Spain in July 1953, whilst eventual World Cup runners-up Hungary had twenty international matches scheduled for 1954 alone, not counting tournament warm-up matches, and that neighbours Brazil and Uruguay were both regularly testing themselves against European opposition. It concluded, 'To count on a seasoned and capable national team is the unanimous yearning, but all this must be well planned and must not continue to be improvised.'[125] *Goles* bemoaned the cancelled tour to Eastern Europe in May 1954 when Argentina were scheduled to play Russia and Hungary as a missed opportunity to reintegrate the country into world football.[126] Argentina finally ended their self-imposed isolation months after Perón was ejected from office at the 1955 South American Championship in Santiago de Chile, which they won.

Ultimately Argentine football's isolation from global competition from 1934 to 1958 was the result of a combination of factors and not the consequence of an overarching deliberate political policy on the part of the Peronist authorities. Although writing ahead of the 1958 World Cup, by which time the Peronist regime had been overthrown by the military, the words of Panzeri are pertinent. He wrote 'To compete in a World Cup supposes two parallel things: total victory and the exposition of a technical physiognomy that shows the prestige of a nationality.'[127] In this context whilst Peronists may have obtained political capital by the AFA not risking adverse results by the Argentine national team on the international stage, the regime was not directly responsible for its absence. However, the Peronist government's indirect role in the failure to end the Players' Strike in a timely manner combined with incompetent administration and diplomacy on the part of the AFA played an equally damaging role. This isolation proved to be severely injurious to Argentine football as the next section investigates.

[125] *El Gráfico*, 18 June 1954, 3.
[126] *Goles*, 15 June 1954, 5 and 18.
[127] *El Gráfico*, 30 May 1958, 38–39.

The 'Disaster of Sweden'

The phrase, 'Disaster of Sweden' was coined by Panzeri to describe the 6–1 defeat to Czechoslovakia at the 1958 World Cup and the cataclysmic effect it had on Argentina's footballing morale and identity in terms of the definitive end of its 'golden era' and notions of *la nuestra* being the best way of playing football.[128]

Argentina finally returned to the World Cup after twenty-four years in 1958, qualifying top of a group containing Chile and Bolivia. Argentine progress was not without its difficulties, losing 2–0 to the unheralded Bolivians in La Paz, leading the British journalist, Brian Glanville, to conclude, 'even if they qualify I do not think they can be rated serious challengers in Sweden next summer.'[129] Expectations were somewhat higher in Argentina, as the annual report of the AFA reflected in 1957, '1958 can signal the definitive consecration of the values of Argentine football, whose goal is the VI Championship of the World, the objective to which we must lead ourselves with all efforts without stopping for anything which could hinder them.'[130] The AFA's optimism proved misplaced, highlighted by Argentina's selection woes ahead of the 1958 World Cup which were largely of their own making. Within months of Argentina clinching the 1957 South American Championship, their famed forward line of Antonio Angelillo, Humberto Maschio and Omar Sívori had moved to Italian clubs—Internazionale, Bologna and Juventus, respectively—whilst goalkeeper Rogelio Domínguez transferred to Real Madrid. In the days of the *rimpatriati* in the 1920s and 1930s, when transatlantic travel took weeks rather than hours, a transfer to Europe meant certain hiatus, if not an outright end to a player's international career with Argentina. Yet with the advent of jet air travel, and the 1958 World Cup being held in Europe where these star players now resided, there was no reason why they should not have been considered for selection for Argentina, with *Goles* printing a front-page headline in February of that year that demanded underneath a picture of the trio, 'Bring them back.'[131] That had been coach Stábile's intention, but his bosses at the AFA turned down the request as a matter of national pride, confirming

---

[128] Bauso (2013, 24–26).
[129] *The Observer*, 13 October 1957, 23.
[130] Asociación del Fútbol Argentino (1958).
[131] *Goles*, 23 February 1958, 1.

in its Bulletin of 31 March 1958, 'By 18 votes it was established that the representative team at the VI World Cup will be constituted of players registered with this Association.'[132]

Whilst not mentioning the *trio de la muerte* ('trio of death') by name, Panzeri indicated that contrary to the attitude of the AFA, their example in playing abroad would be helpful to the development of Argentine football on several fronts. The journalist expressed hope that other Argentine players would be spotted by foreign clubs at the World Cup, firstly to financially benefit Argentine clubs, and secondly to improve the footballing education of the country's players against other playing styles to help the national team in the future. Despite this laudable aim, Panzeri's hopes would not come to fruition until the 1974 tournament.[133] Sívori expressed his disappointment over his non-selection, saying 'I had news that the AFA were going to ask us [Angelillo and Maschio too], but this request was not forthcoming … I wanted to play and they [Juventus] would have given me permission to do so, like they did for [John] Charles.'[134] Other countries at the tournament had no such reluctance about picking foreign-based players, with Wales securing the release of John Charles from Sívori's club, Juventus, Real Madrid's Raymond Kopa playing for France, and hosts Sweden selecting five players contracted to Italian clubs.[135] Notwithstanding the departure of the *trio de la muerte*, a lack of consistency in selection also saw twelve home-based members of the 1957 South American Championship squad discarded for the World Cup, most notably Ángel Schadlein, Juan Guidi and Héctor de Bourgoing.

Argentina travelled to Europe three weeks before the tournament, preparing with friendlies against Italian club sides Internazionale and Bologna, and Roma's youth team. Pedro Dellacha later remembered of the latter, which gave a foretaste of what was to come, 'I knew that Sweden was going to be extremely difficult the day that we played against the juniors of Roma. They were kids, but they made us run like madmen. They had another speed, and another rhythm.'[136] When Roberto Zárate

---

[132] Cited in Barnarde (2018).
[133] *El Gráfico*, 30 May 1958, 38–39.
[134] Ibid., 4–6.
[135] *La Nación*, 4 June 1958, 12; 7 June 1958, 11.
[136] Cited in Levinsky (2016, 103–107).

5 POLITICAL FOOTBALL: THE AGE OF DECLINE? 1931–1958

got injured against Bologna, ruling him out of the tournament, such was the scarcity of resources available to coach Stábile within Argentina, that the veteran River Plate striker, Ángel Labruna—who himself was only just returning from injury—was called up as his replacement, three months short of his 40th birthday.[137]

There was a lack of dedication and focus on the task in hand on the part of the squad, with Dellacha moaning about being cooped up in the team's remote Ramlösa headquarters, saying 'The Argentine players live in a different way in our country. We don't like to be concentrated in a site like this for so many days, without going into the city as a change [of scenery].'[138] Meanwhile, a training ground fight between Federico Vairo and Julio Musimessi was swept under the carpet by Stábile, who refused to even discuss the matter at a pre-competition press briefing.[139] Reflecting on the Vairo–Mussimessi fight, which he considered to be the tip of the iceberg of indiscipline in the Argentine camp, and the antithesis of professionalism, Panzeri wrote 'The only description that can be used is shame. All things admired about Argentina [football] at the end of the twenties has gone.'[140]

Argentina's lack of professionalism contrasted with the performance of tournament winners, Brazil. Under the leadership of João Havelange and Paulo Machado de Carvalho, the Brazilian football authorities left no stone unturned in searching for a winning edge for the 1958 tournament with a strategy 'based in study and planning' in contrast to the 'errors and improvisation' that had gone before as Brazil had flattered to deceive in previous World Cups.[141] Illuminating the key differences between the approaches of Argentina and Brazil, Pedro Escartín wrote in *El Gráfico* that Brazil had combined, 'their classic virtues, ball control, speed of thought, passing to empty space, uniting them with European qualities of physical strength, fighting spirit, shots at goal and team play.'

---

[137] *La Nación*, 2 June 1958, 11.
[138] *La Nación*, 6 June 1958, 13.
[139] *La Nación*, 2 June 1958, 11; *La Nación*, 13 June 1958, 48.
[140] Ibid., 48.
[141] Kittleson (2014, 57–58).

In terms of preparation he noted, 'Brazil has had in its Technical Commission and in [coach] Vicente Feola, intelligent people who left nothing to improvisation, now everything was scrupulous and severely planned.'[142]

For Brazil, victory was the climax of an eight-year journey of developing all facets of their football after their own catastrophe of the *maracanazo* in 1950. In the Argentine press, there was little optimism that Argentina could recover its own sense of footballing identity in a similar timeframe. Even before Argentina played their first match in the tournament against West Germany, Stábile was playing down expectations, claiming that, 'The Germans play too brusquely for us and there exists a danger that my boys lose their step.'[143] It proved to be a self-fulfilling prophecy as the Germans won, with Stábile noting 'The two teams represent such different systems of play. Ours showed virtuosity and The Germans employed a quick and skilled game.' As *La Nación* succinctly put it, 'Quick and strong win by 3–1'.[144] Not only that, but by equating the national team to 'an inefficient *zambo*' the newspaper demonstrated that a racially derogatory discourse remained present in Argentina.[145]

Argentina beat Northern Ireland convincingly in their second game and appeared to have found the necessary backbone to back up their skilful technique. Fidel Horacio Heugas wrote in *La Nación* that, 'Argentina showed a different spirit, one which validated the team's victory. Their men did not wait for the ball, but looked for it, fought for it … The Argentine *garra* prevailed as they arrived at a true and deserved victory.'[146]

Argentina therefore needed just a draw in their final group game against Czechoslovakia to reach the quarter-finals. After watching the Czechs draw with West Germany, an Argentine delegate boldly claimed 'The Czechs are really bad, we will beat them walking.' The lack of preparation was further exemplified when an Argentine journalist covering the tournament, Miguel Ángel Merlo, offered numerous newspaper clippings about the Czechs culled from the German media to Stábile. The offer was

---

[142] *El Gráfico*, 18 July 1958.
[143] *La Nación*, 4 June 1958, 12.
[144] *La Nación*, 9 June 1958, 13.
[145] *La Nación*, 10 June 1958, 16.
[146] *La Nación*, 12 June 1958, 16.

declined on the basis that the information would not contribute anything to the Argentine's preparation. After Czechoslovakia won the game 6–1, Stábile finally admitted that Argentine football had fallen behind that of the rest of the world, 'From now going forward Argentine football must combine technical perfection with the physical strength which we currently lack. The victory of the Czechoslovaks was deserved. They showed how to be strong, compact and their physical superiority was above all doubt.'[147]

Before the team arrived back at Ezeiza airport, the inquest began into the 'Disaster of Sweden' in the Argentine press. In a *La Nación* article entitled 'Everything was Deficient in the Argentine Team,' Heugas attributed the malaise to a decay on the part of both players and administrators. The players were castigated for being undisciplined and displaying a lack of 'professional responsibility' in failing to train sufficiently. He blamed the AFA for a lack of strong leadership, in failing to prepare properly for the tournament, throwing a team together on the eve of the competition, and not taking a firm hand with the players.[148] A lack of administrative transparency and integrity was the root cause of all that was rotten in Argentine football according to Panzeri. He pointed to the disciplinary infractions by players during the World Cup, suggesting that they escaped lightly by receiving just on-the-spot fines from AFA delegates (who had no such authority). Panzeri preferred instead that the miscreants be dealt with by a Disciplinary Tribunal on their return, who had powers to suspend them and block them from playing for the national team for anything up to three years, acting as a deterrent to future misbehaviour.[149]

Beyond the damage done to Argentina's football, the 'Disaster of Sweden' extended to the wider self-confidence of Argentine society, which itself was in a state of turmoil. None of the three main powerbrokers in Argentine politics—the Radicals, the Peronists and the military—were able to mould a national consensus to drive the country forward because as Goebel notes 'each of these three had the power to block the designs of the other two.' *La Nación* wrote on the team's return, 'For football, for our sport, for the fans, for all the country, the Swedish stumble had

---

[147] *La Nación*, 16 June 1958, 12.
[148] Ibid., 12.
[149] *El Gráfico*, 11 July 1958, 30–40.

all the characteristics of a disaster.'[150] *El Gráfico* outlined the centrality of football to Argentine society and how the nature of Argentina's elimination from the World Cup affected the country's sense of self, 'The cafés, the markets, the offices, the street corners, where all human life congregates, all raised the same debate, with incredulity, with lamentations, with criticisms, with indignation. On all sides the popular voice took on the character of national condemnation.'[151] The capitulation in Hälsingborg was also considered a betrayal of Argentina's footballing traditions, 'It was not the physiognomy of a football with antecedents rich in exploits, in stars that achieved an illusion of progress before converting itself into an export market. The defeat captured the feeling of the street ... the defrauding of the public.'[152] The rudderless nature of Argentine football's management and administration was mirroring the country's governing classes by the end of the 1950s.

The period book-ended by Argentina's appearances at the 1930 and 1958 World Cups with wildly differing results was a parable for Argentina's wider decline over three decades from being one of the richest countries in the world with a representative democracy, to a nation in which democracy became a parody of itself, in which the military was always in the background waiting to intervene if anything approaching social revolution was on the horizon.

The introduction of professionalism reinforced power imbalances with the creation of the oligarchical elite of the *grandes* whilst class differences hampered the organisational development of Argentine football in terms of player-employer relations for decades to come. Failure to establish a transparent governance of Argentine football reflected the wider failure of the Argentine polity to establish a meaningful working democracy that itself continued for much of the rest of the twentieth century.

Whilst the 1940s saw Argentine football's so-called Golden Age, with the exploits of River Plate's *la máquina* team and Argentine dominance in the South American Championship being portrayed in the press as the apogee of *la nuestra*, it was an illusion that obscured a number of systemic failures behind the scenes and was sustained by Argentina's privileged geopolitical position at the time. Dislocation from Europe caused

---

[150] *La Nación*, 23 June 1958, 11.
[151] *El Gráfico*, 17 June 1958, 14.
[152] Ibid., 14.

by the Second World War contributed to the idea that Argentine football was the best in the world, enabling hubris to take root with the perception that an everlasting supply of talent would be available with no planning in place for nurturing future generations of footballers within the traditional club system.

The integration of the *cabecitas negras* into the national discourse was a bold progressive move on the part of the Peronist regime in its attempt to achieve a unified national identity based on social justice achieved through cross-class cooperation and the end of exclusion based on racial origin. However, as the *cabecitas negras* became established on Argentine football ground terraces, this alliance was at best brittle as stadiums became fora for expressing class tensions with stadium violence becoming an increasingly prominently feature of the game in Argentina.

Inter-class ambiguities within Peronism were further highlighted by the 1948–1949 players' strike. With a foot in both camps, Peronist authorities were unable to broker a compromise between players and club directors, a failure that proved so destructive to Argentine football's attempts to reinsert itself into a global competition after the end of the Second World War. The resulting exodus of players in search of better remuneration in Colombia and other destinations proved far more grievous than the loss of the *rimpatriati* had been in the 1920s and 1930s.

This exodus created a lack of confidence on the part of Argentina's footballing authorities that the country could be adequately represented, which combined with poor sporting and governmental diplomacy, resulted in an ad hoc withdrawal from international competition between 1947 and 1955. This isolation prevented Argentina from keeping up with new international developments in the world of football so that by the time they finally re-entered global competition at the 1958 World Cup, existing notions of *la nuestra* had been rendered anachronistic when compared to the scientific, athletically based play of the Europeans, not to mention that of the Brazilians, who allied fitness and tactical discipline to their traditional flair.

The 'Disaster of Sweden' was the climactic event that brought all these elements together in a vortex that left Argentine football at its lowest ebb, echoing wider deficiencies in creating a broader national consensus within Argentine politics and society. The issue was neatly synthesised by the contemporary journalist, Lázaro, who later described the defeat to Czechoslovakia as 'the origin of the maelstrom of Argentine thought,' in which a dichotomy of nostalgia for past glories would fight for prominence with a desire for a radical change of mentality.' He speculated 'This bifocal epic will sweep across the world of football transforming it into a fertile field for ethical and political debates.'[153]

References

Alabarces, Pablo. 2007. *Fútbol y patria. El fútbol y las narrativas de la Nación en la Argentina*, 4th ed. Buenos Aires: Prometeo Libros.
Archetti, Eduardo. 1999. *Masculinities: Football, Polo and the Tango in Argentina*. Oxford: Berg.
Asociación Argentina de Football (Amateur y Profesionales). 1932. *Memoria y Balance General 1931*. Buenos Aires: Geronimo J. Pesce y Cia. Impresores.
Asociación Argentina de Football (Amateur y Profesionales). 1933. *Memoria y Balance General 1932*. Buenos Aires: Geronimo J. Pesce y Cia. Impresores.
Asociación del Football Argentino. 1938. *Memoria y Balance General 1937*. Buenos Aires.
Asociación del Fútbol Argentino. 1949. *Memoria y Balance 1948*. Buenos Aires.
Asociación del Fútbol Argentino. 1950. *Memoria y Balance 1949*. Buenos Aires.
Asociación del Fútbol Argentino. 1951. *Memoria y Balance 1950*. Buenos Aires.
Asociación del Fútbol Argentino. 1955. *Memoria y Balance General 1954*. Buenos Aires.
Asociación del Fútbol Argentino. 1958. *Memoria y Balance General 1957*. Buenos Aires.
Barnarde, Oscar. 2018. Una decisión que cambió la historia del fútbol argentino. Clarin.com. 4 April. http://clarin.com/deportes/seleccion-nacional/decision-cambio-historia-futbol-argentino_0_HkA5UF-jM.amp.html. Accessed 5 July 2018.
Barnade, Oscar, and Waldemar Iglesias. 2014. *Todo Sobre la Selección*. Buenos Aires: Club House.
Bauso, Matías. 2013. *Dante Panzeri, Dirigentes, Decencia y Wines*. Buenos Aires: Sudamericana.
Ben Plotkin, Mariano. 2003. *Mañana es San Perón: A Cultural History of Perón's Argentina*. Wilmington: Scholarly Resources Books.
Bertolotto, Miguel Ángel. 2016. *River Plate. Mientras viva tu bandera*. Buenos Aires: Atlántida.
Blanco, Guillermo. 2016. *Los Juegos Evita: la historia de una pasión deportiva y solidaria*. Buenos Aires: Editorial Octubre.
Bunge, Alejandro. 1940. *Una Nueva Argentina*. Buenos Aires: Kraft.

---

[153] Lázaro (1993, 30–31).

Campomar, Andreas. 2014. *¡Golazo!* London: Quercus.
Caparrós, Martín. 2004. *Boquita*. Buenos Aires. Booklet.
Club Atlético River Plate. 1949. *Memoria y Balance 1948*. Buenos Aires.
Club Atlético River Plate. 1950. *Memoria y Balance 1949*. Buenos Aires.
Di Stéfano, Alfredo. 2000. *Gracias, Vieja*. Madrid: Aguilar.
Elena, Eduardo. 2010. Peronism in "Good Taste" (Argentina Magazine) Jan 49 to Jul 50. In *The New Cultural History of Peronism*, ed. Matthew B. Karush and Oscar Chamosa, 209–238. Durham, NC: Duke University Press.
Estévez, Diego, and Sergio Lodise. 2017. *116 Más de un Siglo Rojo y Blanco*. Buenos Aires: Ediciones Continente.
Frydenberg, Julio, and Daniel Sazbon. 2015. La huelga de jugadores de 1948. In *La cancha peronista: Fútbol y política (1946–1955)*, ed. Ranaan Rein, 65–80. San Martín: UNSAM Edita.
Goebel, Michael. 2011. *Argentina's Partisan Past*. Liverpool: Liverpool University Press.
Hawkey, Ian. 2016. *Di Stéfano*. London: Ebury Press.
Hedges, Julie. 2021. *Juan Perón: The Life of the People's Colonel*. London: Bloomsbury.
Hill, Jeffrey. 2002. *Sport, Leisure and Culture in Twentieth Century Britain*. Basingstoke: Palgrave.
Hobsbawm, Eric. 2017. *Viva la Revolución: On Latin America*. London: Abacus.
Holt, Richard. 1989. *Sport and the British: A Modern History*. Oxford: Clarendon Paperbacks.
James, Daniel. 2002. Perón and the People. In *The Argentina Reader*, ed. Gabriela Nouzeilles and Graciela Montaldo, 273–295. Durham, NC: Duke University Press.
Kittleson, Roger. 2014. *The Country of Football: Soccer and the Making of Modern Brazil*. Berkeley: University of California Press.
Lanfranchi, Pierre, and Matthew Taylor. 2001. *Moving with the Ball: The Migration of Professional Footballers*. Oxford: Berg.
Lázaro. 1993. *Doctrina de Fútbol*. Buenos Aires: La Caja.
Levinsky, Sergio. 2016. *AFA. El fútbol pasa, los negocios quedan: Una historia política y deportiva*. Buenos Aires: Autoria Editorial.
Lupo, Víctor F. 2004. *Historia Política del Deporte Argentino (1610–2002)*. Buenos Aires, Corregidor.
Mason, Tony. 1995. *Passion of the People? Football in South America*. London: Verso.
Milanesio, Natalia. 2010. Peronists and Cabecitas. In *The New Cultural History of Peronism: Power and Identity in Mid-Twentieth-Century Argentina*, ed. Matthew B. Karush and Oscar Chamosa, 53–84. Durham, NC: Duke University Press.

Molinari, Alejandro, and Roberto L. Martínez. 2013. *El Fútbol. La conquista popular de una pasión argentina*. Avellaneda: Editorial de la Cultura Urbana.

Montenari, Enrico. 2018. '*¡Hoy no hay fútbol!*' La huelga de futbolistas de 1948 de la prensa Peronista. *Revista Historia Autónoma* 12: 91–204.

Munck, Ronaldo, Ricardo Falcón, and Bernardo Galitelli. 1987. *Argentina, from Anarchism to Peronism*. London: Zed Press.

Pandolfi, Claudia, and Rolando Rivello. 2015. *Futbolistas Argentinos Agremiados 1944–2015: La Lucha Continúa*. Buenos Aires: Ediciones al arco.

Poggi, Carlos, ed. 2009. *Glorias Eternas: 1ra Entrega 1919–1948*, Buenos Aires: Atlántida.

Racines, Rafael Jaramillo. 2011. El Fútbol de El Dorado "El Punto de Inflexion que Marcó la Rápida Evolución del Amateurismo al Profesionalismo". Revista da Asociación Latinoamericano de Estudios Socioculturales del Deporte. Curitiba. v.1. September: 114–120.

Ramos Ruiz, Armando. 1974. *Nuestra fútbol. Grandeza y decadencia*. Buenos Aires: L V Producciones.

Rein, Ranaan. 1998. 'El Primer Deportista': The Political Use and Abuse of Sport in Peronist Argentina. *The International Journal of the History of Sport* 15 (2): 54–76.

Sáenz Quesada, María. 2012. *La Argentina. Historia del País y de su Gente*. Buenos Aires: Editorial Sudamericana.

Scher, Ariel. 1996. *La patria deportista*. Buenos Aires. Planeta.

Scher, Ariel, and Guillermo Blanco, Jorge Búsico. 2010. *Deporte Nacional*. Buenos Aires, Emecé.

Smith, William C. 1989. *Authoritarianism and the Crisis of the Argentine Political Economy*. Stanford: Stanford University Press.

Tischler, Steven. 1981. *Footballers & Businessmen: The Origins of Professional Soccer in England*. New York: Holmes & Meier Publishers Inc.

CHAPTER 6

The Age of Social and Footballing Revolution 1959–1976

During the 1960s and 1970s, Argentina underwent huge political and cultural societal change, as sectors such as the young, women and those living in the interior found their voices in challenging the status quo. Between 1959 and 1973, the military exercised power both explicitly and implicitly, seeking to exclude what it perceived to be a potentially revolutionary working class by banning its representative Peronist movement from political participation. This disconnect between those in power and the governed was highlighted by Argentine writers in the mid-1960s. In 1964, Juan José Srebeli wrote *Buenos Aires, vida cotidiana y alienación* ('Buenos Aires, daily life and alienation'), whilst in 1966 Arturo Jauretche's *El medio pelo en la sociedad argentina* ('The second rate in Argentina') and *Los que mandar* ('Those that give orders') by José Luis de Imoz, both reinforced the discourse of a broken Argentine society.[1] Culturally, football was also immersed in this tumult. In 1977, the sports journalist Osvaldo Ardizzone observed that, 'We exceed ourselves in revolutions.'[2] He was writing about the constant changes in the styles of play within Argentine football since 1958, and the need to find consensus for

---

[1] Sáenz Quesada (2012, 630).
[2] *Goles*, 14 June 1977.

a settled, unified approach, but his words could easily have also been a metaphor for Argentina's polity, forming the theme of this chapter.

The 'Disaster of Sweden' also highlighted an issue that severely impacted Argentina in the second half of the twentieth century, professional emigration or 'brain drain.' From a nation built on mass immigration from Europe, Argentina instead became a country of net emigration from the 1960s onwards due to economic and political instability and better opportunities available elsewhere in the 'developed' world. This chapter analyses the effect this phenomenon had on assessments of national identity in Argentina through the lens of player migration and national team selection policy. Whilst Lanfranchi and Taylor have studied the economic dimension of this period of migration, focusing on its impact on receiving countries, this chapter builds on their work to develop a more specific understanding of perceptions of identity of those going to play abroad from within Argentina.[3]

Through the case study of Estudiantes de Plata's meteoric rise from relegation candidates to arguably the best club side in the world, this chapter demonstrates how through football, Argentine youth was integrated into the discourse surrounding national identity during this turbulent period. Whilst this journey has interested scholars, especially Alabarces, in relation to changes in playing style and the link to the political situation of the time, this chapter goes further, making wider societal connections and focusing specifically on the relationship between football and the emergence of a discernible, radicalised youth culture in Argentina in the 1960s, which broke with existing moral and value systems.[4]

This chapter also revisits the role of the interior, this time in contributing to constructions of Argentine identity during the 1960s and 1970s. Using the case studies of the introduction of the Campeonato Nacional in 1967, and the selection policies of Argentina coach, César Luis Menotti, in the lead-up to the 1978 World Cup, it probes the role that football played in these constructions.

---

[3] Lanfranchi and Taylor (2001, 96–100).
[4] Alabarces (2007, 81–107).

Revolutions: The Battle for Argentina's Footballing Identity

The democratic restoration signalled by Arturo Frondizi's election as president in 1958 briefly saw Argentine society come together after the divisions of Perón's second presidency (1952–1955), and the 'Liberating Revolution' which ousted Perón. Reconciliation with disenfranchised Peronists and a nationalist economic policy of 'developmentalism' based on import substitution, and an export economy geared towards industrial production rather than agricultural products were at the root of such optimism. By 1962, a lack of investment meant that Frondizi was forced to abandon his nationalist credentials and encourage foreign companies to develop Argentina's oil and natural gas resources, attracting political and public opposition. As at the turn of the twentieth century, Argentina again had to sacrifice its economic independence to develop its own resources.

Similarly, Argentina's calamitous first-round exit from the 1958 World Cup prompted a fundamental rethink of how Argentine football should be played as it underwent an identity crisis. It was apparent during a lengthy tour in 1961 against some of the most powerful teams in Europe that the national team had not learned lessons from the 'Disaster of Sweden,' with the 4–1 defeat to Italy in Florence being particularly sobering. As Panzeri wrote in *El Gráfico*, 'We came to Europe "to know where we are." We came back very much with the tail between the legs.' He considered an opening victory against Portugal as counterproductive, marking a return to the pre-1958 hubristic attitude of 'we are the best,' 'we have to win' and 'we cannot lose.' Panzeri concluded that lessons from the tour included the need to subjugate the individual to the collective and not vice versa, claiming, 'We don't have teamwork, we have inspired individuals. Some always inspired. But for himself. He does not adjust for his team-mate when the adversary annuls his game.'[5]

This latest failure provoked further discussion within Argentina about the future direction of its football, just as debates were taking place over the effectiveness of foreign influence in the economy. Policies oscillated according to the performance of the economy and the Argentine national team over the next twenty years, as moves to 'modernise' saw a wholesale appropriation of European-style athleticism compete with Argentine football's own traditions of spontaneity. The most deeply ingrained imported

[5] *El Gráfico*, 12 July 1961, 65.

innovations originated from Italy, where a greater emphasis on defensive organisation was at the core of the nation's football. That Italy should be the model for Argentine football's attempt to regain global relevance is curious, given there were more compelling examples of 'modern' football to aspire to, such as that practised in Eastern Europe, particularly the Soviet Union, and closer to home in Brazil, where athletic conditioning was combined with the traditional improvisation of *jogo bonito* ('beautiful play'). Yet the footballing cultural interchange between the two countries since the 1920s, firstly with Argentine players going to play in Italy, and more recently with the return of Argentine coaches inculcated with tactical ideals from Italy, proved extremely powerful.[6]

Central to this modernising process was Jorge Lorenzo, a coaching icon in Argentina during the 1960s and 1970s, who steadfastly pursued a pragmatic approach to football, becoming an ideological counterpoint to those like César Luis Menotti who defended notions of *la nuestra*. Lorenzo spent five years playing for Sampdoria in Italy between 1947 and 1952, before moving to Spain in 1958 to cut his coaching teeth with RCD Mallorca. After returning to Argentina in 1961, he took over at San Lorenzo before coaching the national team at the 1962 World Cup in Chile, where according to *El Gráfico* expectations of success were not high. The magazine claimed that the team was, 'Badly led. Confounded and wasted in the attempt to be "modern" and "practical".'[7] *El Gráfico*'s doubts were validated as Argentina again made an ignominious first-round exit, after a tedious 0–0 draw with Hungary when they needed a win to progress to the quarter-final. Journalist Ernesto Lazzatti blamed failure on attempts to 'evolve' Argentine football through a 'system assimilated from regions of Europe that play football badly' implemented by 'imported Argentines' like Lorenzo, which was 'lacking in technique, in style, in the personality that characterises us.' In short, it was, 'Football without ambition.'[8] Lazzatti's opinion was well-founded. Italy had not even qualified for the 1958 World Cup and failed to make it past the first round in both 1962 and 1966. Just as attempts to develop Argentina's

---

[6] *El Gráfico*, 20 June 1962, 48.
[7] *El Gráfico*, 1 June 1962, 108–112.
[8] *El Gráfico*, 20 June 1962, 48.

national resources with foreign assistance were unpopular with the Argentine public, so was the progression of Argentine football with foreign ideas.

Pablo Alabarces suggests that the Argentine-born coach, Helenio Herrera was also paradigmatic in this process through his implementation of the *catenaccio* defensive system when in charge of Internazionale during the 1960s, but in reality Herrera's influence on Argentine football was marginal at best, never having played or coached in the country and with little evidence that he was influential to the ideas of coaches like Manuel Giudice and Osvaldo Zubeldia who brought international success to Argentine clubs during this period.[9]

According to Armando Renganeschi—who achieved success as a coach in Brazil with São Paulo—in a 1963 interview with *El Gráfico*, the 1958 debacle was due to the unhealthy clinging to national traits for the sake of it and not absorbing developments in the game elsewhere 'because of a poorly understood nationalism.' He considered that the complete *volte-face* that came immediately afterwards in trying to imitate the Brazilians and Europeans was equally as damaging, in that Argentine football forgot everything it knew, including 'those things we knew how to do well.' In the 1962 World Cup, Renganeschi felt that Argentina's blind copying of their great rivals whilst improving elements such as tactical organisation and physicality, meant that they jettisoned *criollo* virtues like 'precision,' 'skill' and 'manipulation' of the ball. Summing up, he argued, 'We don't reject the good that has come to us from outside. But we must return to being the creators that we have always supposed ourselves to be.'[10] Panzeri considered this transformation nothing short of a modern 'Industrial Revolution' applied to football. Amongst the cultural changes this affected was 'the substitution of the improvised' by 'systemised obedience and the tedium of the predictable' as well as the replacement of the naturally talented idol, by the star 'invented' by those in the press and in television representing the 'industrialisation of the spectacle.'[11]

This changing narrative was reflected in the footballing press as a generational change occurred, especially in the pages of *El Gráfico* as it tried to stay relevant. Traditionalist journalists such as Panzeri, who

---

[9] Alabarces (2007, 82–87).

[10] *El Gráfico*, 3 April 1963, 36–37.

[11] Panzeri (2011, 60–61).

left the magazine in 1962, made way for younger modernisers like Juan Carlos Pasquato, writing under the pen-name 'Juvenal.' Writing of the challenges facing Argentine football after Barcelona's 1963 tour to the country, Juvenal argued the need to dispense with 'this ceremonial football' that was 'boring' and 'slow in ideas,' as it was, 'not in condition to confront dynamic football … that is played in other parts of the world.'[12]

By 1964, modernisation was bearing fruit under new coach, José María Minella, when Argentina played in the Nations' Cup in Brazil, held to celebrate the fiftieth anniversary of the host confederation. *El Gráfico* wrote approvingly of the newly calculating, scientific approach that helped Argentina to obtain the draw against England in their final game that was sufficient to win them the trophy, claiming that: 'Everything was the cold examination of a situation … Against England they worked for this goal: to leave as champions.'[13]

Argentine clubs replicated this success, with Independiente winning the continental Copa Libertadores in 1964 and 1965, and their Avellaneda neighbours, Racing Club, lifting the trophy in 1967. For Juvenal, these were important benchmarks for Argentine identity. Lauding Independiente's 1964 triumph, he wrote, 'Independiente is how Argentine football should be. All of Argentine football. As an expression of strength, vitality, optimism, with a desire to do, and capacity to achieve. Our play can be reasoned, and precise, without losing strength, rhythm, and aggression.'[14] For journalist Horacio de Dios, Independiente's victory had wider lessons in application and focus, showing that, 'Argentines are capable of doing something important: even organising the World Cup.'[15] After Racing's 1967 victory, Juvenal opined, 'The Copa Libertadores has returned to Argentina … We take this Racing as flag-bearer of a footballing revolution … their dynamism together with frantic pace brought us two convincing demonstrations of footballing character in 100 hours.'[16] Central to Racing's victory was the performance of Humberto Maschio, recently returned to Argentina after a near decade playing in

---

[12] *El Gráfico*, 17 July 1963, 28–30.
[13] *El Gráfico*, 10 June 1964.
[14] *Sport*, August 1964, 6–8.
[15] Ibid, 6–8.
[16] *El Gráfico*, 5 September 1967, 34–37.

Italy, who according to Juvenal represented the fusion of the two footballing traditions to a successful end, 'He played with the class and conceptual richness learned in the *potreros* of the south [of Buenos Aires] and at the same time with the professional seriousness and the spirit of practice assimilated in his years in Italy.[17] Physical and mental courage combined with effort as well as skill were what both the country and Argentine football needed to thrive.

'Animals'

By the mid-1960s however, these virtues became corrupted, as Argentina became internationally renowned in the foreign press for brutality, both in the political arena and on the football pitch, as cold calculation took on a more sinister, violent tenor. In 1963, the Radical, Arturo Illia became president with just 25.4% of the vote, in an election in which Peronist candidates were once more excluded. With such a weak mandate, his legitimacy was in constant question, opposed by Peronist-supporting unions and the conservative elites, who felt that he failed to pay sufficient heed to their interests. Illia was removed by a military coup in June 1966 and replaced as president by General Juan Carlos Onganía.

Describing itself as the 'Argentine Revolution,' unlike previous military interventions, this coup sought to restructure Argentine society and sweep away the 'corruption' of civilian politics. As in the foundational years of the Argentine Republic, the military perceived themselves to be the moral saviours of the nation rather than just a means for establishing order and guiding a transition back to democracy. Indeed, 'morality' was a central tenet of Onganía's rationale, acting as the justification for state repression against perceived hotbeds of 'moral degeneracy' in Argentina's universities, exemplified by the 'Night of the Long Sticks' on 29 July 1966 in which police attacked students and professors. This climate of violence extended to the football pitch, most visibly with the Argentine team at the 1966 World Cup, and the participation of Estudiantes de La Plata in the Copa Libertadores and Intercontinental Cup between 1968 and 1970. As sociologist Roberto Di Giano notes, a new emphasis on fighting spirit, great effort and sacrifice during the 1960s brought international successes both 'real or imagined' that the government could

---

[17] *El Gráfico*, 8 May 1973, 42.

link itself to and seek to translate to Argentine society.[18] Even before Argentina met England in their iconic World Cup quarter-final in 1966, there was discomfort in the English press about the change in Argentina's footballing identity, foreshadowing Anglo-Argentine clashes to come, with Bob Ferrier writing in *The Observer*, 'the system and philosophy used by the Argentine team here is totally divorced from anything in their domestic game and is a complete denial of all their history and tradition in football. Argentine fans who saw the win over Switzerland were delighted with the result, bewildered by the play.'[19] Cynicism was actively encouraged by journalists in the Argentine press, recalling recourse to *viveza criolla* ('native cunning') in the origins of *la nuestra*. *Clarín* published an article ahead of the tournament which suggested that 'cynicism and simulation cannot be forgotten in the tactical process of football,' as well as offering advice on 'making games cold' (slowing the pace of the game down to disrupt the rhythm of the opposition).[20] The match against England was marred by numerous fouls by both sides and the expulsion of Argentina's captain, Antonio Rattín for 'violence of the tongue' by referee Rudolf Kreitlein for his persistent haranguing. After Geoff Hurst scored the winner with eleven minutes to go, England's manager, Alf Ramsey, uttered the words that would remain in the public imaginary of Argentine football in both countries for the next decade or more. Ramsey said, 'It seemed a pity so much Argentinian talent is wasted. Our best football will come against the right type of opposition—a team who come to play football, and not act as animals.'[21] The fallout from the encounter and Ramsey's comments significantly coloured relations between Argentina and the United Kingdom, especially in relation to the ongoing sovereignty dispute of the Falklands/Malvinas that ended in the 1982 conflict between the two nations.[22]

In Latin America, elimination from the 1966 World Cup and Ramsey's comments were attributed to a wider imperialist Anglo-Saxon conspiracy on the part of the hosts England, and a Stanley Rous-led FIFA, to prevent South American teams prevailing in the competition. In defence of the

---

[18] Di Giano (2010, 78).
[19] *The Observer*, 24 July 1966, 14.
[20] *Clarín*, 13 July 1966.
[21] McKinstry (2006, 311–13).
[22] Dodds (2002, 96–100).

Argentines, journalist Carlos Fontanarrosa pointed to Kreitlein's partial refereeing in terms of over-penalising Argentina compared to the English, especially given that England committed thirty-three fouls in the match against just nineteen by the Argentines.[23] It was against this background that Onganía welcomed the team home as 'moral champions,' whilst *El Gráfico*'s cover proclaimed, 'Bravo Argentines,' considering the team to be 'men of courage' and 'winners even though beaten.'[24] Panzeri subsequently suggested that the designation of 'moral champions' was predetermined by the Argentine football authorities in advance of the tie to cynically deflect attention from potential defeat. He claimed that Alfredo Di Stéfano had spoken to Dr. Vena of the Argentine contingent, who revealed that, 'In the Argentine delegation, they are planning to leave Wembley as martyrs.'[25] It was a view supported by a team member, Roberto Perfumo, who contested, 'Who invented this title of moral champions that they gave us after the World Cup? ... we didn't have faith in ourselves, and we cooled down [the game] to the point that we could not fight for it when we went 1–0 down.'[26] Perfumo was suggesting that the old failing of the Argentine psyche in lacking self-confidence had once more let Argentina down in a World Cup, just as it had done in the final against Uruguay in 1930. Interviewed by *La Razón* two months later as to why Argentina had failed at the 1966 World Cup, River Plate's psychiatrist, Dr. Handlarz had some interesting revelations from his discussions with the club's players. Rationalising why Argentina lost, Handlarz explained that psychologically the team was focused solely on not losing and lacked the motivation to win.[27]

Ferrier's concern for Argentine football was vindicated in the years following the World Cup. As political repression in Argentina took hold, so Argentine club football echoed its use of violence to achieve results in what became known as *antifútbol*. The epithet was first used by the Brazilian press during the 1968 Copa Libertadores final between Estudiantes de La Plata and Palmeiras, won by the Argentine side.[28]

[23] *El Gráfico*, 26 July 1966, 3.
[24] Ibid, 1.
[25] Panzeri (1974, 271).
[26] *La Nación*, 13 September 1967.
[27] *La Razón*, 22 September 1966.
[28] *El Gráfico*, 21 May 1968, 3.

Intercontinental Cup victories by Racing Club de Avellaneda against Celtic in 1967, and by Estudiantes over Manchester United in 1968 vindicated the validity of this approach in the eyes of the Argentine press, as national pride was satisfied with revenge over 'Perfidious Albion,' and Argentine football sat at the pinnacle of the world game. In January 1969, Juvenal wrote in *El Gráfico*, 'Racing organised and delivered the first great revolution ... Estudiantes continued with the liberating campaign, strengthening that first crusade of Racing ... We have eliminated the improvisation. We have improved and evolved those elements that had contributed to our inferiority.'[29] Racing and Estudiantes were posited in militaristic terms as 'defenders' of Argentina. Whilst Alabarces has alluded to this being a revindication of Argentina's independence from Spain, Juvenal's stance can better be interpreted as a victory over the Anglo-Saxon neo-imperialism exercised in Argentina's oilfields, and other sectors of its economy, a crucial narrative of national identity in 1960s Argentina.[30]

If Estudiantes' win over Manchester United marked the apex of modernisation in Argentine football, Argentina's failure to qualify for the 1970 World Cup—the first time they had failed to so—coupled with revulsion at the violence meted out by Estudiantes when surrendering their Intercontinental title to AC Milan in 1969, proved its nadir was not long in following. Racing Club and Argentina defender, Perfumo, reflected the feelings of players at this juncture when he claimed, 'The Argentine player has lost all joy in playing football. Moreover, those who join the national team know their fate to be only one thing: to be made a fool of.'[31] If players, as football's key protagonists were disillusioned, and *antifútbol* had exhausted itself in achieving sporting success, then it was only a matter of time before debates about the best way to play were reawakened. In its September 1969 post-mortem, *El Gráfico* was explicit in what had gone wrong in trying to erase the memory of the 'Disaster of Sweden' with a defensive football based on a fear of losing, 'The desire to overcome our deficit of speed and physical prowess in the face of the Europeans induced us to indiscriminate imitation, to the detriment of skill and intelligence ... with a mental scheme of fear, we have arrived where

---

[29] *El Gráfico* 7 January 1969, 30.
[30] Alabarces (2007, 95–98).
[31] Cited in Campomar (2014, 317–319).

we are today.'³² References to fun and enjoyment, staple elements of *la nuestra*, represented wider debates in Argentine society, exemplified by the flourishing artistic vanguard of the Instituto di Tella under the directorship of Enrique Obeiza, which stood in stark contrast to the repressive and somewhat joyless 'Argentine Revolution' of Onganía and his military successors, Roberto Levingston (1970–1971) and Alejandro Lanusse (1971–1973), which lost impetus in the face of civil disobedience and guerrilla activity. The military withdrew from power in 1973, giving way to the restoration of democracy and the return of the man whose absence had contributed so much to the polarisation of Argentine society: Juan Perón.

THE RENAISSANCE OF LA NUESTRA

Whilst Estudiantes were besmirching Argentina's image abroad, there were signs domestically that a change of attitude was in the air. Chacarita Juniors' unheralded victory in the 1969 Campeonato Metropolitano indicated something of a renaissance for *la nuestra*. Described by *El Gráfico* as a 'moral bath for all football,' Chacarita's victory was juxtaposed against Argentina's travails in qualification for the 1970 World Cup, with Juvenal observing that, 'the victory of Chacarita symbolises the validity of the values that made Argentina great, just when those values seem to have been forgotten by many of our teams, our players and our coaches.'³³ Brazil's victory at the 1970 World Cup, playing a thrilling brand of *futebol arte* which overcame the Fordist football of Europe reinforced debate within Argentina about recovering its own football traditions. Modifying his own modernist discourse, Juvenal wrote in June 1970, 'Mexico presented us with a tournament that served to rescue the most beautiful and immutable values of the world …We send you an embrace Pelé. Argentines, we must revive ourselves under the spell of this example.'³⁴

Huracán's 1973 Campeonato Metropolitano victory consolidated this revival of tradition, capturing the zeitgeist of the period, with Fontanarrosa eulogising in *El Gráfico* that, 'The triumph of Huracán makes us happy through the way in which they achieved it and through the

---

³² *El Gráfico*, 2 September 1969, 3.
³³ *El Gráfico*, 8 July 69, 3–7.
³⁴ *El Gráfico*, 23 June 1970, 112–115.

example that they leave ... to play with happiness.'[35] Coached by the young, urbane and politically savvy César Luis Menotti, Huracán played with a freedom that not only reflected traditional notions of *la nuestra*, but the democratic opening that saw the Peronists return to power after an eighteen-year interregnum. Menotti's pronouncements about football in this period carried political overtones. When asked what Argentine football lacked, the Huracán coach replied, 'The same as Argentine youth in general: to free itself of some insecurities about the future. Clearly that is linked to what is offered by club directors or those who lead the country,' the inference being that an elected Peronist government would be beneficial for the country. He was equally adroit in his answer about how he maintained discipline in his team, replying, 'I am not much convinced by this "imposing discipline" in the squad. It sounds to me like a military regime and football is another thing ... the thing that concerns me is to count on people who are honest and aren't quiet through fear,' suggesting a distaste for dictatorships more broadly.[36]

Despite the euphoria surrounding Huracán's victory, Juvenal reminded *El Gráfico*'s readers of the esoteric nature of *la nuestra*. Asking rhetorically whether *la nuestra* existed, he argued that it did so, as 'an expression of desires.' Using Menotti's side as an example, he noted that their play was not entirely based on carefree attacking 'fantasy' football: 'In the Huracán of Menotti, the subtlety of Babington and the skill of Houseman are important but the generosity of Brindisi in always going to the front, to put his heart and lungs at the service of the team was vital.'[37]

After Argentina again disappointed at the 1974 World Cup, rendered obsolete for the second time in a generation by the 'Total Football' of Johan Cruyff's Holland in West Germany, Menotti was the stand-out candidate to replace Vladislao Cap as coach of the national team. Menotti immediately caught the popular imagination of Argentine football fans by promising to restore *la nuestra* to the national team. Placing his work in the wider context of Argentine football's historical traditions, Menotti outlined his plans to win the 1978 World Cup, to be held in Argentina, in a five-point manifesto published in *El Gráfico* in August 1975. The first four points referred to the need to combine technique and mental agility

[35] *El Gráfico*, 18 September 1973, 67.
[36] *El Gráfico*, 1 May 1973, 24–26.
[37] *El Gráfico*, 8 May 1973, 40–43.

to athleticism and tactical awareness, but it was the fifth that said much about Menotti's philosophy. He said, 'It is important to have a sense of belonging to a footballing tradition with great heroes.'[38] Menotti felt it incumbent on his team to demonstrate that there was a continuum in Argentine football, as in Argentine history more broadly, in which it was necessary to pass on national traditions from one generation to the next 'because it is definitively a way of life.'[39] He challenged his players to express their skills and earn their place in the Argentine footballing pantheon alongside the likes of Pedro Calomino, José Manuel Moreno and Omar Sívori, establishing what Vic Duke and Liz Crolley describe as 'an affinity with dead generations.'[40] For Menotti, restoring the identity of Argentine football mattered as much as winning matches, as he later wrote in 1980, 'I thought that was the secret: we had lost our identity: we lived running behind the "last word" in football, trying to catch the last system or recipe that lay behind the last triumph and this way, we forgot what our idiosyncrasy was.'[41]

The difficulties of achieving the balance sought by Menotti were highlighted in a match against reigning world champions West Germany in July 1977, one of a series of seven matches against European opposition designed to replicate the demands of tournament football. Menotti argued with the German coach Helmut Schön in the post-match press conference about the perceived shortcomings of Argentina's footballing style, and European superiority to it. Schön observed that Argentina would need to 'adapt themselves to European football to be at the same level' and that Di Stéfano was the model Argentine player to aspire to because in addition to his Argentine attributes of 'mentality, impetuousness and dynamism,' he adapted to European football. In reply, Menotti asserted that to do so he would need to bring in 'eleven Germans,' arguing, 'Each country has its own characteristics, not only in football, but also as a way of life … Argentina must play like Argentina and achieve a constant dynamism.'[42]

---

[38] *El Gráfico*, 1 August 1975, 2.
[39] Menotti (1986, 18).
[40] Duke and Crolley (2014, 4–5).
[41] Menotti (1980, 15).
[42] Cited in Bauso (2018, 146).

By entering this essentialist discourse, Menotti was echoing the Borocotian ideals of *la nuestra* of the 1920s and 1930s, becoming its self-appointed curator. By invoking Di Stéfano, who had achieved unparalleled success with Real Madrid, Schön was highlighting how powerful the fusion between Argentine spontaneity and European professionalism and athleticism could potentially be. However, there was a perception in the press that Menotti's team were no different to Argentine sides of the previous two decades, as players fought—sometimes literally—to gain their World Cup place. Vicente Pernía's dismissal for punching Scotland's Willie Johnston in the face in June 1977 exemplified the problem, with *El Gráfico* headlining, 'This No! The expulsion of Pernía. The attitude that injures our image. The aggression that everyone reproves,' before going on to editorialise that the pressures of the series were proving counterproductive in terms of the attitudes of the players, noting, 'the philosophy of Menotti has suffered a rude contrast in the soul of his players. Because they try to stay in the national team at any price. If they are not capable of playing well, they revert to violence and thuggery.'[43]

In Menotti's 1977 winter of discontent, Argentina's footballing identity stood at a critical juncture. With sections of the press and the footballing public concerned about the nation's ability to win the upcoming World Cup, some called for Menotti's replacement by Jorge Lorenzo, especially the fans on the terraces of the Bombonera who chanted his name. As *Goles* noted when the Argentine national team played Boca in a Summer tournament in early 1977, 'The game between Boca and Argentina has generated a lot of interest. It is because Menotti and Lorenzo are the axes of a controversy that thrives on a depressed football.'[44] Since 1966, Lorenzo had rehabilitated his reputation with success at San Lorenzo, Atlético de Madrid, Colón de Santa Fe and most recently Boca Juniors, with whom he won the Copa Libertadores in 1977. Lorenzo remained unapologetically pragmatic, arguing, 'If you win you are the king, but if not, you are hated by everyone … they brought me to Boca to finish as champion.'[45]

The AFA kept faith with Menotti, but contemporary press coverage indicates what the effect would have been had he been replaced by

---

[43] *El Gráfico*, 21 July 1977, 1–3.
[44] *Goles*, 22 February 1977.
[45] Cited in Caparrós (2004, 181).

Lorenzo. Within a month of Argentina winning the 1978 World Cup, Lorenzo's Boca team, including six players discarded from the national team by Menotti, beat Borussia Mönchengladbach 3–0 in West Germany to win the Intercontinental Cup. *El Gráfico* wrote, 'Just as we criticise Boca Juniors for failing to provide a spectacle in its own stadium, today for the same reasons of objectivity and fair play we must congratulate Boca. We congratulate them as an Argentine team that has won abroad ... Boca were worthy in all senses: as "ambassador" and as footballing expression of the world champion country.'[46] Had Lorenzo been in charge for the World Cup and won it using his pragmatic style, his team would likely have been fêted in the same way as Menotti's.

The real test of whether Menotti's team reproduced *la nuestra* came with the tournament itself. To foreign observers, there was clearly a move away from the pragmatic style of the previous twenty years. Bobby Charlton—an opponent of Argentina in the 1962 and 1966 World Cups, and Estudiantes in 1968—enthused after Argentina's opening victory against Hungary, 'This was the best performance by an Argentine team that I have seen in my life ... If the Argentines can maintain the rhythm, the skill, and this determination that they have shown it is very possible that they can end up with the cup.'[47] Within Argentina, a series of nervy first-round performances against Hungary, France and Italy aroused doubts about whether Menotti could complete his mission. Although already qualified for the next round, a 1–0 defeat to Italy did little to inspire confidence that Argentina would attain the ultimate tournament triumph, let alone in the style of *la nuestra*. *El Gráfico* was underwhelmed, 'It seems that in the face of the demands of the World Cup, the national team has forgotten the fundamentals in which its play was supported during the preparatory process. For this, more than asking for a change, we ask for a return to the fountain.'[48]

It was not until the second round that Argentina began to display anything like the flowing football promised by Menotti, as mercurial forward, Mario Kempes, finally found form with two goals against Poland. A 0–0 draw against Brazil in the next game, in which seventeen fouls were committed by both sides in the opening ten minutes brought back

[46] *El Gráfico*, 8 August 1978, 3.
[47] *El Gráfico*, 6 June 1978, 89.
[48] *El Gráfico*, 13 June 1978.

notions of the 'animals' trope and a reversion to *antifútbol*. A sweeping 6–0 victory over Peru, which Colin Malam likened to the 'Ride of the Valkyrie' marked the apotheosis of Menotti's vision of *la nuestra*.[49] After victory in the final against the Netherlands, the Argentine press had completely changed their tune from the first round. *La Prensa* claimed, 'It was a triumph of those that dare, of the valiant, of the bold. They leave behind the dark negative tactics, the egoists expounding from the rear-guard [Lorenzo], the fearful closed systems, without air, without soul.'[50] For its part, *Clarín* editorialised, 'Argentine football is the best in the world ... But the success of Menotti is bigger. His style won.'[51]

According to Menotti, 'we had done justice to the old and beloved Argentine football. That which had been made great by Adolfo Pedernera, "Charro" Moreno, Antonio Sastre and so many others. We had been loyal to this glorious past and should be proud.'[52] The battle for Argentine football's soul between Lorenzo and Menotti had been decided decisively in Menotti's favour.

Vendepatrias: Migration and National Identity in Argentina

In the event, Argentina won the 1978 World Cup with just one overseas based player in its squad, Mario Kempes, but over the previous two decades player drain abroad became a serious issue affecting Argentine football. As identified in previous chapters, the emigration of Argentine footballing talent was a recurring theme throughout the twentieth century, although there were specific factors that led to previous exoduses. The restrictive import practices of the 1920s and 1930s which made dual national *rimpatriati* players from Argentina valuable commodities for Italian clubs, and the coinciding of an Argentine players' strike in 1949 with the formation of a rebel league in Colombia, were self-contained situations. What set the departure of the *trio de la muerte* of Omar Sívori, Antonio Angelillo and Humberto Maschio apart after helping Argentina to the 1957 South American Championship, was that it was the beginning

---

[49] Malam (1978, 96–107).
[50] *La Prensa*, 26 June 1978.
[51] *Clarín*, 26 June 1978.
[52] *El Gráfico*, 3 October 1989, 128.

of a broader, ongoing process of economic globalisation and liberalisation that not only affected the strength of domestic Argentine football, but also raised questions about the perceived patriotism of those who left Argentina. Investigated in a 1961 article entitled 'Is this the way?' *El Gráfico* placed the Argentine situation in the wider global context, showing that countries such as Brazil and Britain were equally affected by the emigration of football talent. The magazine concluded that government intervention was required to maintain the strength of Argentine sport as a 'vehicle for social happiness.'[53] In reality, there was nothing a democratic Argentine state in a state of economic precariousness could do to assist.

These debates were most persistent every four years when press attention was concentrated on selection of the Argentine World Cup squad. When it was suggested in the press that Sívori should play for Argentina at the 1966 World Cup despite still playing in Italy for Napoli, *El Gráfico* strongly supported the idea whilst berating nativist opposition to it as a 'grave error,' arguing, 'It is closing the eyes to a reality as big as the triumph of Sívori in Europe, where he won with his football from the *potrero*.'[54]

Sívori was not selected for the trip to England, and in succeeding years Argentina haemorrhaged talented players such as Carlos Bianchi, Roberto Perfumo and Rafael Albrecht at a concerning rate as the country's economic situation militated against Argentine clubs' ability to match salaries on offer in Europe, Brazil and Mexico. By the time Argentina next qualified for the World Cup in 1974, the dispersal of many of their best players around the world was reflected by a major policy reversal, as Vladislao Cap's squad included seven foreign-based players. The late arrival of the Atlético de Madrid pair of Ramón Heredia and Rubén Ayala, who only joined days before the competition after playing for Atlético in the European Cup final, made a mockery of integrating them into a functioning team situation.[55]

The lessons from 1974 were not lost on Cap's successor, Menotti. *El Gráfico* summed up the task facing Menotti in terms of restoring a sense of identity to the national team, editorialising, 'We have the most

[53] *El Gráfico*, 3 May 1961, 42–43.
[54] *El Gráfico*, 10 May 1966, 3.
[55] *The Guardian*, 21 May 1974, 31.

orphaned team in the world.'[56] Menotti's attempt to form a coherent team from the best Argentine talent available was a recurring matter of controversy over the next four years. Argentina's second scheduled European tour in 1976 was aborted as the perennial issue of losing players to European clubs returned to the fore, with *Goles* headlining, 'The Dollars against Argentina: The National Team Disintegrates.'[57] Of the 26 players selected for the tour, eight—Mario Kempes, Marcelo Trobbiani, Héctor Scotta, Padino, Norberto Alonso, Miguel Brindisi, Oscar Ortiz and Jorge Valdano—were playing in Europe the following season, earning up to ten times their existing salaries.

Before the AFA called off the tour, *El Gráfico* made some telling interpretations about the emigration of Argentina's footballing talent and its effect on national identity. Anticipating the coming exodus, the magazine asked, 'Why are we making the tour to Europe? So that the players can gain experience? Or to use it as a shop window to be able to sell them?' Acknowledging the economic reasons for the players to go, it recognised, 'We know it is mean to deny the departure of a youth of twenty-two to earn in a month that here he is not going to earn in a year. But the coach must do it because something as important as the World Cup [in Argentina] is in play.'[58] The interpretation was that these young men should subjugate their personal financial situation to a greater patriotic project, despite the risk that they may not make the final squad and that their sacrifice could be for nothing. The article concluded by making it clear that Argentina must be represented by its best players, preparing at home, a complete *volte face* from when the magazine advocated the recall of Sívori from Italy ten years earlier. Again, the implication, expressed subtly if not explicitly, was that those going abroad or who spent the most sporting and economically productive years of their careers there, were *vendepatrias* (literally 'nation sellers'). Sections of the press considered these players as unpatriotic, selling their nationhood in order to profit financially, rather than staying and helping Argentina in the great national task of winning the World Cup on home soil. Betraying his carefully cultivated libertarian reputation, Menotti persuaded the AFA to draw up a list of players deemed to be 'untransferable' to foreign clubs until after

---

[56] *El Gráfico*, 20 November 1974, 3.
[57] *Goles*, 6 April 1976, 1.
[58] *El Gráfico*, 17 August 1976, 3.

the World Cup which came into force in February 1977. By doing so, Menotti denied young men the opportunity to earn good wages for their families in a climate of high inflation and a collapsing Argentine economy, an extension of the restriction of civil rights enforced by the military *junta* on society more widely. Not only that, but Menotti was denying players the opportunities he took himself in 1967 when going to the United States to play for New York Generals and then Santos in Brazil in 1969.

In 1977, as the Argentine team struggled in their World Cup preparations, there was a popular campaign to bring back star players such as Mario Kempes, Enrique Wolff, Carlos Bianchi and Osvaldo Piazza from abroad. As *Goles* reminded its readers of the 1974 experience in the World Cup held in West Germany, 'The so-called repatriation served very little at that time.'[59] In that campaign, aside from the logistical problems of integrating players from far and wide in a short period, there was also jealousy from those who saw their places usurped at the last minute by players returning from abroad, especially when they had 'served their country' by ensuring Argentina's World Cup qualification in the first place. As Osvaldo Piazza argued when it was reported that Menotti would call him back from St. Etienne for the competition, 'I haven't come to rob the place of anyone. I am going to win it by working. I don't want what happened in 1974 to happen to Kempes and myself, with those coming from abroad being received like parasites.'[60]

The repatriation of players from abroad was given as one reason for the unexpected resignation of Argentina's captain, Jorge Carrascosa in January 1978. According to Carrascosa's teammate, Leopoldo Luque, it was a principled decision based on the decision to bring Mario Kempes back from Spain to re-join the World Cup squad, having already told the squad that he would resign from the team if anyone was brought into the squad who was playing abroad.[61] Menotti made his feelings clear on the issue of repatriating players for the national cause, saying in a 1977 interview, 'If I cannot get the players I need here [in Argentina], I will go to the players performing abroad.'[62] Despite planning to call up three foreign-based players—Enrique Wolff, Osvaldo Piazza and Mario

---

[59] *Goles*, 5 July 1977.
[60] *Somos*, 4 April 1978.
[61] Bauso (2018, 322).
[62] *El Gráfico*, 15 February 1977, 61–64.

Kempes—ultimately only Kempes made the World Cup squad after the AFA failed to secure Wolff's early release from Real Madrid and Piazza had to return to France after his wife was involved in a serious car accident. Even then it cost the AFA US$25,000 to ensure Kempes' release from Valencia to join the squad before the end of the Spanish season.[63] Although as an organisation, the AFA was all but bankrupt, the military regime was happy to underwrite the sum as a statement of their intent that Argentina be represented in the best way possible at the World Cup, including on the pitch. This counters Lanfranchi and Taylor's argument that 'the composition of the national squad reflected the autarkic views of the regime.'[64] As Admiral Lacoste, a key figure in organising the tournament claimed in November 1977, 'Argentina must face the World Cup with the best players … Politically for the country it is convenient that there is a great footballing performance. The players that the coach considers necessary must come.'[65]

Whether to select foreign-based players for the national team was just one side of the debate relating to national identity and footballers migrating from Argentina. The other side was the selection of Argentine-born players by other nations on the strength of dual nationality or naturalisation through residency, and the potential conflicts that could arise from their playing against the country of birth. Whilst erstwhile Argentine internationals, Humberto Maschio and Omar Sívori represented Italy, Néstor Combin played for France and Alfredo Di Stéfano had been selected for the Spanish squad at the 1962 World Cup, the vagaries of the draw ensured that none were compelled to play against their native country. Combin did appear against Argentine opposition in the shape of Estudiantes in the 1969 Intercontinental Cup final whilst playing for AC Milan. After leaving Argentina as a teenager, Combin joined Lyon thanks to his dual French ancestry, before progressing his career at Milan, with whom he won the European Cup. Whilst in France, Combin took French nationality and fulfilled his civic duty by completing his military service. Combin's reception was a study in revenge for those who had supposedly sold out their country. Having boasted before the game to opponent, Ramón Alberto Aguirre Suárez, 'I can earn in one month what you do in

[63] Malam (1978, 14).
[64] Lanfranchi and Taylor (2001, 100).
[65] Cited in Bauso (2018, 305).

two years,' Combin was sought out by the Estudiantes player for violent retribution, breaking the Frenchman's cheekbone. To compound the sense of vengeance, Combin was arrested as he was stretchered from the pitch: his crime, not completing his Argentine national service. Combin returned to Italy without further action being taken.[66]

The price for being a *vendepatria* was the hatred of one's people. Where once the likes of Renato Cesarini were seen as emissaries of *la nuestra* to other lands, or the likes of Sívori had wanted to represent Argentina after joining a foreign club only to be rebuffed by the AFA, for players now to refuse the call of the *patria* and move abroad for money was seen by some Argentine fans as akin to treason.[67]

ESTUDIANTES THE ICONOCLASTS

As in other parts of the western world, debates over national identity in Argentina during the 1960s cut across not just class and political boundaries but also generational ones. In matters of culture, ideology and dress, Argentine youth became political actors for the first time in response to the lack of democracy and an ambience of repression within Argentina under successive military regimes. Inspired by revolutionary liberation movements in places like Algeria, Cuba and Vietnam, they joined activist groups like the Tucuara, and by the end of the decade the Montoneros.

This political awareness and activism amongst the young were as the product of a better educated society which saw a growing percentage of the working class now attending university. Thanks to Peronist reforms in the 1950s, student numbers multiplied from 81,000 in 1950, to 181,000 in 1960, to 322,000 in 1971, before reaching 620,000, half of whom were women, in 1977. By the end of the 1970s, Argentina had more university students per capita than any other country, and twice as many as the UK.[68] Professional football, like other industries, had players studying in the evenings in addition to their day jobs. In Carlos Bilardo and Raúl Madero, Estudiantes de la Plata had two players who went on to qualify as medical doctors, whilst future national team players Carrascosa and

---

[66] Campomar (2014, 308).
[67] Alabarces (2007, 89–90).
[68] Goebel (2011, 155).

Osvaldo Ardiles studied law at university.[69] Access to higher education also made players more politically aware. Interviewed in 1973, Carrascosa said, 'My objective is to learn, to acquire knowledge. To me it is important to be a protagonist of my time, to take part.'[70] Student and worker-led resistance to the military government of Onganía and his successors coalesced around Peronism, described by Goebel as 'the agent of an emancipatory revolution.'[71] Later in the decade and into the 1970s, political resistance crystallised into the formation of a number of armed guerrilla groups of which two, the Trotskyite Ejercito Revolucionario del Pueblo (ERP), and the Montoneros, gained significant popular support.

In her study of identity construction in Chilean football, Brenda Elsey has argued that youth was thrust into the vanguard of popular culture. Young people were targeted not just politically but as consumers in the wider context of rejuvenating football through commodification, something that also happened with the emergence of Pelé in Brazil.[72] In Argentina, the projection of youth into football took a different form, with Estudiantes at the vanguard. In 1961, Panzeri announced prophetically—in the context of what Estudiantes would achieve—that 'Argentine football can only save itself from decline if it concerns itself with the formation of the player, the mentality of the player.'[73] Whilst clubs had always taken on and developed talented junior players in the hope that they would one day become first team stars, few teams went about it in the systematic, scientific and ultimately successful way that the La Plata club did. During the mid-to-late 1960s, Estudiantes completely transformed their sporting fortunes, winning their first league title, the Metropolitano in 1967, and achieving three consecutive Copa Libertadores triumphs between 1968 and 1970.

In 1962, with Argentina in the depths of recession, the club's hierarchy fundamentally changed its playing structure, focusing exclusively on youth development as the future of the first team, as it sought to trim wage costs by dispensing with the reserve squad. It was calculated that by removing these established professionals, with a wage bill of

[69] *El Gráfico*, 8 August 1967, 11–12.
[70] *El Gráfico*, 10 April 1973, 24–26.
[71] Goebel (2011, 155).
[72] Elsey (2011, 209–212).
[73] *El Gráfico*, 12 July 1961, 65–68.

600,000 pesos (£2,654) per month, Estudiantes could instead accommodate and develop thirty youth players at a combined monthly cost of just 225,000 pesos (£962).[74] Directing the project was youth coach, Miguel Ignomiriello, charged with instilling in these young men an *esprits de corps* and technical knowledge based as Pepe Peña wrote in *Sport*, on the 'philosophy of the Argentine player: their vices, their virtues, their defects, their capacity for integration.' To these virtues were added the latest advances in scientific physiological preparation provided by physical education teacher, Carlos Omar Cancela.[75] In addition to their educational lessons, the scholars trained twice a day from Tuesday to Friday, and from 10am to 12pm on a Saturday. Beyond their footballing abilities, players were also assessed on their behaviour, which if not professional enough, resulted in their being expelled from the programme. The club felt that such maturity, combined with a rigorous training schedule, meant that any of the eighteen-year-old scholars called upon to step up to the first team would immediately be mentally and physically prepared to deal with the demands of professional football.[76]

The returns for Estudiantes were not long in coming. By 1965, several youngsters including Oscar Malbernat, Juan Ramón Verón and Juan Echecopar had been promoted to the first team by the coach Osvaldo Zubeldía. Nicknamed *La tercera que mata*, 'The Killer Juniors,' a number later established themselves as star players or internationals.[77] It was from this point that Estudiantes established themselves as the popular resistance to the traditional hegemony of Argentine football's *grandes* in the second half of the 1960s, reaching the apex of world football. Estudiantes became renowned for exerting psychological pressure on opponents to generate favourable refereeing decisions, pushing the spirit of football's laws to their absolute limits, through 'ungentlemanly conduct.' Their pragmatism led to accusations of Estudiantes practising *antifútbol*, leading Andreas Campomar to assert that the team's play reflected Argentine football's brusque British roots.[78] It can equally be argued that it was instead an interpretation of traditional *viveza criolla* taken to extremes. Reflecting

[74] *Sport*, September 1965.
[75] Ibid.
[76] Ibid.
[77] Ibid.
[78] Campomar (2014, 303–308).

on their performances, *El Gráfico* likened the players to their working-class peers in the factories, 'Estudiantes continue producing points just as they manufacture football: with more mechanism than talent.'[79] Whilst the team did not represent the traditions of Argentine football, *El Gráfico* acknowledged its effectiveness as contemporary icons, 'Their style does not convince, but their campaign is convincing. It is not a squad of "luxury" [players], but instead a good team. With the conviction of a winning group, with the work [ethic] of a modern team and with the conviction of a big club.'[80] The role played by youth in the club's rise to prominence was eulogised by Juvenal as 'the triumph of the new mentality,' one that was served by 'young, strong, disciplined, dynamic, vigorous, spiritually, and physically whole men.'[81]

Alabarces has suggested that these attributes of spiritual and physical fortitude made Estudiantes' players archetypal of the type of young Argentine that Onganía's government was trying to nurture, although he concedes that by 1971, they had come full circle to occupy the place of 'enemy *par excellence*' inviting comparisons with the Montonero armed struggle.[82] By contrast, Estudiantes can instead be interpreted from the outset as a metaphor for the student-led resistance, who with a fresh outlook, used the tools available to them, including violence, to overcome the hegemony of the establishment in the shape of the *grandes* and traditional South American powerhouses from Brazil and Uruguay and create a new order. As Ardizzone wrote after the club won their second Copa Libertadores in 1969 against Nacional de Montevideo, 'Estudiantes go out to destroy, to defile, to irritate, to negate the spectacle, to use all the illegal subterfuges of football … I, for my part surrender … If it serves to win it must be good. In all cases, it must be better than that football which lost.'[83] The insinuation was that as in Argentine society more widely, the ends justified the means, and that aesthetically pleasing football had not brought Argentine football such continental hegemony since the bygone days of the 1940s.

---

[79] *El Gráfico*, 3 May 1967, 63.
[80] Ibid, 63.
[81] *El Gráfico*, 20 July 1967, 8.
[82] Alabarces (2007, 95–102).
[83] *El Gráfico*, 27 May 1969, 25–26.

Yet, Estudiantes' monstrous reputation was not entirely deserved, giving a lie to Bayer's assertion that, 'Zubeldía, prepared his players exclusively to win games and not provide spectacle.'[84] They had the capacity to play enterprising, attacking football that at times called to mind some elements of *la nuestra*. As Juvenal noted, 'the super-utilitarian football of Osvaldo Zubeldía at Estudiantes' made room for the exquisite skills of Raúl Madero and the inventive plays of Juan Ramón Verón.'[85] After playing in their renowned pragmatic style for the majority of their successful 1967 Metropolitano campaign, for their last three games, including the final, they switched from type. Juvenal was suitably impressed, highlighting how in their last three games Estudiantes 'achieved the miracle of erasing the image of a team that defended but did not attack,' whilst also admiring the 'sportingly agreeable' nature of their final win over Racing that was a 'convincing demonstration of creative-attacking aptitude.'[86]

Estudiantes were most polemical in their representation of Argentina abroad. Argentine journalists closed ranks in support of the team against attacks from the Brazilian and British press, the significant others against which Argentina's football was projected in the second half of the twentieth century. Despite evidence to the contrary, in May 1968, Fontanarrosa preferred to focus on defending Argentine honour against foreign denigration in *El Gráfico*, claiming that whilst 'their play is more solid, it is not enough to describe this authentic football of mass production and the convincing results that Estudiantes have achieved as *antifútbol*.'[87]

The Intercontinental Cup final against Manchester United in 1968 exemplified this conflict, coming just two years after the clash between England and Argentina which left so much mutual bad blood. If Ramsey's description of the Argentina team as 'animals' in 1966 was provocative, then reaction in the British press to Estudiantes' Intercontinental Cup first leg victory over Manchester United in 1968 left no doubts about how Argentine football was viewed abroad. Comparing the team's aggression in the first leg to the social violence prevalent in Argentina and throughout Latin America at the time, Hugh McIlvanney wrote, 'The

---

[84] Bayer (2016, 111–12).
[85] *El Gráfico*, 8 May 1973, 24–26.
[86] *El Gráfico*, 8 August 1967, 8.
[87] *El Gráfico*, 21 May 1968, 3.

students of Mexico City are fighting the battle as if it were a game, Estudiantes de la Plata approached a game as if it were a battle.'[88] Not that the Argentine press took such a slight passively. *El Gráfico* retorted in anti-imperialist tones, 'The absurdity. The pressure of some Englishmen to transmit a climate of violence before starting to report the game, with an almost infantile fickleness, as if Buenos Aires were virgin jungle or the next territory to be colonised.'[89] After the second leg, Manchester United's manager Matt Busby called for Argentine teams to be banned from international football, 'FIFA should really step in and stop them. If the Argentinians cannot behave, they should not be allowed to compete until they do.'[90] As in 1966, the Argentine press claimed that their compatriots had been unfairly maligned. A picture of José Medina leaving the pitch at Old Trafford sheltering from a barrage of projectiles after being sent off for fighting with George Best was captioned, 'The animals protect themselves from the gentlemen.'[91] Constancio Vigil editorialised in *El Gráfico*, 'We have now reached the limit of our capacity for indignation ... We would prefer to be animals in our simple, open, human, and frank Argentine manner than be gentlemen like them.'[92]

For a brief, twelve-month window Estudiantes, the erstwhile country cousins from provincial Buenos Aires and upstart resistance to the hegemony, were considered by the press as ambassadors at large not just for Argentine football, but also the nation more widely. President Onganía sought to link himself with the triumphs of Estudiantes, asking during a reception for the team after they had won the 1968 Intercontinental Cup against Manchester United, 'What can we do to maintain this team, which is an example to everyone?'[93] Yet, just a year later, he firmly distanced himself from the team as some of its players were jailed in Villa Devoto prison following a violent Intercontinental Cup clash with AC Milan, which saw two visiting players stretchered off. Under pressure from Onganía, the AFA took swift and decisive action, banning goalkeeper Alberto Poletti for life, Ramón Alberto Aguirre Suárez for thirty

---

[88] *The Observer*, 29 September 1968, 18.
[89] *El Gráfico*, 26 September 1968, 29.
[90] *The Guardian*, 28 September 1968, 16.
[91] *El Gráfico*, 22 October 1968, 71.
[92] Ibid, 3.
[93] Ibid, 68–71.

games and Eduardo Manera for twenty matches. Although Estudiantes also won the 1970 Copa Libertadores, it was the excesses committed against Milan which irrevocably lost the team support within Argentina as a beacon of national identity and altered their reputation to that of 'urban guerrillas.' Ahead of the tie, Zubeldía forewarned what was to come, claiming, 'The players of Estudiantes have been living with too much intensity, the obligation of being the saviours of Argentine football after they eliminated us from Mexico.'[94] No longer Onganía's 'moral champions,' those representing Argentina at the highest level, were now cast as depraved, damaging the country's image. As *El Gráfico* wrote two months later in its annual review, 'Television carried to all the world the deformed image of football converted into urban guerrilla warfare.'[95] It was the ultimate expression of football as resistance from Estudiantes the iconoclasts.

Pioneras

If the political wakening of Argentina's youth owed much to some of the more progressive policies of the 1946–1955 Perón presidency, the same could be said of the emancipation of women in Argentine society, with the promulgation of female suffrage in 1947. Indeed, the Peronist regime was keen to associate itself with successful sportswomen, not least the tennis player Mary Terán de Weiss, who won three medals at the 1951 Pan American Games in Buenos Aires.

The greater presence of women in universities and in the workplace began to promote greater female participation in football, something that became noticeable in the late 1960s. Amongst the first to organise were the Cerro Porteño club from the Greater Buenos Aires *barrio* of Aviación, where future World Cup player Teresa Suárez played her first game as 13-year-old in a match between married and unmarried players. Other clubs included San Fernando, Tigre, All Boys and Sarmiento de San Martín.[96] Brenda Elsey and Josh Nadel submit that Argentina's biggest clubs were the main engine of growth for Argentine women's football at the turn of

---

[94] *El Gráfico*, 21 October 1969, 75.

[95] *El Gráfico*, 17 December 1969, 15.

[96] *La Nación*, 6 September 2019; *La Nación*, 18 August 2019; Elsey and Nadel (2019, 10).

the 1970s. Certainly, established men's clubs had women's sides too, but they tended to come from those of a lower profile such as All Boys and Tigre, whilst the prominence of Universitario suggests the importance of university students in this process.[97]

In 1966, women's teams representing Boca Juniors and River Plate travelled across northern Argentina through the provinces of Catamarca, Tucumán, Salta and Jujuy by bus on a tour organised by Juan Doce. The two sides were pictured on the front page of Tucumán newspaper, *La Gaceta* on 15 March under the headline 'Boca Juniors and River Plate will be opponents today in women's football,' although there is little evidence of this being part of wider efforts by either club to establish a regular women's team at this juncture.[98] Doce was later at the centre of an attempt to establish a more enduring women's tour, taking twenty-two female players to take part in exhibition matches throughout the interior and north of Argentina through cities like Tucumán, Santiago del Estero, Córdoba and San Luis which at this point were largely denied top-flight football in the men's game. The women left Buenos Aires on Friday evenings and returned in the early hours of Monday morning to resume their regular jobs.[99] Further evidence that women's football was gaining prominence in Argentina came in 1970 when a tournament involving Universitario, Real Torino, Sporting and Rosario was played at the Independiente stadium and broadcast on TV by Canal 13, achieving very high ratings according to Elsey and Nadel.[100]

An Argentine team appeared at the second women's world football championship in 1971 held in Mexico with sponsorship from the Cinzano drinks company. With no institutional backing from the AFA, it was instead left to the recently founded Argentine Association of Women's Football to arrange the team's participation. Lack of resources meant the team prepared for the tournament playing in training shoes, not being able to afford proper football boots, which they wore for the first time at the tournament itself. The team did receive help in the form of a donation of playing kit by the Unión Tranviarios Automotor (UTA), who also allowed them to practise on the union's recreation pitches.

[97] Ibid, 55–58.
[98] *La Gaceta*, 15 March 1966.
[99] *La Nación*, 6 September 2019.
[100] Pujol (2018); Elsey and Nadel (2019, 55–58).

As a warm-up for the competition, Argentina played a friendly against Mexico—which they won 3–2—at the 50,000-capacity stadium of Nueva Chicago in the Mataderos *barrio* of Buenos Aires, a full-blooded event which saw Argentina's Betty García and Irma Mancilla of Mexico sent off for fighting. The game was a box office success with receipts of 438,350 pesos demonstrating that women's football could be economically viable as a form of entertainment, and as importantly was of a good playing standard.[101] To get the support of the local crowd, the Argentine team appeared for one half in the shirts of Nueva Chicago, but it appears that many of the male spectators did not attend to admire the footballing prowess of the players. Instead, it was reported that more than one fanatic wanted to 'come on the pitch with mad desires of offering caresses to the girls, the majority of spectacular physique,' demonstrating that male attitudes had progressed little since the 1920s.[102]

Argentina opened the tournament against Mexico, going down 3–1 to the hosts in front of 110,000 spectators. Their biggest achievement at the tournament was in beating England 4–1 on 21 August in front of almost 100,000 in Mexico City's iconic Azteca Stadium, the first time an Argentine football team had done so in a World Cup, with all four goals coming from Elba Selva. Most of the players were factory workers or students, having to secure time off from work and university to take part. For example, the team's twenty-year-old number four, Teresa Suárez worked on the production line at the Texas Instruments factory, who kept her job open until she returned from Mexico. The Argentines finished fourth after losing a third-place play-off 4–0 against a technically superior Italy team. As team-member Betty García remembers of the tournament, 'We were without a coach, without boots and a shirt that fell apart with the first wash.' They also travelled without a team doctor or physiotherapist, and such was the youth of goalkeeper, Marta Soler—aged just seventeen—that her parents had to sign a letter of authorisation for her to travel to play in Mexico.[103] That Argentina's women footballers should have participated and played at the Azteca was supremely ironic given the failure their male counterparts to qualify for their own World Cup at the same venue a year previously.

[101] Ortiz (2018).
[102] Pujol (2018).
[103] *La Nación*, 6 September 2019; *La Nación*, 18 August 2019.

The team's exploits went largely unreported in the Argentine press, and even when they were, it was usually with disdain. In one such article published in *Clarín* by Diego Lucero entitled 'Football is not for pussies,' the Uruguayan journalist mocked the female players' 'insufferable slowness,' claiming football 'is only a thing for men with hair on their chest and strong yolk.' Lucero did temper his macho rhetoric enough to close the piece by recognising the ability of the women to attract 90,000 fans to the Azteca, exhorting readers to 'Salute the girls of the ball.'[104] The team's performance was belatedly recognised after years of campaigning by *las pioneras* 'the female pioneers' by the Buenos Aires city legislature, which in 2019 declared 21 August—the date of the win over England—as 'Day of the Female Footballer' (providing a neat symmetry with Perón's designation of Argentina's men's victory over the English in 1953 as 'Footballer's Day').[105]

The team's participation in Mexico was to have been the motor for the start of a six-team women's league, something promised by the vice president of the Association, Raúl Rodríguez before the World Cup. By the mid-1970s, however, the progress of the previous decade was undone by the incoming military dictatorship of General Julio Videla and its 'Process of National Reorganisation' which sought the return of women to traditional family roles and restricted university and union-run activities.[106]

The hands-off approach of the AFA towards women's football finally ended on 27 October 1991 when it assumed institutional responsibility for it, forming an eight-team league including River, Boca and Independiente.[107] This reflected a global inattention to women's football by FIFA, who failed to organise a women's World Cup until the 1991 tournament held in China (a competition Argentina would not qualify for until 2003). Part of the reason for this belated intervention by FIFA was as part of a wider strategy to maximise its commercial revenue and grow football in less traditional football markets.[108] Indeed, it was not until 1998 that Florencia Romano became the first woman to referee an official game

---

[104] Cited in Pujol (2018).
[105] *La Nación*, 21 August 2021.
[106] Elsey and Nadel (2019, 10 and 55–58).
[107] Pujol (2019, 34 and 42).
[108] *La Nación*, 28 July 1996.

under the auspices of the AFA when she took charge of the Primera D division match between Victoriano Arenas and Muñiz.[109]

Off the pitch, women started taking more active roles on the terraces, including membership of *barra brava* hooligan groups. This was exemplified by the leadership roles held by María Esther Duffau and Haydée Luján within the hooligan gangs of Boca Juniors and River Plate, respectively, during the 1960s. According to Brenda Elsey and Josh Nadel, the pair 'abandoned their female identities to become "real fans".' As such, they were able to enter the masculine sphere by sublimating their femininity and embracing a homophobic and misogynistic terrace culture.[110]

'Fomenting National Integration': Football and the Incorporation of the Interior into the Argentine Mainstream

As Chapter 3 highlighted, the power balance between Buenos Aires and the Argentine interior had always been heavily weighted towards the former. By the late 1960s, the government's austerity policies hit the interior provinces disproportionately, as subsidies were reduced or eliminated to key industries. The 1966 closure of sugar mills decimated the economy in Tucumán, whose capital was depopulated by 230,000 inhabitants between 1965 and 1970 as a result, leaving for other cities in search of work. In 1967, the cotton industry in the Chaco and tobacco cultivation in Misiones were similarly affected, causing disaffection with the federal authorities in Buenos Aires.[111] In Córdoba that disillusion turned into open rebellion, with the *cordobazo* uprising of May and June 1969. The strength of feeling unleashed in the insurrection took the government by surprise. It had taken provincial acquiescence in Córdoba for granted, with the Minister of Economy, Krieger Vasena, expressing disbelief at the action taken by some of the best paid workers in Argentina who were employed in the most modern factories, although there had long been disquiet amongst metal workers in Córdoba about getting paid less than their peers in Buenos Aires for doing the same job. The violence

---

[109] Scher et al. (2010, 555).
[110] Elsey and Nadel (2019, 51–52); Binello et al. (2000, 33–56).
[111] Sáenz Quesada (2012, 623–624).

unleashed by the *cordobazo* also spilled into the footballing sphere. On 9 June 1969, three of the five scheduled matches in the Liga Cordobesa, which functioned as the qualifying tournament for the Campeonato Nacional, were suspended due to disorder on the terraces. The worst of the violence came in the fixture between Racing and Belgrano, where the away fans, seeing their team 2–1 down took the opportunity to take out their frustration on the police, whose numbers were reduced due to dealing with the rebellion in other parts of the city.[112]

It was in this context that in 1967, as the continental Copa Libertadores took precedence amongst the big clubs, the AFA sought to rejuvenate the domestic league competition by splitting it into two shorter competitions. The first called the Campeonato Metropolitano was open to the traditional teams from Greater Buenos Aires and Rosario; the second called the Campeonato Nacional, was ground-breaking, including provincial teams in a national league for the first time (although they had taken part in the short-lived Copa Ramírez knockout cup competition in the 1940s). The idea of the Nacional was credited to AFA *interventor*, Valentín Suárez, with the aim of 'fomenting national integration' and to financially develop the clubs from the interior so that they could eventually challenge the established clubs from the capital. As an appointed acolyte of the military regime, Suárez claimed 'the government will never lower the curtain on football,' leading to Sergio Levinsky's suggestion that the move was a backhanded way of attracting government subsidy in the form of a television contract with the state television channel *Canal 7* worth 7 million pesos.[113] Paradoxes arose from the innovation. Whilst the AFA were thinking of the financial appeal of full stadiums in the provinces as River visited Mendoza or Boca played in Córdoba, the idea of Atlanta from the capital playing Aldosivi from Mar del Plata was box office poison. The short-sightedness of this business model was also reflected in the reduced attendances resulting from so many matches switched to the evening to suit television schedules. In that first season of the Nacional, the game between River and Unión de Santa Fe moved to a weekday night in the middle of winter attracted just 391 paying customers.[114]

---

[112] Farias (2012).

[113] Asociación del Fútbol Argentino (1968); Scher et al. (2010, 402); Levinsky (2016, 131–132).

[114] Mitre (1993, 404).

The Nacional fed notions of *porteño* supremacy, as provincial teams, who were amateur or semi-professional at best, were no match for their big city opponents, with no thought given by the authorities as to how this chasm in class might be bridged. In the inaugural season, River's 8–0 thrashing of San Martín de Mendoza and Vélez Sarsfield's 8–1 whipping of San Lorenzo de Mar del Plata highlighted this gulf in class. An *El Gráfico* article in December 1969 entitled 'The Performance of the Provincials' reflected on three years of interior participation in the Nacional, bemoaning that no team had managed to average more than one point per game. Although the performances of Belgrano and Talleres from Córdoba, Argentina's second most populous city, were singled out for praise, they were the exception from the 'general mediocrity' of the rest.[115] Press coverage of teams from the interior called to mind the condescending reportage of the 1920s. Victories by interior teams over the *grandes* were routinely described in the press as 'historic' or as 'heroic backs against the wall' efforts. For example, San Martín de Tucumán's win over Boca Juniors in September 1968 was headlined in *El Gráfico*, 'San Martín: The Heroic Defence of a Goal.'[116]

Within a decade, though, teams from the interior became serious contenders in the Nacional, with Talleres de Córdoba coming to the fore. The shortened tournament format allowed provincial clubs to put a run of results together and challenge for the title, which would not have been possible in an extended competition, in which teams with greater resources would have had time to rein in any such advantage. After entering the Campeonato Nacional for the first time in 1969, Talleres won nine consecutive games on the way to finishing runners-up in 1977, only losing the final on away goals to Independiente, earning entry to the following season's Copa Libertadores. For *El Gráfico*, Talleres' achievement was a 'historic landmark' which 'strengthened the tournament,' signalling that for the first time interior clubs were competing with their peers from the capital on an equal footing.[117] As standard-bearers for the interior, Talleres broke the domination of the capital and the littoral provinces, and for the first time were considered part of the footballing

[115] *El Gráfico*, 23 December 1969.
[116] *El Gráfico*, 24 September 1968.
[117] *El Gráfico*, 18 May 1982, 3.

mainstream as players such as Luis Galván, Humberto Bravo and Daniel Valencia became regular members of the national team.

The success achieved by Talleres from the mid-1970s was an important outlet for the interior to obtain recognition and position itself positively in the national discourse. From the *cordobazo* in 1969, the provinces were seen by federal authorities as a disruptive hotbed of subversion, harbouring the guerrillas of the ERP and Montoneros. The suspension of Congress following the 1976 military coup meant that the provinces no longer had a voice in national government as the *junta* centralised power on Buenos Aires.

By April 1976, provincial teams had come so far in proving themselves competitive in both a sporting and economic sense, that *El Gráfico* was advocating doing away with the two-league system in favour of 'a true national championship with the most prestigious clubs from Greater Buenos Aires and the interior.' The magazine argued, 'A club like Talleres de Córdoba has the necessary solvency to play all year in a strictly national championship, with an inter-provincial championship providing a pathway to participation in the National [tournament].'[118]

By the early 1980s, provincial performance in the Nacional reached its apex with Racing Club de Córdoba reaching the final against Rosario Central in 1981, whilst in 1982 more than half of the quarter-finalists in the Nacional came from the interior, outnumbering teams from Greater Buenos Aires and Rosario for the first time, prompting *El Gráfico* to proclaim, 'Football in the interior has developed itself, it is on a plain of equality, moving closer to competition equilibrium.'[119]

The legitimacy of the interior's place at the heart of Argentine football was cemented by the selection policies of Menotti after becoming national team coach in September 1974. Historically, Argentine national squad selection had come almost exclusively from those players playing for clubs from the Federal Capital or the littoral provinces of Buenos Aires and Santa Fe, but this changed radically under Menotti (see Fig. 6.1).

As part of his plan to develop a side capable of winning the World Cup being staged in Argentina in 1978, Menotti proposed working with four groups of players: a 'traditional' national team drawn from players with the big clubs from Buenos Aires; a team of up-and-coming junior players

---

[118] *El Gráfico*, 14 April 1976, 32–33.
[119] *El Gráfico*, 18 May 1982, 3.

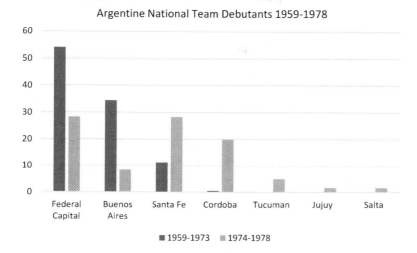

Fig. 6.1 National Team Debutants 1959–1978 by Province of Club as percentage[120]

in their late teens; a Santa Fe side comprised of players from Rosario and Santa Fe; and most revolutionary of all, a team from the interior—as he worked with an initial 80 players to be whittled down to 22 in less than four years. As Menotti noted in January 1975, 'The interior team was the one that most enthused me. I had people scouting for me in all the provinces.' He trained the team, composed of players who played competitively for only three months of the year in provincial tournaments unless their clubs qualified for the Nacional, in the northern city of Salta, further lessening the Buenos Aires-centric nature of the national team.[121] According to Ricardo Villa's memoirs, Menotti's move was a bold one which was well received by players in the interior who had been hitherto ignored.[122]

By 1977, provincial players were making Menotti's first-choice team on merit. In the Mar del Plata summer tournament, five players from the successful Talleres de Córdoba team were selected for the Argentine

---

[120] Compiled from data in Macias (2011).
[121] Bauso (2018, 106–8).
[122] Villa and Miller (2010, 65).

side at the expense of players from more popular Buenos Aires clubs such as Boca Juniors, who also competed in the competition. According to Humberto Bravo of Talleres, their selection was met with hostility by the capital-based press and fans in Buenos Aires province, 'The fans wanted us to lose, journalists didn't stop criticising us … It was not [fun] for anyone.'[123] Menotti was unrepentant, justifying his selection policy on the basis that he would not pick players because of popular clamour for short-term gain, saying, 'I have time to elaborate an organic piece of work. Then I can look for the player I need wherever I will find him. For example, I picked Villa from Atlético Tucumán because he was a Number 10 and Alonso had gone [abroad] and Bochini was unavailable.'[124]

Five of those called up for the Interior team that participated in the 1975 Pan American Games—Villa, José Valencia, Ardiles, Miguel Oviedo and Luis Galván—featured in the final World Cup squad. Argentina's tournament victory reaffirmed Menotti's belief that it could be achieved with the best talent from *all* the country.[125]

Argentine society has long been the battleground for competing visions of national identity, whether to open the country to the world and accept foreign help in modernising and developing its economy or to focus on its traditional values and export of agricultural goods to sustain it. During the period 1959–1976, this dichotomy was never more apparent, with oscillations between the two according to economic cycles driving the political discourse, and numerous military interventions when no common ground could be found in society, leading to this chapter's description as this being the Age of Revolution. This lack of commonality gave the military, as Argentina's 'moral guardians,' a veneer of legitimacy following the 1966 coup to try to fundamentally reshape Argentine society. The lack of democratic accountability left little recourse for opposition except violence or silent acquiescence.

Therefore, football became a critical arena in which underrepresented and suppressed sectors of Argentine society, women, youth and the interior could challenge the establishment on their own terms and project themselves into the public imaginary.

[123] Bauso (2018, 138).
[124] *El Gráfico*, 15 February 1977, 61–64.
[125] Bauso (2018, 106–108).

For women, the gains made from a fine showing at the 1971 World Cup were marginal. The limited press coverage afforded to the team's exploits confirmed that for the media, football remained a masculine sport in which representations of Argentine identity could only be represented by the men's national team and espoused by men as women also remained excluded from the telling of the national story through football in the pages of newspapers and magazines. As Ayelén Pujol notes, even fifty years later to try and do an internet search of the heroes of 1971, virtually no information would be returned.[126]

The 1967 inauguration of the Campeonato Nacional, although initially established for opportunistic reasons, did eventually see the meaningful integration of the interior into Argentine football, to the point that by the late 1970s, a measure of equality had been attained by clubs like Talleres de Córdoba with their counterparts from Greater Buenos Aires, paving the way for a single unified league championship from the early 1980s. Meanwhile, the selection policies of César Luis Menotti ahead of the 1978 World Cup legitimised the validity of players from the interior in terms of representing Argentina, with five of them forming part of his World Cup-winning squad.

In terms of playing style and wider representations of Argentine identity, the 1958 'Disaster of Sweden' was a catalyst for the modernisation of the country's football, with Juan Carlos Lorenzo acting at its vanguard. As with other sections of Argentine society, short-term results, both positive and negative, resulted in numerous changes of approach and leadership, as World Cup performance damned the modernist way, but paradoxically Copa Libertadores success by Argentine clubs in the mid-to-late 1960s appeared to validate the approach. The evolution of footballing ideologies, principally from Italy, saw the creation of something that became considered uniquely Argentine: *antifútbol* in which the ends justified the means. Although interpreted at the time in several ways, as both the antithesis of *la nuestra* and as the overdue modernisation of the Argentine game, this evolution can be described as a continuation, albeit a genetic mutation, of Argentine football's *criollo* traditions. It could be seen as a footballing response to the wider climate of repression in Argentine society, in which violence was perceived as the only way of achieving one's ends. The *pibes* of the 1920s had now been more formally educated

---

[126] Pujol (2019, 102).

in the ways of the world, although their sense of fun and spontaneity had been systematically stifled as football mirrored the authoritarianism that dominated the country at the end of the 1960s.

The constant stream of Argentine players to foreign markets reflected the wider international movement of skilled human capital known as 'Brain Drain,' in which individual free will is expressed in a global marketplace for talent. Whilst this benefited those with the economic resources to pay for this talent, it also served to simultaneously create a 'poverty trap' in countries like Argentina in which the local competition was diminished by the effects of emigration.

References

Alabarces, Pablo. 2007. *Fútbol y patria. El fútbol y las narrativas de la Nación en la Argentina*, 4th ed. Buenos Aires: Prometeo Libros.

Asociación del Fútbol Argentino. 1968. *Memoria y Balance General 1967*. Buenos Aires.

Bauso, Matías. 2018. *'78 Historia Oral del Mundial*. Buenos Aires: Sudamericana.

Binello, Gabriela, Mariana Conde, Analía Martínez and María Graciela Rodríguez. 2000. Mujeres y fútbol: ¿Territorio conquistador o a conquistar?. In *Peligro de gol: Estudios sobre deporte y sociedad en América Latina*, ed. Pablo Alabarces, 33–56. Buenos Aires: CLACSO.

Bayer, Osvaldo. 2016. *Fútbol Argentino*. Buenos Aires: Sudamericana.

Campomar, Andreas. 2014. *¡Golazo!* London: Quercus.

Caparrós, Martín. 2004. *Boquita*. Buenos Aires: Booklet.

Dodds, Klaus. 2002. *Pink Ice: Britain and the South Atlantic Empire*. London: Bloomsbury.

Duke, Vic, and Liz Crolley. 2014. *Football, Nationality and the State*. Abingdon: Routledge.

Elsey, Brenda. 2011. *Citizens & Sportsmen: Fútbol & Politics in 20th Century Chile*. Austin: University of Texas Press.

Elsey, Brenda, and Joshua Nadel. 2019. *Futbolera*. Austin: University of Texas Press.

Farías, Gustavo. 2012. El Cordobazo del fútbol. La Voz del Interior. 29 May. www.mundodlavoz.com.ar/futbol/cordobazo-futbolwww.mundod lavoz.com.ar/futbol/cordobazo-futbol. (Accessed 27 August 2019).

Goebel, Michael. 2011. *Argentina's Partisan Past*. Liverpool: Liverpool University Press.

Lanfranchi, Pierre, and Matthew Taylor. 2001. *Moving with the Ball: The Migration of Professional Footballers*. Oxford: Berg.

Levinsky, Sergio. 2016. *AFA. El fútbol pasa, los negocios quedan: Una historia política y deportiva*. Buenos Aires: Autoria Editorial.
Macias, Julio. 2011. *Quién es quién de la Selección Argentina: diccionario sobre los futbolistas internacionales: 1902–2010*. Buenos Aires: Corregidor.
Malam, Colin. 1978. *World Cup Argentina*. Glasgow: Collins.
McKinstry, Leo. 2006. *Sir Alf*. London: Harper Collins.
Menotti, César Luis. 1986. *Fútbol Sin Trampa*. Barcelona: Muchnik.
Menotti, César Luis. 1980. *Fútbol, juego, deporte y profesión*. Buenos Aires: El Gráfico.
Mitre, Bartolomé, ed. 1993. *Historia del Fútbol Argentino*. Buenos Aires: La Nación.
Ortiz, Pablo. 2018. La hazaña de la Selección femenina en el Mundial 1971. *Ahora*. 30 August. https://ahora.com.ar/la-hazana-la-seleccion-femenina-futbol-el-mundial-1971-n4158362. (Accessed 26 June 2019).
Panzeri, Dante. 2011. *Fútbol Dinámica de lo impensado*. Madrid: Capitan Swing.
Panzeri, Dante. 1974. *Burguesia y gangsterismo en el deporte*. Buenos Aires: Libera.
Pujol, Ayelén. 2019. *¡Qué jugadora! Un siglo de fútbol femenino en la Argentina*. Buenos Aires: Ariel.
Pujol, Ayelén. 2018. El día que Argentina jugó su primer Mundial de fútbol. *Página 12*. 12 May. https://www.pagina12.com.ar/114143-el-dia-que-argentina-jugo-su-primer-mundial-de-futbol-femini. (Accessed 26 June 2019).
Sáenz Quesada, María. 2012. *La Argentina. Historia del País y de su Gente*. Buenos Aires: Editorial Sudamericana.
Scher, Ariel, Guillermo Blanco, Jorge Búsico. 2010. *Deporte Nacional*. Buenos Aires, Emecé.
Villa, Ricardo, and Joel Miller. 2010. *And Still Ricky Villa: My Autobiography*. Kingston-upon-Thames: Vision Sports Publishing.

CHAPTER 7

In the Shadow of the Proceso 1976–1983

Despite Argentina's most recent military dictatorship (1976–1983) being of a relatively short duration, its psychological effect on Argentine society continues to reverberate to this day. Its self-styled Proceso de Reorganización Nacional (National Process of Reorganisation), in which up to 30,000 perceived opponents of the regime were murdered or disappeared by the state, coincided with two of the biggest events to involve Argentina during the twentieth century: hosting the 1978 football World Cup and the 1982 'recapture' of the Malvinas/Falklands. This period also saw the emergence of a player, Diego Maradona, who over the remaining quarter of the twentieth century came to be conflated as *the* personification of the Argentine nation. This chapter investigates how football was central to expressions of Argentine identity at a time when its society was more polarised than ever. It charts how Maradona came to represent the different facets and complexities of the Argentine people as well as becoming a global symbol of Argentine excellence, as well as unwittingly becoming the face of Argentina's military adventure in the South Atlantic.

Hosting the FIFA World Cup in June 1978 was important in terms of Argentine self-perception of national identity and its projection to the rest of the world. Whilst a vast historiography on the subject exists, much has been written since Argentina's democratic restoration in 1983, positioning events and actions in the context of new cultural norms

© The Author(s), under exclusive license to Springer Nature Switzerland AG 2023
M. Orton, *Football and National Identity in Twentieth-Century Argentina*, Palgrave Studies in Sport and Politics, https://doi.org/10.1007/978-3-031-20589-7_7

underpinned by the freedom of a functioning democracy. Indeed, Duke and Crolley have suggested that 'opinions previously unvoiced because of censorship were then made known.'[1] By contrast, this chapter concentrates on contemporary media accounts, particularly from abroad given the censorship in place in Argentina, to assess how narratives of national identity were constructed against a background of a polarised society in a state of extreme tension. Building on works such as Matías Bauso's oral history of the competition, these sources enable an understanding of how this was accomplished, thereby giving a different perspective to the existing literature by engaging with how national identity was perceived within Argentina and interpreted internationally at the time.[2] Focusing on how three key actors: the state, the Peronist Montonero opposition and human rights activists in the shape of the Madres de la Plaza de Mayo, projected their idealised version of Argentine society to a national and global audience, this section assesses the degree to which each group was successful in the tug of war for the support of 25 million Argentines through the medium of football, not the ballot box or the battlefield.

Whilst the emergence of Maradona as the *pibe de oro* ('golden boy') in terms of maintaining the traditions of Argentine football and *la nuestra* has been amply investigated by scholars such as Pablo Alabarces and Eduardo Archetti, less academic attention has been paid to other elements of the player's influence on constructions of national identity and perceptions of Argentina in the rest of the world, something addressed by this chapter.[3]

Similarly, the juxtaposition of football and the Malvinas/Falklands War has scarcely been explored beyond linking military defeat in the conflict to Argentina's lacklustre defence of their title at the 1982 World Cup. By contrast, this chapter argues that football played an important role in maintaining morale during the conflict and in efforts to position the legitimacy of Argentina's actions in 'recovering' the islands to the international community.

---

[1] Duke and Crolley (2014, 113).
[2] Bauso (2018).
[3] Alabarces (2007, 133–60); Archetti (1999, 180–9).

'25 Million Argentines Will Play for the World Cup': Mundial'78 and Argentine Identity

Hosting the World Cup had been coveted by Argentine governments of all political hues since the 1930s, with the decision to award the 1962 competition to Chile and the 1970 tournament to Mexico being particularly injurious to national self-esteem due to Argentina's self-perception as a regional superpower. As damaging as the 1958 'Disaster of Sweden' for Argentina's self-confidence was FIFA's decision at its 1956 Lisbon congress to award the staging of the 1962 World Cup to neighbouring Chile. Whilst the decision came as a surprise to some, especially in Argentina, Chile's comfortable win by 32 votes to 10 was an admonishment by the rest of the world for the perceived arrogance of Argentina's isolationist stance in boycotting previous tournaments from 1938 to 1954. It was a feeling consolidated when the Argentine delegation concluded their presentation by saying, 'We can have the World Cup tomorrow. We have it all.'[4] Argentina was finally awarded the 1978 tournament World Cup on 6 July 1966 at FIFA's 35th congress in London. Given Argentina's history in international football and the fact that it was the only major Latin American nation yet to host the competition, it was as David Lacey described, 'the logical venue' from a footballing perspective.[5] The ongoing political turbulence that followed Perón's overthrow in 1955, and which contributed to Argentina losing the 1962 race, made FIFA's decision to grant the country organisation of the 1978 World Cup a risky one.

Five years on from that decision, inertia on the part of the authorities in the face of economic and societal pressures meant that nothing had been done to progress preparations. *El Gráfico* lamented that, 'Argentina 78 must already be an organisation on the march. And those taking responsibility have yet to be named. Argentina has lost ground as a host simply because there is no entity to coordinate the project. It seems a deception.'[6] In 1973 the first organising committee was formed by the Peronist government, not that this placated *El Gráfico*, who feared that Argentina's international reputation was being compromised. 'We are so behind

---

[4] Elsey (2014, 162–84).
[5] *The Guardian*, 14 January 1977, 17.
[6] *El Gráfico*, 7 December 1971, 3.

in the organisation of our World Cup that we doubt that we will be able to do things with dignity in the time remaining that such an important event for our country deserves.'[7]

At the heart of the magazine's concerns were racial perceptions of Argentina in the developed northern hemisphere, that despite Argentine self-identification as 'European,' positioned the country like the rest of Latin America as an indolent 'land of *mañana*.' This perception overshadowed previous global events held in the region. In 1930, the Centenario stadium in Montevideo remained unfinished until after the initial World Cup games had taken place elsewhere in the city, whilst in 1950 games were played at Rio de Janeiro's Estadio Maracanã whilst still under construction. Even in the years leading up to the 1968 Mexico City Olympics, the US press was continually critical about the lack of progress in the building of associated infrastructure.[8]

The death of Argentina's president, Juan Perón in July 1974 further hampered progress. His demise triggered a political crisis, as the governing movement fractured into factionalism without the personal control of its founder, one that his successor as president and third wife, Isabel Martínez de Perón, was unable to control. Beyond these political differences, the global economic recession triggered by OPEC oil price rises hurt Argentina too, producing a sharp reduction in economic output and an upsurge in unemployment, adding further to societal tensions. With Martínez de Perón unable to maintain control, the extra-judicial Alianza Anticomunista Argentina (AAA) comprising elements of the state security forces under the direction of the Minister for Social Welfare, José López Rega began a campaign of kidnappings and assassinations against those considered to be attempting to overthrow the state, such as the Montoneros, and the ERP as well as students and trade unionists. In this climate of virtual civil war, the military overthrew Martínez de Perón in March 1976 to try and restore order to Argentina.

In this milieu of chaos, numerous concerns were raised by European football associations that Argentina was not fit to host the tournament, with suggestions made that there should be a joint Dutch-Belgian staging instead. Ironically, given their previous dealings with FIFA, footballing geopolitics came to Argentina's rescue. FIFA's recently elected president,

---

[7] *El Gráfico*, 15 January 1974, 3.

[8] Jawad (2009, 28–9); Campomar (2014, 221); Zolov (2005, 191–6).

João Havelange confirmed at a meeting in Zurich in February 1975 that Argentina would indeed host the 1978 tournament, appeasing his power base in the developing world which had elevated him to power a year earlier. A *Goles* editorial declared, 'Now, the happiness; going forward the work,' describing the decision as a victory for justice in the face of agitation from the other side of the Atlantic.[9] But by the time the Peronists were ejected from office in a 1976 military coup headed by a three-man *junta* led by General Jorge Videla, nothing substantive had been done.

As with the Onganía coup of 1966, the military once more charged themselves with a long-term project to 'correct' the social disintegration afflicting Argentina. The 'cure' for this 'disintegration' was the *junta*'s self-styled Proceso de Nacional Reorganización, a return to Christian moral values and national traditions which would be enshrined in an educational system that 'consolidates the cultural values and aspirations of being Argentine.'[10] This ideology underpinned claims of legitimacy for the regime's 'crusade' against those they claimed were trying to subvert the traditional Argentine, Catholic way of life—including Montoneros (despite sharing the importance of Catholicism to its movement), socialists and trade unionists—in an institutionalisation of human rights violations and extra-judicial murder known as the 'Dirty War.' Officially 8,960 were registered as disappeared during the 1976–1983 dictatorship but estimates by human rights groups put the figure at around 30,000 murdered or disappeared.[11]

When it took power, opinion was divided within the *junta* as to whether hosting the World Cup was an essential part of its re-organisational agenda. There were compelling economic and social arguments for resigning the tournament. For example, the 1976 Argentine Grand Prix was cancelled for the lack of the US$500,000 needed to organise it, despite an Argentine, Carlos Reutemann being one of the leading racing drivers in the world at the time. Dante Panzeri claimed, 'The 1978 World Cup shouldn't be held in Argentina for the same reason that someone who can't afford gasoline for a Model "T" Ford shouldn't buy a Ford Torino.'[12] It was a theme continued by Finance Secretary Juan

---

[9] *Goles*, 11 February 1975, 3.
[10] Goebel (2011, 183).
[11] Comisión Nacional Sobre la Desaparición de Personas (1984).
[12] *The Guardian*, 14 January 1977, 17.

Alemann, who claimed in February 1978 that had the *junta* known that the cost of the tournament would be US$700 million rather than the original estimate of between US$70 million and US$100 million, they probably would not have gone through with it.[13] His assessment was reinforced by foreign journalists such as Hugh McIlvanney, who wrote of one of the 'white elephant' infrastructure projects, 'Flying into an airport that looks like one vast building site, it was easy to see Alemann's point about priorities.'[14]

By contrast, Admiral Massera advocated using the tournament as a means to show a new 'Argentine image to the world.'[15] The link between the World Cup and the Proceso was made explicit by Economy Minister, José Alfredo Martínez de Hoz, 'We must carry on playing the great game of the National Process, in which the final triumph is going to depend not only on the government, but instead on the effort and participation of each Argentine.'[16] The tournament therefore became a way for the regime to try and ally its aims to a popular mobilisation. A new organising committee, the Ente Autárquico Mundial'78 (EAM), was created by the *junta* in July 1976 to get Argentina prepared for the World Cup. Without any hint of irony, given that it was in the hands of the military dictatorship, *El Gráfico* highlighted that, 'The entity (EAM) will be independent and will have full liberty to exercise its rights and contract obligations.'[17] The designation of officials to lead the EAM reflected conflicts within the dictatorship over the scale the tournament. EAM president, Omar Actis, representing the army, argued that it should be an 'Austerity World Cup' in recognition of the reality of Argentina's economic and social situation, in a similar way to how the 1948 London Olympics were positioned by the International Olympic Committee (IOC) as an act of post-war reconstruction.[18] By contrast, his deputy, Captain Carlos Lacoste, dutifully reflected the opinion of Massera, his superior in the navy, that the tournament should positively project Argentina as widely as possible. When Actis was assassinated before the first EAM meeting had been convened, he was

[13] *The Guardian*, 16 February 1978, 7.
[14] *The Observer*, 28 May 1978, 24.
[15] Alabarces (2007, 111–26).
[16] Cited in Lanata (2003, 589–94).
[17] *El Gráfico*, 13 July 1976, 3.
[18] Alabarces (2007, 111–26).

officially replaced by another army appointee General Antonio Merlo, although Lacoste became the EAM's de facto leader, giving a lengthy speech at its opening press conference, reflecting the navy's dominant role in organising the World Cup.[19]

Through the EAM, the military regime sought to present Argentina as a united and capable nation, able to take its place amongst the advanced developed nations of the world. To help them burnish their image, the Argentine government hired American public relations company Burson-Marsteller, at a cost of US$5.5 million between 1976 and 1980.[20] Writers such as Eduardo Galeano have focused on the company's attempt to positively market Argentina in the same way as a consumer product.[21] But Burson-Marsteller's report was more nuanced and critical than otherwise suggested. The report's opening remarks got straight to the heart of the *junta*'s image problem, 'The majority of journalists consider the Argentine government as oppressive and repressive, a military dictatorship that only deserves condemnation.' The report suggested that the way to improve their image was to conform to the norms of Western society, 'The manner of eradicating terrorism that counts on global support (or said another way, that which gives a good image) must respect human rights and individual liberties of the terrorists of the right or left. Otherwise, the repression will always evoke the Gestapo of Nazi Germany.'[22] It was advice that the military ignored to the detriment of its international reputation.

To demonstrate Argentina's modernisation, the government invested US$60 million in a state-of-the-art television centre, Argentina Televisora Color, enabling the country to broadcast in colour for the first time.[23] Colour transmission proved extraordinarily successful. The images of blue and white tickertape cascading on to the pitch when Argentina played were some of the most iconic images of the tournament, capturing the passion of the home fans and encapsulating the symbiotic relationship between football and Argentine national identity. Certainly, these images

---

[19] Ente Autárquico Mundial 1978, Boletín No 1, November 1976.
[20] Bauso (2018, 250–2).
[21] Galeano (1997, 153–4).
[22] Cited in Bauso (2018, 250–2).
[23] Ente Autárquico Mundial 1978 (1976, 4).

were more representative of this link than Videla's speech at the tournament's opening ceremony which was met with lukewarm applause inside the stadium. His most telling words referred to, 'the confrontation on the sporting field, the friendship in the field of human relations that allow us to affirm that it is possible *even today, in these days* [my emphasis], to live together in unity and diversity, the only way to control the peace,' the opposite of what was really happening under the Proceso in 1978 Argentina.[24]

Elsewhere, whilst Menotti was espousing his restoration of *la nuestra*, some of its mythical building blocks, such as the *pibe* and the *potrero* were simultaneously being eroded due to a combination of societal change and social engineering on the part of the military government. Changes in social habits, especially in the consumption of leisure time, saw the reduction of street-kids or *pibes* kicking a ball around from dawn to dusk in the *potrero* as other entertainments such as television gained favour instead. Panzeri identified one key common factor between eras. Where once these *potreros* were populated by first-and-second generation European immigrants, now they were inhabited by the offspring of migrants from the interior, particularly the poor northern provinces, the origin of numerous quality contemporary Argentine players such as René Houseman and Diego Maradona, whose families hailed from Santiago del Estero and Corrientes, respectively.[25]

The case study of René Houseman is paradigmatic of these shifting sands. A key member of Huracán's 1973 championship-winning team, Houseman's international career represented all the complexities and contradictions inherent in the mythical *pibe*. Born in La Banda in the northern province of Santiago del Estero, Houseman moved with his family to Buenos Aires in the 1950s at the age of two, his father being a *cabecita negra*, attracted to the capital by the possibilities of work arising from Peronist industrialisation. Proud of his upbringing in the *villa* of Baja Belgrano in the north of Buenos Aires, Houseman claimed, 'I am a *villero*. This is what I have been all my life, and this is what I will be until I die.'[26] With freedom to play spontaneous football, Houseman honed his skills in the *potrero* between calle Ramsey and calle La Pampa,

---

[24] Cited in Bauso (2018, 389).
[25] Panzeri (2011, 81–3).
[26] Boisson (2018).

hustling for a handful of pesos, just as Borocotó's archetypal *pibe* had done in the 1920s, representing the traditions of Argentine football that Menotti vowed to restore. Paradoxically, as a product of poverty with an associated lack of education, Houseman also exemplified the lack of discipline that Menotti considered to be hindering Argentine football. Houseman smoked before matches, and as his Huracán and Argentina colleague, Osvaldo Ardiles, remembered of him, 'When he had to run, he looked like a cripple, but with a ball in front of him, he cured himself miraculously and was the quickest.' Even when he turned professional with Defensores de Belgrano, Houseman continued to live in the *villa*, drinking with his friends and living a carefree lifestyle.[27] Despite these flaws in terms of the behaviours expected of a professional footballer in the 1970s, Houseman's talents were undoubted. Described by Menotti as a mix between 'Maradona and Garrincha,' Houseman was a rare shining light in Argentina's disastrous World Cup campaign in 1974, eliciting a 50,000-strong standing ovation in Stuttgart after his virtuoso performance against Italy, and prompting numerous offers to play abroad which he rejected, arguing, 'Why would I leave Buenos Aires, the most beautiful city in the world?'.[28]

The 1978 World Cup produced another irony. With Houseman predicted to be the shining star of Menotti's team, the environment in which those skills flourished was being systematically demolished as part of a wider policy of state-sponsored social engineering. Commentary on the removal of *villas miserias*—home to 213,823 in 1976 in Greater Buenos Aires alone—in Argentina's biggest cities in the months and years leading up to the tournament has largely followed Simon Kuper, who has viewed it in the context of the military government trying to beautify city venues to impress the anticipated thousands of foreign visitors to the country.[29]

A decade in the planning, the villa clearances accelerated in advance of the competition. Positioned by the authorities as correcting health and safety breaches in construction by rehousing the *villa* dwellers in more suitable accommodation in their places of origin where there were

---

[27] Ibid.
[28] *El Gráfico*, 25 June 1974, 86–9; Boisson (2018).
[29] Kuper (1996, 173–8); Cordolcini (2018, 37).

'appropriate work opportunities,' the reality was more sinister.[30] The military regime was attempting to reverse the internal migrations of *cabecitas negras* that gained traction during the 1946–1955 Peronist era, and return them to the poor northern provinces, where they would be out of sight and out of mind, as well as returning 'undesirable' *mestizo* immigrants back to the Andean republics of Bolivia and Peru from whence they came. The aim was to restore Buenos Aires to the Europeanised, white and bourgeois city it had been half a century earlier.[31] Having attempted to criminalise the *villeros* as tax evaders, the capital's Director General of the Municipal Housing Commission, Guillermo del Ciappo argued before the World Cup that, 'To live in Buenos Aires is not for anyone but instead for those who deserve it … We must have a better city for the better people.'[32] There were economic reasons too for the municipality of Buenos Aires to reclaim the *villas*. Where the *villas* had been established from the 1940s onwards on the periphery of the city-centre, was now prime real estate, and the authorities sought to benefit from the sale of this unregistered 'public land.' Amongst the *villas* cleared was that of Bajo Belgrano where Houseman had grown up. Bajo Belgrano's early eradication owed much to its proximity to the Estadio Monumental, the showpiece venue of the World Cup. According to official statistics, the demolition of Bajo Belgrano alone resulted in the clearance of 7.2 hectares of land for rebuilding, and the relocation of 2,021 people.[33] Houseman recalled his sadness at returning to Bajo Belgrano after two months at a national team training camp, 'When I returned, I found rubble. To see all this made me cry huge tears … It killed me … If I had the money today and the possibility of doing so, I would return to rebuild the same *villa*, in the same place and bring all my friends back.'[34] Whilst it is impossible to discern for certain the impact this news had on the player's form, Houseman's impact on the 1978 World Cup receded the longer the tournament went on, as he went from first-choice starter to substitute.

[30] Comisión Municipal de Vivienda (1977).
[31] Larraquy (2018).
[32] Cited in Bauso (2018, 371–3).
[33] Antunes de Moraes (2019, 50).
[34] Cited in Ibid, 50.

Despite this contradiction, the regime was assisted in propagating a narrative of unity by a supplicant press, not least the magazines of the Editorial Atlántida publishing house, owned by the historically conservative Vigil family which represented staple reading for Middle Argentina, the biggest supporters of the 1976 coup. The dictatorship benefited from the breadth of population that could be reached through the pages of Atlántida's biggest selling magazines: *El Gráfico, Para Ti, Gente, Somos* and *Biliken*. Full page advertisements appeared in *El Gráfico* on the part of the EAM under the headline, '25 Million Argentines will play the World Cup. We will not have this opportunity again for 100 years,' although this was popularly altered to '25 million will *pay for* the World Cup.'[35] Whilst Alabarces has focused on the unifying motif of the first half of the slogan, of there being an all-inclusive 'us,' there was also an implicit threat in the second part, warning of the consequences of non-compliance in this patriotic venture.[36] Remarkably, it was through the pages of those magazines that did not appeal openly to 'traditional' masculine football audiences, that the propaganda campaign was most interactive in widening the link between the World Cup and all sectors of Argentine society in the creation of a shared identity. Despite not usually being associated with football, the women's glossy magazine *Para Ti* included within its pages a series of postcards in the weeks leading up to the World Cup, which readers were encouraged to send to human rights groups in Europe and to relatives abroad—bearing in mind that most Argentines had familial links to Italy or Spain—urging them to 'Defend your Argentina' and to use the cards as an 'opportunity to show all of the world all the truth of a country that lives in peace.'[37] Even youngsters were targeted by this approach. The children's magazine *Biliken* encouraged its young readership, 'With your Mum, with your Dad, with your brothers and sisters, you also send cards abroad. Help to show the true Argentina.'[38] However, giving that the people of Europe were fully aware of the *junta*'s appalling human rights record, the campaign had no resonance outside of Argentina and was effectively purely for domestic consumption.

[35] Kuper (1996, 173–81).
[36] Alabarces (2007, 111–26).
[37] Cited in Lanata (2003, 589–94).
[38] *Biliken*, August 1978.

Elsewhere in the national press, not supporting the national team in its patriotic quest was considered 'anti-Argentine.' Even detachment was deemed disrespectful to the *patria*. *Clarín* argued in June 1978, 'When a World Cup is played, and is situated in our own country, it makes it difficult to understand the attitude of those that remain voluntarily marginalised from the popular fervour in an almost depreciative attitude.'[39] Scholars such as Bill Smith and Alabarces have contended that such articles reflected state control of the press in which even criticism of the team was prohibited as being anti-patriotic, with journalists adopting 'genuflecting and obedient' positions.[40] Such claims are overstated. Even during the tournament, there was criticism of the team's performances, especially in the nervy opening games. After the first game against Hungary, *La Razón* reported, 'Silence, the Argentine fans kept themselves in closed silence for practically all of the game. Only with the goals and with the entrance of Alonso did they make themselves heard.'[41]

Given the authoritarian nature of the Argentine government presiding over the World Cup, writers such as Bayer and Levinsky have sought to position the 1978 World Cup as a repetition of Mussolini's use of the 1934 World Cup and Hitler's exploitation of the 1936 Olympics for their own propaganda purposes.[42] Such claims are similarly exaggerated. The use of multinational sporting events to illustrate aspects of national identity are not unique to totalitarian regimes, as the 1951 Pan American Games held in Buenos Aires under the first Juan Perón presidency exemplifies. The new stadiums constructed for the 1978 tournament were no more than functional sporting stadia; they were not the architectural representations of the regime that Italy's World Cup venues were in 1934.[43] Despite failing to manage Argentina's social breakdown, the democratically elected Peronist presidencies of 1973–76 had sought to gain political capital from staging the competition as a means of uniting a

---

[39] *Clarín*, 23 June 1978.

[40] Smith (2002, 67–88); Alabarces (2007, 111–26).

[41] *La Razón*, 3 June 1978.

[42] Bayer (2016, 135); Levinsky (2016, 189); Galeano (1997, 153–4); Lanata (2003, 58–94); Molinari and Martínez (2013, 201).

[43] Ente Autárquico Mundial 1978 (1976, 9).

divided nation. As the journalist Richard Gott noted just before the tournament, 'if General Perón were still alive and running, the World Cup would be even more of a jamboree.'[44]

A more telling comparison can be found with a more recent major sporting event, the 1968 Olympics in Mexico City. As Gott asked rhetorically eighteen months before the tournament, 'Will it be able to ensure that matches are played in a comparatively peaceful atmosphere, or will Argentina 78 go down in the history books much as Mexico 68 and Munich 72 have done—occasions when politics erupted into sport with a frightening degree of violence?'[45] In projecting Argentina as technologically and organisationally developed, the *junta* copied President Gustavo Díaz Ordaz' government in seeking to place Mexico amongst the world's advanced countries through hosting the 1968 Olympics. Set against this laudable ambition was the fact that Mexico, like Argentina, was a country of extreme income inequality, and for many, the Games and the World Cup that was due to be held two years later were an expense the country could ill-afford. Opposition crystallised into student protests in the summer of 1968 involving up to 500,000 students and teachers, reflecting wider student mobilisation in favour of social change. Protests met with state repression on 2 October, when 10,000 people gathered in the Plaza de las Tres Culturas to protest Mexico's hosting of the Games. In front of the world's media, Mexican security forces opened fire on the largely peaceful crowd, leaving 267 dead and 1,200 injured.[46] Again, the Argentine regime learned lessons from the Mexicans, abstaining from overt repression in the lead up to and for the duration of the World Cup.

As such, comparisons can be made with the position of the Montonero guerrilla opposition in Argentina, who committed themselves to not interfering with the public's enjoyment of the World Cup as it was the 'Festival of the People.'[47] One of the Montonero leaders, Fernando Vaca Narvaja, claimed in December 1977, 'We would not want to damage such an excellent opportunity to address a large audience,' before adding that the group would encourage 'public expression' in the stadiums, as 'Argentina's youth has no place but the football stadium to express

---

[44] *The Guardian*, 17 May 1978, 19.
[45] *The Guardian*, 14 January 1977, 17.
[46] Miller (2012, 183).
[47] Biriotto del Burgo (1995, 61–3).

[political] feelings.'[48] Previewing the tournament, Gott reported that the *junta* were in fear of Peronist and Montonero infiltration of games, where the singing by just a few activists of the *Los Muchachos Peronistas* anthem might catch on around the stadium to the great embarrassment of the regime.[49] The group's campaign to influence the foreign press achieved a measure of success, especially amongst more politically attuned sports journalists. Hugh McIlvanney wrote shortly before the tournament, 'the voice we are happy to hear in Argentina this week is that of the Montoneros,' who, 'have declared that they will observe a truce over the next month and leave the championship unmolested.' It was a decision he said, 'underpinned by political common-sense in a country where football is almost an alternative religion, and [where] anyone who interferes with the masses' enjoyment of it is inviting an instant flood of resentment.'[50] During the tournament, the Montoneros were able to pull off one audacious publicity coup when they managed to intercept the transmission of the Argentina v Poland game by *Channel 10* in Mar del Plata, inserting a propaganda message during the half-time advertisements.[51]

The third strand of this battle for international attention represented those who effectively had their national identity and citizenship stripped from them by the state, as well as their lives in many cases: the disappeared. A combination of open and clandestine repression, known as the 'Dirty War' in which perceived enemies of the state were 'disappeared' and imprisoned before being extra-judicially killed without friends and families knowing of their whereabouts, had an invidious effect on Argentine society. As *Nunca Más*, the official report into the Dirty War recorded, the use of disappearances succeeded in 'paralysing protest,' by, 'ensuring the silence of the relatives. By giving them hope that their loved ones might be alive, in the nebulous category of missing persons, an ambiguity was created which forced relatives into isolation, frightened to do anything which might annoy the government.'[52] Those who questioned the regime either went into exile or lived in constant fear of their own disappearance.

---

[48] *The Guardian*, 15 December 1977, 6.
[49] *The Guardian*, 27 May 1978, 19.
[50] *The Observer*, 28 May 1978, 24.
[51] *El País* (Madrid), 16 June 1978.
[52] Comisión Nacional Sobre la Desparición de Personas (1984).

A brave exception were the Madres de la Plaza de Mayo, a group of mothers, who from 1977 paraded around the main square in front of the Casa Rosada presidential palace, demanding to know the whereabouts of their sons, daughters and other relatives that had been 'disappeared' by the state. It was a request that *The Buenos Aires Herald*, which held no great sympathy for the *junta*, considered in a 1978 editorial as being 'not too much to ask.'[53] Even national footballing heroes were similarly given short shrift. Alberto Tarantini recounted that, 'I had three friends who disappeared at the time of the military, and I went to ask about them. They didn't pay me the slightest bit of notice, didn't even give me the time of day.'[54] As well as the fear of infiltration and disappearance by the state security apparatus, the Madres had to withstand the hostility of some members of the public carrying the Argentine flag who considered them terrorist sympathisers.

The 1978 World Cup brought an estimated 5,000 members of the foreign press to Argentina, giving groups like the Madres opportunity to draw attention to their plight to the wider world, something denied to them within their own country due to press censorship.[55] This engagement brought opposing reactions in the Argentine press. *The Buenos Aires Herald* reported how despite being ignored by the local press, the story of the 'Mad Mothers of the Plaza de Mayo' formed an integral part of foreign media reporting during the World Cup, remarking, 'What prejudices the country is their clamour: "We only want to know if our sons are alive or dead".'[56] Whilst *Para Ti* was berating the foreign press for 'lying' about what was going on in Argentina, it was simultaneously happy to embrace the use of the term 'madwomen' to describe the Madres by those same 'liars' to denigrate the group to an Argentine audience.[57] One tactic used by the Madres was a very public boycott of the World Cup, staging demonstrations at the same time as games were being played, starting with the opening match at 3 pm on 1 June. Juxtaposed against local live television coverage of the opening ceremony was the presence of dozens of foreign journalists in the Plaza de Mayo reporting on the

---

[53] *The Guardian*, 25 May 1978, 13; MacLachlan (2006, 145–9).
[54] Hunt (2006, 181–3).
[55] *The Guardian*, 20 February 1978, 4.
[56] *The Buenos Aires Herald*, 17 May 1978.
[57] *Para Ti*, 24 June 1978.

Madres. The attendance of these journalists and television crews lent the group a level of protection, as watching police held back from disrupting the demonstrations for fear of being portrayed as violent and repressive on European TV stations. Yet, the disappearances continued out of the view of the cameras. According to press conference given by the Argentinian Commission for Human Rights in Brussels just after the World Cup, 48 people were disappeared, with spokesman, Rodolfo Matarolo claiming, 'The World Cup was a manoeuvre to change the image of the Videla government. The dictatorship has not changed. We are fighting a regime which is practising state terrorism.'[58]

By explicitly ignoring the World Cup, the Madres signified a split within Argentine society that did not necessarily run along ideological lines, but instead between those who were directly affected by state repression in terms of torture and disappearances, and those that were not, who could avert their gaze from it and enjoy the tournament. By protesting openly and peacefully in plain defiance of the regime in front of the world's press for the duration of the World Cup, the Madres were paradoxically the biggest winners of the World Cup public relations campaign outside Argentina, whilst within the country their actions were heavily censored and criticised. There were contradictions even within those directly affected by the 'Dirty War.' As the leader of the Madres, Hebe de Bonafini, whose son had been disappeared, later argued, 'How am I not going to understand the people if in my own house, whilst I am crying in the kitchen, my husband is shouting for the goals in front of the television.'[59] Human rights activist, Adolfo Pérez Esquivel, imprisoned by the dictatorship in August 1977 and freed two days before the final, on 23 June 1978, encapsulated the dilemma thrown up by a World Cup held during a dictatorship, 'It was strange, but in shouting goal the prisoners and the guards were united. It gave me the sensation that at this moment, then in the situation through which we lived, was the feeling throughout Argentina.'[60]

For the military regime to get full value for hosting a successful World Cup, ironically it had to rely on something over which it could not exercise control (despite a surfeit of conspiracy theories relating to Argentina's

---

[58] *The Guardian*, 7 July 1978, 7.
[59] Cited in Molinari and Martínez (2013, 207).
[60] Cited in Ibid, 205–6.

6–0 win over Peru which secured their place in the final): the performance of the Argentine team led by Menotti, who in other circumstances could quite possibly have been a victim of the military task groups because of his left-wing political sympathies.[61] As such Menotti was representative of the contradictions and complexities that existed within Argentine society at the time. Numerous writers in the democratic era suggest that Menotti connived with the military regime, some even arguing that the junta 'ordered' Menotti to play an expansive, attacking style of play, despite ample evidence that Menotti's coaching philosophy predated the Videla regime by many years.[62] Such accusations were refuted by Menotti. An educated man with a clear grasp of not just history but class relations. Menotti said of Argentina's predicament in 1978, 'I have a good political formation. I am not a moron who can be linked to it [the military] easily. I know very well that historically the Argentine Armed Forces are the armed group of the oligarchy since when they killed the Indians. They were always the armed group of economic power.'[63] Menotti was also aware of the limits of what a World Cup could achieve, although very subtly suggesting that the formation of a good football team was a metaphor for better collaboration between all the political classes. As he opined a month before the tournament, 'I know what our situation is politically and economically, but I also know that these problems will not solve themselves by playing football. The only possibility that football has is to improve the man as individual: to make him understand the collective sense of life, the need to respect the rights of the others, the importance of disciplined work.'[64] Regarding his essentialist viewpoint about Argentina's footballing traditions, Alejandro Molinari and Roberto Martínez have interpreted Menotti's claim to General Videla, that, 'we not only come to bring a style of play, but also a country's way of life,' as clearly linking him to the dictatorship.[65] Whilst Menotti's declarations

---

[61] For more about the claims and counter-claims relating to the match being 'fixed' by the military *junta* see Miller (1978, 143–4); Ardiles (2010, 64–5); Hunt (2006, 181–3); Kuper (1996, 173–81).

[62] Smith (2002, 77); Galeano (1997, 153–4).

[63] Molinari and Martínez (2013, 207).

[64] Bauso (2018, 799–800).

[65] Molinari and Martínez (2013, 208).

about his preferred style of play appeared to appeal to nationalist sentiment, he was careful to clarify his words, arguing in April 1977 that, 'playing we do not defend our borders, the Fatherland, the flag. With the national team nothing essentially patriotic dies or is saved.'[66]

Given the human rights abuses committed by the dictatorship and his political leanings, there was an expectation that Menotti would say something more definitive on the subject. Pérez Esquivel was particularly critical, suggesting that the coach could have used his unique position to publicly raise the issue of the disappeared.[67] Yet, at the time it would have been prejudicial to Menotti's own position and safety to explicitly speak out against the dictatorship. Given the hold the military had over the levers of power at the AFA at the time, it is likely that he would have been summarily removed from his post, let alone the possibility of him joining the ranks of the disappeared as well. Menotti's response was unequivocal, 'Many people say that I have coached teams during the time of dictatorships, in an epoch when Argentina had governments with which I had nothing in common, and even more, they contradicted my way of life. And I ask what should I have done? Coach teams to play badly, to base everything on tricks, to betray the feelings of the people? No of course not.'[68] As he told his players before the final, 'We look to the stands. We play for those who are there. We defend a style, without tricks, without lies, with dignity, playing for a history that today belongs to us: our football.'[69]

Inconsistencies in Menotti's rhetoric remain. Two weeks before the tournament began Menotti was drawn into the contradiction affecting many in Argentina at the time, of not actively supporting the military dictatorship but simultaneously not accepting criticism of Argentina from outside. He told a press conference of a contretemps he had with a Dutch journalist after seeing flyers handed out in Europe urging a boycott of the World Cup, 'I made him understand that the World Cup is something strictly sporting, that nobody has the right to hinder it because its exclusive protagonist is the public ... I hope nobody tries to use the World Cup as a political weapon because it is a loathsome manoeuvre: the World Cup

---

[66] *El Gráfico*, 19 April 1977, 65.
[67] Molinari and Martínez (2013, 208).
[68] Menotti (1986, 27).
[69] Ibid, 18.

is, above all the biggest party of the people, and as such belongs at the margin of any political manipulation, wherever it comes from.'[70]

The reaction of wider Argentine society during the World Cup reflected a genuine expression of spontaneous national identity and pride that was not reliant upon state direction or manipulation, but instead on a shared love of football. At the outset of the tournament, the Spanish newspaper, *El País* opined, 'The problems [of the country] have been postponed for a month. Argentina is united more than ever in these times thanks to the World Cup. The opinion of the street in this respect is unanimous.'[71] The Argentine people remained impervious to state choreographed public displays of nationalism. Previewing the competition, Gott highlighted the difficulties that the *junta* faced in this regard, describing it as, 'an uphill task since the Peronist movement, for all its faults of omission, commission and division, remains the only genuine voice of Argentine nationalism.'[72] Observing state-sponsored attempts to celebrate the 25 May public holiday, commemorating the establishment of Argentine self-government from Spanish colonial rule in 1810 which received little popular enthusiasm, Gott noted, 'Never have the people of the capital appeared so exhausted, silent, and morose. Perhaps there will be a tremendous explosion of latent nationalism and capacity for enjoyment for which the Argentinians are famous when the football matches begin next week.'[73]

Gott's analysis proved prescient. Watching the opening game against Hungary, Colin Malam wrote of 'Argentina's raging desire to win the World Cup for the first time and on their own soil,' that manifested itself with, 'chants of "Ar-gen-tina, Ar-gen-tina" battering the senses into submission and the ticker tape coming down from the packed tier of this majestic stadium like a blizzard.'[74] The emotions released inside the stadium were a foretaste of the spontaneous celebrations on the streets of Buenos Aires and other towns and cities around Argentina after each match. Technically against the *junta*'s regulations, these mass gatherings enabled people to come together regardless of political affiliation in

---

[70] Bauso (2018, 244–5).
[71] *El País* (Madrid), 6 June 1978.
[72] *The Guardian*, 25 June 1978, 19.
[73] Ibid, 13.
[74] Malam (1978, 8).

what writer Ernesto Sábato described as a 'popular mobilisation marked by generosity and altruism.'[75] As the British *chargé d'affaires* reported back to London, 'the nationwide celebrations after the final reflected not only the fierce popular pride in victory but also … a growing sense of national identity.'[76] It was a theme reprised by *The Buenos Herald*, 'Argentine society, deeply weakened by decades of frustration and then savagely wounded by the terrorist onslaught and its terrible aftermath, may be gradually recovering its inner forces.'[77] After the final, the same newspaper claimed, 'The jubilation was so great that the massive celebrations of 1945 for the end of the war in Europe paled before the frantic joy that seized the twenty-six million inhabitants of the country.'[78]

As such, it was a victory representing a *criollo* identity constructed over nearly two centuries and its essentialist traditions, not transient political ideologies of left or right. As Archetti has argued, 'the victory of a style was transformed into "the victory of the race" over foreign influences and powers,' equating it to a validation of the *junta*'s nationalist discourse in which profession of the Catholic faith was an integral part.[79]

As anticipated, the regime attempted to bask in the reflected glory of Argentina's victory, commissioning a film, *La fiesta de todos*, directed by Sergio Renán, and released in 1979, to immortalise the 'symbolic coming together of the country in common cause.' The closing monologue of the film's narrator, Félix Luna encapsulates all that the *junta* hoped to achieve from the World Cup, 'These delirious, clean, unanimous multitudes are the most that I have seen in my life, a mature, fulfilled people vibrating with a common feeling without anyone feeling defeated or marginalised. And for the first time in this country, without the happiness of some signifying the unhappiness of others.'[80] Whilst the crowd scenes and cascades of tickertape did reflect popular acclamation for the national team, as Patrick Ridge notes, Renán's employment of fictitious comic sketches to underline the *junta*'s nationalist discourse fundamentally undermine

---

[75] *La Razón*, 13 June 1978, 4.
[76] Goebel (2011, 198).
[77] *The Buenos Aires Herald*, 4 June 1978.
[78] *The Buenos Aires Herald*, 26 June 1978.
[79] Archetti (1996, 213–16).
[80] Renán (1979).

the film's value as a documentary of the time.[81] Havelange's words in FIFA's report on the tournament served to validate the *junta's* attempt to project Argentina as a modern, capable country, 'After the political and economic changes the country went through ... the Argentinian authorities ... rendered a near perfect organisation of the 1978 FIFA World Cup possible.'[82]

Whilst the intensively lived experience of winning a home World Cup generated a feel-good factor that cut across all classes and political persuasions, and genuine sense of national pride in Argentina being the best in the world in its most important cultural phenomenon, existential questions soon resumed their habitual importance once the tournament was over. Contrary to the hopes expressed by *The Buenos Aires Herald* that the peaceful image of Argentina conveyed during the tournament would lead to 'measures that will consolidate that peace—the release of people held without charges; an end to "disappearances"; and the healing of all wounds (particularly the question of thousands of people who had disappeared) left by war,' the status quo soon re-emerged.[83] The search for disappeared friends and relatives, so nobly continued during the World Cup by the Madres de la Plaza de Mayo clashed more forcefully with the authorities who were no longer under the intense gaze of the world's press. The worsening economic situation, with an annual inflation rate of 192% eroding living standards also restored a sense of reality that was resistant to empty footballing metaphors used by the Economy Minister, Martínez de Hoz, who claimed that the reduction of inflation required 'intense and persistent discipline, like that shown by the national soccer team.'[84]

PIBE DE ORO: THE EMERGENCE OF DIEGO MARADONA AS NATIONAL ICON

In the mid-1970s, a player emerged who would not only be the archetypal Argentine footballer, but over the remainder of the century became the personification of *argentinidad*: Diego Armando Maradona. Born

---

[81] Ridge (2016, 109–27).
[82] Courte (1980), 4.
[83] *The Buenos Aires Herald*, 10 June 1978.
[84] *The Guardian*, 1 July 1978.

in 1960 in Lanús, Maradona grew up in poverty in Villa Fiorito in the southern suburbs of Greater Buenos Aires, the son of migrants from the northern province of Corrientes. In the best traditions of *la nuestra*, he learned his football in the *potrero*, recalling in his autobiography, 'They were enormous patches of waste ground; some pitches had goals and some didn't … There was no grass, synthetic or otherwise, but to us it was wonderful. The pitches were made of earth, really hard earth. When we started running we stirred up so much dust that we felt as if we were playing at Wembley in the fog.'[85]

Maradona first came to prominence playing for the schoolboy side Los Cebollitas ('little onions') in the prestigious Evita Championship, a tournament that was revived following the Peronist restoration in 1973. So good were the team that they were signed up *en bloc* by Argentinos Juniors to play for their junior team, with Maradona making his senior debut for the club in October 1976 aged just fifteen.[86] In 1973, *El Gráfico* profiled Los Cebollitas, interviewing a 12-year-old Maradona, who highlighted the contradictions that would come to reflect his life and career. Despite being born in Lanús and growing up in poverty in nearby Villa Fiorito, Maradona claimed a provincial provenance, saying that like his father he was a Correntino, moving to Greater Buenos Aires when he was aged four, showing a capacity for personal reinvention that was not restricted to the pitch.[87]

Maradona had made his Argentina debut in February 1977 aged just sixteen but was left out of Menotti's final squad for the 1978 World Cup due to his perceived emotional immaturity. A year later, in September 1979 Maradona was captain and focal point of the Argentine team at the World Youth Cup. The team captured the public imagination despite Argentines having to rise at 4am to watch the matches due to the time difference, coverage of which was heavily censored by the government, who successfully blocked opposition chanting and slogans in the stadiums. The team's delegation in Japan was headed by Julio Cassanello, the Mayor of Quilmes under the dictatorship, who excitedly called President Videla to tell him, 'We have the conviction that we have really been able to

---

[85] Maradona (2004, 6).
[86] Blanco (2016, 65–71).
[87] *El Gráfico*, 21 August 1973, 20–1.

show through our state [of play] here the way of being free, the way of thinking, the way of living of all the Argentine youth, today as always.'[88]

Argentina's victory in Tokyo coincided with the visit to Argentina by a delegation from the Organisation of American States (OAS) to the country to investigate human rights abuses. It was a perfect opportunity for the regime to get the people onto the streets to show that they were at one with the *junta*'s national project. The famous radio commentator José María Muñoz exhorted his listeners to go to the Plaza de Mayo to show the visitors that Argentines were, 'Human and Right.' They came in their thousands, jostling the Madres de la Plaza de Mayo who were waiting their turn to give evidence to the investigators from the OAS.[89]

On his return from Japan, Maradona along with Juan Barbas was due to start his year's conscription in the army. After having his hair cut short and being symbolically pictured in army uniform saluting the flag, he and his *compadré* were given an honourable discharge and allowed to continue with their footballing careers, with his commanding officer leaving Maradona in no doubt was expected of him as an example to the youth of Argentina 'as part of the great enterprise' of the *proceso*.[90] It was not the last time that the *junta* sought to link themselves with Maradona's international profile. President Galtieri made a highly publicised visit by helicopter to the Argentine team's training camp just outside Mar del Plata on 21 February 1982, making sure to single out and embrace the side's new superstar and international symbol of Argentine excellence, Maradona. When asked for his political views, the youngster dutifully trotted out, 'All I want is for my country to be the best in the world.'[91]

Even before he left Argentina, Maradona had before the age of twenty became emblematic of the commercialised road that football was travelling globally. The Argentine airline Austral underwrote his contract at Argentinos Juniors in order to put their logo on the club's strip, as Maradona became the Argentine face of global brands like Coca Cola, Agfa and Puma.[92] In 1981 with Maradona's club, Argentinos Juniors incapable of keeping up with his spiralling wages, they sought to cash

---

[88] Cited in Scher et al. (2010, 459).
[89] Ibid, 459.
[90] Burns (2010, 53).
[91] Cited in Burns (2002, 269–72).
[92] Maradona (2004, 26–7).

in on their prize asset, allowing him to join his boyhood idols Boca Juniors on loan for a fee of US$4 million until after the World Cup when a transfer abroad could be concluded. In his first season with Boca, Maradona helped the club to win the 1981 Metropolitano, their first league title since 1976.

As international interest rates rose, Argentina became unable to meet its debt servicing obligations on the cheap loans it acquired during the late 1970s, something that found an echo in the position of its brightest footballing jewel, Maradona. Despite having been described as national patrimony, Maradona's contract denominated in US dollars became unsustainable, requiring an exhausting schedule of exhibition games to be played by Boca with Maradona in the side to keep up with what the club owed him in wages. By the time of the 1982 World Cup, it became inevitable that the country's brightest star would depart for foreign fields. Despite Boca's fans chanting each Sunday for their idol not to be sold, the insolvency of Argentine football matched that of the country. As Maradona recalled in his autobiography, '…it was obvious that Argentinian football would not be able to afford me for ever—partly because of the economic situation the country was in at the time and partly because Europe is always where our top players end up.'[93] The need for Argentines to 'prove' themselves in the lands of their forefathers was increasingly forming part of the national psyche. In June 1982, Maradona joined Spanish club Barcelona for a world record fee of US$7.6 million. As Argentina's debt crisis reached its nadir in the summer of 1982, the country would need to sell the equivalent of six thousand five hundred Maradonas to clear its borrowing.

Malvinas Y Mundial

Victory in the 1978 World Cup gave national team coach César Luis Menotti almost dictatorial powers, an uncomfortable situation in the context of the ongoing military rule. Anything he wanted from the AFA to aid Argentina's defence of the trophy in 1982 he got, from the suspension of the league so the national team could train together, to the ban on current internationals from being transferred abroad and the insistence on a four-month training camp in advance of the finals. If Argentina were

---

[93] Ibid, 41.

not to succeed in their quest, it certainly would not be for the lack of anything requested by Menotti. Significant sums were made available to local clubs to repatriate top players, for example Kempes and Tarantini were brought back from Europe by River Plate despite not having the financial wherewithal to finance the transfers on their own.

In April 1982 Argentina's defence of the World Cup was overshadowed by a much larger patriotic undertaking: the retaking of the Falkland Islands, which had historically been claimed by Argentina as Las Islas Malvinas since independence from Spain. Britain's continued presence from 1833 after the Argentine garrison had vacated the archipelago two years earlier, and the establishment of a British population there was seen as a colonial usurpation, which only added to anti-British sentiments constructed through later bilateral economic relationships. Over the previous two decades Britain had sent mixed signals to Argentina over their resolve to maintain sovereignty of the islands in the long term, with Argentine diplomats pointing to a 1968 memorandum in which the British 'would recognise sovereignty of the Republic of Argentina' as part of a conclusion to the issue.[94] The decommissioning of the navy patrol vessel HMS Endurance and overtures by British minister, Nicholas Ridley to Falkland Islanders to consider closer links to Argentina added to Argentine belief that the UK was not committed to retaining the Falklands. Indeed, football lay at the root of improved relations during the 1970s when a tournament between Argentine construction workers on Port Stanley airfield and British servicemen attracted a crowd of 500.[95]

General Videla retired from the presidency in 1981 to be replaced by General Roberto Viola. When Viola started a process of engagement with the political opposition about a return to civilian rule, he was usurped in a palace coup that December by a faction of ultra-nationalists in the army led by General Leopoldo Galtieri, who assumed the presidency. In contrast to the politically savvy Viola, Galtieri cast himself as the 'saviour' of the *proceso* after returning from a stint as military attaché to the United States. In Washington, Galtieri had won friends within the Reagan administration for his key support of American efforts to subvert the left-wing government of Nicaragua and in helping El Salvador's military government in that country's civil war against the socialist Farabundo Martí

---

[94] Embajada Argentina Londres (2013, 2).
[95] Campomar (2014, 373).

National Liberation Front (FMLN), providing Argentine advisers who had gained anti-guerrilla experience in its own 'Dirty War' against alleged subversives. It was assistance that led the Reagan government to lift sanctions imposed against Argentina by his predecessor President Carter in 1978 to punish human rights abuses.

In March 1982, the Argentine people began to protest the military government's handling of the economy. An already troubled economy in which deficit spending on projects such as the 1978 World Cup had fuelled spiralling inflation, was worsened by the onset of 1981 global debt crisis leaving Argentina on the verge of default as it struggled to keep up with repayments. Meanwhile the implementation of neo-liberal monetarist economic policies, mirroring those used by Ronald Reagan in the United States and Margaret Thatcher in the UK, in a policy of 'shrinking the state to make the nation larger,' increased unemployment, vastly reduced living standards and left millions of Argentines in poverty.[96] For the first time since the 1976 coup, the Argentine people felt angry and courageous enough to take to the streets to demonstrate against the government only to be harshly repressed by the security forces who fired teargas to disperse them and arrested two thousand of the protesters. It was in this context that Galtieri's government sought to gain public popularity by mounting a military 'recovery' of the Malvinas/Falklands.

News that Argentine forces had taken the islands on 2 April was met with spontaneous demonstrations of support in the Plaza de Mayo that recalled the scenes of celebration following the Argentina's 1978 World Cup victory. Milking the adulation, Galtieri called out to the crowd in response to British Prime Minister, Margaret Thatcher's assertion that Britain would retake the islands by force if necessary, 'If they want to come, let them come, we will present them with battle!'.[97]

As the country went to war in the South Atlantic, Maradona was held up as the archetype of the young men, conscripts in the main, who were doing the fighting. During a live link-up with soldiers on the islands, *ATC Canal 7* anchor-man José Gómez Fuentes referred to a poster of Maradona behind them, saying, 'Dieguito Maradona. Never have we wanted him so much as in this moment, a little because he expresses the *pibe* in all of us, but also because he is a symbol of the nation that makes

---

[96] Sáenz Quesada (2012, 671).
[97] Cited in Gustafson (1988, 146).

Argentines recognise ourselves in each other.'[98] Fuentes was making the case that the two were sharing a common cause. As the soldiers were 'recovering' the Malvinas to fulfil Argentina's destiny, so Maradona was going to the World Cup for the same higher national purpose.

As the arrival of British forces in the South Atlantic meant the dispute over the Malvinas/Falklands turned to war, there were debates over whether Argentina should participate at the World Cup in Spain for which three teams from the United Kingdom: England, Scotland and Northern Ireland had also qualified. The chances of meeting England or Northern Ireland were remote, with Argentina only able to face either in the final, but there was a realistic possibility of playing Scotland in the second phase. Answering questions about a possible British boycott of the tournament FIFA president, João Havelange told a press conference on 23 April, 'In FIFA we deal with sport and not conflicts between nations and sovereignties.'[99] On the Argentine side, AFA president Julio Grondona declared on 7 May that, 'Argentina will be present, unless the military *junta* decides otherwise. So only in the case of a considerable aggravation [of the situation] could we contemplate a withdrawal.'[100] From his self-imposed exile in Spain where he was coaching Real Madrid, Alfredo Di Stéfano publicly called for Argentina to withdraw, feeling it was improper for the team to play in a sporting jamboree whilst Argentine blood was being spilt for *la patria*, saying that, 'It is not logical that whilst some play for their life in the Malvinas, others participate in the World Cup to entertain the people.'[101] For the most part, participation in the tournament was seen by the squad as their patriotic duty in support of their comrades on the battlefields of the Malvinas. Across the Atlantic, British government minister Michael Heseltine noted that any thoughts of withdrawing British sides from the tournament, 'would be seen as a morale boost for the Argentinian forces, and a defeat thousands of miles away, such as the government backing down on this, would see our own forces' heads drop.' By contrast, Heseltine suggested, 'In the present situation we believe that ministers can continue to argue that Argentina is the

---

[98] ATC Canal 7 (1982c).
[99] *El País* (Madrid), 24 April 1982.
[100] Clarín.com (2012).
[101] ESPN.com (2013).

aggressor nation and the onus of withdrawal lies in that direction and not with us.'[102]

One player particularly conflicted by the dispute was Osvaldo Ardiles, who played his last match for his English club Tottenham Hotspur against Leicester City in an FA Cup semi-final on the day after the invasion, before returning to join the Argentine World Cup training camp. As he wrote in his autobiography, 'I never imagined war would break out between the two countries that mattered so much to me, my two countries, my birthplace and my home.'[103] On the terraces, there was equanimity between those Tottenham supporters who expressed support for their Argentine stars Ardiles and Ricardo Villa, and the Leicester City fans who booed them throughout, although this must be seen in the context of the phoney war, before a shot had been fired in earnest save for the early resistance of the small marine detachment defending Port Stanley on the day of the invasion. Ardiles recalled, 'It was quite amazing to hear the fans chanting "Argentina! Argentina!" around the stadium. There was even a banner saying something like "Argentina, you keep the Falklands and we'll keep Ardiles." Quite something.'[104] For Ardiles, the war had another very personal resonance. His cousin, 1st Lt José Leonidas Ardiles was killed on 1 May when the Dagger C-433 that he was flying was shot down by a British Sea Harrier.[105]

On an ideological basis, the national team players were no different from the wider Argentine population in supporting the 'recovery' of the Malvinas, posing with a banner declaring '*Las Malvinas son Argentinas*'— 'The Falklands are Argentine.'[106] According to Ardiles, 'Without doubt we supported the fact that Argentina should recover the islands. In Argentina we are born believing those islands are ours, that they have been stolen from us and therefore to recover the islands is a matter of national pride.'[107] The players were willing supporters of the war effort, helping with the *24 horas por Malvinas* fundraising telethon on the public broadcaster's, *Canal 7*, acting as glorified cheerleaders for the regime's

[102] Cited in Jordan (2017, 186–7).
[103] Ardiles (2010, 124–5).
[104] Ibid, 124–5.
[105] Periodismo Deportivo (2011).
[106] Burns (2010, 89).
[107] Hunt (2006, 194).

military adventure. Some players such as Maradona justified playing in the World Cup as a way of providing succour to the Argentine armed forces. As he later recalled, 'We have talked about it a lot between the boys and that we can best support them from there [Spain], playing as well as possible to cheer up our soldiers.'[108]

Whilst preparing in Argentina, the squad believed the government propaganda that their compatriots were winning the war, but Argentine players based abroad soon acquainted them with the truth. Prime amongst them was the eloquent and well-educated forward, Jorge Valdano, who arrived late to the squad after playing for his Spanish club-side, Real Zaragoza. He challenged the official version of the conduct of events, saying, 'What the Argentine media were saying about the war had nothing to do with the information I had read in Spanish papers and when I wanted to talk about it, I received rather aggressive reactions, some of them a bit violent, even within the squad. I was accused with a very fashionable epithet at the time: anti-Argentinian.'[109] It was an accusation also levelled against Ardiles' Tottenham team-mate Villa, who no longer being a member of the national team, remained in England to finish the season with his club. Seeing the truth of the losses sustained by his countrymen in the conflict, Villa made clear his opposition to the war, and his hope for a negotiated settlement during a telephone interview with the famous Argentine broadcaster Bernardo Neustadt. To which Neustadt replied, 'If you ever decide to come back to Argentina, we will forgive you.'[110]

Within days of their arrival in Spain, it was clear that the Argentine delegation accepted Valdano and Villa's version of events, as they saw uncensored news reports of military reverses for themselves, rendering a psychological blow that undermined the team's performance at the tournament. Despite the news from the battlefront, the team of reporters sent to Spain by *El Gráfico* to cover the tournament went with the intention of highlighting Argentina's ideological claim to the islands, with one editorial claiming, 'We are living through the most difficult days of our times, the world needs to know what happened because of our defence against

---

[108] Zanoni (2006, 75–7).
[109] Cited in Hunt (2006, 200).
[110] Villa and Miller (2010, 186–7).

the British imperialist attack. The reason for our fight. Sport cannot be unconnected to this crucial moment in our history.'[111]

Domestic football in Argentina continued unabated as a way of maintaining a sense of normality at home during the two-and-a-half-month conflict. In a patriotic move, the 1982 Campeonato Metropolitano was initially renamed 'Argentine Malvinas' and later 'Argentine Sovereignty in the Malvinas' by the AFA, who also donated 100 million pesos to the National Patriotic Fund. The players' union the FAA raised a further 190 million pesos to support Argentine servicemen twelve days later by staging a charity match.

Football was also to be part of the civilian integration of the Malvinas into the Argentine Republic, with Grondona claiming, 'Close to one hundred footballers take part in the Falkland Islands Football League, which will soon pass to the control of the AFA.'

It was even suggested that the *superclásico* between River Plate and Boca Juniors could be transplanted to the Malvinas in an exhibition match to entertain the troops. Boca's President, Martín Benito Noel argued, 'I believe that it is a patriotic duty of the (football) leaders to bring happiness to our boys in the islands.'[112]

During the early part of the conflict, the government was able to use censorship and control of the media to their advantage, combining nationalist slogans promoting its adventure in the Malvinas with footage of Argentina's 1978 World Cup win. Indeed, some commentators most notably Nicolás Kasanzew of the *ATC Canal 7* TV channel, reporting from the islands, used footballing analogies in their description of the prosecution of the war.[113] The only subject to break up reporting of the war on *ATC Canal 7*'s primetime show *60 minutos* fronted by José Gómez Fuentes, was coverage of Argentina's pre-World Cup friendlies. For example, the 14 April edition was interrupted to go live to the game against the Soviet Union, where a minute's silence was being held for, 'those lost in defence of the Fatherland.'[114] On 5 May, three days after the ARA Belgrano had been sunk with the loss of 323 dead, Gómez Fuentes began the programme by saying, 'as is tradition in our programme, we

---

[111] *El Gráfico*, 25 May 1982, 3–8.
[112] Burgos (2014).
[113] Burns (2010, 91–2).
[114] ATC Canal 7 (1982b).

would be informing everybody what happened in the battle in our Malvinas, but now we must go abruptly to another subject, that which is to see the great fiesta of Argentine football,' before cutting to Menotti's team's game against Bulgaria.[115]

Enmity towards the British even extended to coverage of the British sides playing at the World Cup, especially England. After declining to show England's first game against France live, despite having trailed it several weeks in advance, *Canal 2* and *Canal 11* instead broadcasted West Germany versus Algeria (British TV stations did the same, choosing not to show Argentina's and the World Cup's opening match live for fear of upsetting public opinion). Things reached an absurd level when commentary of the second-round tie between England and West Germany on 29 June, made no mention of the English at the instruction of broadcasters Radio Rivadavia. Instead, commentator Juan Carlos Morales referred to the English team as 'the reds,' 'the rivals of Germany,' and on one occasion in reference to the recently concluded conflict, 'the pirates.'[116]

In a foretelling of Argentina's forthcoming fate in the war, *La Nación* had published an article ahead of the World Cup entitled 'Knowing How to Lose' referring to the national euphoria generated by the invasion of the Malvinas/Falklands, comparing it to the 1978 World Cup win, warning of the 'progressive disintegration of Argentine optimism, causing a real national neurosis.'[117]

As the War reached its conclusion in the battles for the mountains surrounding Port Stanley, some of the Argentine troops sought solace in their trenches by listening to radio commentary of Argentina's opening World Cup match in Barcelona against Belgium. For conscripts like Marcelo Rosasco, football generated mixed feelings. Whilst listening to games in the trenches had provided distraction from fighting in a war, the business-as-usual attitude on the Argentine mainland, partially engendered by the continuation of football, was a cause of bitterness for those doing the fighting, who felt forgotten by their civilian compatriots on the mainland. As he recalled, 'It shocked us that the people were more worried by Maradona's injury, and we were here dying. In the country

---

[115] ATC Canal 7 (1982a).
[116] Taveira (2013); Lisotto (2012).
[117] Cited in Femenia (1996, 64).

everything carried on the same ... The cold of the Malvinas was not the worst, but instead that from continental Argentina.'[118]

To general surprise, Belgium won the game 1–0. Criticism of the performance was unremitting in the Argentine press the following day. *La Nación* led with the headline, 'A formula for defeat: little conviction and no direction,' a metaphor for Argentine propagation of the war itself. Whilst *Clarín* split its front page with misinformation from the front, 'Bombardment of British Troops,' sharing space with 'Failed Debut in the World Cup.'[119] *El Gráfico* was more emollient, cautioning against using words like tragedy and horror to describe defeat to Belgium in deference to 'the soldiers that defended the Malvinas [that] are incorporated in our souls.' Instead, the loss was 'no more than a disappointment' and 'nothing more than a defeat.'[120]

Even after the Argentine surrender, football continued to play an important part in the lives of the soldiers. Prisoners of war on board SS Canberra caused such a commotion when they heard that Argentina had defeated Hungary 4–1 in their second group game that their British guards trained their weapons upon them for fear that a riot was taking place.[121]

The end of Argentina's reign as world champions came in a comprehensive 3–1 defeat to dazzling Brazil. Not that Argentina's humiliation was yet over. In a fit of pique that summed up Argentina's frustration in this World Cup and a wider sense of Argentine impotence, Diego Maradona was sent off with five minutes to go for a petulant kick into the midriff of Brazilian substitute Batista. Elimination left the squad devastated. When the recriminations began, some players like Ardiles blamed the effect that losing the Falklands War had on morale, whilst others such as Valdano, blamed the cliques that developed inside the squad; the 1978 veterans, and the 1979 youth team newcomers that failed to gel. The Argentine press in Spain freed from the constraints of home were particularly scathing. They were highly critical of what they felt were a bunch of prima donnas, wholly out of touch with what the people back home had been going through. The team's indiscipline, poor motivation and

[118] Periodismo Deportivo (2011).
[119] Burns (2002, 269–72).
[120] *El Gráfico*, 25 May 1982, 3.
[121] Periodismo Deportivo (2011).

lack of leadership were seen as a metaphor for the failings of the military campaign in the Malvinas. Menotti, the hero of 1978, was castigated for appearing to spend more time carousing with a German model at the team's hotel than training the team, whilst the players were accused of being more interested in which European team they would be playing for after the tournament. Indeed, *El Gráfico*, accused the team of 'staying in Buenos Aires.'[122]

In its own way, simply hosting the World Cup in 1978 was a huge boost to Argentine self-esteem. Despite its much-declined economic situation and vacillating body politic, the tournament was a revindication of Argentina's self-image as a modern, sophisticated nation, no longer inflicted with the perceived *mestizo* and *criollo* indolence of its Latin American neighbours as attempts were made to clear the *villas* with their *cabecita negra* inhabitants and redistribute them to their provinces of origin, out of the way of foreign visitors.

Notwithstanding the travails encountered during the first round of the competition, subsequent victories over Poland, Peru and Holland in the final brought the illusion of the superiority of *la nuestra* as a playing style and the long overdue fulfilment of the country's footballing destiny that remained resilient to wholesale appropriation by the military government as a 'victory of the race' in support of its own agenda to 'reorganise' Argentine society.

A sense of national pride extended to the whole population, even conflicting those directly affected by state repression, as the excitement of hosting the tournament in which Argentina were successful after twenty years of disappointment, and the pride in showing foreign visitors that the country could organise it as well as any European country, was something that many could celebrate, and did not need to be state-led. At the time of the World Cup, an uneasy sense of peace existed as Argentina entered a national 'time-out' in which political differences and economic problems were put on hold if not forgotten about, in which Montonero terrorism was absent, and state repression was drastically scaled back from levels seen beforehand, although it patently still went on. As Goebel notes, 'Paradoxically, the public displays of unanimous national consciousness during the football World Cup and the South Atlantic war were paralleled by a growing recognition of the nation's plurality, whether in

---

[122] Burns (2010, 94–5); Campomar (2014, 374–5).

political, ethno-cultural or gender terms.'[123] For the regime, the effect on the national mood was transitory, as the reality of Argentina's declining economy and determining the fate of the 'disappeared' regained public focus. Being champion of the world did not put food on the table or find the whereabouts of a missing son or daughter.

The *junta* was more successful in allying the 1978 World Cup victory to its military 'recovery' of the Malvinas, a historic patriotic aim that long preceded the 1976–1983 dictatorship. However, the Argentine team's listless defence of the World Cup came to symbolise Argentina's ultimate surrender of the islands to British forces that represented such a crushing blow and sounded the death knell for the military dictatorship as it lost whatever perceived authority that it held. Meanwhile the departure of the *pibe de oro*, Diego Maradona, held to be part of the 'national patrimony' to Barcelona reflected the weakness of the Argentine economy as the country entered the world's hitherto biggest debt default.

References

Alabarces, Pablo. 2007. *Fútbol y patria. El fútbol y las narrativas de la Nación en la Argentina*, 4th ed. Buenos Aires: Prometeo Libros.

Antunes de Moraes, K. Helena 2019. Modernidade e Segregação da Villa 29 Através da Cap do Albúm Bajo Belgrano. *Revista Latina-Americana de História*. Vol. 9. No. 21. Jan/Jul: 49–68.

Archetti, Eduardo. 1996. In search of national identity: Argentinian Football and Europe. In *Tribal Identities, Nationalism, Europe, Sport*, ed. J.A. Mangan, 201–219. London: Taylor & Francis Ltd.

Archetti, Eduardo. 1999. *Masculinities: Football, Polo and the Tango in Argentina*. Oxford: Berg.

Ardiles, Ossie. 2010. *Ossie's Dream*. London: Corgi Books.

Bauso, Matías. 2018. *'78 Historia Oral del Mundial*. Buenos Aires: Sudamericana.

Bayer, Osvaldo. 2016. *Fútbol Argentino*. Buenos Aires: Sudamericana.

Blanco, Guillermo. 2016. *Los Juegos Evita: la historia de una pasión deportiva y solidaria*. Buenos Aires: Editorial Octubre.

Boisson, René. 2018. René Houseman: vida de un villero. Panenka. 22 March. www.panenka.org/miradas/rene-houseman-vida-villero/ (Accessed 16 July 2019).

---

[123] Goebel (2011, 218–20).

Burgos, Andrés. 2014. Jugar en guerra, El Gráfico.com. 7 June. www.elgrafico. com.ar/2014/06/07/C-5325-jugar-en-guerra,php. (Accessed 2 June 2015).
Burns, Jimmy. 2002. *The Land That Lost its Heroes*. London: Bloomsbury.
Burns, Jimmy. 2010. *Maradona: The Hand of God*. London: Bloomsbury.
Campomar, Andreas. 2014. *¡Golazo!* London: Quercus.
ATC Canal 7. 1982a. 60 minutos. 5 May. http://www.youtube.com/watch?v= KuWU-2n2hg4. (Accessed 26 June 2015).
ATC Canal 7. 1982b. 60 minutos. 22 April. http://www.youtube.com/watch? v=vXss7SPUnBk. (Accessed 26 June 2015).
ATC Canal 7. 1982c. 60 minutos. 14 April. http://www.youtube.com/watch? v=LMZiVYPAUXQ. (Accessed 26 June 2015).
Clarín.com. 2012. *La selección que jugó el Mundial en medio de la Guerra*. 2 April. La Selección que jugó el Mundial en medio de la guerra (clarin.com). (Accessed 2 June 2015).
Comisión Municipal de Vivienda. 1977. 'Ordenanza municipal No. 33.652'. 13 July.
Comisión Nacional sobre la Desapararición de Personas. 1984. *Nunca Más (Never Again)*. Buenos Aires.
Cordolcini, Alec. 2018. *Pallore Desaparecido: L'Argentina dei generali e il Mondiale del 1978*. Turin: Bradipolibri Editore.
Del Burgo, Biriotti, and Maurice. 1995. Don't Stop the Carnival: Football in the Societies of Latin America. In *Giving the Game Away, Football, Politics & Culture on Five Continents*, ed. Stephen Wagg, 52–71. London: Leicester University Press.
Periodismo Deportivo. 2011. El fútbol y la Guerra, a proposito de Malvinas. 30 March. http://perio.unlp.edu.ar/pd/?q=node/318. (Accessed 2 June 2015)
Duke, Vic, and Liz Crolley. 2014. *Football, Nationality and the State*. Abingdon: Routledge.
Elsey, Brenda. 2014. Football at the "End" of the World. The 1962 World Cup. In *The FIFA World Cup 1930–2010: Politics, Commerce, Spectacle and Identities*, eds. Stefan Rinke and Kay Schiller, 162–84. Göttingen: Wallstein.
Emabajada Argentina Londres. 2013. *Islas Malvinas, Argentina, sus derechos y el diólogo necesario*. London: Embajada Argentina Londres.
Ente Autárquico Mundial 1978. 1976. *XI Campeonato Mundial de Fútbol: Obras de Infrastructura*. Buenos Aires.
ESPN.com. 2013. Una guerra que terminó en el Mundial. 18 October. Una guerra que terminó en el Mundial (espn.com.pa). (Accessed 2 June 2015).
Femenia, Nora A. 1996. *National Identity in Times of Crises: The Scripts of the Falklands-Malvinas War*. New York: Nova Science Publishers. New York.
Galeano, Eduardo. 1997. *Football in Sun and Shadow*. London: Fourth Estate.
Goebel, Michael. 2011. *Argentina's Partisan Past*. Liverpool: Liverpool University Press.

Gustafson, Lowell, and S. 1988. *The Sovereignty Dispute Over the Falkland (Malvinas) Islands.* New York: Oxford University Press.
Hunt, Chris: 2006. *World Cup Stories: The History of the FIFA World Cup.* Ware: Interact.
Jawad, Hyder. 2009. *Four Weeks in Montevideo.* Abbots Langley: Seventeen.
Jordan, Gary. 2017. *Out of the Shadows: The Story of the 1982 England World Cup Team.* Worthing: Pitch Publishing.
Kuper, Simon. 1996. *Football Against the Enemy.* London: Orion.
Lanata, Jorge. 2003. *Argentinos.* Buenos Aires: Sudamericana.
Larraquy, Marcelo. 2018. René Houseman y El Mundial '78: cómo la dictadura desalojó a su familia de la villa del Bajo Belgrano para "embellecer" la Ciudad. Infobae.com. 18 June. www.infobae.com/historia/2018/06/18/rene-houseman-y-mundial-78-como-la-dictadura-desalojo-a-su-familia-de-la-villa-del-bajo-belgrano-para-embellecer-la-ciudad/. (Accessed 19 November 2019).
Levinsky, Sergio. 2016. *AFA. El fútbol pasa, los negocios quedan: Una historia política y deportiva.* Buenos Aires: Autoria Editorial.
Lisotto, Pablo. 2012. Mundial 82: el recuerdo del relato en el que se evitó nombrar los ingleses. La Nación.com. 8 June. http://canchallena.lanacion.com.ar/1479772-mundial-82-recuerdo-del-relato-en-que-se-evito-nombrar-a-los-ingleses. (Accessed 14 June 2015).
Malam, Colin. 1978. *World Cup Argentina.* Glasgow: Collins.
Maradona, Diego A. 2004. *El Diego.* London: Yellow Jersey Press.
Menotti, César Luis. 1986. *Fútbol Sin Trampa.* Barcelona: Muchnik Editores.
Miller, David. 1978. *World Cup: The Argentina Story.* London: Frederick Warne and Company.
Miller, David. 2012. *The Official History of the Olympic Games and the IOC Athens to London 1894–2012.* London: Mainstream Publishing.
Molinari, Alejandro and Roberto L. Martínez. 2013. *El Fútbol. La conquista popular de una pasión argentina.* Avellaneda: Editorial de la Cultura Urbana.
Courte, René, ed. 1980. *Official FIFA Report World Cup Argentina 78.* Munich: proSport Gmblt & Co.
Panzeri, Dante. 2011. *Fútbol Dinámica de lo impensado.* Madrid: Capitan Swing.
Sáenz Quesada, María. 2012. *La Argentina. Historia del País y de su Gente.* Buenos Aires: Editorial Sudamericana.
Renán, Sergio. 1979. *La fiesta de todos.*
Ridge, Patrick T. 2016. ¿La fiesta de todos o pocos?: Representaciones fílmicas del Mundial '78 de la Argentina. *Studies in Latin American Popular Culture.* 34: 109–127.
Scher, Ariel, Guillermo Blanco, Jorge Búsico. 2010. *Deporte Nacional.* Buenos Aires, Emecé.

Smith, Bill L. 2002. The Argentinian Junta and the Press in the Run-up to the 1978 World Cup. *Soccer and Society.* 3 (1): 69–78.

Taveira, F. 2013. España 1982: El Mundial de las Malvinas. infobae.com. 5 July. http://blogs.infobae.com/mundialistas/2013/07/05/espana-1982-el-mundial-de-las-malvinas/. (Accessed 14 June 2015).

Villa, Ricky and Joel Miller. 2010. *And Still Ricky Villa: My Autobiography.* London: Vision Sports and Publishing.

Zanoni, Leandro. 2006. *Vivir en los medios.* Buenos Aires: Marea Editorial.

Zolov, Eric. 2005. The Harmonizing Nation, Mexico and the 1968 Olympics. In *In the Game,* ed. Amy Bass, 191–217. New York: Palgrave Macmillan.

CHAPTER 8

False Dawn: From Democratic Restoration to Economic Armageddon 1983–2002

Following the dual disappointments of being ejected from the Malvinas/Falklands and the World Cup at the second phase stage in June 1982, both Argentina and its national football team were under new leadership by the end of 1983. The surprise winner of Argentina's first democratic presidential elections in a decade was the UCR candidate Raúl Alfonsín. Alfonsín set about re-establishing the country's democratic institutions and trying to heal the divisions within civic society through political pluralism and what Luis Romero describes as 'cultural modernisation' which tried to pick a path through the extremes of *mitrismo* and revisionism in constructions of national identity.[1] This chapter shows how football represented the initial optimism engendered by this democratic restoration, particularly in international competition culminating in 1986 World Cup victory in Mexico. However, failure to control inflation and continued economic inequality in Argentina resulted in an increase in social instability that revealed itself over the course of the 1980s and 1990s through football in the form of hooliganism, as the neo-liberal economic model applied during Carlos Menem's 1989–1999 presidency set Argentina on a course towards the economic crash of 2001–2002.

---

[1] Romero (2004, 263–265).

A process of cultural modernisation was applied to Argentina's football following César Luis Menotti's resignation as national coach, as his successors beginning with Carlos Bilardo attempted to chart a course through a rapidly globalising football world. This chapter assesses the extent to which this process led to a dislocation between the national team and the people it sought to represent, whilst showing how simultaneously the Argentine junior team, led by José Pekerman from the second half of the 1990s, more loyal to a traditional *criollo* style play enjoyed unprecedented international success and popular acclaim.

Diego Maradona's transfer to Barcelona in 1982 was also paradigmatic of the changing nature of Argentina's position in the global economy with repercussions about how football represented identity. The commodification of his image and consequent conflation with the Argentine nation at large was an outlier for the globalisation and commercialisation that not only transformed football in the final quarter of the twentieth century but represented the weakness of Argentina in the global economy.

Using the case study of Boca Juniors, this chapter examines how the initially successful neo-liberal economic policies applied by the Menem government accelerated this process during the 1990s, as well as investigating how the transfer of Argentine players served as an example of Argentina using its 'comparative advantage' in producing quality players for export. It concludes by probing how the Argentine team's first-round defeat in the 2002 World Cup highlighted the bankruptcy of Argentina as a nation following its 2001–2002 financial clash, illuminating the disconnect between its millionaire European-based players and the millions of Argentines recently plunged into poverty that they purported to represent.

Azteca Gold

After the failure of the military in the Falklands/Malvinas War, with Argentina's foreign debt at an unmanageable US$44,000 million, and GDP at a lower level than it had been a decade earlier, General Galtieri was replaced as de facto president by General Reynaldo Bignone, a moderate whose role was to oversee the transition to civilian rule.[2] Radical leader, Raúl Alfonsín was inaugurated as Argentina's first democratically

---

[2] Sáenz Quesada (2012, 678–681).

elected president for a decade on 10 December 1983, a dozen days before his beloved Independiente were crowned league champions. This was mirrored by Julio Grondona being re-elected to a second term as AFA president. Although first elected in 1978 during the dictatorship, Grondona was no puppet of the regime but a Radical political ally of Alfonsín.[3]

Liberated by the political freedom that came with Alfonsín's election, Argentine cultural production re-asserted itself on the international stage, with *la historia oficial* directed by Luis Puenzo becoming the first Argentine film to win an Oscar in 1986. It was no different in the realm of football. A Ricardo Bochini-inspired Independiente won their seventh Copa Libertadores title in 1984, following it up with victory over all-conquering Liverpool in the Intercontinental Cup Final. A year later, the attacking play of Argentinos Juniors dazzled South America as they succeeded Independiente as Copa Libertadores champions, and only lost on penalties to Juventus in the Intercontinental Final in one of the best games of the decade. Such was the quality of Argentinos' play that Horacio Pagani wrote in *Clarín*, 'It was a great game … Because Argentinos showed our [style], that which our people enjoy … Argentine football is again in the shop window of the world. We salute them.'[4] River Plate made it a hat-trick of Argentine victories in 1986 as they finally became continental champions after near-misses in 1966 and 1976 before going to add the Intercontinental Cup after beating Steaua Bucharest.

Argentina's economic situation undermined attempts to embed democracy amid rising unemployment and poverty. In a bid to arrest this decline, Economy Minister, Juan Vital Sourrouille launched the Plan Austral in June 1985, an audacious combination of Keynesian and monetarist economic policies designed to stimulate economic growth whilst keeping a lid on inflation. A new currency, the austral, was gradually introduced by Sourrouille as part of a progressive devaluation to make Argentine exports more competitive. The Plan Austral was initially successful, the reduction in inflation from late 1985 helping to increase the UCR majority in Congress at the mid-term elections before worsening again in 1986.

---

[3] Lewis (2002, 75–76, and 154–158).

[4] Scher et al. (2010, 509).

In July of that year another World Cup victory temporarily helped the Argentine people forget their economic woes. Argentina's qualifying campaign for the 1986 World Cup was a troubled one, with the host of fresh players failing to gel and the team relying on new captain, Maradona's individual skill to drag the team through to qualification. Only a late Ricardo Gareca equaliser in the final qualifier at home to Peru secured Argentina passage to the finals in Mexico. A seven-match winless run after qualification that ended with a 7–2 victory over Israel did little to relieve the pressure on Bilardo's position as coach. Roberto Saporiti, coach of the Argentinos Juniors side which won the Metropolitano Championship in 1984, went as far as to say it would be a retrograde step for Argentine football if Argentina won the World Cup in such a manner. Criticism of Bilardo extended into the political sphere. President Alfonsín was said to be unhappy about the composition of the squad, whilst the Secretary for Sport, Rodolfo O'Reilly—a former Argentine rugby international—put pressure on the AFA to axe Bilardo. Maradona claimed that he was phoned by O'Reilly in April 1986 late in the evening to be told of Bilardo's imminent departure, to which the Minister was told in no uncertain terms that if the Argentine coach left, the captain would go too.[5]

After Argentina's 2–0 victory over Bulgaria in their final group game, the team's World Cup challenge gathered momentum, as the Argentine journalist, Juvenal wrote, the Bilardo's team played to, 'A European rhythm with a creole swagger.'[6] Victory over *rioplatense* neighbours Uruguay in the second round set up a quarter-final at Mexico City's iconic Azteca Stadium with another old rival: England. It was the first football international between the two countries since the Malvinas/Falklands War ended four years earlier. In an atmosphere of great tension ahead of the match, one group of Peronist Senators implored President Alfonsín to pull the Argentine team out of the game as a mark of respect to Argentina's war dead. The Argentine press also did their bit to stir pre-match passions. 'We're coming to get you pirates!' screamed the headline on the front page of *Crónica*, who had sponsored a PR stunt invasion of the Malvinas/Falklands in the 1960s.[7]

---

[5] Maradona and Arcucci (2017, 1–2).

[6] Cited in Maradona (2004, 124).

[7] Burns (2002, 279–280).

Behind the scenes the Argentine and British governments worked together to reduce tensions that they feared would spill over into trouble on the terraces—somewhat forlornly given that gangs of Argentine hooligans or *barras bravas* had flown to Mexico intent on confronting English fans to avenge the deaths of their compatriots in the conflict. President Alfonsín phoned Bilardo to instruct that he come to an unwritten agreement with his opposite number, English coach Bobby Robson to only talk of footballing matters before the game and not the war, and for their players to do the same. Maradona, as captain, showed due circumspection declaring in a final press conference, 'When we go on to the field it is the game of football that matters and not who won the war.'[8] In private, Maradona's views were completely different, writing later in his autobiography of his desire to avenge the Argentine dead from the conflict, 'shot down like little birds …. It was like recovering a little bit of the Malvinas.'[9]

A match that had been unexciting in the first half, caught fire five minutes into the second half with the most controversial moment of the whole tournament. Maradona challenged English keeper, Peter Shilton who had a clear height advantage, in the air for the ball but a touch from Maradona's fist put it beyond the Englishman and into the goal. Maradona claimed that he headed the ball, deceiving the Tunisian referee, Ali Ben Naceur into awarding the goal. It was a goal straight from the *potrero*, the *pibe* Maradona using *viveza* to defraud his opponent, not just any opponent but Argentina's most hated adversary at that point in time. When asked after the game whether he handled the ball, Maradona disingenuously replied that it was, 'A little of the hand of God, and a little of the head of Maradona.' It was another two decades before he confessed the truth, writing, 'it was the hand of Diego! And it felt a little bit like pickpocketing the English.'[10]

If Maradona's first goal was pure *viveza* then his second four minutes later was a devastating essay on the effectiveness of the *gambeta*. Maradona received the ball in his own half with his back to goal and with one neat turn and flick took Peter Beardsley and Peter Reid out of the play before setting off on a dribble accelerating all the while,

---

[8] Ibid, 279–280.
[9] Maradona (2004, 127–128).
[10] Ibid, 130.

slaloming his way past Terry Butcher and Terry Fenwick, the ball stuck to his foot as if magnetised, using Jorge Valdano as a decoy, before inducing an early dive from Shilton by switching from his left to his right foot, and calmly slotting the ball past the England keeper into the empty net. As Jonathan Wilson highlights, the goal prompted Uruguayan journalist, Víctor Hugo Morales to elicit a commentary that has entered Argentine folklore in synthesising the feelings of a nation, 'I'm so sorry, it brings tears to your eyes, in a move for all time …You barrel-chested cosmic phenomenon … From what planet did you come to leave so many Englishmen in your wake, to turn the country into a clenched fist screaming for Argentina?'[11] The edition of *El Gráfico* dedicated to coverage of victory over the English sold 800,000 copies, the most in the magazine's illustrious history, reflecting the zeitgeist of the moment: redemption for the Malvinas and the majesty of Maradona.

After beating Belgium in the semi-final with another virtuoso performance from Maradona, Argentina met a West Germany side in the final who had progressed through the World Cup through sheer resilience rather than by playing dazzling football. As Hugh McIlvanney wrote of Maradona's contribution ahead of the game in *The Observer*, 'Never before in half a century of World Cups has the talent of a single footballer loomed so pervasively over everybody's thinking about the final …Maradona's impact goes far beyond the simple realization that he is indisputably the best and most exciting player now at work in the game.'[12] Maradona had moved from being a national icon to a global one and a metaphor for his country.

When the team arrived back in Argentina an estimated two million people lined the streets of Buenos Aires and the road to Ezeiza Airport to greet them in stark contrast to the handful of people that waved them off just two months earlier. What should have been a 45-minute journey from the airport to the Casa Rosada in the city-centre took six hours as police struggled to keep the road clear of the crowds for the bus to proceed along its way. When they finally got to the presidential palace, Maradona handed the trophy to President Alfonsín who kissed it before handing it back for Maradona to step onto the balcony where Eva Perón had enthralled the crowds over thirty years earlier and take

---

[11] Wilson (2016, 356).

[12] Cited in Burns (2010, 154–155).

the acclaim of the throng in the Plaza de Mayo below, whilst he retired from the limelight. It was a gesture appreciated by the players after the *junta* had hogged the attention when in the same position after Argentina's first World Cup victory eight years earlier. Not only that, but it was also symbolic of Maradona assuming the mantle of 'spiritual leader of the nation' once held by Evita. As *El Gráfico* later reported, he became the personification of the country in eyes of the rest of the world, 'Argentina? Ah, the country of Maradona.'[13]

Whilst celebrations of a second World Cup victory momentarily lifted national morale, they were marred by a spate of looting that left four dead, echoing the deep economic morass afflicting Argentina. As Maradona reflected after the tournament, 'all that happened was that a team of Argentine footballers won a few matches. No more. The price of food stays the same. If going to play football in Mexico could change social conditions in the world then I would go and live there permanently! But a handful matches do not answer anything.'[14]

Argentines did not enjoy the satisfaction of having the world champion football team and a restored democracy for long. By 1987, the Austral had proved not to be the panacea to the ills of the Argentine economy as investment remained stagnant and Alfonsín's government failed to convince Argentine citizens of the benefits of low inflation. A poor harvest in 1988 exacerbated Argentina's trade imbalance which saw the Argentine Central Bank exhaust most of its foreign currency reserves in February 1989 trying to maintain the value of the Austral, bringing it to the verge of bankruptcy. Within two months, the Austral plummeted on the international currency exchanges and the annual inflation rate reached 5,000%.[15]

In 1987, Argentina again had the opportunity to display its credentials as a well-organised country as it hosted the Copa América. Half empty stadia—even those involving the hosts—compared unfavourably with the tickertape fervour engendered during the 1978 World Cup, whilst the Peruvian team had to practice in a public park because adequate training facilities could not be provided by tournament organisers, reflecting the poor organisation of the country more widely. The Argentine team

---

[13] *El Gráfico*, 3 October 1989, 26.

[14] *World Soccer*, December 1986, 5.

[15] Lewis (2002, 154–158); Goebel (2011, 202–203); Romero (2004, 263–265).

performed poorly in front of their own fans, losing at the semi-final stage with attendances shrinking accordingly, due to spectator disillusion with the style of play and the effects of the country's declining economy pricing many out of affording tickets. This was evidenced by Argentina's third-place play-off defeat against Colombia, which like the national morale was shrouded in a thick fog, played out in a funereal atmosphere witnessed by just 5,000 in a Monumental Stadium with capacity for fourteen times that number.

As the 1990 World Cup in Italy approached, Argentines elected a new populist president, Carlos Saúl Menem in May 1989 after Alfonsín's government had failed to control inflation, which devoured savings and sent prices spiralling. Despite being the candidate of the Peronist Party, Menem soon underwent a chameleon-like change from left-winger to free marketer and darling of the IMF, overseeing massive liberalisation and privatisation of the Argentine economy, at the expense of his working-class support who saw their welfare and labour rights reduced. Menem argued that this massive structural adjustment was needed to restore economic stability and Argentina's place as a key figure in the global economy, something that hadn't been the case since the 1920s.

Menem wasted little time in ingratiating himself with the national team to maintain his popular appeal, going as far as playing 90 minutes with the side in a charity match in front of 55,000 at the Vélez Sarsfield stadium shortly after coming to power. Fulfilling a childhood dream of playing for his country, he claimed, 'Football is the thing that formed me physically and it has given me a great deal of spirituality.'[16] Attempting to identify his presidency with the national team's status as reigning world champions, Menem made an offer to Diego Maradona to become an honorary Ambassador for Sport with full diplomatic privilege, publicly awarding the player with his diplomatic passport at a pre-World Cup press conference in Milan. Menem was profuse in his praise of Maradona, 'We are here to inaugurate a new form of accreditation, a new type of diplomatic image ... Plato said sport makes wise and careful men – the type of men the world needs now.'[17] To which Maradona replied, 'Thank you. I will represent and defend Argentina ...on the pitch.'[18] The identification of

---

[16] Cited in Mason (1995, 75).

[17] Cited in Burns (2002, 491–495).

[18] Maradona (2004, 153).

Maradona with the Menem presidency was not coincidental. Maradona's social mobility from impoverished childhood in Villa Fiorito to one of the most famous people on the planet was the very essence of Peronism, whilst his gauche wedding at Luna Park in 1989—televised live—would embody the crass consumerism of the Menem presidency.

An embarrassing defeat to Cameroon in their first game of their World Cup defence prompted Bilardo to challenge his players, 'Either we reach the final, or let's hope the plane carrying us back to Argentina falls out of the sky.'[19] Despite some wretched performances in subsequent matches, Argentina recaptured their form during the semi-final to eliminate hosts, Italy in a penalty shoot-out. It was a victory that led Menem to claim was an example for the Argentine people (much like Juan Carlos Onganía's assertion that Argentina were moral victors in 1966). Attempting to unite citizens behind his tough socio-economic policies he appealed, 'we have 11 titans inside the pitch. Now we need 33 million to take Argentina from this situation.'[20] It was a reclamation that had an uncomfortable parallel with José Alfredo Martínez de la Hoz' exhortations after the 1978 World Cup victory which sought to deflect from the inefficacy of government economic policy by placing failure on the Argentine people to 'step-up' and play their part in national austerity.

NATIONAL TEAM FOR ALL?

The relationship between the national team as standard-bearers of national identity and the Argentine people which fractured after the 1958 'Disaster of Sweden' was gloriously reconnected during the successful 1978 World Cup campaign. The decadent failure of Menotti's side at the 1982 World Cup renewed debates about the effectiveness of *la nuestra* that were reinforced by the appointment of Carlos Bilardo as his replacement. The complete antithesis of the urbane Menotti, Bilardo was an arch-pragmatist in the mould of Osvaldo Zubeldía, under whom Bilardo had played for the notorious Estudiantes de La Plata side of the late 1960s that won three Copa Libertadores in succession between 1968 and 1970. After retiring early from playing in 1970 to pursue a medical career as a gynaecologist, Bilardo later returned to football as a coach, with spells in

---

[19] Cited in Wilson (2016, 373).
[20] *La Nación*, 14 July 1990, Sec. 2, 5.

charge of Deportivo Cali in Colombia, San Lorenzo de Almagro, and the Colombian national team before winning the Campeonato Nacional with Estudiantes in 1982.

After taking over as coach, Bilardo was soon reminded of the new democratic Argentine landscape he was now working in. He had wanted to prohibit the transfer abroad of 40–45 of the country's top players to make it easier to work with them in the national team as Menotti had before him, arguing that such transfers would only 'serve to enrich agents,' but was told by AFA Treasurer, Julián Pascual that, 'Legally, one could not deny the freedom to work to anyone, as set out in the constitution.'[21]

Overhauling the team that had failed in Spain, Bilardo's first three years in charge were marked by tactical confusion as his team won just three of his first 15 games in charge. Argentina exited the 1983 Copa América at the group stage and were beaten by China in the Nehru Cup in 1984, a competition in which Héctor Onesime wrote of Bilardo's team, 'What a pity, the football didn't appear.'[22] As Argentina set off on a tour of Europe in late 1984, Bilardo's job was in jeopardy. When he named three central defenders on the team-sheet for the opening game against Switzerland, in a pre-cursor of the revolutionary tactics that would win the World Cup less than two years later he was widely assumed to have made an error. Argentina subsequently rolled over Switzerland and Belgium 2–0, before beating 1982 World Cup finalists, West Germany 3–1 in Düsseldorf.

Bilardo was unrepentant in the face of sceptics, arguing that the Argentine footballing public was living in the past and were ignorant of developments in European football. He claimed, 'Even my father keeps asking me why I don't play with classical wingers, but there aren't really outstanding forwards in Argentina now and certainly no wingers.'[23] Bilardo was now almost ready to employ the 3–5–2 formation that he had trailed with some success on that European tour. His argument was that if no teams played with designated wingers, then what use were fullbacks? According to Bilardo the two extra players could be more usefully deployed further up the pitch in wide midfield positions.

---

[21] *El Gráfico*, 27 September 1983, 54–55.
[22] *El Gráfico*, 17 January 1984.
[23] *World Soccer*, April 1986, 20.

Like Menotti before him in 1978, and the great Brazilian sides of 1958 and 1970, Bilardo was fully aware that attending to the slightest detail could make the difference to winning or losing the World Cup. Argentina was the first team from abroad to arrive in Mexico having already spent time acclimatising to playing at altitude in the Andean town of Tilcara, with Bilardo wanting to spend a full month in the country to acclimatise and work with his team as well as having the benefit of being away from the pressures in Buenos Aires.

It was in the iconic quarter-final against England that Bilardo unveiled his tactical trump card, instituting the 3–5–2 formation that would bring out the best in the players at his disposal. Abandoning the four in a line defence in favour of two markers at the back and a *líbero* or sweeper, enabling him to add another player, Héctor Enrique in midfield, freeing Maradona to roam wherever he needed to create havoc in the opposition half.

Such was the singularity of Maradona's performance in the tournament that it permanently solidified Maradona's status in the Argentine imaginary as the *pibe de oro* ('Golden Boy') and archetype of the Argentine nation as he reached the peak of his profession donning the sky-blue and white shirt. Argentina's victory was also the fitting fulfilment of a childhood premonition on Maradona's part. Interviewed as a precocious, ball-juggling 12-year-old by TV celebrity, Pipo Mancera, Maradona revealed that his ultimate dream as a footballer was, 'to wear the shirt of the Argentine national team in a World Cup and to win it.'[24] When the team returned to display the trophy to the assembled throng in Buenos Aires' Plaza de Mayo, amongst the banners of support was a huge one saying, 'Sorry Bilardo, we forgive you' by way of public apology on behalf of the fans for doubting his tactical methods.[25]

Bilardo was a divisive figure for Argentine commentators and fans. His defensive style was considered overly negative and contrary to the tenets of *la nuestra*. In response, Bilardo retorted, 'I could never understand what the fans wanted, nice play or good results? ... What I'm sure of is that people want to win.'[26] He argued that it was impossible to make comparisons between styles and eras, simply that football just like

---

[24] Cited in Archetti (1999, 182–184).
[25] *World Soccer*, May 1989, 11.
[26] Ibid, 11.

society had evolved. Ironically, despite his perceived defensive proclivities, his greatest gift was in getting the best out of the most creative Argentine player of all-time, the mercurial Maradona, whose brilliance lit up the 1986 World Cup and almost single-handedly dragged his team to the 1990 final.

Alfio Basile replaced Bilardo as coach after the 1990 World Cup, as football entered a more globalised and commercial phase. As a player, Basile was a member of the great Racing Club de Avellaneda side of the mid-1960s which won the 1967 Copa de los Libertadores and Intercontinental Cup. His brief international career was less illustrious, coming at the nadir of the Argentine national team's fortunes when failing to qualify for the 1970 World Cup. He paid tribute to his predecessors for restoring the standing of playing for the national team, 'I'm lucky now, thanks to Menotti and Bilardo. Before they came little importance was given to the national team. I remember as a player around the 1960s, when I had to choose between club and the national team, I chose the security of the former.'[27]

One of Basile's first achievements in charge of Argentina was to reverse the negative stereotypes about Argentine football that had arisen during the team's sterile run to the 1990 World Cup Final under Bilardo by employing a more attacking style, with Daniel Arcucci remarking in *El Gráfico* after an initial 2–0 victory over Hungary, 'The first step invites us to dream.'[28] Basile started to reconnect the national team with the Argentine public, who had felt estranged during the Bilardo era. Not only did the side play far more friendly games at home under Basile but he also picked more locally based players such as Sergio Vázquez, Leonardo Rodríguez and Leonardo Astrada. The selection of Deportivo Mandiyú's Dante Unali for Basile's opening game against Hungary in Rosario evoked Menotti's strategy of using the best talent from the whole of Argentina and taking the national team to all corners of the nation.

Basile's approach achieved instant success with his new-look team, winning the 1991 Copa América—their first for 32 years—without the presence of Maradona, who had announced his international retirement after the 1990 World Cup. With Claudio Caniggia and Gabriel Batistuta as the spearhead of the attack, Basile constructed a side which captured

---

[27] *World Soccer*, October 1992, 16–17.
[28] *El Gráfico*, 26 February 1991, 24–25.

the imagination of the press, playing with a *joie de vivre* not seen for many years, with *El Gráfico* claiming, 'We have not played like this since '86.'[29]

Despite Argentina successfully defending their Copa América title in Ecuador in 1993 and being on an unbeaten run stretching to 29 matches, Basile's team appeared to be a side in decline, rather than a potential winner of the World Cup as they began their qualifying campaign for the 1994 tournament a month later. Erratic results during qualification meant Argentina had to beat Colombia in their final game to make sure of reaching the tournament in the United States, whilst the Colombians required only a draw to progress.

What happened in that match on 5 September 1993 was beyond Argentina's worst nightmares as they endured their heaviest home defeat since 1910, losing 5–0, a result that rocked Argentine self-confidence like no other since the 6–1 loss to Czechoslovakia at the 1958 World Cup. To add insult to injury for the Argentine players, the home crowd started cheering every Colombian touch after the fourth goal went in and applauded them off the pitch after Adolfo Valencia completed the rout in the final minutes of the game. Not only that, the familiar tribal chant of 'Maradó, Maradó, Maradó,' also reverberated around the stadium as the fans were in no doubt who could redeem the team from this disgrace: Diego Maradona, who had by now reversed his decision to retire from international football. Such was the magnitude of the defeat that for its edition published after the game, *El Gráfico* printed its front cover in black, the colour of mourning, with a headline of 'Shame!'.[30]

Part of the reason that Argentines felt such humiliation was that they had played such an important role in the development of Colombian football, especially during the formative years of professionalism in the 1940s and 1950s, and now the 'pupils' had taught the 'masters' a lesson. Not only that, but the Colombians had done so in a style that was the essence of *la nuestra*, meaning that the Argentine players were neither able to defend the national colours, nor the national style.

Fortunately for Argentina the result of the other game in the group, a 2–2 draw between Peru and Paraguay went in their favour, and they were given a second chance of qualification in a two-legged repechage against Oceania group winners Australia. After the debacle against Colombia,

[29] *El Gráfico*, 16 July 1991, 8–9.
[30] *El Gráfico*, 7 September 1993, 1.

Basile had no choice but to accede to the clamour for the restoration of Maradona to the team. Whilst Pablo Alabarces has compared Maradona's return to the national colours as being like a post-modern San Martín, consolidating his role as 'Father of the Nation,' a more compelling comparison would be the return of Juan Perón in 1973 when he was considered the only person capable of galvanising Argentina, albeit unsuccessfully.[31] In the first leg in Sydney, Argentina gained an all-important away goal through Abel Balbo in a 1–1 draw despite not playing well, with *El Gráfico* reporting, 'The footballing fatherland must continue to be thankful to Diego Armando Maradona.'[32] Two weeks later in the return match in the Monumental, Gabriel Batistuta scored the winner in a hard-fought victory over the Australians to clinch World Cup qualification.

Despite the blind faith placed in him by the Argentine nation on the based on past exploits, serious questions marks were raised about the fitness and condition of Maradona ahead of the 1994 World Cup in the United States. With his career in severe decline following a 15-month suspension for drug-taking in 1991, Maradona was once more without a club after parting company with Newell's Old Boys after just five months and seven games played. His psychological state was also called into question when he fired an air-rifle at journalists camped outside his residence in an upmarket northern Buenos Aires suburb. Those doubts appeared dispelled after Argentina's opening match in the competition against Greece in Boston's Foxboro Stadium. Having lost over a stone, Maradona looked the fittest he had been for years and showed that he had lost none of his precision passing ability, prompting Argentina's best moves. Maradona's virtuoso performance was capped by a fine goal that put Argentina 3–0 ahead; however, it was the manic goal celebration in which his contorted face roared into a television camera that alerted the world to the fact that something was amiss. Events in the immediate aftermath of the game against Nigeria in Dallas sealed Argentina's fate at the tournament as Maradona was separated off from his colleagues and led away by a nurse to conduct a routine drugs test. It was Maradona's last action not just at the World Cup, but also in the blue and white jersey of Argentina as he tested positive for several banned substances including

---

[31] Alabarces (2007, 151).
[32] *El Gráfico*, 2 November 1993, 8.

ephedrine. Following the fallout of the Maradona scandal, morale within the Argentine squad evaporated. After losing their final group match to Bulgaria, Argentina were eliminated after defeat by Romania in the second round.

Reaction in Argentina was one of stunned disappointment, sad for the downfall of a great hero rather than anger at his selfishness in letting down the team and the country. Some compared the national mood to the death of Juan Perón in 1974 and the loss of the Malvinas War in 1982. In *Clarín*, Fontanarossa jokingly claimed that for Argentine fans, the tragedy of Maradona's downfall in Dallas was akin to the assassination of President Kennedy there in 1963.[33] Maradona's human frailties were the flipside of his invocation as the embodiment of *argentinidad*. As Andreas Campomar identifies, 'his more objectionable traits, which came in the guise of those twins, hubris, and self-pity, were a reflection of Argentina. In many ways, hatred of Maradona was simply a form of Argentinian self-loathing.'[34]

Part of the reason for the lack of outright condemnation of Maradona within Argentina was the propensity to push rules to the limit, with the phrase, 'I obey but I do not comply,' being an article of faith in attitudes to authority in Argentine society since Spanish colonial times.[35] As Eduardo Archetti notes, Maradona's status as the archetypal *pibe* also allowed for a greater measure of forgiveness as a trade-off for the enjoyment of his outrageous talent.[36]

After Argentina's humiliation against Colombia and subsequent failure at the 1994 World Cup, Basile was replaced as national coach by 41-year-old Daniel Passarella. A double World Cup-winner, Passarella made his coaching reputation by winning trophies with River Plate over a four-year period since retiring as a player in 1990, simultaneously promoting young talents such as Ariel Ortega, Roberto Ayala and Marcelo Gallardo. When interviewed for the role by the AFA, Passarella presented his vision of the future in a document entitled 'National team for all,' something he later clarified in a magazine article, 'All the players who come into the squad will first of all have to understand what it means to wear the

---

[33] *Clarín*, 2 July 1994, 24.
[34] Campomar (2014, 378).
[35] Bonner (2007, 16).
[36] Archetti (1999, 184).

national colours, be serious, professional and responsible and that they will start at zero. Nobody will play because of their name. They will have to show every day why they are in the national team.'[37] Passarella's assertion that his players should wear their hair short as a sign of personal discipline had some observers scoffing, not sure whether he was joking or not, given the uncomfortable echoes of similar demands made by the military dictatorship barely two decades before. It was soon confirmed when two players with flowing locks; Fernando Redondo and Claudio Caniggia found themselves outside the national squad, whilst Gabriel Batistuta who had sported an equally impressive mane thought it prudent to trim a couple of inches off the bottom to show compliance.

As he had done with River, Passarella promoted young talents to the national team, such as Javier Zanetti, Juan Sebastián Verón and Hernán Crespo as Argentina won the silver medal at the 1996 Olympic Games and had a trouble-free qualification for the 1998 World Cup in France. Counter to claims made by Pablo Alabarces, Alan Tomlinson and Christopher Young, that, 'the hyperbolic tone of the media was not remotely matched by the popular response,' elements of the Argentine press railed against Passarella's team despite it only losing two games *en route* to France.[38] *El Gráfico* were more critical than popular daily newspapers. One of the key accusations made by the magazine was that the team—playing its first World Cup campaign for twenty years without Diego Maradona—was 'lacking geniuses' as Ariel Ortega, Marcelo Gallardo, Pablo Aimar and Juan Román Riquelme all failed to live up to Maradona's heights in the *albiceleste* number ten shirt.[39] Mocking Passarella's 'National Team for All' motif, *El Gráfico* described the side as 'the team of nobody,' claiming that the side had 'neither football nor personality,' before arguing that 'the national team is in debt with the people.'[40]

Whilst Alabarces and others have sought to present press coverage of the tournament as an attempt to ascribe a national dimension to the squad's composition, in reality it was no more than a representation of the central pampean belt rather than being 'a metaphor of the nation,

---

[37] *World Soccer,* November 1994, 12.
[38] Alabarces et al (2001, 547–561).
[39] *El Gráfico,* 22 July 1997.
[40] *El Gráfico,* 17 December 1996; *El Gráfico,* 29 April 1997.

and of all of its component parts,' especially in comparison with the squad selected by Menotti two decades earlier.[41] Argentina ultimately exited the tournament at the quarter-final stage having won all three of their first-round games and participated in the competition's two best matches; against England and the Netherlands. Nevertheless, Passarella tendered his resignation with the criticism of the Argentine press ringing in his years, who complained that his team was too narrow and mechanical. Indeed, before the game Menotti had prophesied, 'If Holland lose, they only lose a game, but not their style.'[42] In his favour, though, Passarella had created the nucleus of the side that would serve Argentina well over the next decade.

On taking over as national coach in 1994, Daniel Passarella argued that Argentina had some of the best young players in the world, and later that same year AFA president, Gondona appointed José Pekerman to develop those players as national youth coach. Rather than having a different coach at each age-group, an integrated youth development programme was initiated with Pekerman charged to generate a production line every two years of players ready for the full national team, from under-15 through to under-23 level. Pekerman had previously trained the youngsters of Chacarita Juniors, Argentinos Juniors and Colo Colo in Chile and came to the role with the aim of achieving results by recovering the identity of the Argentine player in terms of technical capacity, imagination and skill. Passarella's claim was corroborated with Argentine victory a year later at the World Youth Cup in Qatar. A delighted Pekerman said after the final against Brazil, 'We're happy for the whole country. Argentina expected this and we've fulfilled that wish. We've grown as a side throughout the tournament and today we showed how much we've progressed.'[43]

Argentina's victory in Qatar was repeated in Malaysia in 1997, with the emergence of another crop of young players who would go on to shine at senior level including Juan Román Riquelme, Esteban Cambiasso and Walter Samuel. As the team's playmaker, Riquelme was symbolic of a return to the mythical origins of *la nuestra*, a perception further accentuated when he came on as substitute for Maradona in the latter's

---

[41] Alabarces et al (2001, 547–566).
[42] Scher et al. (2010, 546).
[43] *World Soccer*, June 1995, 36–37.

last official game on 25 October 1997 in what was seen by commentators as a generational changing of the guard. In many ways, Riquelme was a throwback to an earlier age when players had more time on the ball to express their skills, and he would not have been out of place in Stábile's South American Championship-winning teams of the 1940s. The main weapon in his armoury was the use of *la pausa,* a staccato move associated with the tango in which the ball was stopped to enable a change of direction and the fooling of the opposition player. Yet, in the fast pace of modern football, Riquelme's lack of pace was a luxury that could be ill-afforded according to a succession of national coaches such as Passarella and Marcelo Bielsa, hindering his senior international opportunities for the rest of the decade. Argentine excellence at junior level was further confirmed in 2001 when the team won the World Youth Cup for the third time in four editions on home soil. The side containing future internationals like Javier Saviola, Andrés D'Alessandro and Maximiliano Rodríguez breezed through the tournament, winning all seven of their games, scoring 27 goals and delighting the capacity crowds along the way.

Attempts by Argentine coaches to stay loyal to *la nuestra* whilst remaining contemporary continued to be doomed to failure, compounded by Marcelo Bielsa's attempt to find a middle way between Menottismo and Bilardismo, when he took the reins of the national team in 1999. Bielsa claimed there were merits in both approaches, 'I spent 16 years listening to them. For eight years I listened Menotti, a coach who emphasises inspiration. For eight years I listened to Bilardo, who emphasises functionalism. And I took the best from both.'[44]

Famed for his permanently dishevelled track-suited appearance, Marcelo Bielsa preferred a cerebral approach that seemed out of place in Menem's slick consumer society. Bielsa's high-tempo play was exemplified by his Newell's Old Boys team that won the 1998 Clausura championship. They attempted to press the life out of opposition teams whilst imposing his team's own counter-attacking offensive play. Eulogising the contemporary Dutch approach of continually keeping the ball moving in search of an attacking opportunity as the blueprint for his Argentina team, Bielsa recognised that this went against the taste of the Argentine press and fans. He conceded, 'In Argentina, people wouldn't accept

---

[44] *World Soccer,* November 2001, 69.

the team being so calm. We can be betrayed by our own anxiety. I've always wanted to mix our ability with European discipline.'[45] That Bielsa should seek to incorporate European influences was a pragmatic response to the fact that the vast majority of his squad were now playing across the Atlantic, something reflected by Marcelo Gallardo, another member of Bielsa's team who considered himself, 'enchanted with the mixture of European dynamism and Argentinian technique.'[46] Amongst fans and press in Argentina there was what journalist Tim Vickery described as resistance to the fact that, 'European-style hard running had taken the place of traditional artistry – a natural response from a proud football nation embittered at not seeing its idols on a weekly basis.'[47] Indeed, it was only by the end of Argentina's successful qualifying campaign for the 2002 World Cup in Japan and Korea that Bielsa won over these key constituents.

That said, Bielsa was not beyond invoking Argentina's gaucho past—just as Nationalists had done in the 1920s and 1930s—to galvanise his players. Facing a tricky away tie against Colombia, Bielsa evoked the knife-fights to the death of gauchesque folklore in his pre-match team-talk, 'boys, there are two ways of looking at this. There are those who see blood, recoil and run away from it and there are those who want more and seek it out. I can tell you that out on that pitch and in the stands, there is the smell of blood.'[48] The motivational tactic worked, as Argentina won in what had traditionally been a hostile venue where they had rarely prospered. Even the visit to the 12,000 feet altitude of La Paz, where Argentina had struggled so many times over previous decades elicited a positive 3–3 draw, fighting back from 3–1 down with just two minutes to play, displaying a resilience rarely seen by the Argentine national team before without recourse to football's dark arts. Bielsa's side qualified with ease, suffering just one defeat, away to Brazil in São Paulo. According to national team midfielder, Juan Pablo Sorín when interviewed in 2001, 'We're playing every game as if it were our last. When we lose the ball we put real pressure on our opponents to get it back, and then comes the

---

[45] *World Soccer*, Summer 1999, 26.
[46] *World Soccer*, November 2001, 69.
[47] Ibid, 69.
[48] Rich (2020, 109–116).

big effort to move and give options to the man in possession. Bielsa is the most attacking coach in the world.'[49]

THE ARGENTINE FOOTBALL FACTORY: MENEM, MACRI AND NEO-LIBERALISM

The export of Argentine footballers following the lifting of restrictions after the 1982 World Cup was but one prong of the transition of both Argentine society and its football brought about by globalisation over the final quarter of the twentieth century. The neo-liberal transformation of Argentina's economy into a consumer-led economy saw a hitherto unseen level of commercialisation in Argentine football. AFA president, Julio Grondona argued that it was simply the culmination at a local level of a process begun by the election of João Havelange as FIFA president in 1974. As part of his mandate to grow the grassroots of the game worldwide, the Brazilian vowed to maximise the commercial income from FIFA's flagship event the World Cup in terms of attracting sponsorship from the likes of Coca Cola, as well as television broadcasting rights. So successful was Havelange's policy that by the 1994 World Cup in the United States, the Argentine team was in receipt of half a million US dollars per game that they played in the tournament.[50]

As seen in previous chapters, Argentine football clubs were owned by their members, but by the 1990s membership rolls were dwindling to half of what they were at the beginning of the 1980s at big clubs such as River Plate, Boca Juniors and Vélez Sarsfield. Matchday attendances declined on a similar downward curve as crowd violence combined with unaffordable ticket prices for the popular classes drove fans away. First Division attendances declined from an average of 15,056 per game in 1954 to just 3,883 in 1978 (although this did not include *socios*, who paid for the equivalent of a season-ticket), and by the mid-1990s some matches involving the top flight's lesser lights saw as few as 200 tickets sold.[51] This combined with inept, and in some cases corrupt management—a common theme to both Argentine football and national politics—meant that most clubs were heavily indebted and in need of alternative sources

---

[49] *World Soccer*, December 2001, 69.
[50] *La Nación*, 28 July 1996.
[51] *World Soccer*, April 1996, 40.

of finance. By 1996 three of the *cinco grandes*; River, Boca and Racing Club were each at least US$10 million in debt.[52] Whilst elsewhere in the world, insolvent clubs like this were being declared bankrupt and expelled from the league, as happened with Newport County and Aldershot in the English Football League, Argentine clubs were able to avoid a similar fate due to political protection as forming part of the 'national patrimony.'

One solution suggested by Grondona was for clubs to abandon the membership model and become privately owned as happened in England, thereby mimicking a key plank of Menem's economic plan which saw the privatisation of Argentina's airports, utilities and telecommunications services, principally sold to Spanish companies such as Telefónica, Endesa and Aguas de Barcelona.[53] When this was briefly tried in the mid-1990s after a TV company took over Argentinos Juniors, there was general opprobrium when the club was relocated to the city of Mendoza, 1,400 km away from the club's home in Buenos Aires, emulating the franchise model of American sports. The experiment was swiftly abandoned as a failure after just one season whilst attempts to do so at San Lorenzo and Deportivo Español were flatly rejected by the respective clubs' members. The latter being an attempt in 1993 by Mauricio Macri to move the Español 'franchise' to Mar del Plata and form a super team coached by César Luis Menotti.[54]

Whilst matches in Argentina had been televised since 1951, technological advances in satellite broadcasting which facilitated the advent of cable television in the 1990s transformed the coverage and consumption of football. With Argentines becoming the biggest consumers of cable television in Latin America, new competitors seeking subscribers like *Torneos y Competencias* (*TyC*) entered the marketplace, leading to revenue from league broadcasts rising tenfold in less than a decade, from US$600,000 a year in 1985 to US$6 million in 1994.[55] By 1997, football matches were the ten highest rated television programmes in the country.[56] What the negotiations did was to reinforce the economic power within the Argentine game of the *cinco grandes*, who by 1995 shared two-thirds of the

---

[52] Ibid, 40.
[53] Vázquez-Rial (2002, 198–200).
[54] *World Soccer*, April 1996, 40; Giulianotti (1999, 96).
[55] *El Gráfico*, 11 April 1995, 49–58.
[56] Wilson (2016, 400–4011).

US$20 million received by the AFA, with the remainder divided by fifteen clubs. This differed from the situation in Europe where leagues negotiated such contracts on a collective basis based on equality.[57] Furthermore, whilst these figures were huge in the Argentine context, they were still four times less than deals negotiated by the English, Spanish and Italian leagues, hindering the bargaining power of Argentine clubs in the global transfer market.[58] Cable television also introduced an element of exclusion to the consumption of football on television in Argentina. On the one hand, subscription meant that those at the lower end of the socio-economic scale were now unable to afford to watch their favourite teams on TV, whilst provision of cable television was restricted to the major urban conurbations, leaving large swathes of the rural interior without access to televised football.

The screening of national team matches proved similarly lucrative. The AFA made just US$30,000 per game in the mid-1970s, but two World Cup victories in the intervening years made the side a more marketable commodity, and two decades later the AFA was able to command a 25-fold increase per match instead.[59] Increased television interest in the national team was also reflected in the coverage of the 1994 World Cup Finals, with all five of the major channels covering the finals, and *Canal 13* deploying nearly 100 people in putting together their broadcasts. *Canal 13* also committed themselves to hiring Diego Maradona as a pundit for the tournament once his playing participation in the competition was over.[60] These deals became even more profitable following the decision by the regional governing body, CONMEBOL to change the qualifying format for the World Cup to an all versus all league competition. This meant for the 1998 World Cup, each country was guaranteed to play 16 matches in qualification (Brazil qualified automatically as holders), and 18 matches for the 2002 tournament, with the AFA earning US$1 million per game in TV rights. Furthermore, these earnings were enhanced by deregulation in European markets, which saw greater interest in broadcasting South American matches on sports only subscription channels. As *World Soccer* noted in 1997, 'South America has attempted to take

---

[57] *El Gráfico*, 11 April 1995, 49–58.
[58] *La Nación*, 28 July 1996.
[59] Ibid.
[60] Mason (1995, 141–151).

advantage of global developments, but the traffic runs both ways with overseas interests moving into the marketplace.'[61] Despite the inequalities brought to the consumption of football on television within Argentina, the uncomfortable truth is that had the TV companies not invested such sums, and continued to do so, the very survival of top-level football would have been in jeopardy, 'desolate without television money,' as David Goldblatt notes.[62]

Broadcast of the national team escaped exclusive subscription access, even during the Menem presidency. As the sociologist Richard Giulianotti observed, 'football is much too important a public service to be allowed to come under an economic model that has left half the population out in the cold.'[63] It was a policy continued by the Eduardo Duhalde government ahead of the 2002 World Cup, with the president declaring in recognition of the centrality of football to Argentine society and its capacity to deflect the people from the financial crisis, 'All Argentinians, from Quiaca in the north to Tierra del Fuego in the polar-facing south, must be given the right to watch football, their great passion. Argentina needs football, so as to forget, even for a few hours. It needs to watch its team and feel proud of something once again.'[64]

These TV contracts, denominated in US dollars, became even more precious when combined with the introduction of the dollar peg in 1991 which stabilised the Argentine economy and temporarily erased the problem of high inflation. The centrepiece of Menem's economic restructuring—the Convertibility Plan—was put in place in April 1991 by Economy Minister, Domingo Cavallo. Aside from opening the economy, the plan's principal measure was to tie a new currency, the peso (equivalent to 10,000 australes) at one-to-one with the US dollar, preventing the government and Central Bank from printing extra pesos to stimulate the economy with the attendant risks of inflation. This new stability meant that creditors could demand settlement in debts in either pesos or dollars. In its early years, the Convertibility Plan succeeded in its aims, with GDP growing at 8% pa and consumer price inflation declining from

---

[61] *World Soccer*, January 1997, 16–17.
[62] Goldblatt (2007, 776).
[63] Giulianotti (1999, 96).
[64] *The OECD Observer*, May 2002, 63.

84% in 1991 to just 3.9% in 1994. It also helped Argentina to withstand external shocks such as the Tequila Crisis of December 1994 which affected many emerging markets and saw an attack on the peso in the currency markets. Deposit guarantees and the re-appearance of foreign-owned banks on Argentine high streets reinforced the sense of stability in the financial sector, factors which helped Menem gain re-election as president in 1995.[65]

In 1996 *Grupo Clarín* revolutionised the written press by launching a daily tabloid sports newspaper, *Olé* in the mould of now defunct magazines like *La Cancha*. Loosely modelled on similar titles in Spain such as *Marca* and *As*, the new entrant focused on football—although other sports such as rugby, basketball and hockey featured extensively too when making international headlines over the coming decades—especially the national team and the trials and tribulations of Argentina's two most popular clubs, Boca Juniors and River Plate, as reportage occasionally reached the banal. Sports journalism was now seen as a serious branch of the profession with the likes of Ezequiel Fernández Moores and others teaching university classes and the establishment of the Deportea school for sports journalists in Buenos Aires, as graduates rushed to fill gaps in deregulated radio broadcasting as well as produce content for the nascent internet era of mass communication as it became more democratised, offering the possibility for alternatives ideas of collective identity to be presented and challenge those proposed by established outlets.[66]

It was not just from media coverage that income from commercialisation increased, shirt sponsorship became another important revenue source. Again, these proceeds coalesced around the *cinco grandes* who economically pulled further away from the other clubs in Argentina, in terms of resources. Whilst clubs like River Plate and Boca Juniors could command up to US$5 million a year for shirt sponsorship, lesser lights were only receiving $US300,000 per annum.[67]

One club in particular, Boca Juniors, symbolised this commodification of football in Argentina. From 1995, under the presidency of youthful Columbia University educated building magnate, Mauricio Macri, Boca became poster boys of Menem's neo-liberal transformation,

[65] Lewis (2002, 162–165).
[66] Scher et al. (2010, 536–537).
[67] *El Gráfico*, 11 April 1995, 49–58.

with an annual turnover of US$40 million. Described by journalist Jorge Palomar as a 'postmodern football entrepreneur,' Macri re-signed Diego Maradona for Boca in 1995, not for his footballing prowess which had long since waned, but for the merchandising opportunities and extra tickets the club could sell with the legend on the squad.[68] Other signings like that of Juan Sebastián Verón were made not just to improve the team in the short term, but because of the anticipated increase in transfer value. Signed for US$1.5 million from Estudiantes de La Plata in January 1996, Verón was sold to Italian club Sampdoria for US$7 million just six months later. This model of player development and value incrementation was central to the club's plans to amortise its debts. Not only that, but the need to win trophies to maintain Boca's commercial attractiveness, with Macri claiming, 'We want to put Boca Juniors among the half-dozen most important clubs in the world. I want to make Boca the Ajax of South America. But it will take time.'[69] Summing up the dichotomy between commercialisation and sporting passion, Macri said in a 1996 interview with *La Nación*, 'The formula is simple: intelligence from Monday to Saturday and passion on Sundays,' and when asked when he believed Boca would be a big corporation, Macri replied, 'I believe that Boca is going to be profitable when it develops other lines of business, like merchandising, like alternative tournaments and above all when it has its own nursery and turns into a club that is a net seller of players.'[70]

In sporting terms, Macri's plan started to bear fruit under the coaching reins of Carlos Bianchi. In 2000, Boca won the Copa Libertadores, and more importantly the Intercontinental Cup, beating Real Madrid, giving not just the Boca brand, but Argentine football global visibility. As Bianchi said after the game, 'This victory is not only for Boca but for the people of Argentina. We were able to prove tonight that Argentinian soccer is the best in the world.'[71]

Reflecting a desire to emulate the gentrification of football going on in post-Taylor Report England, Macri argued, 'spectators have to be given more comfort, and I would like to see whole families go early, having lunch at stadium restaurants, with good bathrooms available, watch a

---

[68] *La Nación*, 28 July 1996.
[69] *World Soccer*, May 1997, 49.
[70] Ibid.
[71] *World Soccer*, January 2001, 6.

good match and have some sort of show during the interval – with no incidents.'[72] The Boca president had already spent US$6 million in 1996 on remodelling the club's Bombonera stadium, including the construction of 32 hospitality boxes in place of the old balconies. Each box with space for six people had its own parking space, lift, air-conditioning, catering and televisions for watching replays, and could be rented for a ten-year period at a rate of $US12,500 per person. On the external walls of these new constructions, two new murals designed by renowned Argentine artist, Miguel Pérez Célis were positioned linking them to the *populares* section of the stadium inhabited by the club's traditional working-class support giving the illusion of cross-class unity in support of Boca and its illustrious past.[73]

This further emphasised a moving away of the top clubs from the concerns of their working-class fanbases who were at the same time feeling the pain of Menem's economic reforms through unemployment and recession, whilst football was engaged in the 'dance of the millions,' something that Macri reasoned was no different to other places in the world where some lived in luxury whilst others died of hunger, and that the largesse in football could be justified by the 'provision of circus to those who didn't have bread.'[74] Grondona took a more nuanced view to Macri, fearing over-commercialisation could dissipate the passion of the fans as their heroes appeared in front of them for progressively shorter periods before being sold abroad. Whilst this was good business for the clubs, it did nothing for the fans who were the 'thermometer' of the game.[75] By the end of 2000 Macri had succeeded in his aims, Boca were now out of debt and with their world champion status had become the first Argentine club to establish themselves as a global brand.[76]

Menem's metamorphosis into a paragon of neo-liberal economics was also reflected by the mass migration of Argentine footballers to other markets as the country became an exporter of football talent *par excellence*. The matter was already of concern to Bilardo, who claimed in 1989, 'When I took over as coach people told me "Argentina is an exporter

---

[72] *World Soccer*, May 1997, 49.

[73] *La Nación*, 28 July 1996; Caparrós (2004, 308–310); Di Giano (2010, 117–126).

[74] *La Nación*, 28 July 1996.

[75] Ibid.

[76] *El Gráfico*, 20 November 2000, 93–95.

of soccer players and that is going to be your main problem," and they were right. Most of my first team are now playing abroad so that they can rarely train together and often, as soon as I pick a new player he is transferred abroad.'[77] Defending himself against complaints over poor results achieved by his team outside of major competitions—including a 4–1 loss to Australia in 1988, Bilardo argued, 'For the many friendly internationals and friendly tournaments we play in, we cannot get our players with foreign clubs so that we field virtual B teams ...while these friendly internationals are very useful in every aspect to blood new players, one cannot expect to win all the time.'[78]

Basile reprised the theme on replacing Bilardo as national coach in 1991. He expressed an age-old Argentine concern about the impact of his players being transferred to Europe on team building, saying, 'I can't be against players moving to a better future, but hope the work we have done will not go to waste six months before we go to compete. I therefore hope that the FA will ban transfers abroad from next year's Olympic Games until the World Cup qualifying games the following year.'[79] Basile's pleas fell on deaf ears, in Argentina as in many places around the world, deregulation was *de rigueur*, not the restriction of markets. No sooner had his Argentine team won the 1991 Copa América in Santiago de Chile, seven of his squad including tournament top-scorer Gabriel Batistuta, had transferred abroad from their Argentine clubs. By 1995, an estimated 324 Argentine players were plying their trade outside of the country.[80]

The successful development of elite youth players decisively changed the nature of the Argentine transfer market, with players departing for foreign clubs at ever younger ages. Ironically, it was not Pekerman's intention for young Argentines to go abroad, but the success of his programme was such that his wishes were soon overtaken by market forces. In a 2001, interview Pekerman spoke of the advice given to youngsters under his charge, 'The first thing I tell my players, is not to rush into a move abroad, not to dive in at the best offers, because this is the best school they can have. Argentina has the best qualities in the world to develop

---

[77] *World Soccer*, May 1989, 11.
[78] Ibid, 11.
[79] *World Soccer*, May 1991, 31–35.
[80] *World Soccer*, April 1996, 40.

players.'[81] Watching Barcelona scouts were so impressed with Javier Saviola's performances at the 2001 World Youth Cup that they paid River Plate £19 million for his services, a world record fee for a teenager. Like his colleagues, Saviola was a seasoned starter for his club, his opportunity hastened by the sale of Juan Pablo Angel to Aston Villa and the difference in experience compared to their opponents was notable, as the Dutch coach Louis van Gaal commented, 'Argentina has order, discipline and individual skill which makes the difference. They play like grown-up professionals.'[82]

A 15 December 1995 ruling on a case brought before the European Court of Justice by the journeyman Belgian footballer, Jean-Marc Bosman had huge ramifications for the Argentine game. The case rested on the legality of Bosman's club, RFC Liège being able to demand a transfer fee when he reached the end of his contract, and because his prospective new club was Dunkerque in France, the principal of free movement of European Union (EU) citizens came into play. The European Court not only ruled that players were free to sign for whomever they wished without a fee payable at the end of their contract, but also that leagues in member states could not limit the number of EU players who could play for clubs in any one game. With most leagues limiting foreign players to just three per team, this had huge consequences for the Argentine game, given that many of its players could claim EU citizenship due to Italian and Spanish-born antecedents who came to Argentina in the early twentieth century. From the mid-1990s, hundreds of Argentine footballers were taking this route to a better paid life in the EU, following thousands of compatriots in other professions doing the same. Whilst economic considerations were clearly a factor in players' decisions to transfer to European clubs, some did so paradoxically to further their ambitions to play for Argentina. When joining Italian club Parma in 1996, Hernán Crespo claimed that despite outscoring his rivals Batistuta and Abel Balbo, he remained behind them in selection for the Argentine number nine shirt, 'When I asked them why, they said it was because they were playing in a better class of football and I needed to come to Italy if I wanted to

---

[81] *World Soccer*, November 2006, 30.
[82] August 2001, 16–17.

compete.'[83] Again, Argentine insecurity meant that validation was sought from outside.

It was not just the established internationals how were now coveted by clubs in the EU, but also younger up-and-coming players, whilst good league players also found themselves wanted by in minor European leagues as deregulation and an increase in EU membership opened-up the options available to them. The effect on the balance between European and South American football can be seen in the results of the annual Intercontinental Cup between the best clubs of the two continents. Up until 1995, there were 20 South American wins against 14 by European clubs, after the application of the Bosman Ruling between 1996 and 2022 the tide turned decisively in favour of the Europeans with 19 titles (including the Intercontinental Cup's successor tournament the World Club Championship) against just six for South America, with Boca the only Argentine club to be world champions in the post-Bosman period, most recently in 2003.

With the Argentine football industry generating an estimated US$200 million per year—US$50 million a year coming from the sale of players abroad—and given the parlous state that Argentine club finances remained in, the question being asked was where did the money go? Some of this leakage was attributed to the role of agents which became central to football transfers from the 1990s, with the most famous exponent in Argentina being Settimio Aloisio, who represented over a hundred of the country's top players.[84]

Corruption in the transfer of players by club officials, often colluding with agents—collecting up to 20% of the fee—contributed to clubs not receiving anywhere near the full value of their assets. Indeed, the ownership of players' contracts by individuals and private companies saw a new form of financial market develop in Argentina. Players effectively became commodities in a new futures market, not just traded between clubs on the orthodox transfer market, but also between third parties gambling on future transfer fee values. Whilst in other countries, most notably in the UK where agencies such as Premier Management floated on the London Stock Exchange in 2000, the trade in individual players' contracts in such an institutionalised way became a particularly Argentine phenomenon.

---

[83] *World Soccer*, November 2002, 6.
[84] *La Nación*, 28 July 1996.

Despite third-party ownership being officially banned by FIFA internationally and the AFA in Argentina, it was openly practiced, dominating the Argentine transfer market, aided by those in positions of power within the AFA also being club officials involved in the practice. As Eric Weil opined in *World Soccer* in 1991, 'The rewards are great, however, and this is one reason why Argentine clubs are continually selling players abroad, but at the same time are nearly all in great financial difficulties.'[85] The practice exemplified neo-liberal deregulation in the wider Argentine economy in which academic Eric Hershberg notes, 'private actors were permitted to amass monopolies and oligopolies through which to line their own pockets and those of many of the public officials who were supposed to regulate them.'[86]

In 1997, Macri initiated his own version of this 'futures market' to raise capital for Boca Juniors. Unable to go to the stock exchange in the more orthodox way like British clubs because Boca was a member-owned club, Macri launched an innovative investment fund: *Fondo Boca Juniors*. With the aim of raising £12 million, he sold shares priced at £63 each to fans and investors for Boca to buy the contracts of young players, loan them to the club and then sell them on without the club being obligated to pay transfer fees. The value of the fund rose and fell according to the form of the players whose contracts were pooled and their prospective transfer value. In the event, the fund generated returns of 15% and enabled the club to sign the Barros-Schelotto twins, Martín Palermo and Walter Samuel amongst others.[87]

¡Violencia!

The social instability that accompanied Argentina's economic problems in the final decades of the twentieth century saw an upsurge of hooliganism at Argentine football grounds from the 1980s onwards. Crowd violence had been a feature of Argentine football since becoming a mass spectator sport at the turn of the twentieth century, and between 1922 and 2000,

---

[85] *World Soccer*, April 1991, 36.
[86] *NACLA Report on the Americas*, July/August 2001, 33.
[87] *World Soccer*, November 1997, 32; *World Soccer*, 1998, 8; Caparrós (2004), 312.

161 Argentines had met their deaths in football stadia, including seventy-four crushed at the Monumental during a River Plate v Boca Juniors match in 1968 after police tear-gassed visiting fans.[88]

Hooliganism in Argentina differed from that experienced in Britain because of the inclusion of *barra brava* ('tough gang') leaders into the institutional framework of Argentine football. The term was first used in 1925 by *Crítica* newspaper to describe groups of fans who attended matches with the object of 'manifesting their base instincts,' something that continued in subsequent decades, with club directors and political actors used the gangs both inside and outside of the stadium for intimidation in support of their own personal agendas, not least during the politically charged 1970s. By the 1980s, *barras bravas* resembled organised criminal gangs, with unemployed men armed with knives and guns joining for financial gain, extorting money from fans and ambulant sellers within the stadium.[89]

The main way in which the *barras bravas* integrated themselves within the club framework was in the resale of tickets, given to them by club officials seeking favours from these influential fan groups in gaining re-election. They also benefited from money for banners, travel to away games, even to international tournaments like the World Cups in the United States in 1994 and France in 1998 in support of the national team, something that would be otherwise economically out of reach for gang members who were out of work because of prevailing neo-liberal policies.

The central role taken by the *barras bravas* in the matchday choreography of flag-waving, pyrotechnics and raw passion in a way unmatched outside South America except for the Italian Ultras, has led to some commentators from outside Argentina such as David Goldblatt to ascribe a benign aspect to some of their activities.[90] Far from being 'a radicalized folkloric expression,' as Scher and others have described this kind of interpretation, groups such as *La Doce* ('The Twelfth Man') have become organised criminal gangs lending their services to the highest bidder.[91]

---

[88] *World Soccer*, September 2000, 29.
[89] Frydenberg (2011, 225).
[90] Goldblatt (2007, 802–803).
[91] Scher et al. (2010, 547).

The lack of state action in dealing with violence of the *barras bravas* only emboldened their activities, in what Scher and others describe as a 'fluid relationship' with political, sporting and policing authorities.[92] Police often turned the other way as hooligans got into stadiums for free after selling their own tickets. On the rare occasions that hooligans were brought before the judiciary, a combination of inadequate laws and corruption meant they usually received light sentences. The problem was highlighted in a 1983 *El Gráfico* editorial which bemoaned that the return of democracy had not achieved a 'healthy judiciary' but instead one that derogated its duty by allowing hooligans to act with impunity. The magazine also chastised a similar lack of action by the police who were 'supposed to act in the name of the decent,' before concluding, 'The *barras bravas* – miniscule groups that don't deserve to consider themselves fans – are enemies of football, and we must defeat them with morality, prevention and rigour.'[93]

The personal endangerment of players that saw Claudio Zacarias injured when an industrial firework went off in the San Lorenzo changing room before a match against Instituto de Córdoba in 1988, resulted in players going on strike. AFA president Grondona blamed the problem on a weak judiciary, but his organisation's adherence to union demands for safety guarantees ensured the players were soon back in the stadiums.[94] After the incident, Juan Ángel Pirker, the head of the Argentine Federal Police sought to put part of the blame on the silent majority attending matches for subscribing to a code of *omertà* that ensured that hooligans were able hide amongst them in anonymity, 'through the passivity shown by those who witness these events.' National Deputy, Oscar Alende blamed a toxic masculinity that dominated football grounds highlighting the misogynistic and racist singing directed against Peruvian and Paraguayan immigrants, saying, 'This violence in the stadiums is another symptom of the social decomposition at this very difficult time for the government.'[95]

On 14 December 1990 at a game between Boca and San Lorenzo, Saturnino Cabrera was killed by an iron bar thrown from the upper

---

[92] Ibid, 546.
[93] *El Gráfico*, 9 August 1983.
[94] *El Gráfico*, 17 May 1988; *World Soccer*, July 1988, 36.
[95] *El Gráfico*, 17 May 1988.

terraces of La Bombonera in a battle between rival *barras*, the victim of collateral damage as life became cheap at Argentine stadia.[96] A government commission on the issue the following year proposed improved security measures such as the installation of CCTV cameras to identify perpetrators of violence. These measures made negligible impact with 502 episodes of hooliganism in 1992 alone, although a policing crackdown saw the number of hooligans arrested nearly double to 10,703 a year later.[97]

After a Boca v River match on 30 April 1994, two River fans, Ángel Cabrera and Walter Vallejos were murdered in an ambush by Boca hooligans in a case that horrified the nation. In 1997, the case resulted in the Boca *barra*, La Doce being adjudged an illicit organisation by the courts, with nine of its members condemned to jail terms of up to 20 years each. One of those sent to prison was gang leader José Barritta, known as *el abuelo* ('the grandfather'). The money extorted from players and other criminal activities found its way into the group's 'charitable' fund, Fundación N° 12—a post-modern take on the Fundación Eva Perón—in which investigators found US$3 million. Meanwhile, Barritta's successor as leader, Rafael Di Zeo became a media figure in his own right.[98]

The scale of the problem of hooliganism led to the suspension of Argentine league football for two weeks in May 1998 by court order of the Buenos Aires judge, Víctor Perotta. Such was the outcry from vested interests including clubs and television companies that the suspension was lifted by the authorities without any substantive security measures being implemented. Banning orders served against known hooligans resulted in the unedifying spectacle of miscreants turning up at the stadium with their lawyers arguing that their exclusions were 'unconstitutional.' Attempts by the AFA to penalise clubs for the poor behaviour of their supporters were subverted by the continued power of the *grandes*. After three clubs; Los Andes, River Plate and Racing reached the trigger for a points deduction in 2001, only Los Andes were sanctioned immediately, contributing to their relegation at the end of the season. By contrast, River and Racing had their punishments suspended to a later date, enabling Racing to avoid a relegation play-off.

---

[96] Scher et al. (2010, 546).
[97] Wilson (2016, 419–423).
[98] Ibid, 419–423; Scher et al., 548.

El Crisis

Whilst Argentina's football team and its European-based millionaire players were comfortably confirming their place at the 2002 World Cup, the country itself and its economy was imploding in what Hershberg described as a 'Second Great Depression.'[99] The 'economic miracle' generated by the neo-liberal policies of President Menem in the 1990s and fuelled by foreign investment which soon dried up, went into reverse. The decline was exacerbated by Argentine exporters being rendered uncompetitive by the unsustainable dollar peg which made their goods more expensive as the dollar continued to gain in value. This was particularly relevant given that Argentine companies were competing against neighbouring Brazilian firms benefiting from a managed devaluation in 1999.[100]

As years of growth gave way to four years of recession, the Argentine government—whose external debt stood at an unmanageable US$155 billion—turned to the IMF for an US$8 billion bailout, the price being massive budgetary cuts which saw the reduction of pensions and unemployment benefits and the slashing of public sector employment, sending large swathes of the middle class into joining the 50% of Argentines living in poverty, and the development of a new underclass, exemplified by the *cartoneros* who eked a living by scavenging cardboard and plastic from public bins in order to recycle them for a small amount of cash.[101]

As inflation ate into the savings of the rich and middle classes, those who had any salted them away to the United States and Europe as capital flight severely depleted the country's cash reserves. In a highly unpopular move to stem the flow by President Fernando De la Rúa's government, bank withdrawals were restricted to US$1,000 per month through the hated '*corralito*' ('little pen'), further hitting the rapidly diminishing middle-class and the cash dependent domestic economy. Football was not immune from the crisis, and players in the Argentine League went on strike for ten days on 30 April 2001 over £35 million in unpaid wages. When Argentina's top players, rich beyond the imagination of their compatriots from their lucrative European contracts, returned to

---

[99] *NACLA Report on the Americas*, July/August 2001, 30.

[100] Ibid, 33.

[101] Lewis (2002, 168–171); *The Financial Times*, 20 December 2001; *The Financial Times*, 2 January 2002.

play for the national team, it was clear example of the divide between the haves and the have-nots which only added to their aloofness from Argentine fans.[102] The dispute was only resolved following the intervention of Argentine Labour Minister, Patricia Bullrich when the AFA promised that all outstanding payments would be made with government help by 30 June.[103] According to union leader, Sergio Marchi, 'This has not happened overnight. This goes back a long way. There's only one culprit here and that is the management of Argentinian football, who run things badly and think the party is never going to be over. But the party has ended.'[104] In reality, the debts were only partially paid and by the end of the year many salaries were at least two months in arrears.

One club symbolised Argentina's economic chaos at the turn of the twenty-first century, Racing Club de Avellaneda. Technically bankrupt with debts of US$60 million, Racing had avoided formal liquidation thanks to a series of benevolent court rulings, which also meant evading the threat of relegation that the AFA had threatened to impose at the end of the 1999–2000 season on clubs that were insolvent. Echoing the 1960s boast of Valentín Suárez that the government would never 'lower the curtain' on Argentine football, the Ministry of Sports introduced a bill to Congress that declared the club part of the 'national patrimony,' saving Racing from going bust.[105] A year later, the club was taken into private ownership by a group of Racing supporting businessmen, who formed a company called Blanquiceleste (sky-blue and white, Racing's colours), led by Fernando Marín. In December 2001, as Buenos Aires was literally in flames from the social unrest emanating from the Argentina's economic disaster which saw 20 killed and President De la Rúa forced to resign following the *cacerolazo* protests of the middle-classes, Racing improbably won the Apertura championship, their first league title for 35 years. Victory prompted Marín to claim, 'people said this "privatisation" would not work, and I dedicate this title to those who supported me.'[106] It was to be a rare example of privatisation succeeding in Argentina for the benefit of Argentines, albeit only for Racing fans.

---

[102] *The Financial Times*, 20 December 2001; Lewis (2002, 172–177).
[103] *World Soccer*, March 2002, 63.
[104] *World Soccer*, Summer 2001, 68.
[105] *World Soccer*, May 1999, 4.
[106] *World Soccer*, February 2002, 70.

After an absurd situation in which five men served as president over a thirteen-day period, Eduardo Duhalde was finally chosen by Congress to serve out De la Rúa's remaining term of office. To reinvigorate the economy, Duhalde's government removed the dollar peg to the peso, at a stroke devaluing the currency to 3:1 against the US dollar, which whilst making Argentina's exports more competitive also meant that anyone with savings saw them slashed overnight by two–thirds. This had a devastating effect on Argentina's football clubs, already heavily indebted because of poor management and corruption, who now had to deal with players having contracts and bank loans denominated in dollars whilst income was effectively a third of its previous level. This issue was alleviated months later when a court ruling meant that all local debts should be denominated in pesos rather than dollars. When San Lorenzo sold Bernardo Romeo to German club Hamburg in early 2002, more than a third of the £3.4 million transfer fee went to the player in unpaid wages, with the club's vice-president, Rafael Savino saying, 'The club's situation is desperate. There is no money coming in at the moment. We have almost 90 lawsuits against us and 30 requests for bankruptcy.'[107] Elsewhere in a stunning volte face, the archetype of neo-liberal football economics, Boca Juniors were forced to sell 25 of their players, including key defenders Jorge Bermudez and Hugo Ibarra in the 2001 close season for financial reasons despite winning the Copa Libertadores the previous season. Their coach Oscar Tabarez highlighted the paradox caused by the crash, 'The economic crisis is resulting in a general lowering of standards in the domestic championship. Financial interests are winning the battle over the sporting part, with players continually leaving to go elsewhere. It's so strange that when you try to build a team, you are really working to disband it, because you know as soon as it is successful the transfers will start. It's impossible to keep the same team from one season to the next. The clubs are not even owners of their players, and the agents and businessmen who hold their contracts move from one club to another.'[108]

Meanwhile, Argentina defaulted on its foreign debt, the biggest in history, closing off any further lines of credit.[109] Amongst those affected was national coach, Marcelo Bielsa who not only saw his salary slashed to

---

[107] *World Soccer*, March 2002, 62.

[108] *World Soccer*, August 2002, 64.

[109] Lewis (2002, 79).

a third of its former value, but with the AFA enveloped by the financial crisis engulfing Argentina, he was not getting paid at all and by the time he led the team to Japan in June 2002 for the World Cup, Bielsa had not been paid for almost a year and was owed nearly half a million dollars in unpaid salary and bonuses. After threatening to quit, a compromise was reached whereby the arrears would be paid in dollars and the remainder of his contract would be paid in pesos.[110] The crash in value of the peso hastened the movement of Argentine players abroad, including those of lesser standing who would otherwise have stayed in Argentina as clubs cashed-in on their only saleable assets—their players—in order to stay afloat and players sought to restore the value of their wages. As the agent, Juan Simón argued, 'Obviously if they didn't devalue the currency, not so many players would leave … Today offers appear from markets that until now were unimaginable … The young players are going to exotic countries to use them as a trampoline.'[111] Insecurity of income led players to contemplate previously unconsidered footballing markets such as China, Turkey, Finland and Armenia, indeed anywhere they could earn a living. As another agent, Norberto Recassens commented, 'They want to go any part of the world. Before they were offered a transfer to a club in Russia, and nobody wanted to know. Now as a change, scores go to the Spanish Second Division, Korea, Japan, Australia. They go to anyone that pays in dollars.'[112] The economic situation in Argentina also led to a worsening of social conditions and a rise in crime. Top-level Argentine league footballers, despite being way behind their European-based compatriots' salary-wise, were still rich in domestic terms, and they and their families became targets for express kidnappings. This was seen by the example of Juan Román Riquelme's transfer to Barcelona in 2002. 'Around that time, my brother was kidnapped and that made me feel the time had come to move. It was a bad time.'[113]

The 2002 World Cup was expected to offer some catharsis for beleaguered Argentines, with the team amongst the favourites to win the competition for the first time since 1986 based on its strong qualifying performance, in contrast to traditional rivals like Brazil and Germany

---

[110] *World Soccer*, June 2002, 25; Rich (2020, 118).
[111] *El Gráfico*, August 2002, 44–51.
[112] Ibid, 44–51.
[113] *Four Four Two*, May 2006, 96–103.

who had struggled in qualification. A newspaper poll shortly before the competition suggested that 76% of Argentines believed their compatriots would win the tournament. Argentina's political class very much pinned their hopes on the national team distracting the people from the ongoing crisis. As Santa Fe governor, Carlos Reutemann told a governors meeting, 'There needs to be a solution to the *corralito*, because if they eliminate us from the World Cup and then we don't sort out the *corralito* it is not known what could happen in the country... [in terms of a repeat of the 2001 social strife].'[114]

The first-round meeting against England in Sapporo reflected the downturn in Argentina's economic fortunes. Four years previously, the number of travelling Argentine fans in St. Étienne considerably outnumbered those of the English, but now with the decimation of the Argentine middle-class, the roles had now reversed in Japan with the number of English fans very much in the ascendancy. Despite beating Nigeria in their opening fixture, a 1–0 defeat to England combined with failure to beat Sweden meant Argentina made a shock exit from the tournament at the first-round stage. Verón, who was scapegoated for Argentina's failure exemplified the team's mood, 'I am absolutely devastated. This is the worst moment of my life. We hoped to give the World Cup as a present to the people of Argentina.'[115]

Despite the millionaire status of the players Verón claimed, 'In six months, we didn't get paid a peso nor did it interest us to discuss World Cup prize money.'[116] It was a sentiment elaborated on by Marcelo Gallardo, 'It was a total sadness ... The sensation of feeling totally frustrated for not giving the country what we wanted was terrible. There is not one who felt better than another. With this team we could have gone very far. I have never seen something so hard. The passion that each one of the players in the squad had at this World Cup could not be beaten.'[117]

Despite initial elation, the quarter of a century following the restoration of democracy in Argentina was a great deception for the Argentine people. Whilst political and cultural freedoms were recovered, the succession of financial crises that ended in the crash of 2001 meant that

---

[114] *Página 12*, 1 June 2002, 2.
[115] Rich (2020, 131–137).
[116] *Clarín*, 23 July 2002.
[117] *Olé*, 19 August 2002.

increasingly fewer Argentines were able to make the most of these freedoms. As Di Giano notes, 'It seems that self-destructive tendencies had no limit and that, in a country with such a traumatic history, one could not find the language sufficient to channel pain.'[118] This was potently reflected by the career of Diego Maradona who become the personification of Argentina like a latter-day Eva Perón. His decline from the great redeemer at the 1986 World Cup, to national disgrace just eight years later accurately reflected the downward trajectory of the Argentine nation. As María Sáenz Quesada argued, 'in the final years of the twentieth-century Argentina had seen many of its myths and deeply rooted truths shattered. No longer the granary of the world, neither the promised land of immigration, we did not have going forward a destiny of greatness.'[119]

The commercialism of football in Argentina at the end of the twentieth century can be seen through the prism of the neo-liberal paradigm. The deregulation of labour and the media in the core European markets during the 1990s was bound to have global ramifications which Argentina could not avoid. With the Argentine football industry structurally and financially in disarray, it was inevitable that players would be drawn to the core in ever greater numbers. The concentration of talent and wealth at Europe's top clubs inevitably coalesced with Argentina's ability to produce quality footballers, something reflected in the fact that just two players in Argentina's 2002 World Cup squad were contracted to home-based clubs.[120]

As what Sáenz Quesada describes as 'the cultural globalisation' came to be the dominant force in Argentina, there was a revaluation of identity that harked back to a nostalgia for better times. In football, this was seen with popular affection for the national youth teams who not only succeeded internationally, but in a way that was recognisably 'Argentine.'[121]

---

[118] Di Giano (2010, 93).
[119] Sáenz Quesada (2012, 717).
[120] Goldblatt (2007), 778.
[121] Sáenz Quesada (2012), 720.

References

Alabarces, Pablo. 2007. *Fútbol y patria. El fútbol y las narrativas de la Nación en la Argentina*, 4th ed. Buenos Aires: Prometeo Libros.

Alabarces, Pablo, Alan Tomlinson, and Christopher Young. 2001. Argentina versus England at the France'98 World Cup: Narratives of Nation and the Mythologizing of the Popular. *Media, Culture and Society* 23: 547–566.

Archetti, Eduardo. 1999. *Masculinities: Football, Polo and the Tango in Argentina*. Oxford: Berg.

Bonner, Michelle D. 2007. *Sustaining Human Rights: Women and Argentine Human Rights Organizations*. University Park, Pennsylvania: Penn State University Press.

Burns, Jimmy. 2010. *Maradona: The Hand of God*. London: Bloomsbury.

Burns, Jimmy. 2002. *The Land That Lost its Heroes*. London: Bloomsbury.

Campomar, Andreas. 2014. *¡Golazo!* London: Quercus.

Caparrós, Martín. 2004. *Boquita*. Buenos Aires: Booklet.

Di Giano, Roberto. 2010. *Fútbol, Poder y Discriminación Social*. Buenos Aires: Leviatán.

Frydenberg, Julio. 2011. *Historia Social del Fútbol: Del amateurismo a la profesionalización*. Buenos Aires: Siglo Veintiuno Editores.

Giulianotti, Richard. 1999. *Football: A Sociology of the Global Game*. Cambridge: Polity Press.

Goebel, Michael. 2011. *Argentina's Partisan Past*. Liverpool: Liverpool University Press.

Goldblatt, David. 2007. *The Ball is Round: A Global History of Football*. London: Penguin.

Lewis, Colin, M. 2002. *Argentina: A Short History*. Oxford: Oneworld Publications.

Maradona, Diego A. 2004. *El Diego*. London: Yellow Jersey Press.

Maradona, Diego A., and Daniel Arcucci. 2017. *Touched by God: How We Won the Mexico '86 World Cup*. New York: Penguin Books.

Mason, Tony. 1995. *Passion of the People? Football in South America*. London: Verso.

Rich, Tim. 2020. *The Quality of Madness: A Life of Marcelo Bielsa*. London: Quercus.

Romero, Luis Alberto. 2004. *A History of Argentina in the Twentieth Century*. University Park, Pennsylvania: Penn State University Press.

Sáenz Quesada, María. 2012. *La Argentina. Historia del País y de su Gente*. Buenos Aires: Editorial Sudamericana.

Scher, Ariel, Guillermo Blanco, Jorge Búsico. 2010. *Deporte Nacional*. Buenos Aires: Emecé.

Vázquez-Rial, Horacio. 2002. *El Enigma Argentino (descifrado para españoles)*. Barcelona: Ediciones B.

Wilson, Jonathan. 2016. *Angels with Dirty Faces: The Footballing History of Argentina*. London: Orion Books.

CHAPTER 9

Conclusion

In 1852, the Argentine nation builder Juan Bautista Alberdi prophesied that massive European immigration was needed to transform Argentina into a modern country with a more civilised identity. He wrote, 'By the customs later communicated to our inhabitants, every European who comes to our shores brings us more civilization than a great many books of philosophy … An industrious worker is the most edifying of instruction manuals.'[1] Alberdi's analysis was prescient: migration and assimilation were key to the construction of a new Argentine identity at the turn of the twentieth century. As this book has showed, of the 'customs' introduced to its inhabitants, football proved to be an important cultural element of this transformation, taking root and impacting all sectors of Argentine society.

In reflecting socio-political and economic developments in Argentina, football's arrival and diffusion coincided with the modernisation of Argentina's economy and infrastructure at the turn of the twentieth century, financed by British capital and implemented by mass immigration from Europe. Whilst the game's introduction and incipient organisation by the British community appears at first sight to support existing ideas of British informal empire being exerted over Argentina, two

[1] Alberdi, (2002, 95).

sectors of British influence were important in assimilating immigrants: the railway industry and education. In diffusing football, they functioned as agents for the organic miscegenation of immigrants from diverse backgrounds with the existing *criollo* population. Given the ethnically heterogonous urban expansion of cities like Buenos Aires and Rosario, this agglomeration helped establish multicultural local identities. *Criollo* and immigrant youngsters, including Anglo-Criollos used civic national symbols in naming their clubs as a way of assimilating into Argentine society and occluding their disparate national backgrounds.

However, that is not say that immigrants totally forsook their original national identities as football became an arena for the exhibition of dual identity as the case study of the Italo-Argentine community proves. Whether as major contributors to the Argentine national team or in leadership roles at the country's foremost clubs, the dominant role played by the Italian collective in Argentine football's consolidation phase from the late 1910s until the mid-1930s reflected the social mobility of Italo-Argentines more widely in Argentine society. Tours by Italian clubs to Argentina and vice versa during the 1920s gave Italo-Argentines a chance to celebrate both their *argentinidad* and Italian-ness on the terraces, reflecting a failure to completely assimilate that concerned nationalists preoccupied with the potential threat of Argentina being Italianised. This duality was reinforced by the celebration in Buenos Aires of Italy's 1934 World Cup victory achieved with the help of four Italo-Argentine players. Therefore, football provided an outlet for immigrants to show multiple identities that were not mutually exclusive with being Argentine.

The presence of these Italo-Argentines players in the 1934 Italian team highlighted other key themes, those of emigration and Argentine football's insertion into the global economy. The relocation of Argentine footballers beginning with the *rimpatriati* in the 1910s and 1920s reflected wider professional migration or 'Brain Drain' from Argentina that continued through the long twentieth century. Their departure was symptomatic of Argentina's economic weakness in the global marketplace from the 1920s, reaching critical mass as international successes at the 1928 Olympics, 1930 World Cup and South American Championships of 1947 and 1957 created a global demand for Argentine players. The deregulation of global transfer markets and enforcement of freedom of movement within the European Union during the 1980s and 1990s fundamentally changed the nature of player development in Argentina as the transfer of players abroad became an important part of Argentine clubs' business model.

This emigration of Argentine players underscored wider debates surrounding national identity. For much of the century, a transfer abroad meant the end to a player's international career as administrators considered them unfit to represent their country despite press campaigns for their selection. The reversal of this policy ahead of the 1974 World Cup, with several foreign-based players joining the squad at the last minute changed the tone of the debate. These latecomers were now regarded by the public and in the press as *vendepatrias* who played little part in helping Argentina qualify for the tournament, preferring instead to make more money abroad. It was a trait of jealousy prevalent in Argentine society, whereby talents from all walks of life were criticised at home for seeking validation abroad as in the case of the author Jorge Luis Borges.[2] Yet, by the final two decades of the century, attitudes had changed again, with players encouraged to go abroad and 'prove' themselves good enough to represent Argentina.

Another area in which football illuminated wider Argentine society was in its intersection with the political arena, acting as a pioneer for Argentine democracy and civic engagement. The development of Argentine football clubs as member-owned institutions from the 1890s onwards predated the 1912 Sáenz Peña electoral reforms by almost two decades, meaning that in numerous cases people's first experience of political activity came through football club elections as boardrooms became proving grounds for men with wider political aspirations. However, the 1931 introduction of professionalism did not democratise Argentine football as some have suggested. By contrast, the commodification of football encouraged the development of an oligopoly of five clubs—the *cinco grandes*—who by virtue of their greater economic resources and political connections shaped administrative decisions in their favour. By consolidating their control over the AFA's decision-making process in 1937 with qualified voting, the *grandes* emulated the democratic deficit of Argentina's political system during the *década infame* of the 1930s.

The link between politics and football during the 1946–1955 Peronist era ran deeper than the conventional bilateral relationship as more tangential themes such as industrial relations, foreign affairs and use of

---

[2] *Veintitres*, 30 June 2016, 84–89.

the media have been equally illustrative in analysing this relationship and in demonstrating how the sport highlighted contradictions at the heart of Peronism. The protracted 1948–1949 players' strike highlighted these paradoxes, with players representing Perón's working-class support in dispute with club directors who were part of the middle-class plank of the president's cross coalition. The regime's incapacity to act as mediator due to this conflict of interest ultimately caused significant harm to Argentine football as the strike dragged on for almost a year.

The exodus of players abroad following the strike combined with diplomatic failures by an AFA influenced by the Peronist regime, resulted in Argentina's absence from the international stage between 1947 and 1955. Whilst Tony Mason contends that Perón used the 1951 Pan American Games in Buenos Aires to advance ideals of his 'New Argentina,' the fact that these football tournaments were held overseas meant that he was unable to exert control over Argentina's performance in them, something which could potentially damage Argentina's image abroad, contributing to a policy of isolation.[3] Strained diplomatic relations with Brazil, against whom Perón was contesting regional dominance, contributed to Argentina's absence from the 1949 South American Championship and 1950 World Cup, both held in Brazil. Meanwhile, Perón's own ambitions for hosting the 1962 World Cup were thwarted by his overthrow in 1955.

If Peronist intervention in footballing matters of industrial and foreign relations was unsuccessful, the movement's attempt to promote a 'New Argentina' through the advancement of Perón as *'el primer deportista'* was more effective. Football alongside other sports was the focus of a narrative of national development and unity in the pages of the Peronist magazine *Mundo Deportivo* that resonated with readers by conflating sporting success with the Peronist movement.

The societal decline arising from the infamous decade and the Peronist era that retarded Argentina's economic and political development was also reflected in the country's football, reaching its nadir at the 1958 World Cup with the 'Disaster of Sweden.' Player indiscipline, administrative ineptitude and short-termism concerning player development reflected a decline in Argentine football that the introduction of professionalism was supposed have avoided. Indeed, it is interesting that Aloé and Panzeri, normally writers of opposing views, agreed that Argentine football was

---

[3] Mason, (1995, 67).

more orderly and more faithfully reflected Argentine values during its late amateur period.[4] As the *maracanazo* had done in Brazil in 1950, the 'Disaster of Sweden' represented a greater blow to national identity in Argentina than a simple sporting defeat.

With Argentina unable to arrest its terminal socio-economic decline as short-lived attempts to embed representative democracy were repeatedly interrupted by military coups, the prestige of hosting the 1978 World Cup offered Argentines an opportunity to exteriorise ideas of Argentine identity to an international audience. The tournament contributed more to debates about Argentine identity than simplistic interpretations that General Videla's military regime used the tournament to deflect attention from its repression and to glorify itself as other authoritarian dictatorships had done with the 1934 World Cup and 1936 Olympic Games. Firstly, hosting the World Cup had been something of a holy grail for democratic Argentine governments of different persuasions and had one been in power in 1978 it is certain that they too would have sought to gain political capital from the tournament too. Comparison with Mexico's hosting of the 1968 Olympics is more apposite. The *junta* replicated the strategy employed by President Gustavo Díaz Ordaz' government in terms of distancing themselves from 'indigenous' Latin America and aligning itself with the more technologically advanced nations of the northern hemisphere.

The government's vision of national identity was not the only one expounded during the 1978 World Cup. By directing their campaign of disavowal against Argentina's hosting the tournament towards the foreign press corps, the Madres de la Plaza de Mayo who spoke for the tens of thousands of Argentines whose disappearance by the regime made effectively stateless, emerged as the global propaganda winners of the 1978 World Cup, despite being *personas non gratas* within Argentina according to the regime and its apologists in the press. The Madres later received their deserved respect in Argentine society following the return of democracy in 1983, a development which paradoxically diminished the image of Argentina's winning team and its coach, César Luis Menotti, as revisionist interpretations were applied to the actions of these actors. Rather than their actions being viewed in the difficult social context in which they

---

[4] *Mundo Deportivo*, 9 August 1951, 26; *El Gráfico*, 13 June 1958, 48.

competed, revisionist interpretations have instead looked to undermine them.

Whilst the 1978 World Cup was one way of football demonstrating Argentine identity to the world, the portrayal of an archetypal Argentine way of playing the game over the preceding 60 years did so in a more enduring and metaphorical way. From the late 1920s, the myth of *la nuestra* became established within the Argentine press to define an idiosyncratic Argentine playing style and to project national identity, a myth that has remained resilient to this day. Whilst this construction has been uncritically accepted by scholars, the discourse surrounding *la nuestra* was a piece of nationalist revisionism that usurped existing *mitrista* notions of civic identity to reinforce a narrative of Argentine singularity in the face of large-scale immigration.

La nuestra also supported an anti-colonial rhetoric that sought to remove all British influence from the history and traditions of Argentine football, one that coalesced around the idea of a '*criollo* rebirth' in 1913. However, the revisionist underpinning of this discourse is misleading. Differences of playing style in early twentieth-century Argentina were class-based rather than ethnically based, with Anglo-Criollos—negated in the existing literature—playing a full part in the development of this style. Whilst *la nuestra* has traditionally been conflated as the national Argentine way of playing, it was in fact an urban Buenos Aires construct. By contrast, the variety of climate and topology in the rest of Argentina necessitated the creation of unique styles of play to meet the demands of diverse local challenges. These disparities were highlighted in the Campeonato Argentino each year as provincial teams played those from the capital, with the *porteño* press using these differences to reinforce stereotypes of Buenos Aires' civilisation against the 'barbarism' of the interior.

For *la nuestra* to obtain wider recognition and more fully represent Argentine identity, Argentine teams needed to compete against foreign teams to prove the style's efficacy. Whilst British touring sides had regularly visited Argentina in the decade before the First World War, Argentine football was still in a process of maturation as Uruguay's victory at the 1924 Olympics awakened European awareness of the potency of *rioplatense* football. However, for Argentine football to gain renown, its own teams needed to be seen across the Atlantic. Whilst the pioneering nature of Boca Juniors' 1925 European tour highlighted nascent constructions of Argentine identity through football, Sportivo

Barracas' 1929 tour to Europe was more consequential in terms of representing Argentine identity. The quality of the opposition combined with provincial representation in Barracas' touring party prompted the AFA to extol the tour for having verified the level of Argentine football, and Italian journalists to eulogise the skill of Argentine footballers.

Whilst tours by Argentine teams to Europe, and European teams to the Río de la Plata reinforced ideas of *la nuestra*'s essentialism compared to foreign opponents, Argentine football was also receptive to transnational exchanges of ideas. This was exemplified by links with the Danubian school of football practised in Austria, Hungary and Czechoslovakia, reaching its apogee with Ferencváros' 1929 visit to Argentina. The interplay of the Hungarians won the hearts of Argentine crowds, whilst the fitness and teamwork of players later became a feature of Argentine teams such as Gimnasia y Esgrima de La Plata and River Plate prepared by the Hungarian coach Imre Hirschl during the 1930s.

Projection of *la nuestra* against the 'other' was even more important on a country-to-country basis, with Uruguay being the best opponent against which to make comparisons, given the two nations' intertwined rise to international prominence at the 1928 Olympics and 1930 World Cup. From a shared *rioplatense* identity born of the common enterprise in gaining independence from Spain as the United Provinces of the Río del Plata, their continued rivalry at the highest level of world football needed the differentiation of playing styles between the two countries. Whilst *la nuestra* focused on the aesthetic side of football and the expression of skill, the Uruguayan style relied on *garra charrúa* and the use of willpower to resolve matches in their favour, acknowledging Uruguay's Indigenous heritage.

Earlier interpretations have suggested that *la nuestra* reached its peak execution in the 1940s with River Plate's *la máquina* team. However, *la máquina* were more than an expression of a traditional style; they were also innovators absorbing lessons from the Danubian school from when they were coached by Hirschl, as well as adapting the rotating the rotation of positions from basketball. Indeed, another footballing style achieved remarkable success during the so-called Golden Age of the 1940s: that of Boca Juniors. Despite winning the league three times, Boca were not considered as positively as their counterparts at River Plate. Coverage in *El Gráfico* reflected this dichotomy: its middle-class writers posited *la máquina* as the aesthetically pleasing archetype of Argentine football, whilst at the same time damning Boca with faint praise as the efficient

'Team of the People.' This analysis highlighted the disconnect between the popular classes consuming football on the terraces each Sunday and those who dictated the narrative that defined Argentina's footballing identity.

If the 1940s were considered the zenith of *la nuestra*, then the 'Disaster of Sweden' raised existential questions. Defeat to Czechoslovakia in the 1958 World Cup not only reflected wider debates about the direction of Argentine society, but also what form the modernisation of Argentine football should take exercised journalists and administrators for the rest of the century. The modernising discourse initially coalesced around Juan Carlos Lorenzo, schooled in defensive Italian football and who coached Argentina at the 1962 and 1966 World Cups with underwhelming results. However, at club level this pragmatic approach was achieving results, evidenced by the Copa Libertadores victories of Independiente in 1964 and 1965 and Racing Club in 1967. Initially, this footballing 'revolution' was lauded in the press as expressing the fortitude needed in wider Argentine society to remedy the ills of its dysfunctional democracy. However, as Argentina again succumbed to military rule in 1966 with President Onganía's 'Argentine Revolution,' the country's football reflected the violence emanating from government repression and popular responses to it. Described by journalists outside Argentina as *antifútbol*, this violence was exemplified by the international campaigns of Estudiantes de La Plata in the late 1960s.

Argentina's failure to qualify for the 1970 World Cup ended the flirtation with modernisation as the press lamented the loss of traditional Argentine footballing values, vindicated by Brazil's thrilling victory in the tournament with its own brand of artistic football. A renaissance of *la nuestra* was consecrated by Huracán's 1973 league championship win masterminded by César Luis Menotti, who the following year was charged with revitalising the fortunes of the Argentine national team. Menotti staked his reputation on winning the 1978 World Cup by playing in a way that represented the best of *la nuestra*, challenging his players to join the pantheon of Argentine footballing heroes of the 1920s and 1940s. However, just as Menotti was promoting *la nuestra's* restoration, the military government that seized power in 1976 was simultaneously destroying some its legendary building blocks, most notably the *potreros* of the urban poor as part of a policy of social engineering, returning internal migrants to their home provinces by destroying the shanty towns in which they lived on the margins of Argentina's big cities. Menotti was successful in not only winning the World Cup, but by doing so in a way that invoked the myth of *la nuestra*, although this was a precarious undertaking that only came to fruition in the final games of the tournament.

By the time Argentina tried to retain their world title four years later, hubris had set in, and Argentine football entered a new pragmatic phase under the guidance of Carlos Bilardo, who led the nation to World Cup victory in 1986, and to a second final in 1990. The dichotomy between Menottism and Bilardism represented the battle for the soul of Argentine football in the final decade of the twentieth century which culminated in the 'Third Way' employed by Marcelo Bielsa which whilst initially achieving sporting success en route to qualifying for the 2002 World Cup, failed to stir the passions and taste of the Argentine footballing public, something that ironically was achieved by the national junior team at the same time in winning three World Youth Cups under José Pekerman.

In terms of the contribution of under-represented sectors of society to the creation of Argentine identity through football, the role of women during the twentieth century was marginalised to the periphery at best as the game remained a masculine preserve. Whilst women playing football was not explicitly banned by Argentine football authorities as it was in England, there was little or no support for the development of female football by the AFA, even when it took nominal responsibility for it in 1991. Any progress made by women's football was self-driven as exemplified by Argentine participation in the 1971 Women's World Cup in Mexico. Throughout the century, press coverage of women's football reflected a masculine discourse about the physiological unsuitability of the game for female players, as well as it being a haven of lesbianism. Yet, when given the opportunity to play, Argentine women showed they were skilful exponents of the game that could command decent-sized crowds as the tours to northern provinces in the 1960s showed. However, without the financial and institutional support of male dominated institutions the women's game foundered.

Similarly, the contribution of Afro-Argentine, Indigenous and *mestizo* players has been retarded, although when given opportunity they have made a significant input to Argentine football. Despite their presence being negated in the existing literature, Afro-Argentine players such as Alejandro de los Santos, Juan Manuel Ramos Delgado and Héctor Baley achieved international honours for Argentina. Others such as Julio Benavídez and Ernesto Picot also shone despite the systemic racism directed against players of Afro-Argentine descent by administrators, fellow players and the press. A similar story of negation and denigration was applied to players of Indigenous and *mestizo* origin from Argentina's peripheral provinces. Despite being adored by Huracán fans in the capital and playing for the national team, José Laguna was effectively stripped of his dignity and nationality in an infamous 1920 *Crítica* article. Zini's piece demonstrated positivist attitudes within Argentina of white supremacy over Black and Indigenous peoples, suggesting that it was only due to his extraordinary football skill that the *mestizo* Laguna was brought up to the same level of civilisation as his white teammates. This demeaning discourse was continued in the Buenos Aires press after the introduction of the Campeonato Argentino later that decade, with Santiago del Estero's winning team of 1928 derided as *pelo duros* or 'brush-heads' on account of their indigenous appearance. Such treatment highlighted that in the minds of many in the capital, these players were simply leftovers from the 'Conquest of the Desert,' a state-sponsored exercise in genocide of Argentina's Indigenous population during the 1880s, and not worthy of consideration as Argentines.

Football also offered a way for Argentina's *mestizo* population to it make itself visible following the internal migration of one million people to the country's major cities during the 1930s and 1940s. Disparaged by *porteños* as *cabecitas negras*, the presence of these migrants challenged existing notions held by intellectuals of Argentina being a white, Europeanised country. As the lowest echelon of the working class that had habitually populated the football terraces of Argentine clubs, *cabecitas negras* were held to blame by journalists for the increased violence at matches due to their lack of 'civilisation' and education, and for creating class tensions by making stadiums a less appealing space for middle-class supporters who found refuge in other forms of entertainment such as television.

The *villas miserias* or shanty towns in which the vast majority of *cabecitas* lived became the breeding ground for the continuum of the myth of the *pibe* or street-kid in more modern interpretations of *la nuestra*, replacing the tenement blocks of European immigrants at the turn of the twentieth century. As the case study of René Houseman shows, by the 1970s the sons of provincial migrants were fast becoming amongst the best footballers in Argentina. Stereotyped as the heir to earlier graduates of the *potrero* such as José Manuel Moreno, Houseman represented a maverick archetype for whom playing was meant to be fun and not subject to tactical rigour.

Another under-represented area of Argentine society whose contribution to national identity through football came to the fore during the 1960s was that of Argentina's youth. The widening of university provision, particularly to the working class during the Peronist era created a more educated Argentine youth which reached maturity during that decade. During this heady period of increased political awareness not just in Argentina, but across the Western world, young people joined in narratives of national identity for the first time, which by the end of the decade manifested itself in a student-led resistance to the military regime of General Onganía which took power in 1966.

As the case study of Estudiantes de La Plata between 1965 and 1970 exemplifies, this awakening of youth in Argentina was also represented through football. A change in the age profile of Estudiantes' playing staff saw the wholesale promotion of a group of teenagers to the first team—including two university undergraduates in their ranks—taking a pragmatic scientific approach to the game that helped their transformation from relegation candidates to world club champions in three years. In the process, Estudiantes established themselves as the youthful resistance to the hegemony of the *grandes* in Argentina and the traditional Uruguayan and Brazilian powerhouses of South American football. The methods employed by Estudiantes, including the targeted use of violence to obtain results was akin to the student-led resistance in Argentina which later morphed into armed groups like the Montoneros, rather than reflective of the repression of the Onganía regime as others have alluded. This progression to 'urban guerrillas' was cemented by the brutality of the team in losing the 1969 Intercontinental Cup Final to AC Milan. Just like the radical student movement more widely, Estudiantes burned brightly for a few short years before returning to relative obscurity in the early 1970s.

Whilst Estudiantes de la Plata were a provincial outfit, the club's proximity to Buenos Aires meant that their successes of the late 1960s could not be considered as a breakthrough for the positive representation of the interior in Argentine football. Indeed, the Argentine football authorities' treatment of the provinces was resonant of the neglect of the interior by the national government. Whilst Jeffrey Richey optimistically argues that the introduction of the inter-provincial Campeonato Argentino in the 1920s was definitive in aligning provincial football with the power base of Buenos Aires and making the game truly federal and national, the reality was less impressive.[5] Despite Argentine football administrators positioning the competition as a paragon of federalism, debates aroused by the victory of Santiago del Estero in the 1928 tournament confirmed that those from the interior continued to be considered second class citizens by power brokers in the capital, who mocked the provincials as *chacareros* or 'peasants.'

The 1967 establishment of the Campeonato Nacional by AFA interventor, Valentín Suárez once again gave the illusion of a new dawn for federal football in Argentina as provincial clubs were finally drawn into a national league competition for the first time. The Argentine League had become secondary in importance to the continental Copa Libertadores, and the need to attract new television revenue through a rejuvenation of the tournament was of greater significance to the AFA than genuinely improving the standard of the game in the interior, as it took almost a decade for the semi-professional provincial sides to become competitive against teams from Buenos Aires and Rosario, when Talleres de Córdoba reached the final of the 1977 edition. A bigger contributor to the inclusion of the interior into the national mainstream were the selection policies of national team coach, Menotti, in preparing the Argentine team for the successful 1978 World Cup campaign. This highlighted the talent available in the interior at a national team level for the first time and in a manner that has been rarely employed since.

This book, therefore, argues that during the long twentieth century football became a cultural signifier for Argentine identity that cut across ethnic, class and provincial barriers. In shared schools, workplaces and heterogeneous neighbourhoods, the game functioned as an agent for the successful assimilation of millions of immigrants into a national whole that went far beyond its origins within the British community. Equally, the sport has paradoxically been an instrument of exclusion, with significant sectors of Argentine society, women and those originating from non-white backgrounds and the interior being deliberately excluded from the national narrative by the media and those in positions of footballing authority. Football's clearest role as a cultural signifier has been in its faithful reflection of the breakdown in Argentine society that culminated in the paradoxes emanating from victory in the 1978 World Cup in the context of a government at war with sectors of its own people and the

---

[5] Richey (2013, 117–119).

mass emigration of Argentine talent emanating from the failed neo-liberal economic policies that culminated in the fiscal crisis of 2001–2002 which marked the end of the long twentieth century for Argentine society.

REFERENCES

Alberdi, Juan B. 2002. Immigration as a Means of Progress. In *The Argentina Reader*, ed. Gabriela Nouzeilles and Graciela Montaldo, 95–101. Durham, NC: Duke University Press.

Mason, Tony. 1995. *Passion of the People? Football in South America*. London: Verso.

Richey, Jeffrey W. 2013. *Playing at Nation: Soccer Institutions, Racial Ideology and National Integration in Argentina 1912–31*. unpublished PhD thesis. Chapel Hill: University of North Carolina.

Index

0–9
1928 Olympics, 112
1930 World Cup, 111
1934 World Cup, 99
1936 Olympics, 220
1948–1949 Players' Strike, 10, 165
1950 World Cup, 154
1955 South American Championship, 158
1957 South American Championship, 159
1962 World Cup, 158, 172, 211
1966 World Cup, 176
1968 Olympics, 221
1971 Women's World Cup, 8
1974 World Cup, 180
1978 World Cup, 7, 211, 217
1982 World Cup, 232
1986 World Cup, 250
1990 World Cup, 258
1991 Copa América, 273
1994 World Cup, 260, 268
2002 World Cup, 280, 283

A
Abyssinia, 118
Afro-Argentines, 57, 78, 82
Alberdi, Juan, 34
Alfonsín, Raúl, 247, 248
Aloé, Carlos, 138, 142, 155
Alumni, 28, 49, 62
Andrade, José Leandro, 108
Anglo-Criollos, 9, 65
Animals, 176
Antifútbol, 6, 177, 178, 191
Ardiles, Osvaldo, 236
Argentine Association Football League (AAFL), 28
Argentine Association of Women's Football, 196
Argentine identity, 47
Argentinidad, 3, 44, 229
Asociación del Football Argentino (AFA), 131, 147, 152, 276
Asociación Mutualista de Footballers, 69, 129
Assimilation, 41

Austral, Plan, 249
Avellaneda Law, 38

B
Bacigaluppi, José, 37, 70
Banfield, 33
Barings Crisis, 19
Barras bravas, 277
Basile, Alfio, 258
Batistuta, Gabriel, 262
Battle of Caseros, 19
Bianchi, Carlos, 271
Bielsa, Marcelo, 264, 282
Bilardo, Carlos, 189, 255, 256
Blanquiceleste, 281
Boca Juniors, 64, 135, 141, 232, 270, 282
Boca Juniors' 1925 European tour, 98
Bombonera stadium, 272
Borocotó, 60
Bosman Ruling, 275
Brazil, 79, 161
British referees, 143
British-run schools, 25, 31
Brown, Alfredo, 49
Buenos Aires English High School (BAEHS), 27
Buenos Ayres Cricket Club, 23

C
Cabecitas negras, 140, 165
Campeonato Argentino, 58, 85
Campeonato Nacional, 90, 200
Carrascosa, Jorge, 187
Cereijo, Ramón, 150
Chacareros, 89
Chacarita Juniors, 179
Cinco grandes, 131, 146, 267
Civic identity, 4
Colombia, 149, 259
Combin, Néstor, 188

Convertibility Plan, 269
Córdoba, 35
Cordobazo, 199
Crespo, Hernán, 274
Criollización, 59
Criollo, 40
Criollo rebirth, 63
Crisol de razas, 61
Crítica, 104
Czechoslovakia, 163

D
Danubian school, 101, 102, 106
Day of the Female Footballer, 198
De los Santos, Alejandro, 80
Diffusion, 42
Dimayor, 149, 152
Disaster of Sweden, 10, 159, 163, 171
Di Stéfano, Alfredo, 181, 235
Dual identity, 56
Duhalde, Eduardo, 269

E
Elba Selva, 197
El Gráfico, 11, 219, 252
El Mundo Deportivo, 12
Emigration, 170, 184
Ente Autárquico Mundial '78 (EAM), 214
Escuela Rosarina, 89
Esquivel, Adolfo Pérez, 224
Estadio Monumental, 218
Estudiantes de La Plata, 10, 170, 195, 255

F
Ferencváros, 102, 103
Fernando De la Rúa, 280
Ferro Carril Oeste, 33

Festival of Britain, 156
FIFA, 212
First World War, 66
Footballers' Day, 157
Forrester, Arturo, 47
Frondizi, Arturo, 171
Fútbolistas Argentinos Agremiados (FAA), 145

G
Gaelic Athletic Association (GAA), 45
Gallardo, Marcelo, 284
Gallegos, 39
Galtieri, Leopoldo, 233
Garra charrúa, 111, 135, 162
Gauchesque folklore, 265
Gaucho, 59
Genoa, 72
George Drabble, 21
Golden Age, 125, 136, 138
Grondona, Julio, 249, 266

H
Hälsingborg, 164
Heald, William, 13
Hiberno-Argentines, 22
Hirschl, Imre, 133
Hogg, Thomas, 23
Hooliganism, 276
Houseman, René, 216
Huracán, 45, 179

I
Ignomiriello, Miguel, 191
Imagined political community, 2
Immigration, 38
Independiente, 174
Indigenous populations, 84
Informal empire, 20, 58
Intercontinental Cup final, 193

Interior, 87, 202
Invented tradition, 3
Ireland, 22
Isolation, 152
Italian immigration, 39
Italo-Argentines, 67, 71, 99, 113, 116

J
Juvenal, 174

K
Kempes, Mario, 183, 188

L
La Bombonera, 279
Labruna, Ángel, 161
Lacoste, Carlos, 214
La década infame, 124
La Doce, 277, 279
La fiesta de todos, 228
Laguna, José, 78
La máquina, 133, 134, 164
La Nación, 11
Land-owning elite, 19
La nuestra, 61, 106, 119, 164, 179, 183
Las Islas Malvinas, 233
Law of Public Education, 29
Law of Social Defence, 68
Lesbianism, 75
Liberating Revolution, 171
Libonatti, Julio, 113
Liga Argentina, 152
Lorenzo, Jorge, 172, 182
Los Cebollitas, 230
Lunfardo, 72

M
Macacos, 8, 79

Macri, Mauricio, 267, 270, 272, 276
Madero, Raúl, 189
Madres de la Plaza de Mayo, 210, 223, 231
Malvinas, 234, 238, 240, 250
Maradona, Diego, 1, 209, 230, 234, 251, 252, 254, 257, 259, 261
Menem, Carlos, 247, 255
Menotti, César Luis, 180, 182, 203, 216, 225, 232, 241
Migration, 272
Mitrismo, 41
Montevideo, 107
Monti, Luis, 117
Montoneros, 190, 222
Moreno, José Manuel, 145
Mundo Deportivo, 126, 142
Muscular Christianity, 26

N
National Patriotic Fund, 238
New Argentina, 144
Newbery, Jorge, 46
Nicolini, Oscar, 148

O
Olé, 270
Onganía, Juan Carlos, 175
Orsi, Raimundo, 104

P
Padlock Clause, 129
Panzeri, Dante, 123, 213
Passarella, Daniel, 261, 263
Pekerman, José, 263, 273
Pelota, 43
Per Henrich Ling, 74
Peronism, 5, 140
Perón, Juan, 126, 127, 212
Pibe de oro, 210

Pico, Ernesto, 82
Plymouth Argyle, 100
Poletti, Alberto, 194
Polideportivos, 74
Porteño, 24
Pozzo, Vittorio, 116
Privatisation, 267
Professionalism, 128, 132

R
Race, 57
Racing Club de Avellaneda, 62, 147, 281
Railways, 32, 35
Ramos Delgado, José Manuel, 81
Rattín, Antonio, 176
Renganeschi, Armando, 173
Rimpatriati, 113, 115
rioplatense identity, 108
Riquelme, Juan Román, 263, 283
River Plate, 37, 69, 77, 130
Romano, Florencia, 198
Romero Brest, Enrique, 30
Rosario Central, 34
Rugby union, 65
Rugilo, Miguel, 156
Ruiz, Armando Ramos, 124

S
Sáenz Peña Law, 42
Sailor myth, 18
Sánchez Terrero, Eduardo, 132
Santiago del Estero, 83, 87
Sarmiento, Domingo, 86
Scotland, 21
Segundo Luna, 88
Sívori, Omar, 117
Social mobility, 5
Social question, 58
South American Championship, 136, 137

Southampton FC, 48
Sportivo Barracas, 98, 104
Sportsmanship, 106
Stábile, Guillermo, 115
St. Andrew's Athletic Club, 24
Suárez, Valentín, 5, 154, 200

T
Talleres de Córdoba, 201, 203
Tarantini, Alberto, 223
Ticker tape, 227
Torneos y Competencias (*TyC*), 267
Trio de la muerte, 160, 184

U
Urquiza, Justo José, 18
Uruguay, 97, 107, 108, 110

V
Valdano, Jorge, 237

Vargas, Getulio, 126
Vélez Sarsfield, 71
Vendepatrias, 186
Videla, Jorge, 213
Villas miserias, 141, 217
Vladislao Cap, 185

W
Watson Hutton, Alexander, 26, 44
Women's football, 74, 76
Works' teams, 31

Y
Yrigoyen, Hipólito, 85

Z
Zacarias, Claudio, 278
Zubeldía, Osvaldo, 191, 193